CONTENTS

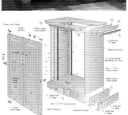

CHAPTER 1 **an introduction to home storage** 5

Four Steps to Conquering Clutter 6

Sizing Up Your Home 6

Advantages of Building a Storage Unit 7

Plans and Illustrations to Ensure Your Success 9

CHAPTER 2 **material options** 10

Wood-Buying Basics 11

Guide to Sheet Goods 14

Basic Fasteners, Hardware, and Open Shelving 19

Preventing Shelf Sag 22

CHAPTER 3 **finishing guidelines** 24

Staining Guidelines 25

Four Clear Finishes That Make It Hard to Fail 30

Applying a Paint Finish 34

CHAPTER 4 **cabinet storage** 36

Shaker Cabinet 37

Pine Hutch Cabinet 40

Traditional Sideboard 50

CHAPTER 5 **centers for great entertainment** 61

Country Entertainment Center 62

Showtime Storage 68

Cabinet Combination 74

CHAPTER 6 **organizing your library** 84

Barrister's Bookcase 85

Shelving Showcase 94

One Bookcase, Three Ways 100

CHAPTER 7 **storage solutions for your homework** 111

Drop-Front Writing Desk 112

Hideaway Home Office 119

Storage Cabinet 128

CHAPTER 8 **showcases for collectibles** 133

Collector's Cabinet 134

Country Plate Rack 139

Lighted Showcase 144

CHAPTER 9 **stowaway storage** 155

Country Hall Seat 156

Cedar-Lined Heirloom Chest 163

CHAPTER 10 **super shelves and storage centers** 169

Knockdown Cabinet System 170

Laundry Center 180

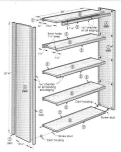

Index 188

Metric Equivalents 191

Credits 191

WOOD

WITHDRAWN
FROM STOCK

Magazine ®

home
storage
solutions

STERLING PUBLISHING CO., INC.
NEW YORK

Editor: Peter J. Stephano
Designer: Christine Swirnoff

Library of Congress Cataloging-in-Publication Data

Wood magazine's home storage solutions: 19 space-saving solutions Edited by Peter J. Stephano
   p. cm.
 Includes index.
 ISBN 1-4027-1176-X
 1. Cabinetwork. 2. Storage in the home. 3. Shelving (Furniture) I. Title: Home storage solutions.
 II. Better homes and gardens wood.
 TT197.W83 2005
 684.1'6--dc22

                          2004022845

10   9   8   7   6   5   4   3   2   1

Published by Sterling Publishing Co., Inc.
387 Park Avenue South, New York, NY 10016
This edition is based on material found in WOOD® magazine articles
© 2005 by WOOD® magazine editors
Distributed in Canada by Sterling Publishing
c/o Canadian Manda Group, 165 Dufferin Street
Toronto, Ontario, Canada M6K 3H6
Distributed in Great Britain by Chrysalis Books Group PLC
The Chrysalis Building, Bramley Road, London W10 6SP, England
Distributed in Australia by Capricorn Link (Australia) Pty. Ltd.
P.O. Box 704, Windsor, NSW 2756, Australia

Printed in China

Sterling ISBN 1-4027-1176-X
For information about custom editions, special sales, premium and
corporate purchases, please contact Sterling Special Sales
Department at 800-805-5489 or specialsales@sterlingpub.com.

an introduction to home storage

STORAGE MEANS A LOT MORE THAN HIDING THINGS *you don't know what else to do with. It means taking advantage of unused and otherwise wasted space; putting your belongings away in an organized manner; and making ordinary storage space do double duty—to point out just a few definitions.*

In this book you'll find a least nineteen solutions for storage, and long before you reach the end you'll have learned an important lesson: Organization and storage go hand in hand. Some people think that organization stifles creativity. But how can you be creative when you're always searching for what you want, and tripping over other things as you do so? Bringing order to your chaos actually frees you up to do the things you really enjoy, whether they're creative or not.

This versatile cabinet system has cam-lock knockdown hardware, which allows you to alter your furniture as needed. See Chapter 10 to learn how to build it.

1–1.

FOUR STEPS TO CONQUERING CLUTTER

You may not be aware of it, but there are professionals who specialize in helping people clear away clutter. And if you rounded up them all in a room, they would agree on the following steps to an organized home. Briefly summarized, they are:

1. Sort the items.

Room by room, space by space, group the items to see exactly what you have. In your garage, for example, you might have groupings by use, such as lawn equipment, garden tools, sports gear, and so on.

To more fully utilize your floor-to-ceiling shelving, you may want to build this collector's cabinet, which has a drop-down panel that conceals a storage compartment. See the instructions in Chapter 8.

1–2.

2. Evaluate the items.

Get some large, moving-style boxes and label them as to what you should do with the contents: Give Away/Sell, Put Away, Needs Fixing, Throw Away, Undecided. Then look at the items you've grouped and evaluate each by its usefulness. Place it in the appropriate box—and don't take long with your decision.

3. Purge.

Toss the unneeded stuff in the Throw Away box. Dispose of other items in the Give Away/Sell box. Store items that need repair in the Needs Fixing box. Close the Undecided box, date it, store it, and come back to it as you need things that it contains. If after a year you've not retrieved anything from it, give away its contents.

4. Rearrange the items.

Now that you've cleared away the things you don't or can't use, you have more room for the remaining items. And you can turn to the projects in this book for interesting and attractive ways to store them.

SIZING UP YOUR HOME

Okay, you've gone through the four steps just summarized and it still seems that you have too much stuff and too little place to put it. Now it's time to size up your home. There's a very good chance that you're not presently making the best use of the space you have. If you look carefully, you will discover storage areas and sites that hadn't occurred to you.

For instance, you can look to the ceiling. For each square foot of floor storage, you actually have about eight square feet if you build up to the ceiling. Shelving and cabinetry will get your things up off the floor and provide you with more storage space. The collector's cabinet in **1–2** has shelving meant to display your favorite collectibles. The distinctive bookcase in **1–3** holds a mini-library of your favorite books.

As you go from room to room, think about strategically placing your belongings. In other words, try to store items where you'll use them. If you pay bills and do other work at home, gather and store everything you use to do that in one unit in a special place in your home. In Chapter 7, you'll find a hideaway home office and super-nice desk that fit the bill.

With the same strategy in mind, three cabinet plans are included in Chapter 4. The hutch unit (shown on *page 8*) and the traditional sideboard will fit perfectly in your dining room, so you can store tableware and linens where they are used.

Naturally, we have taken the same approach with the two entertainment centers in Chapter 5. Both are designed to maximize storage space. There's even a CD/DVD cabinet to go with them.

1-3.

Talk about floor-to-ceiling storage space! You can build this majestic, traditional bookcase from the step-by-step plans you'll find in Chapter 6.

to mention what you'll have to pay. You'll be able to build any of the projects in this book for pennies on the dollar compared with what they'd cost at retail. And with the detailed plans and emphasis on sturdy construction, you'll end up with quality items. And think about all the choices you have by doing it yourself.

You can select the material and hardware that best fits your budget and decorating scheme. Choose from durable sheet goods and classic woodworking woods—not what happens to be on the showroom floor. You'll be able to make informed decisions regarding materials after you read Chapter 2. You'll understand the advantages and disadvantages of sheet goods (**1–4** and **1–5**), as well as the

ADVANTAGES OF BUILDING A STORAGE UNIT

As you well know, you can buy nearly any type of storage unit ready-made (or ready to assemble) at furniture stores, office suppliers, and home centers. However, be prepared to do a lot of aisle-walking or Internet searching, because no one place will have exactly what fits your needs and space requirements. That's not

1–4.

Plywood has some quirky tendencies. That's why there is a special section in Chapter 2 that will help you saw it to perfection.

1–5.

The exposed edges of plywood and other sheet goods require special attention. Turn to Chapter 3 to see what the pros do.

characteristics of popular hardwoods and softwoods. There are woodworking tips in the following pages to help you work with these woods.

Finishing is not one of a woodworker's favorite activities. That's because a great finishing job takes roughly two thirds of the time it takes to build the project. Don't worry about that aspect, though. Chapter 3 will show you how to do a

1–6.

Want your project to reflect the wood's natural beauty? Learn how to stain, finish, and paint like a pro in Chapter 3.

1–7.

See the plans and step-by-step instructions for building this hutch in Chapter 4.

professional-looking job with stains, clear finishes, and paint (**1–6**). It also discusses how to professionally prepare the project for the finish—an essential step. You'll also learn how to select the right finish for durability, ease of application, and visual appeal.

All in all, after you've read the material and reviewed the illustrations in Chapters 2 and 3, you'll be ready to tackle some great projects.

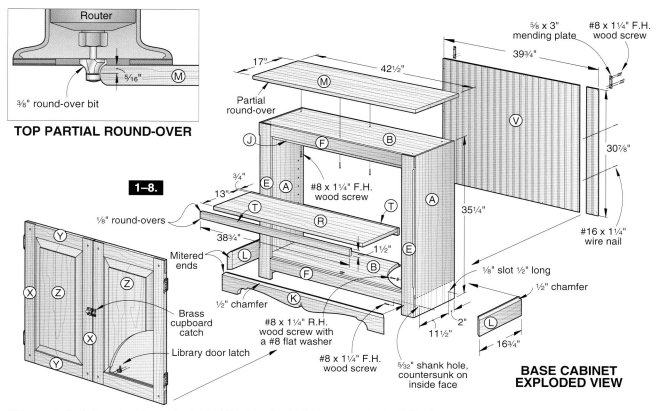

TOP PARTIAL ROUND-OVER

1–8.

**BASE CABINET
EXPLODED VIEW**

This exploded-view drawing is typical of the hundreds that appear in the following pages.

PLANS AND ILLUSTRATIONS TO ENSURE YOUR SUCCESS

The nearly two dozen projects in this book represent years in the workshop, the photo studio, and at the "drawing board" (read that as "computer"). Each project was actually built in the *WOOD*® magazine shop by on-staff craftsmen. The builder's notes were then carefully read by a project editor, and transformed into easy-to-follow, step-by-step instructions. Draftsmen tediously created highly accurate, detailed plan drawings, and photographers and/or artists then added their skills to show you the project in progress.

That's why, even if you're not a highly experienced woodworker, you'll be able to succeed with any and all the projects in this book you choose to build. You'll find precise cutting diagrams and materials lists, too, so you'll never have to guess.

The exploded-view drawing shown in **1–8** is typical of the hundreds that can be found on the following pages. Where a part or process requires further explanation, there's always a detailed drawing to provide it. To help you further, you'll find project-in-progress photos, such as the one shown in **1–9**. Sometimes, in lieu of a photo, an artist's illustration does the work. There are also plenty of shop tips, so enjoy this book!

1–9.

Each project in this book is accompanied by detailed photos of the work in progress.

material options

NO MATTER WHETHER YOU'RE PLANNING to build shelves, chests, or storage cabinets, you have numerous options as to choice of material and hardware for creating them. In fact, there are more choices than you'll find in any furniture store. And that's part of why making them yourself is so satisfying.

The other advantage to building storage units in your own shop is the opportunity to get exactly what you want at a price that fits your budget. However, that advantage means you need a sound understanding of the materials you'll be working with. This chapter is devoted to giving you just that.

First, it is important to explain the difference between softwood and hardwood, how they're sold, and what types of projects are best suited to the most readily available species.

Of course, these days many if not most furniture pieces and cabinets are built with a combination of solid stock (boards) and sheet goods, such as plywood. Today, though, plywood isn't your only option in sheet goods. See page 14 for your choices, and for pointers on sawing.

Finally, we have furnished information to help you build sturdy shelves and use the hardware needed to support them.

WOOD-BUYING BASICS

Hardwood and Softwood

What makes a wood "hard" or "soft"? Carvers love the softness of basswood and butternut under their knives. Sure, they're soft in that respect, but technically they're hardwoods. That's because hardness isn't the quality that spells the difference between hardwood and softwood lumber. Instead, it's determined by the type of tree that the wood comes from.

Hardwood is produced by broad-leaved deciduous trees that (in the world's temperate zone) lose their leaves each fall. Softwood, on the other hand, is produced by the evergreen, cone-bearing, needle-leaved trees called conifers. Neither term has anything to do with hardness, although the wood from deciduous trees generally proves to be harder than that from coniferous trees.

Because of its beauty, stability, strength, predictability when machined, and resistance to denting, hardwood is the choice for most furnituremaking. Few softwoods offer the same positive characteristics. Bald cypress, redwood, and western red cedar are occasional exceptions. See "Guide to Key Woods and Their Uses" at *right* for a selection of the most commonly used hardwoods and softwoods.

Hardwood Grades

Because hardwood trees are less abundant than their softwood counterparts and their lumber more valuable, great care is taken to minimize waste from a log. This means you'll find boards of differing quality—even if they came from the same log. Therefore, the National Hardwood Lumber Association (NHLA) assigns specific quality grades to all hardwood boards (2–2). Each grade reflects a classification according to the percentage of clear material the grade is expected to yield. The greater the percentage, the higher the grade and value of the board. Let's look at the top four standard grades of hardwood lumber.

▦ **Firsts & Seconds (FAS)**. This grade features long and wide

2–1.

A selection of softwoods and hardwoods.

cuttings. The board sizes measure from 6" and wider to 8' and longer. Graded from the poorer side, FAS boards produce minimum cuttings of 4" x 5' or 3" x 7'. Clear-face cuttings must yield no more than 16% waste. These highest-quality boards are most often used in tabletops, moldings, or where long, clear boards are required.

GUIDE TO KEY WOODS AND THEIR USES

		PRIMARY USES	OTHER USES
HARDWOODS	Alder (red)	cabinets, simple furniture	
	Ash (white)	cabinets	sporting goods
	Basswood	carved items	
	Birch (yellow)	cabinets, furniture	flooring
	Butternut	carved items	
	Cherry	cabinets, fine furniture	moldings
	Hickory	chairs	tool handles, cabinets
	Mahogany	classic furniture	outdoor furniture
	Maple (hard)	durable tables & chairs	cabinets, moldings
	Oak (red)	cabinets, furniture	moldings
	Oak (white)	outdoor & indoor furniture	barrels
	Poplar	utility furniture	painted items
	Teak	furniture	boat decks & trim
	Walnut (black)	fine furniture, cabinets	moldings
SOFTWOODS	Bald cypress	outdoor & indoor furniture	
	Cedar (western red)	outdoor furniture	decks, fences
	Pine (ponderosa)	country furniture	interior construction
	Pine (white)	country furniture	interior construction
	Pine (southern yellow)	flooring	treated for outdoor use
	Redwood	outdoor furniture	decks, fences

The examples below show the minimum clear yield (shaded areas) needed to make each grade. The unshaded areas contain defects and are not used in calculating the yield. Woodworkers possibly could rip and crosscut the lumber in a different way, and use portions of the boards in the unshaded areas.

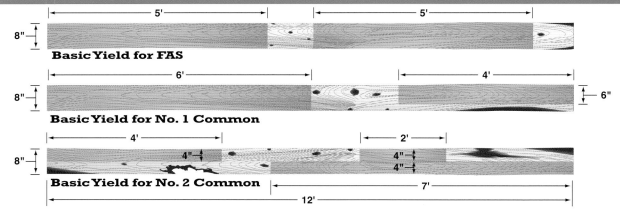

Basic Yield for FAS

Basic Yield for No. 1 Common

Basic Yield for No. 2 Common

Tip: If you're looking for consistent color and grain in long boards, say for making a piece of fine furniture or cabinetry, go with a Select or Better grade. If, however, you're building a small project that you plan to paint, a lesser grade will save you 30 to 50% in wood cost.

■ **FAS 1-Face (FAS1F) or Selects.** FAS1F is graded like FAS, except that the boards are graded from the better side, or the clearer face, of the board. The back side of the board will be graded no lower than No. 1 Common grade.

No difference exists between FAS1F and Selects except for minimum dimensions. The minimum board size for FAS1F boards is 6" x 8'. Selects measure at least 4" x 6'. The select grade applies to woods, such as birch or hickory, that yield narrower and shorter boards.

■ **No. 1 Common.** Graded from the poorer side, common boards measure 3" and wider, 4' and longer, with minimum cuttings of 4" x 2' or 3" x 3'. Clear-face cuttings must yield two-thirds or more usable wood. You'll find this grade in the shorter pieces of cabinets or furniture.

■ **No. 2A.** Most often found in flooring, boards of this grade yield at least 50% clear wood in cuttings at least 3" wide and 2' long.

Softwood Grades

Like hardwood, softwood lumber of furniture and cabinet quality (not for building construction) is graded on the number of cuttings a board will yield. Softwood grades fall into three main categories—Select, Shop, and Common. A board's best side determines the grades for all but 5/4 (1¼") and thicker shop grades. One-inch lumber generally is sold in 2" width increments (1 x 2, 1 x 4, etc.), and 1¼" lumber comes in random widths and lengths. Several rules and regulations govern sofwood grades. Here's a simplified rundown.

■ **C and Better Select.** The clearest grade available from most American mills, many C and Better Selects have a B and Better face

with backs of a slightly lower grade that have minor imperfections, but no knots.

■ **D Select.** A good practical grade for many projects, D Selects have only minor defects, such as small, tight knots.

■ **Molding Stock.** A special grade offered by a few mills, molding stock yields more than 70% clear rippings 1" and wider, 6' and longer. As the name implies, this grade is used to make moldings because of its narrow yields.

■ **Shop Grades.** The highest shop grade, in 1¼" and thicker dimensions, No. 3 Clear offers only a few well-placed defects, allowing for a very high yield of clear, two-faced stock.

Beyond No. 3 Clear, shop lumber falls into three other categories: No. 1 Shop, No. 2 Shop, and No. 3 Shop. Widths run 5" and wider; lengths run 6' to 16'.

No. 3 Clear yields 70% clear cuttings. In contrast to this, No. 1 Shop yields 50% clear cuttings and No. 2 Shop yields just 33⅓% clear cuttings.

■ No. 2 and No. 3 Common.

No. 1 Common is no longer graded and sold separately. Instead, it's included with No. 2 Common and sold as No. 2 & Better Common. Referred to as the knotty or shelving grade, No. 2 Common is the most popular utility grade. Similar to No. 1 Common, No. 2 Common allows more pronounced knots and other defects. No. 3 Common includes boards of less uniform appearance than the higher grades. Common grades include the designation "S-Dry," meaning they have 18 to 20% moisture content. All higher, more expensive softwood grades are kiln-dried to less than 10% moisture content.

Air-Dried vs. Kiln-Dried Lumber

Both hardwood and softwood lumber begin as "green" boards sawn at mills from the logs of freshly felled trees. The moisture content of a green board runs 28% or greater. This makes it unsuitable for woodworking because all wood shrinks, warps, and splits as it dries.

To remove moisture from green boards, most manufacturers air-dry, then kiln-dry them. Air-drying lumber reduces its moisture content to 12 to 19% naturally—workers stack and separate the boards so that air circulates between them. Moisture content in the teens

2–3. HOW TO DETERMINE BOARD FEET

Whether you measure a board's length in inches or feet, calculating board footage for that piece of lumber is simple math.

$$\frac{T'' \times W'' \times L''}{144} = \textbf{board feet}$$

1" x 6" x 96" = **576**
576 ÷ 144 = **4 board feet**

$$\frac{T'' \times W'' \times L'}{12} = \textbf{board feet}$$

1" x 6" x 8' = **48**
48 ÷ 12 = **4 board feet**

is okay for outdoor construction, but is inadequate for interior projects, such as furniture and cabinets. The reason is that the wood will shrink further in a drier interior environment, playing havoc with project glue joints and finishes.

Kiln-drying takes over where air-drying leaves off. Large oven-like kilns with carefully controlled temperatures reduce the moisture to 6 to 9%, the ideal range for interior projects. Kiln-dried lumber won't absorb moisture readily, which means that it offers more stability.

Board Feet Guidelines

Dealers typically price softwoods by the running (lineal) foot and hardwoods by the board foot (a volume measurement). A board foot includes thickness, width, and length measurements that equal 144 cubic inches. "How to Determine Board Feet" *above* provides some sample calculations.

The thickness of lumber, especially hardwoods, is referred to in quarters of an inch, such as 4/4 ("four/quarters" or 1"), 5/4 (1.25"), 6/4 (1.5"), 8/4 (2"), and so on. However, these hardwood thicknesses are designated and the board footage calculated before surfacing. Although you'll pay for the full designated thickness, what you'll actually get in lumber surfaced two sides (S2S) is shown in "Effects of Planing" *below*. Also, in a lumber store, the board footage is rounded up or down to the nearest one-half board foot, except for more costly exotic or imported wood. Exotic wood is calculated to the inch, and will be rounded to the nearest hundredth of an inch.

2–4. EFFECTS OF PLANING

When you buy lumber, you pay for its rough thickness before surface-planing on two sides (S2S). Here's how planing affects the thickness of purchased boards. You can save money by buying full-thickness rough stock from mills that offer it, then plane it yourself.

	Hardwood thickness after S2S	Lumber rough thickness	Softwood thickness after S2S
	13⁄16"	4/4 = 1"	¾"
	1 1⁄16"	5/4 = 1¼"	15⁄32"
	1 5⁄16"	6/4 = 1½"	1 13⁄32"
	1¾"	8/4 = 2"	1 13⁄16"
	2¼"	10/4 = 2½"	2⅜"
	2¾"	12/4 = 3"	2¾"

GUIDE TO SHEET GOODS

Most woodworkers know the major virtues of plywood: strength, stiffness, size, and stability. You may not be nearly as familiar, though, with the wide array of other sheet goods available today (**2–5**). No matter the project, you'll find a type of sheet stock ideally suited for the task at hand.

Engineered Wood

All sheet goods, including plywood, fall into a broad category called engineered wood. Unlike solid lumber, which is simply cut from the tree and dried, engineered products are further altered during the manufacturing process to enhance or suppress certain properties.

Plywood, for example, consists of multiple thin layers glued together, with the grain of one layer running at a right angle to the neighboring layer. This arrangement enhances strength, decreases dimensional changes, and allows desirable wood to be placed only on the visible outer faces.

While plywood remains prevalent, more and more sheet goods are produced from ground wood chips or wood pulverized into powder, mixed with adhesives and additives, and then pressed into sheets. This, in turn, becomes such products as medium-density fiberboard (MDF) and particleboard. Even traditional plywood has changed, with the addition of new core materials, face coverings, and increasingly popular "high-density" varieties made up of ultra-thin plies.

You can familiarize yourself with the uses, properties, costs, and sources of ten contrasting sheet goods using the information in "Matching the Sheet Stock to the Project and Budget" on *pages 16* and *17*.

Note: We have purposely excluded some materials that are designed for building construction and have limited usefulness in the shop.

Cutting Plywood

You don't have to settle for rough, splintered edges when cutting plywood; nor do you have to wrestle large, awkward pieces while placing your back at risk. Just use these simple tricks to get great results.

1. Raise the height of the tablesaw blade

When cutting plywood on the tablesaw, raising the blade height can make a big difference

---

SHOP TIP

Surefire Steps to Using Sheet Goods Successfully

1 Always measure the thickness of sheet goods before machining mating pieces. Plywood, for example, is $\frac{1}{32}$" thinner than its stated thickness.

2 When cutting sheet goods on the tablesaw, place the good face up to prevent tear-out. Place the good face down if using a handheld circular saw.

3 If you work with particular sheet goods often, invest in saw blades designed for that material to get the smoothest cuts and the least chip-out.

4 Rather than wrestle a sheet onto the tablesaw, lay 2" rigid foam insulation on the floor, place the sheet on it, and rough-cut the sheet using a circular saw.

2–5.

Left: *When cutting sheet goods on a tablesaw, ensure one edge runs firmly along the saw's fence.*

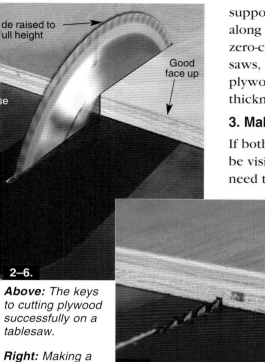

2–6.

Above: *The keys to cutting plywood successfully on a tablesaw.*

Right: *Making a low scoring pass.*

2–7.

support to the workpiece edges along the cutline. You can buy zero-clearance inserts for most saws, or make one to fit, from plywood of the appropriate thickness.

3. Make a low scoring pass

If both faces of the plywood will be visible on your project, you need to minimize chip-out on each side. Do this by making a scoring pass first, with the blade raised only about ¹⁄₁₆" to ⅛", as shown in 2–7. Then raise the blade, as advised in *Step 1*, and make another pass to cut completely through the workpiece.

4. Use the proper saw blade

The blade you choose makes a difference in the quality of your cuts. Illustration 2–8 shows a few options.

On the tablesaw, a combination blade, because of its split-

personality design, cuts smoothly if you keep it sharp and use a slow feed rate. To get the best-quality cuts, invest in an 80-tooth blade ($40 and up) designed for sheet goods. The small teeth take little bites to reduce chip-out and are steeply beveled at their edges to score the veneer face. You'll have to slow down your feed rate, but the result will be a much smoother edge.

Most handheld circular saws come equipped with a blade that is best suited for making rough cuts in construction lumber. Ditch it fast, and then invest in a carbide-tipped plywood blade (about $15); or use disposable thin-kerf steel blades that sell for just a few dollars.

5. One rout to clean edges

So you've tried everything, and just can't get a clean cut. What remedy do you try now? Cut your plywood from ¹⁄₁₆" to ⅛" oversize, and then trim it to final size, as shown in 2–9, with a router by

in the quality of the cut (**2–6**). Most of the time, safety dictates setting the blade low, but this cuts away the underlying plies first, leaving the top face unsupported as the teeth slice through. For a cleaner cut, raise the blade a couple of inches, as shown in **2–7**. The teeth impact the sheet while moving almost straight down, so the face veneer is better supported by the interior plies.

2. Get proper clearance

Before cutting plywood, swap your tablesaw insert plate for a zero-clearance model, as shown in **2–6**, to dramatically reduce chip-out on the underside of the sheet. The blade cuts the opening in this type of insert to match its thickness, offering

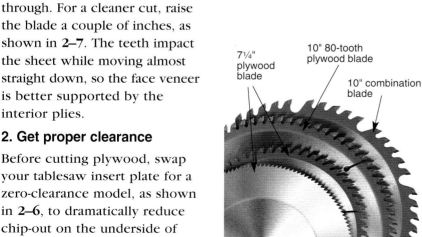

7¼" plywood blade

10" 80-tooth plywood blade

10" combination blade

2–8.

A few tablesaw blades that can successfully cut plywood.

2–9.

Trim plywood to final size with a router and flush-trimming bit.

MATCHING THE SHEET STOCK

MATERIAL	DESCRIPTION	USES	AVAILABLE SIZE
 **PARTICLEBOARD**	Wood shredded into tiny chips (essentially sawdust, often from waste wood), combined with adhesives, then heated and compressed to form sheets.	Widely used as a substrate for flooring and countertops, and for building inexpensive knockdown furniture and cabinetry. Also suitable for some shop fixtures.	Sold in ¼", ½", ⅝", ¾", 1", and 1⅛" thicknesses. Half and quarter sheets are available.
 **MELAMINE**	Particleboard faced with paper impregnated with melamine resin, a type of plastic. Paper on low-cost types is simply adhered. Higher-cost sheets are thermally fused (essentially melted together).	Great for making cabinet carcases because it wipes clean easily. Use it as well for shop fixtures or to make an economical router-table top.	Sold in 49 x 97" oversize sheets in ¼", ½", ⅝", and ¾" thicknesses.
 **HARDBOARD**	Ground wood pulp combined with resins and pressed into sheets. May be smooth on one or both faces.	Excellent for shop fixtures and jigs (especially the variety with two smooth faces) and benchtops. Use perforated hardboard for hanging tools.	Available in two thickness: ⅛" and ¼" in 4 x 8' sheets.
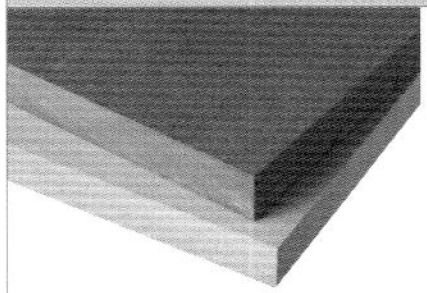 **MEDIUM-DENSITY FIBERBOARD (MDF)**	Cellulose fibers combined with synthetic resin and formed under heat and pressure.	Excellent for shop jigs and fixtures, cabinets, painted projects, molding and millwork, furniture, and as a substrate under veneer and plastic laminate.	¼", ⅜", ½", ⅝", ¾", and ⅞" thicknesses in both 4 x 8' and 49 x 97" sheets.
 **SOFTWOOD PLYWOOD**	Face-glued layers of thin softwood veneer.	Outdoor projects (exterior rated), carpentry and construction, shop cabinets, substrates, underlayment for floors and countertops.	¼", ⁵⁄₁₆", ¹¹⁄₃₂", ½", ⅝", ²³⁄₃₂", and ¾" thicknesses in 4 x 8' sheets.
MEDIUM-DENSITY & HIGH-DENSITY OVERLAY PLYWOOD (MDO/HDO)	Exterior-rated softwood plywood covered on both faces with resin-impregnated fiber (paper).	Used extensively for highway signs; great for outdoor projects, siding, painted projects, watercraft, cabinets, shop fixtures, and concrete forms.	¼", ⁵⁄₁₆", ⅜", ½", and ¾" thickness in 4 x 8' sheets.
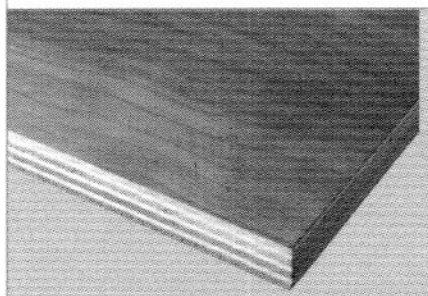 **HARDWOOD PLYWOOD**	Veneers (soft- or hardwood) glued in layers with alternating grain and covered with hardwood veneer.	The traditional sheet wood of choice for everything from furniture and cabinets to wall paneling and boxes.	¼", ½", and ¾" are most common. Occasionally, you'll find ⅛", ⅜", and ⅝" in some species.
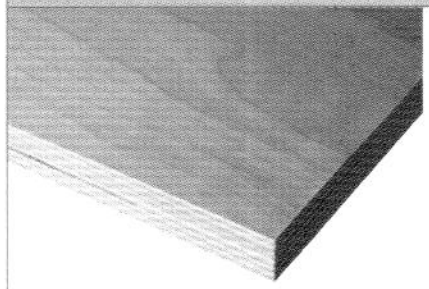 **BALTIC AND FINNISH BIRCH**	Made from ultra-thin (¹⁄₁₆"), void-free birch veneers. Finnish birch is like Baltic, but is made with exterior adhesive for outdoor use.	Used to create shop jigs and fixtures, cabinets, drawer sides, furniture, and as a substrate.	In millimeters: 4 (⅛"), 6.5 (¼"), 9 (⅜"), 12 (½"), 15 (⅝"), and 18 (⅜") in 60 x 60" sheets.
 **APPLEPLY**	American version of Baltic birch with alder and birch core plies and quality veneer faces. Birch face is standard, but other woods are available.	Same uses as Baltic, above, plus applications where a fine-hardwood face veneer is needed.	Available in ¼", ⅜", ½", ¾", 1", and 1¼" thicknesses, in 4 x 8' sheets.
 **BENDABLE PLYWOOD**	Plywood with a single face veneer and core plies with all grain running perpendicular to face to allow cross-grain bending.	Used mostly as a substrate for building cabinets, etc., with rounded corners. Sheets with clear face veneers are suitable for furniture.	⅛" and ⅜" are common, though thicker sheets are produced. Sold in 4' sheets.

TO THE PROJECT AND BUDGET

COMMON GRADES	PROS	CONS	WHERE TO FIND IT	PRICE (¾" X 4' X 8' SHEET unless otherwise noted)
PBU—for floor underlayment, M-S, M-1, M-2, M-3 industrial grades are best for making shelving and countertops.	PBU grade is readily available and inexpensive. Particleboard cuts easily and is fairly stable.	Low stiffness, heavy, holds fasteners poorly, not moisture resistant.	Home centers carry ¼" to ¾" PBU grade. "M" grades (mostly M-2) are found at building-material and millwork suppliers.	$12+ per sheet for PBU grade. "M" grade prices range about 20 percent higher.
There are no standard grades for melamine, but there are "vertical" and "horizontal" types. Higher-priced sheets generally feature thermally fused coatings and are made with thicker paper.	Inexpensive, readily available, easy-to-clean surface, available in a variety of colors and in wood-grain patterns. Also available with kraft paper or real-wood veneer on one face.	Not moisture-resistant, heavy, edges chip easily when cutting unless you use blade designed for cutting laminates.	Home centers carry ½" and ¾" sheets, shelves, and closet parts. Colors other than white and patterned papers are available by special order.	$25+ for adhered-surface, vertical-grade white sheets common in home centers. Colors and wood-grain patterns cost slightly more. $40+ for thermally fused sheets.
Service (2 green strips) Standard (1 green stripe) Service-tempered (2 red stripes) Tempered (1 red stripe) S1S (smooth one side) S2S (smooth two sides).	Readily available, easy to cut, relatively stable, available with two smooth sides or one, takes paint well.	Standard and Service grades are susceptible to moisture, can't sand faces, flexible, edges easily damaged, hold fasteners poorly.	Home centers carry 4 x 8' sheets plus half and quarter sheets in standard and tempere grades. Look for the edge stripes.	$10 (¼" 4'x 8', tempered). Perforated sheets are also available at a similar price.
One main grade: Industrial. Lower grades, which aren't commonly available, carry "B" or "Shop" grade. Also classified by density: Medium-density (MD) is standard; low-density (LD) is a lightweight version.	Flat, no face or core voids, consistent thickness, glues easily, has machinable edges.	Heavy (100 lbs. per sheet in MD grade; low-density [LD] version weighs approximately 60 lbs.), standard wood screws hold poorly.	Home centers carry medium-density (MD) ¾" sheets. Low-density (LD) is available through millwork suppliers and some hardwood retailers.	$20+ for both MD and LD.
Veneer grades: A, B, C, D. Panel grades: include sheathing and "Sturd-I-Floor." Exposure: Exterior, Exposure 1, Exposure 2, Interior.	Less expensive than hardwood ply, readily available, face veneers can have a nice appearance in higher grades.	Built more for performance than appearance; thick plies reduce stiffness; interior plies may have voids, face veneers often patched.	All home centers and building-supply stores carry an array of softwood plywood for construction.	$25+ for A-C sanded; varies by type and material.
Follows softwood plywood grading. Face and back plies (which are covered with paper) rate as B grade or better; inner plies are C grade.	Resistant to weather and water; flat, smooth, surface is easily paintable, machines easily, and is very durable.	Not widely available, heavy.	Some home centers, wood specialty stores, sign shops.	$35+ for medium-density overlay; high-density overlay costs slightly more.
Face: AA, A, B, C/D/E, Special. Back: 1, 2, 3, 4. Core: J, K, L, M. Panel types: Technical type, Type I, Type II (Type II most common for interior use).	More stable and less expensive than solid wood, widely available, made in a variety of species, and with many choices for veneer matching on faces.	Thick sheets are heavy; exposed ply edges may mean you'll have to band with solid wood; thin face veneers (1/32") or less are easy to sand through and damage.	Home centers carry a few species, such as oak, birch, maple. Turn to building suppliers and hardwood retailers for other species.	$35+ to $100+. Prices vary greatly due to species, face and back grades, ply count, and cut of veneer. A/2 o r B/2 is reasonably priced and suitable for furniture.
No standardized grades, but manufactured with void-free plies and face veneer carrying a grade of B or better.	Stiff, stable, consistent thickness, no voids, nice-looking edges, holds screws.	Hard to find, costly, odd (60 x 60") size sheet, available only with birch face.	Woodworking-supply stores, hardwood retailers, mail-order catalogs (small sizes).	$45+ for standard-size 60 x 60" sheets.
No standardized grades, but manufactured with void-free plies and face veneers carrying a grade of B or better.	Stiff, stable, void-free, nice-looking edges, holds screws, offer a variety of face veneers.	Difficult to find, costly, requires large order to get optional veneers.	You'll find distributor information at www.statesind.com.	$50+
Able to conform to tight radii without splitting or cracking with no need for kerf-bending or steaming.	Flexibility allows for radiused corners, decorative shapes.	Not designed for structural use; quality of face veneer varies greatly.	Building-supply stores and hardwood suppliers.	$35+ (⅛" 4' x 8' sheet)

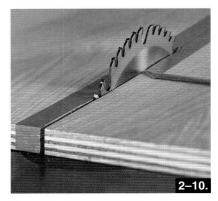

Covering the cutting line with masking tape helps to prevent minor tear-out.

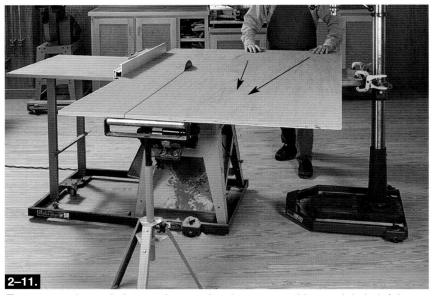

2–11.

To support plywood sheets when cutting them on a tablesaw, it is helpful to use a roller (or a sawhorse outfitted with a proper-height support) that is placed in line with the planned saw kerf. The roller will hold the end of the sheet steady at outfeed.

running a bearing-guided pattern bit along a straightedge.

6. Cover the cutting line with masking tape

Even if you eliminate major chip-out, you may still get minor tear-out of small fibers. Combat this problem by covering the cutline with masking tape, as shown in **2–10**. The blue, low-adhesion variety works best because it holds the fibers in place but peels away easily without grabbing splinters. Be sure to press the tape down firmly.

7. Support the sheet

Cutting plywood sheets on your tablesaw is possible if you support the sheet well throughout the cut. As **2–11** proves, you don't need fancy equipment or a huge saw table, either. A roller (or a sawhorse outfitted with a proper-height support) placed in line with the planned saw kerf holds the end of the sheet steady at outfeed. To support the side of the sheet, be creative by positioning your drill-press table, as we did, or maybe clamp a

piece of scrap stock to your jointer to match the saw table's height.

8. Push your way through

Even with your sheet well supported on a saw table, for best results you have to concentrate on keeping it firmly against the fence as you cut. Push from one side of the blade, as shown in

2–11. The hand that is nearer the blade pushes straight forward. With the hand that's farther from the blade, you should push harder, toward the cutline at the outfeed end of the sheet. As you near the end of the cut, reposition your hands to straddle the cutline so you can push the cut-off pieces through.

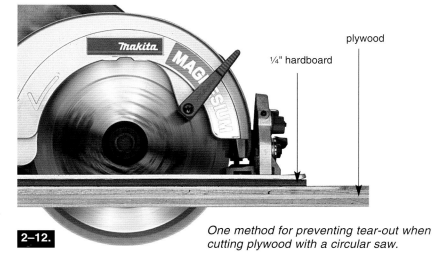

2–12.

plywood

¼" hardboard

One method for preventing tear-out when cutting plywood with a circular saw.

9. The zero difference

If your circular-saw blade causes tear-out, try the method shown: Cut a piece of ¼" hardboard to match the size of the shoe. Retract the blade, lift the guard out of the way, and attach the hardboard using double-faced tape (**2–12**). Start the saw, then slowly lower the blade to create a zero-clearance blade opening. Cut with a slow feed rate and use extra caution because of the exposed blade.

10. A slick jointer pointer

To trim small plywood pieces from rough to final size, try running them across the jointer. But don't just throw on the sheet and run it through—you may get chip-out at the trailing corner. Instead, place one face against the fence, and joint 2" or 3" along the edge you wish to trim. Then place the opposite face against the fence, and joint the remainder.

11. Should you place the board's good face up or down?

If you're cutting plywood on a tablesaw, the blade's teeth enter the wood from the top and exit the face that's against the table. This is where chip-out will most likely appear. So, keep the good face up on the tablesaw.

With a handheld circular saw, on the other hand, remember that the blade's teeth enter the workpiece from underneath, and exit at the top. It's where the teeth exit that you'll have chip-out and splintering. For this

reason, place the good face down to get a clean cut.

12. Floor it!

A sheet of ¾" hardwood plywood can weigh 60 or 70 pounds, and it's difficult to move around. If wrestling a sheet that heavy onto the tablesaw sounds daunting, rough-cut it into manageable hunks first, using a circular saw. Just lay a 4 x 8' sheet of 2" foam insulation board on the floor, and place your plywood on top of that, as shown in **2–13**.

13. Use a shop-made straightedge guide

Many of us are a little challenged when using a handheld circular saw to cut a straight line. Sure, expensive store-bought guides are available, or you can make a shop-made straightedge guide if you cut lots of sheets. But a simpler solution exists as close

as your scrap bin. Make a guide using the factory edge of a 10"- to 12"-wide scrap of plywood or hardboard. Clamp it in place for your saw's shoe to ride against, as shown in **2–13**. If you're cutting on foam, simply chop out notches to create clearance for the clamp heads.

Fastening materials, hardware, and other components for building the solutions for your storage problems vary considerably with the type and extent of your project.

Basic fasteners include nails and screws (**2–14**). For general construction, use box or

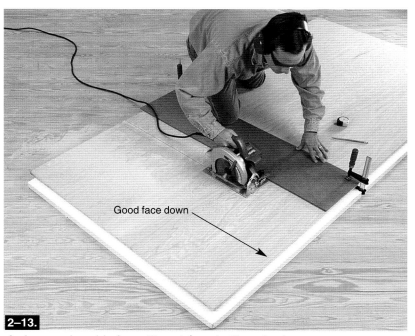

2–13.

A shop-made guide for cutting plywood with a circular saw.

Good face down

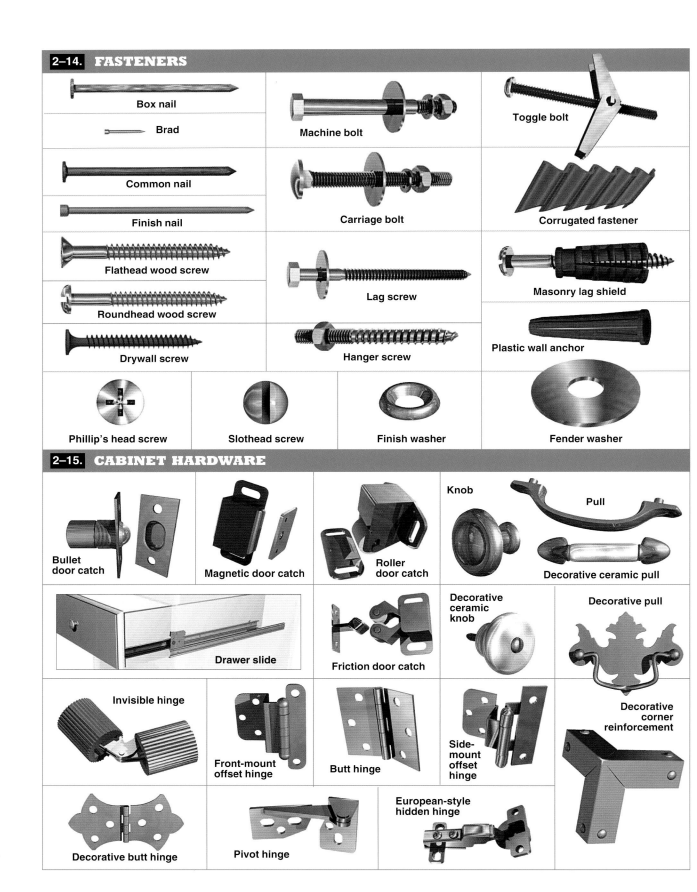

2–14. FASTENERS

Box nail

Brad

Common nail

Finish nail

Flathead wood screw

Roundhead wood screw

Drywall screw

Machine bolt

Carriage bolt

Lag screw

Hanger screw

Toggle bolt

Corrugated fastener

Masonry lag shield

Plastic wall anchor

Phillip's head screw

Slothead screw

Finish washer

Fender washer

2–15. CABINET HARDWARE

Bullet door catch

Magnetic door catch

Roller door catch

Knob

Pull

Decorative ceramic pull

Drawer slide

Friction door catch

Decorative ceramic knob

Decorative pull

Invisible hinge

Front-mount offset hinge

Butt hinge

Side-mount offset hinge

Decorative corner reinforcement

Decorative butt hinge

Pivot hinge

European-style hidden hinge

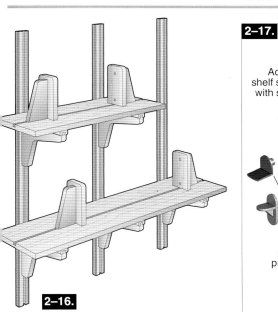

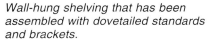

Wall-hung shelving that has been assembled with dovetailed standards and brackets.

2–17.

Adjustable shelf standard with shelf clip

Adjustable shelf standards and brackets

Adjustable shelf standard with shelf clip

Shelf clips for predrilled holes

Just a few of the many shelf-bracket systems.

common nails. For finish work, use finish nails or brads, sinking their heads below the surface with a nail set.

Wood screws are made with flat, oval, or round heads. When the head will be exposed to view, use ovalhead or roundhead screws with trim washers. Use flathead screws when they will be countersunk. Screwhead types include slotted, Phillips, or square-drive styles. Phillips are perhaps the easiest to drive and can be driven with an electric drill. To fasten projects to walls, you may need lag screws, hanger screws, machine bolts, toggle bolts, hollow-wall anchors, or masonry anchors.

You can strengthen joints with angle brackets, flat corner irons, T-plates, or mending plates. Corrugated fasteners, wooden dowels, or biscuits also can be used to strengthen miter, butt, or dado joints.

The variety of shelf-bracket systems ranges from basic closet-pole brackets to several styles of slotted, adjustable standards and accompanying interlocking shelf brackets (**2–16** to **2–19**). You also can support shelves by simply drilling parallel sets of holes and inserting one of many types of pin supports. You can learn more about open shelving in Chapter 6.

If you're building a cabinet, you may need to select hinges and catches for the doors, slides for the drawers, and pulls and knobs for both. In **2–15**, you will find examples of many types of available fasteners and hardware.

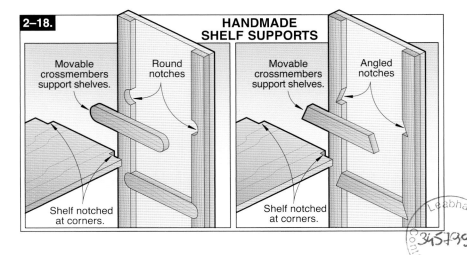

2–18. **HANDMADE SHELF SUPPORTS**

Movable crossmembers support shelves.

Round notches

Shelf notched at corners.

Movable crossmembers support shelves.

Angled notches

Shelf notched at corners.

2–19. WALL-HUNG SHELVING STANDARDS AND BRACKETS

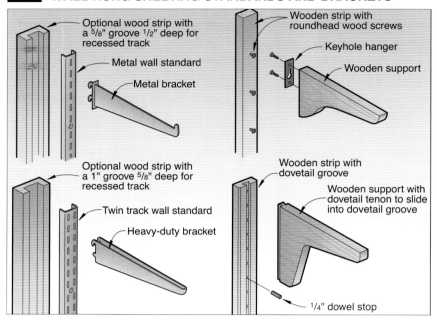

Optional wood strip with a ⅝" groove ½" deep for recessed track

Metal wall standard

Metal bracket

Optional wood strip with a 1" groove ⅝" deep for recessed track

Twin track wall standard

Heavy-duty bracket

Wooden strip with roundhead wood screws

Keyhole hanger

Wooden support

Wooden strip with dovetail groove

Wooden support with dovetail tenon to slide into dovetail groove

¼" dowel stop

PREVENTING SHELF SAG

Any shelf will sag if you over-load it. A shelf's span limit—the distance it can span between supports without sagging or breaking—varies according to the material used.

Architects use books (at 25 pounds per cubic foot) as the standard for determining span limit. Span limits for some typical shelf materials appear in 2–20.

As noted in 2–20, hardwood shelves sag less than other mate-rials, but the amount of sag varies among hardwood species. Oak, maple, beech, and birch rank as the stiffest, followed by ash, cherry, walnut, and mahogany. By comparison, ¾" softwoods, such as white pine,

can only span 36" under load without sagging.

To span longer distances, you need to use thicker material—solid or laminated—or reinforce the shelves using one of the methods shown in 2–21. Reinforcing both edges can boost spans up to 40%.

Similarly, small aluminum channels fitted over the edges of glass or acrylic shelves add strength without affecting the limited visual impact of clear display shelving.

Although solid hardwoods provide you with longer spans, they cost considerably more than veneered plywood. And, plywood reacts less to seasonal humidity changes than does solid wood, making plywood less likely to warp and twist.

Plywood also saves you from edge-joining solid boards to achieve greater widths. And, by applying veneer tape or gluing facing strips to exposed plywood edges, you still get the look of solid wood.

Medium-density fiberboard (MDF) provides a stable, inex-pensive alternative to veneer plywood for shelves you plan to paint. This material will span nearly the same distance, and you can machine and sand its edges smooth. But be sure to use

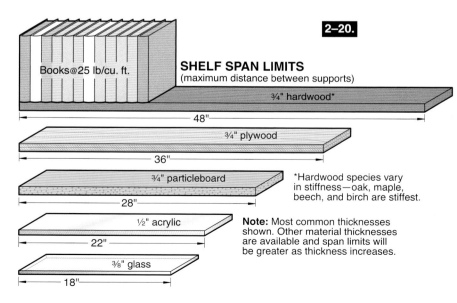

2–20.

Books@25 lb/cu. ft.

SHELF SPAN LIMITS
(maximum distance between supports)

¾" hardwood*

48"

¾" plywood

36"

¾" particleboard

28"

½" acrylic

22"

⅜" glass

18"

*Hardwood species vary in stiffness—oak, maple, beech, and birch are stiffest.

Note: Most common thicknesses shown. Other material thicknesses are available and span limits will be greater as thickness increases.

SIZE UP YOUR SHELVING NEEDS

Once you've settled on a type of shelving, it's time to figure out how much shelving you need. Books, especially, vary greatly in size. The following guidelines provide some general dimensions, but measure your particular components for precision planning.

The books in your home library come in many sizes, and the chart shown at *right* shows typical shelf depth and height requirements for the different types.

As a general rule, a running foot of shelf space holds 8 to 10 books. That same space will hold 10 to 12 children's books, but plan on fitting only five reference books per foot of shelving.

These guidelines provide general dimensions for determining how much shelving your books need.

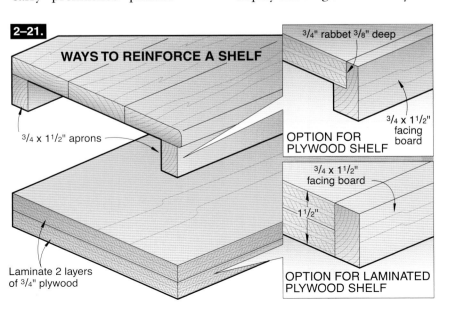

TYPICAL BOOK DIMENSIONS

Type	Height Between Shelves	Shelf Depth
Children's books	8"	8"
Paperbacks	8"	10"
General reading	11"	12"
Large hardbound	15"	12"
Reference	10"	14"

an oil-based primer coat prior to painting MDF because the water in latex primer causes the fibers to swell and separate.

Particleboard provides an even lower-cost option, making it ideal in utility applications where appearance isn't as critical. Many home centers carry "prefinished" particle-board shelving in 8", 10", and 12" widths that has a rounded front edge and a thin, wood-grained or white, vinyl covering. These same outlets also stock this material predrilled for shelf-support pins for use as shelving unit sides.

Glass and acrylic work well for display shelving because they allow light to pass through, and their thin, transparent edges don't detract from the objects on display. Use glass that is at least ¼" thick, and have the edges seamed—or sanded—to make the glass safer to use and handle. For longer spans, or to hold heavier objects, use ½" or thicker glass, but expect to pay substantially more.

Acrylic provides a lightweight alternative to glass where breakage could present a hazard to small children. However, it scratches easily, and costs as much as or more than comparably sized glass.

2–21.

WAYS TO REINFORCE A SHELF

³/₄ x 1¹/₂" aprons

Laminate 2 layers of ³/₄" plywood

³/₄" rabbet ³/₈" deep

³/₄ x 1¹/₂" facing board

OPTION FOR PLYWOOD SHELF

³/₄ x 1¹/₂" facing board

1¹/₂"

OPTION FOR LAMINATED PLYWOOD SHELF

finishing guidelines

IF THERE'S ONE THING TO remember from this chapter, it's that you can't rush a fine finish. Once the glue dries on an assembled project, many woodworkers feel the urge to get it finished quickly and put it into service. However, to achieve a finish deserving of the project you just spent days building, you need to fight this urge. Ask professional woodworkers and they'll tell you that they consider a project at the finishing stage only about two-thirds complete! Keep on asking about their finishing process and they'll tell you the following.

Adding a dye stain. **3–1.**

1. Plan ahead

Just as they plan a project's cutting and assembly steps, pros plan the finishing stage as well. Some pieces, such as inside drawer surfaces or intricate moldings, receive a finish sanding before assembly. In even harder-to-reach areas, mating surfaces get masked off with tape and the finish applied prior to glue-up. To sand round knobs and drawer pulls, simply chuck them in a drill press; then apply finish before installing these parts.

2. Clean up glue squeeze-out

During assembly, clean up excess glue squeeze-out to save yourself additional sanding and avoid finishing problems. You should wipe off excess glue immediately with a wet rag, and rinse the rag often so glue residue doesn't build up. You also can let the glue dry slightly, then scrape off the surplus with a cabinet scraper before it hardens.

3. Don't scrimp on sanding

Although random-orbit sanders have made sanding less painful, there's still no substitute for hand sanding. Use a firm sanding block, such as a cork-faced piece of wood, to keep workpiece edges crisp and to prevent streaks caused by fingertip pressure.

4. Control your environment

Apply your finishes in a clean, well-ventilated environment. Airborne dust raises havoc with trying to achieve a smooth finish. Also, finish fumes pose health risks if inhaled and can ignite if exposed to a spark or flame, such as a pilot light. Keep in mind, too, that faster-drying finishes are less apt to collect airborne dust.

Now that you understand the basics of preparation for whatever kind of finish you choose, here are your two basic choices: a clear finish or paint. Normally, projects built as furnishings that employ expensive hardwoods and hardwood plywood require staining and the application of a clear finish. We'll tell you all about staining beginning on this page. Then, on *page 30*, we'll explain the pros and cons of four popular finishes and how to best apply them.

Paint is traditionally used on projects made from less costly woods and softwood plywood or other sheet goods. However, this doesn't mean that painted projects can't adorn your living room! And just because paint is the easiest finish to apply does not mean that there is less preparation involved. That is why we've included some tips for achieving a perfect paint job on *page 34*.

STAINING GUIDELINES

You've assembled and sanded your project, the can of varnish sits within reach, but this time you want something different than the usual look. You want this piece to match the top-end furniture in the best store in town or the antique in the living room.

Or maybe you want to even out the varying colors of different boards that you've used, make a common wood look exotic, or add richness and depth to your project's appearance. If you have any of these goals in mind, it's time to do some staining.

Staining relies on two types of colorants: pigment and dye. We'll help you choose the right product for the job, and apply it correctly.

Dyes and Pigmented Stains

In **3–2**, shown on *page 26,* you can see the difference between dyes and pigmented stains. The oak board *above* received a coat of golden oak dye, while the other board *below* was tinted with a golden oak stain.

Like paint, a pigmented stain goes on the surface of the wood and penetrates very little. Paint contains enough pigment to make it opaque. Stain has similar pigments, but in lesser amounts, so that it is relatively transparent.

Pigments are suspended in a binder—an additive that dries and thereby creates a seal between the stain and the wood. The most common oil-based binder is linseed oil. Water-based stains employ a non-oil binder. Whether oil- or water-based, all pigmented stains have to be stirred thoroughly to mix the pigments with the binder, or you will get streaky coloring.

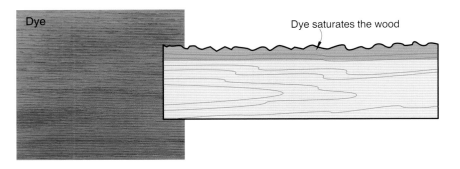

Dye

Dye saturates the wood

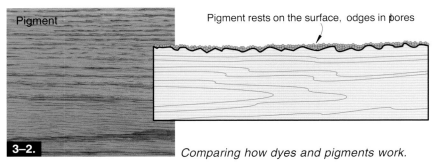

Pigment

Pigment rests on the surface, odges in pores

3–2. *Comparing how dyes and pigments work.*

Applying a Stain

Applying a stain is essentially the same with either a pigment or a dye. Test the stain on a scrap piece, then flood the surface of your project, and wipe off the excess to even out the color.

After wiping, allow the stain to dry completely and wipe the surface again to remove any residue. Remember that the appearance changes when the stain dries and then changes again when you apply a clear topcoat, as shown in 3–3.

You can use either liquid or powder when you choose to dye

3–3.

One of the keys to staining is learning to allow for changes in color from wet stain to dry. Often a woodworker will notice the change and decide that additional coats of stain are necessary—usually a mistake. If the wet color was correct, leave it alone. The wet color of the stain will return as soon as a coat of finish is applied, as shown here.

Some stains dry faster than others, and once the stain dries, you'll have more difficulty removing the excess. Water-based pigment stains tend to dry faster than oil-based pigment stains. Often, the color will get a dry powdery look when the stain dries; it's nothing to worry about.

Dyes differ greatly from pigmented stains. Dyes are transparent, penetrate into any kind of wood, and give it an even tone all over.

You can buy dyes premixed, powdered, or as liquid concentrates. Manufacturers design each powdered dye or liquid concentrate to dissolve with a particular solvent: water, alcohol, or a petroleum product, such as paint thinner. You must use the proper solvent with each type of dye. A dye intended to be dissolved in water usually can't be dissolved in alcohol.

Concentrated liquid dyes will work with more than one solvent. Alcohol-based dyes dry the fastest—perhaps too fast for general use. Water-based dyes are the easiest to apply and the safest to use.

Pigmented stains offer the most flexibility in your choice of

a topcoat. Once the stain dries, you can apply almost any finish over it. For example, you can use an oil-based or water-based finish over either a water-based or an oil-based stain.

The stain must be dry before you proceed with finishing. The temperature, humidity, and moisture content of the wood all affect drying time, so don't rely on the can instructions. Use your nose. If you can smell the solvent, the stain isn't dry.

Dyes are a bit more dicey. If you brush or wipe on a finish containing the same dissolving solvent, you can cause streaking and will partially lift the dye into the finish. This can create a wonderful depth to the color, but might lighten it, too. If you have the necessary equipment, you can spray on the topcoat without causing any problems.

3–4.

3–5.

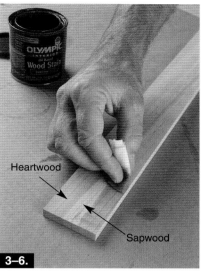

Heartwood

Sapwood

3–6.

When you mix a powdered dye with water or alcohol, no matter how thoroughly you stir, some of the dye particles never will dissolve, so after mixing, allow the dye to settle. Stir it again, and then filter the mixture through a coffee filter, cheesecloth, or nylon hose to remove those undissolved particles. Always wear a protective mask or respirator when working with dry dyes, which become airborne easily. They can cause respiratory problems and even allergic reactions in some people.

You can mix stains and dyes for a custom color, as long as they have the same solvent. For best results, mix the same type and brand of product. Also, mix each color separately before combining them. Don't add a powder or concentrate of one color to the mixed version of another.

Water-based stains and dyes tend to "raise the grain" of wood: Tiny fibers swell up and remain standing like whiskers. If you apply a coat of finish over those whiskers, it will feel like sandpaper.

The easiest way to deal with raised grain is to make it happen before you apply a water-based stain or dye, then eliminate it. First, wet the wood with water from a spray bottle, and allow it to dry completely. Second, sand or scrape off the fuzzy raised grain. For a simple and efficient scraper, just remove the blade from a utility knife. Hold the blade almost vertically, as shown here, and gently scrape the surface.

Wood varies in color, and no stain will even out those differences completely with one coat. The biggest problem occurs in such woods as cherry and walnut, in which the sapwood is a much lighter color than the heartwood.

If you want a dark color on the entire project, apply your stain just to the sapwood, as shown on this piece of cherry. After it dries, apply a coat of the same stain everywhere. If you want a natural finish, find a stain that's the same color as the heartwood, and use that stain to tint only the sapwood.

a piece of wood. Make sure to mix powdered dyes thoroughly, and then filter them, as shown in **3–4**. Generally, the color you apply to a piece of wood will remain the same regardless of the number of coats. The dye color will darken but remain transparent. By contrast, pigmented stains become darker and more opaque with each application.

Preventing and Solving Staining Problems

Even though the actual application is easy, things can still go wrong. But you can avoid most problems once you know what to expect.

Raised grain. The biggest problem with water-based products is that they "raise the grain" of the wood. Go ahead and raise the grain intentionally, but then carefully remove the resulting whiskers, as shown in **3–5**.

Uneven color. A perfectly good board might vary in color, and most stains won't cover up the differences. See **3–6** for a discussion on evening out color.

Blotching. Some woods acquire an uneven look when stained. Apply a conditioner first, and you'll get a much more consistent result. Check **3–7** for examples that illustrate the blotching problem.

Dark end grain. End grain absorbs more pigmented stain than does the rest of the board. To compensate, sand end grain to one grit higher paper than you use on the other surfaces. Then, coat the end grain with a conditioner. Applying a dye stain to the end grain solves the uneven coloring problem without the need for conditioner.

Wrong color. Sometimes you won't be satisfied with the look of a stain on your project. If it's the right shade, but too light, apply another coat of the same

Woods such as pine, cherry, maple, and birch vary significantly in density within a single board. This inconsistency can create "blotch" when you apply stain. Softer areas absorb pigmented stain more readily than do harder areas, making the soft spots darker and more opaque. You can minimize or prevent blotching by using a conditioner before you stain. A conditioner is a coating that seals the pores of the wood, and makes the difference shown here. We applied a conditioner, then red oak stain to the pine sample above right, while the one below received only the stain.

You also can make your own conditioner. For example, if you're going to finish a piece with polyurethane varnish, make a conditioner from five parts thinner and one part poly. Apply this conditioner, allow it to dry, sand it gently with 220-grit sandpaper, remove the dust, and then apply your stain.

With Conditioner

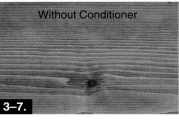

Without Conditioner

3–7.

EXPLORING ANOTHER WORLD OF COLORS

Most woodworkers will find all the colors they need in the standard assortment of cans sold at a home center. But if you have a specific custom look in mind, or you just want to experiment, you can fine-tune those colors. One way is to mix the standard products, always making sure to combine only those with like solvents.

A more controllable approach is to add basic colors to the commercial products, or apply them directly onto the wood. You can either use Japan colors or artist's oils if your stain and topcoat are oil-based, or mix acrylic artist's colors into a glazing medium if you're using water-based products. Art stores and hobby stores carry

artist's oils, acrylic artist's colors, and glazing medium. You can buy Japan colors from a woodworking supply store for about $10 per half-pint.

A color wheel will help you figure out how to arrive at the hue you have in mind. A traditional color wheel shows you how to use red, yellow, and blue to make all of the other colors. You can buy a 9¼" version for about $6.50 from art supply stores.

However, furnituremakers rely more on the earth tone shown on the wheel pictured here. A wheel like this is available from a finishing supply retailer for around $15. Various combinations of raw umber, burnt umber, raw sienna, burnt sienna, Van Dyke brown, white, and black will produce

a range of beautiful furniture colors. Experiment on a storyboard, and write down the recipe as you go along.

When you start dabbling in custom-look colors for your projects, here is a basic approach that many woodworkers don't consider. Illustration **3–8** shows items that can help you create the exact color you need to turn a standard-issue project into something special.

A premixed glaze, available at home centers, plus acrylic colors were used to get the results shown in **3–9.** The left piece received a coat of raw sienna, the middle one got an application of burnt umber, and the sample on the right blends the two colors together.

3–8.

The acrylic colors at left, the artist's colors at right, and the color wheel can help you create the exact color you need to turn a standard-issue project into something special.

A premixed glaze was used to get the results on these oak pieces. The left piece received a coat of raw sienna, the middle one got an application of burnt umber, and the sample on the right shows what happens when you blend the two colors together.

Raw Sienna

Burnt Umber

Raw Sienna Plus Burnt Umber

3–9.

stain. If it's the wrong shade, you can hide it by applying a darker wood stain.

If your stain is too dark, and still wet, you can remove much of it by scrubbing the surface with the appropriate thinning solvent. Use water for water-based stains, and rely on mineral spirits for oil-based stains.

If the stain already has dried, and it's water-based, you'll have to strip it all off with water and start over. You can remove some or all of a dried oil-based stain with lacquer thinner. If not enough comes off to suit you, remove it all with a stripping product, bleach out any remaining spots, and start over.

You can remove some of the color from a dry dyed surface by wiping it with the appropriate solvent. Be careful, though. You run the risk of creating streaks in the color.

Other Staining Products

So far, we have concentrated on pigments and dyes, but five other types of staining products also deserve discussion: In certain situations, you might consider applying a dye/pigment stain, a colored oil/varnish mixture, a gel, an all-in-one product, or a nongrain-raising (NGR) dye. The most versatile of these are the dye/pigment types, as shown in **3–10**. And in some situations, a gel is the best way to get a beautiful result, as shown in **3–11**.

Colored oil/varnish mixtures often are referred to as Danish oils. They combine oil, varnish, thinner, and a dye-like colorant. Easy to apply, they offer a fairly even penetration into the wood and a moderately durable binder that will serve as a finish.

All-in-one products are finishing materials, such as polyurethane varnish, with color added. They

3–10.

Dye/pigment stains contain both kinds of colorant, and usually have separated by the time you take them off the store shelf: The dye is in solution and the pigment has settled out. They require complete stirring to remix the pigment and achieve the intended color.

You can determine if you have a dye/pigment stain by inserting a stick into the unstirred can. If the stick has color along its body and a glob on the end, as shown here, it's a combination product. The dye penetrates the harder portions of a piece of wood, and the pigment settles into the grain and pores. A dye/pigment stain tends to soften blotching, but to really minimize blotch, use a conditioner first.

A dye/pigment stain offers you several staining options. Unstirred, the upper portion of the can will provide a dye type of stain. You can apply it as a stain or add it to a compatible finish to use in toning.

Stir the stain a bit, and you'll get a slightly different shade of the same color; stir it completely for yet another shade. Finally, the settled pigment, left unstirred, works great for glazing.

Gels are pigments, dyes, or a combination of the two, combined with oil-based or water-based finishing materials. Essentially, a gel is a type of paint, coating the surface without penetrating.

Gels tend to obscure the grain, but they do reduce blotching, as you see here. The sample board on the left received a standard stain, while the one on the right was coated with a gel.

Gel stains also work well for "glazing." The technique of glazing allows you to apply color between coats of finish, or to apply an artificial grain to literally any surface. For example, you can make two different woods look alike, or make cardboard look like oak.

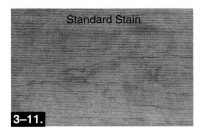

Standard Stain

3–11.

Gel Stain

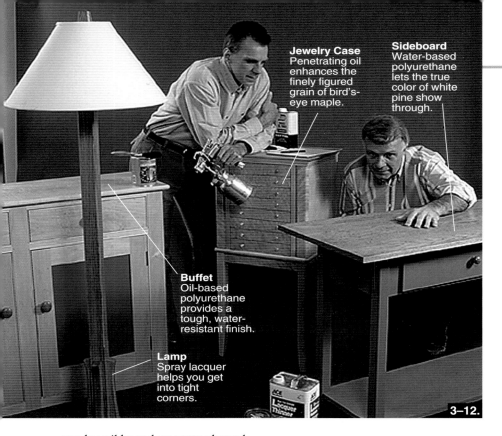

Jewelry Case
Penetrating oil enhances the finely figured grain of bird's-eye maple.

Sideboard
Water-based polyurethane lets the true color of white pine show through.

Buffet
Oil-based polyurethane provides a tough, water-resistant finish.

Lamp
Spray lacquer helps you get into tight corners.

3–12.

The project type and the wood used help determine the choice of finish. The buffet shown here received water-resistant, oil-based polyurethane. The lamp received spray lacquer because of difficult-to-reach areas, and the jewelry case got penetrating oil to highlight the figured maple. The sideboard received paint; then water-based polyurethane was applied to the top to let the true color of the pine show through.

can be oil-based or water-based, and the colorant can be dye or pigment. They are designed to color and finish wood with a single application. These are generally surface products and perform much like paint. They can be tricky to apply because they tend to dry quickly and can be overworked very easily. Successive coats make them darker and more opaque. Lap marks are very difficult to avoid. In short, avoid these products for general finishing.

Non-grain-raising dyes are water-based products that you thin with alcohol or lacquer thinner, making them compatible with oil-based finishing materials. They dry very quickly, matching one of the advantages of a typical water-based dye. Most home woodworkers can get along just fine without them.

FOUR CLEAR FINISHES THAT MAKE IT HARD TO FAIL

Don't let a mediocre finishing job detract from your careful craftsmanship. Choose one of the following clear finishes to ensure success.

Depending on the project, *WOOD*® magazine's craftsmen get great results using oil-based polyurethane, lacquer, penetrating oil, or water-based polyurethane. Each finish has unique properties suited for particular projects, as shown in **3–12**.

The two polyurethanes stand up to both wear and moisture, making them good choices for tabletops, toys, and other heavily used objects. Oil-based poly

flows out more evenly than water-based, but it gives off more fumes and takes much longer to dry. However, an advantage is that the oil-type also imparts a golden tone that enhances the natural color of woods like pine, oak, and cherry.

Lacquer, while durable, works best on projects that won't receive heavy wear or exposure to moisture. It lends itself to spray application, either with a spray gun or aerosol can, and can cover large surfaces rapidly, as well as small, intricate parts. It dries quickly, so you can build up several coats in short order. Lacquer dries clear, letting the wood's true color show through.

Penetrating oil goes on the easiest, but requires the most sanding preparation. Like lacquer, it's better suited to pieces that will not be exposed to heavy wear or moisture.

Water-based polyurethane dries clear, so the wood's true color shows through. It cures hard, but lacks the resilience of an oil-based finish.

While these four finishes vary, some basic principles apply to each one. The following recommendations will help ensure a fine finish no matter which one you decide on.

Oil-Based Polyurethane

The advantages of oil-based polyurethane are that it is water and alcohol resistant, resilient, and it resists wear. The disadvantages are that it takes a long time to dry and is somewhat difficult to apply and repair.

For a heavily used surface, such as a casual dining room tabletop, nothing works better than oil-based polyurethane. Tough and scratch-resistant, it stands up well to water, alcohol, and other beverages that might get spilled on it. Clear polyurethane gives a warm, golden glow to most woods, although a number of companies sell polyurethane with stain mixed in.

You'll have success with any number of brands, although the fast-drying type shortens finishing time. A long drying time— one of oil-based polyurethane's biggest drawbacks—makes working in a relatively dust-free environment even more important because dust has a longer time to settle onto a surface.

Applying an Oil-Based Polyurethane Finish

Here is how to apply an oil-based polyurethane finish:

Preparation. Finish-sand the surface with 180-grit sandpaper, but no finer than 220-grit because a surface that's too smooth will cause bonding problems. Vacuum off the sanding dust,

and then wipe the piece down with a clean rag or tack cloth.

Application. You can use a poly-foam brush, but many woodworkers prefer a good natural bristle brush. Such a brush costs $10 to $20, lays finish down smoothly, and won't shed bristles. For small or intricate pieces, oil-based polyurethane comes in aerosol cans.

First coat. Even if you want a satin finish, use gloss polyurethane on the first coat because it lets the wood grain show through and reveals uneven spots better. It also rubs out easier than satin. If you put it down over stain, apply a second coat, with no sanding between applications.

Between coats. Allow the finish to dry overnight, then use 220-grit sandpaper to rub the entire surface to a uniform dullness. Wipe the piece with a clean, dry cloth.

Final treatment. Apply gloss or satin polyurethane, depending on the desired finish, and let the piece dry for a couple of days. On flat surfaces, you can lightly drag a dull cabinet scraper across

the surface to knock off the dust bumps, as shown in **3–13**. Buff the finish using a light-duty (white) cleansing pad. You can set your random-orbit sander on the pad and apply only light pressure to speed up the buffing process. For a mirror-like finish, buff the finish using an automotive-type polishing compound and a power buffer.

Maintenance. Minor surface scratches buff out easily, but deep gouges require sanding and reapplying finish to the entire wood surface.

Spray Lacquer

The advantages of spray lacquer are that it is fast drying, builds quickly, and is easily repaired. The disadvantages are that it is not water resistant and that it contains highly volatile solvents.

When you're working against a deadline, reach for quick-drying lacquer. The solvents in lacquer, primarily acetone, evaporate quickly, allowing you to apply four or more coats of finish in a single day. These solvents slightly dissolve the previous coat, making a strong bond between coats.

3–13.

Dragging a scraper across a surface to remove dust bumps.

Applying a Spray Lacquer Finish

To apply a spray lacquer finish, do the following:

Preparation. Begin by sanding down the entire project, progressing from 100- to 180- and finally to 220-grit sandpaper. Vacuum off the sanding dust, then wipe down the piece with a clean rag or tack cloth. If you apply a stain, follow the stain manufacturer's directions to ensure that the stain dries evenly and thoroughly.

Application. Lacquer's properties make it ideal for spraying. A high-volume, low-pressure (HVLP) spray gun works well for large projects, while lacquer in spray cans are able to cover small projects. Brushable lacquers dry slower but require you to use a natural bristle brush because the solvents in lacquer can dissolve synthetic bristle and poly-foam brushes. Whether you spray or brush it on, wear an approved respirator and work in a well-ventilated area.

First coat. Apply a heavy, wet coat and allow it to dry. On stained surfaces, apply a second coat as soon as the first coat dries to the touch.

Between coats. Sand lightly between coats with 320-grit sandpaper to knock off the high spots; then wipe the surface with a clean dry cloth. Normally, you want to give most projects three coats.

3-14.

Preparing a board for a penetrating oil.

Final treatment. Generally, a light buffing takes care of any surface blemishes, although rubbing out lacquer with polishing compounds produces a mirror-like sheen people will want to touch.

Maintenance. To remove scratches, buff or lightly rub them with lacquer thinner; then recoat and rub out the finish to match the surrounding area. On stained wood, be careful not to sand down to bare wood.

Penetrating Oil

The advantages of penetrating oil are that it is easy to apply and repair and enhances figured wood grain. The disadvantages are that it is not water resistant and bleeds on open-grained wood.

Nothing equals a hand-rubbed oil finish for putting a warm glow on a piece of fine furniture. Penetrating oil brings out the highlights in wood and enhances the figure of the grain. Although well-suited to tightly grained woods, such as maple, cherry, and walnut, penetrating oil tends to bleed back out of the deep pores of oak. It lacks the durability of the other finishes, but makes up for it in ease of application and maintenance.

Brands of penetrating oil are offered in clear and in several darker shades. Some, though, take only two coats to build up a finish while others require three or more.

Applying a Penetrating Oil Finish

To apply a penetrating oil finish, do the following:

Preparation. Oil finishes require the most sanding preparation. Progress through 220-grit sandpaper, then go back over the piece with 320 or finer grit, as shown in **3–14.** Vacuum off the sanding dust, and then wipe the piece down with a clean rag or tack cloth.

Application. Use a bristle or poly-foam brush to apply the oil to the wood. Small parts can be dipped in a container of finish.

First coat. Lay on the oil. When it just starts to feel tacky, wipe off the excess with a clean, lint-free cotton rag. If it dries too quickly, re-oil lightly, and then wipe it clean.

Between coats. Let the finish dry overnight, then rub it down with an ultrafine (gray) abrasive pad. Rub with the grain to prevent cross-grain scratches. Wipe the piece clean, then reapply oil as before.

Final treatment. When the second coat dries, buff the finish with a soft, clean cloth. For added luster, apply paste wax, then polish it.

Maintenance. To maintain an oil finish, periodically recoat it with the same oil originally used to finish the piece. This replenishes the surface and hides scratches. Wipe waxed finishes with mineral spirits before applying more oil. Dirty finish can be removed using an ultrafine pad dipped in oil finish.

Water-Based Polyurethane

The advantages of water-based polyurethane are that it is tough, durable, water resistant, cleans up with soap and water, and does not emit any fumes. The disadvantages are that it is difficult to apply evenly and that it raises the wood grain.

3–15.

Applying water-based polyurethane.

While well-suited for many of the same projects as its oil-based cousin, water-based polyurethane has very different properties. First, it dries clear, so the color of the wood will not yellow, as illustrated by the pine sideboard in the photo on *page 30*. Because it contains water, this finish raises the wood grain. To minimize grain raising, wipe down the piece with a wet rag, letting it dry; then sand off the raised grain.

Water-based polyurethane dries much faster than does oil-based polyurethane, but this makes it harder to brush out evenly. Its water composition also requires that you use only synthetic abrasive pads, because the particles left behind by steel wool will rust and leave dark stains in the wood.

Finally, water-based polyurethane is low on fumes and cleans up with water, making it a good choice for shops where adequate ventila-tion for solvent-based finishes presents a problem. You can achieve good results by applying it with a synthetic-bristle brush.

Applying a Water-Based Polyurethane Finish

To apply a water-based polyurethane finish, do the following:

Preparation. Finish-sand the project with 220-grit sandpaper, wipe it off with a wet rag or sponge, and allow it to dry. Sand just enough with 220-grit to remove the raised grain.

Application. Brush water-based polyurethane on in thin coats using a quality synthetic bristle brush. Some brands work with an HVLP sprayer, but follow the can directions for thinning information.

First coat. Apply a thin coat, and don't overbrush it (**3–15**). If you get foam, dab it up with a clean cloth, then brush out any marks. (Never, never shake the can! That causes bubbles.)

Between coats. After the first coat cures, sand it lightly with 220-grit sandpaper to remove any raised grain. Vacuum off the sanding dust, then wipe the piece down with a water-dampened rag.

Final treatment. Apply a second thin coat and repeat the steps above. After a final application, allow the finish to cure, and then buff it with a white mesh pad and/or polishing compound.

Maintenance. Minor surface scratches will buff out, but deep scratches call for sanding and reapplying finish to the entire workpiece surface.

3–16.

After filling the edges of plywood with the mixture described below, you'll find a sanding block to be ideal for sanding it smooth and flat.

APPLYING A PAINT FINISH

If you know how to prepare a project for painting and then apply the paint, your work will pass for a factory-made job. And these tips apply to paint both sprayed from a can and brushed on.

Fill and sand the project. No matter how hard you try, a small gap, dent, or scratch can remain on a project after final sanding. To level out problem spots such as these, use mixable, powdered water putty. But instead of mixing the powder with water as called for on the can, mix it with yellow woodworker's glue. By doing this, the filler will set up faster and harder, and won't crumble.

After mixing the powder and glue to the consistency of sour cream, use a putty knife to apply the putty to the depression. The smoother you apply and level the putty now, the less sanding you'll have to do later. Let the putty dry thoroughly (about an hour), and sand smooth the repaired area. As shown in **3–16**, a sanding block works well. If the area is not perfectly smooth and flat, repeat the process.

Apply the primer coats. A white primer coat on bare wood plays many roles in a silky-smooth finish. Primers contain more solids than paints do, making them ideal for sealing and filling a finely sanded surface. Acting as a uniform color backer for the paint to bond to, the primer also allows the true color of the paint to show through. For smaller projects, you can spray on a sandable white primer. Larger projects will require brushing (or more cans of primer). Sprayed directly onto bare wood, paints tend to darken or become slightly more yellow than their natural color. A primer coat also may raise the grain slightly. If it does, sand lightly to smooth the surface. It's better to have the primer raise the grain than the paint.

Note: It is critical that you use a paint that's compatible with the primer. For instance, if you want to use a lacquer-based paint, use a lacquer-based primer. And, although you can spray an enamel paint over a lacquer primer, the solvents in a lacquer paint will dissolve an enamel finish, causing the paint to wrinkle.

To sand the primer, turn to 320-grit sandpaper. Not only does sanding level any little imperfections in the primer, it also highlights imperfections that are easier to smooth out now than later during the painting process.

Plan on giving most projects one or two coats of primer. Porous end grain may need more primer to build up a smooth surface onto which you can spray or brush the paint. Additional primer also is needed if you sand through the primer.

Now, check for imperfections. One of the best ways we know to do this is to shine a work light onto the surface and view the project from a low angle.

Paint the Project. The importance of spraying (or brushing) on light coats of paint cannot be stressed enough. With a spray can, keep the paint can nozzle the same distance from the project at all times. If you spray on too much paint at

3–17.

A can of spray paint in one hand and a bright light in the other are a perfect combination for laying down even coats of paint.

one time, you greatly increase the odds of runs and sags—problems that are difficult and time-consuming to even out. As shown in **3–17**, a bright light gives you a better idea of just how much paint you're putting

on. But be careful, too, that you don't put too little paint on the surface. If your painted surface feels coarse, you're probably not laying down enough paint.

REPAIRING A PAINT JOB

If a scuff, fingerprint, or other surface imperfection mars your painted project, there's still hope. To remove tiny bumps left by shop dust, wet-sand painted surfaces with 600-grit wet/dry sandpaper. Be careful to keep the area being sanded and the sandpaper moist, as shown in **3–18**. Keep a tray of water on hand for this operation. It takes only about six light passes to smooth out the roughness. When doing this, be extremely careful not to apply too much pressure or make too many passes, thereby rubbing through the thin layer of paint.

If the paint balls up under the sandpaper, the paint is not dry enough. If you notice lots of paint on your sandpaper, your paint is not dry enough or you're not using enough water.

After wet-sanding a painted surface, dry it with a clean cloth. The wet-sanding not only removes the dust bumps, it also leaves dull spots. To restore the shine, follow these steps. First, rub the entire painted surface with #0000 steel wool (ultrafine mesh pads, the gray-colored ones, also work fine). Again, use a light touch,

being careful not to rub through the paint to the primer. Then, wipe off the dust with a tack cloth, apply a paste wax with another clean cotton cloth, and buff the surface by hand to bring back the sheen.

3–18.

Keeping the project and sandpaper wet, use 600-grit wet/dry sandpaper to sand away imperfections or runs.

CHAPTER 4

cabinet storage

F O R   C E N T U R I E S ,   H O U S E H O L D S   H A V E turned to cabinet storage, for several reasons. One is that it protects the contents from dust, dirt, and moisture. Another is that it conceals its holdings. And lastly, cabinets can be attractive additions to your home's furnishings. The latter reason is primarily why we've chosen the three cabinets you'll see in this chapter.

Begin with the clean and simple Shaker wall cabinet shown on the next page. Its distinctive, straightforward design will make it seem at home in any room of your house. As a bonus, it's easy to build following our step-by-step instructions.

The heirloom hutch on page 40 raises the cabinet storage solution several notches. It is beautiful in naturally finished knotty pine and offers you two options: Build only the handsome sideboard, or add the glass-doored upper unit for a complete hutch. We've broken down the instructions into two easy options.

If you're looking for a good-looking yet serviceable cabinet with plenty of storage for fine dinnerware and linens, you'll like the oak sideboard on page 50. Its traditional lines are a pleasure to look at, and its joinery is basic.

SHAKER CABINET

With its classic Shaker lines, this cherry unit is not only good-looking, but can be built in a couple of evenings. You will need some thin cherry stock, so plan on resawing or planing thick stock to size.

MATERIALS LIST FOR SHAKER CABINET

PART		FINISHED SIZE			MTL.	QTY.
		T	W	L		
CABINET						
A	sides	¾"	5¼"	22"	C	2
B	shelf	¾"	5"	12"	C	1
C	top and bottom	¾"	5⅞"	14¼"	C	2
D	back	¼"	4¹⁄₁₆"	22¾"	C	3
DOOR						
E	stiles	¾"	1¹⁵⁄₁₆"	17⅝"	C	2
F	rails	¾"	1¹⁵⁄₁₆"	7½"	C	2
G*	panel	¼"	8⅜"	14⁹⁄₁₆"	EC	1
SHELVES AND DRAWER						
H	shelves	½"	4⅛"	11¼"	C	2
I	front	¾"	3⅜"	11⅜"	C	1
J	back	½"	3⅜"	10⅞"	C	1
K	sides	½"	3⅜"	4⁹⁄₁₆"	C	2
L	bottom	¼"	4⅛"	10⅞"	C	1

*Parts initially cut oversized. See the instructions.
Materials Key: C = Cherry; EC = Edge-joined cherry.
Supplies: #4 x ½" flathead wood screws; two 8" pieces of ⅜" cherry dowel (available from crafts stores).
Hardware: One ¾"-diameter and one 1"-diameter Shaker knob; one pair of 1½"-long no-mortise hinges; magnetic catch; strike plate.

This clean and simple cherry cabinet makes a nice addition to almost any wall that needs to be dressed up.

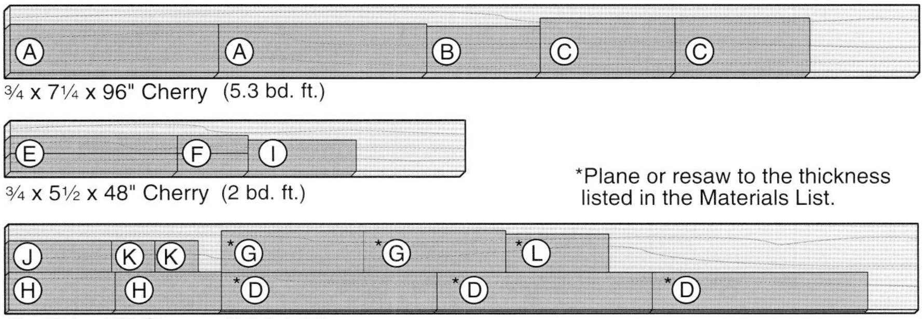

Make the Basic Case

1 From ¾"-thick cherry, cut the sides (A), fixed shelf (B), and top and bottom (C) to the sizes in the Materials List.

2 Mark the locations and cut a ¾" dado ¼" deep on the inside face of each cabinet side (A). Then, cut or rout a ¼" rabbet ⅜" deep along the back inside edge of each cabinet side.

3 Mark the shelf-hole center-points and drill ¼" holes ½" deep on the inside face of the side pieces (40 holes total).

CUTTING DIAGRAM FOR THE SHAKER CABINET

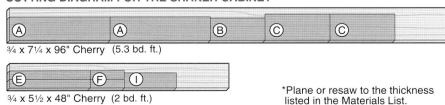

*Plane or resaw to the thickness listed in the Materials List.

¾ x 7¼ x 96" Cherry (5.3 bd. ft.)

¾ x 5½ x 48" Cherry (2 bd. ft.)

½ x 9¼ x 96" Cherry (3.3 bd. ft.)

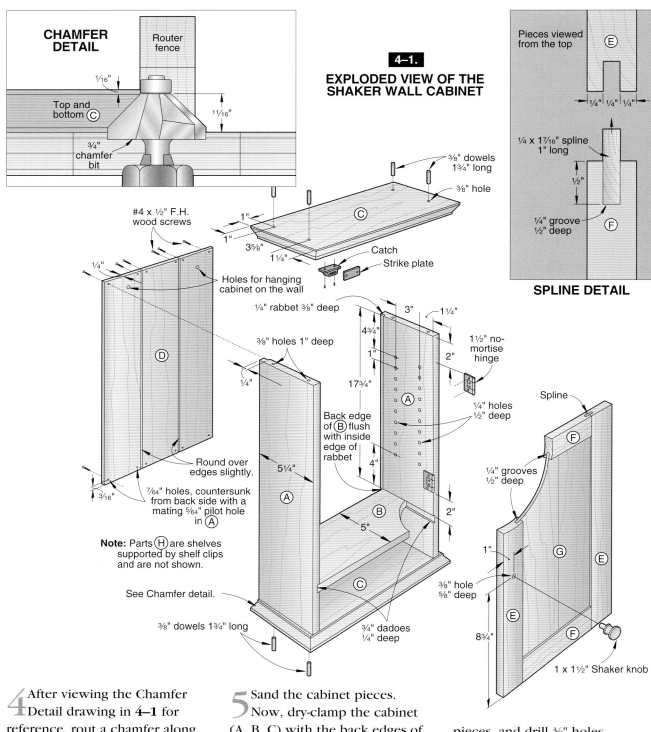

CHAMFER DETAIL

Router fence

1/16"

Top and bottom C

11/16"

3/4" chamfer bit

4–1.
EXPLODED VIEW OF THE SHAKER WALL CABINET

Pieces viewed from the top

E

1/4" 1/4" 1/4"

1/4 x 17/16" spline 1" long

1/2"

1/4" groove 1/2" deep

F

SPLINE DETAIL

3/8" dowels 13/4" long

3/8" hole

C

#4 x 1/2" F.H. wood screws

1"

1"

35/8"

11/4"

Catch

Strike plate

1/4"

Holes for hanging cabinet on the wall

1/4" rabbet 3/8" deep

3"

11/4"

3/8" holes 1" deep

43/4"

1"

11/2" no-mortise hinge

2"

D

1/4"

17 3/4"

A

1/4" holes 1/2" deep

Spline

F

Back edge of B flush with inside edge of rabbet

Round over edges slightly.

51/4"

A

4"

B

1/4" grooves 1/2" deep

7/64" holes, countersunk from back side with a mating 5/64" pilot hole in A

3/16"

5"

2"

G

E

Note: Parts H are shelves supported by shelf clips and are not shown.

B

1"

C

3/8" hole 5/8" deep

See Chamfer detail.

E

3/8" dowels 13/4" long

3/4" dadoes 1/4" deep

83/4"

F

1 x 11/2" Shaker knob

4 After viewing the Chamfer Detail drawing in **4–1** for reference, rout a chamfer along the front and side edges of the top and bottom pieces (C).

5 Sand the cabinet pieces. Now, dry-clamp the cabinet (A, B, C) with the back edges of A and B flush; check for square. Mark the dowel-hole center-points on the top and bottom

pieces, and drill 3/8" holes through the top and bottom and 1" into the ends of the side pieces. Remove the clamps.

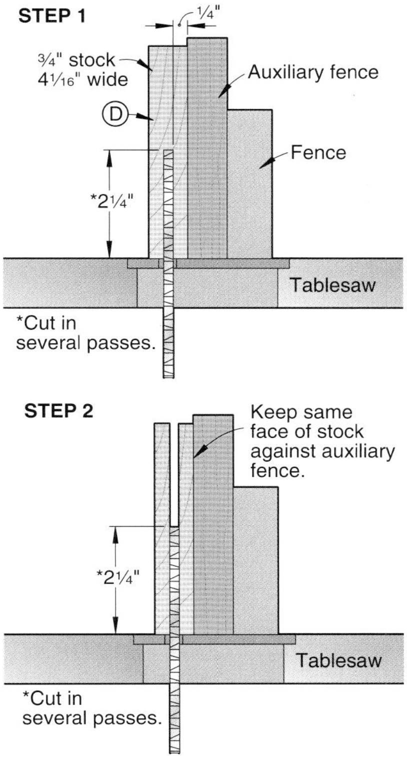
STEP 1
¼"
¾" stock
4¹⁄₁₆" wide
D
Auxiliary fence
Fence
*2¼"
Tablesaw
*Cut in
several passes.
STEP 2
Keep same
face of stock
against auxiliary
fence.
*2¼"
Tablesaw
*Cut in
several passes.

4–2. **RESAWING THICKER STOCK TO SIZE**

6 Cut eight ⅜"-diameter dowels 1¾" long. (We used cherry dowel stock.) Next, glue, dowel, and clamp the cabinet assembly (A, B, C) together, checking for square. Wipe off excess glue with a damp cloth. Trim and sand the protruding end of each dowel flush with the cabinet surface, being careful not to mar it.

7 Mark the location and fasten the hinges to the right-hand cabinet side (A).

Add the Back

1 Cut three pieces of ¼"-thick cherry to 4¹⁄₁₆" width by 22¾" length for the back panel (D). Sand a slight round-over on the front edges of each piece. (Illustration. **4–2** shows the method used to resaw thicker stock to size on a tablesaw.)

2 Rout a ¼" rabbet ⅜" deep along the inside edge of the top and bottom pieces (C) to match the rabbet previously cut in the side pieces. Use a sharp chisel to square the corners where the rabbets meet.

3 Lay the cabinet face down. Position the three back pieces (D) in the rabbeted opening. Drill and countersink holes in the back-panel pieces to the sizes shown in the Exploded View drawing in **4–1**.

Make the Door

1 Cut the door stiles (E) and rails (F) to size. Then, cut two pieces of cherry to 4½ x 15". Plane or resaw the pieces to ¼" thick for the door panel (G). Glue and clamp the pieces edge to edge, with surfaces and ends flush.

2 Cut or rout a ¼" groove ½" deep along one edge of each rail and stile, where shown in the Spline Detail drawing in **4–1**. From ¼" cherry, cut four splines to size.

3 Test-fit the door pieces; the panel should be slightly undersized, about ¹⁄₁₆" in each direction to allow it to expand without splitting the assembled door. Then, glue and clamp the door. Allow the panel to float inside the frame without glue.

4 Mark the centerpoint, and drill a hole for installing the Shaker knob.

5 Cut to size the adjustable shelves (H) shown in the Cutting Diagram on *page 37*.

4–3.

EXPLODED VIEW OF DRAWER

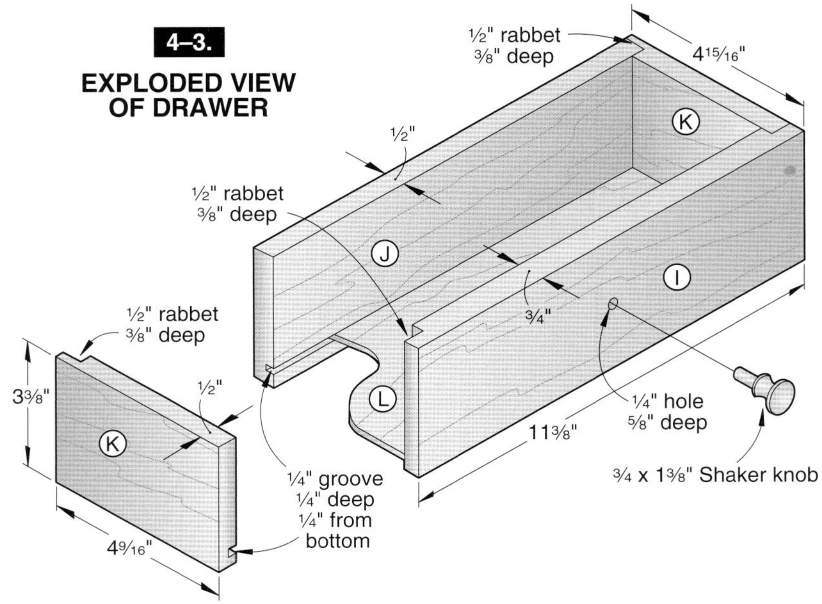
½" rabbet
⅜" deep
4¹⁵⁄₁₆"
K
½"
½" rabbet
⅜" deep
J
I
¾"
½" rabbet
⅜" deep
3⅜"
½"
K
L
¼" groove
¼" deep
¼" from
bottom
4⁹⁄₁₆"
11⅜"
¼" hole
⅝" deep
¾ x 1⅜" Shaker knob

Finally Add the Drawer and Apply a Finish

1 Cut the drawer front (I), back (J), sides (K), and bottom (L) to the sizes in the Materials List.

2 Cut a ¼" groove ¼" deep and ¼" from the bottom edge of the front, back, and side pieces, where shown in **4–3**.

3 Cut ½" rabbets ⅜" deep on both ends of the front piece (I) and the back end of each side piece (K). (See **4–3**.)

4 Draw diagonal lines from corner to corner to find the center of the drawer front. Drill the hole for the knob.

5 Dry-clamp the pieces and check the fit of the drawer in the opening. Then, glue and clamp together the drawer parts.

6 Drill a pair of mounting holes through the cabinet back, where shown on the Exploded View drawing in **4–1**.

7 Sand the cabinet, back, door, and drawer. Apply the finish to the cabinet and knobs. (We left the cherry natural and brushed on several coats of polyurethane.) Add the knobs. Finally, secure the door to the cabinet with the hinges, and mount the magnetic catch and strike plate.

PINE HUTCH CABINET

Create this piece of classic furniture for your home, and in the process, learn a super-simple way to make doors with glass inserts or raised panels using just your tablesaw.

Made entirely of affordable ¾"-thick knotty pine lumber and ⁵⁄₁₆"-thick beaded planking, this handsome piece has a classic country look that's enhanced by such details as its pegged doorframes and antique glass. And by all means, don't try to hide the knots—they're a big part of this piece's rustic appeal!

This pine hutch cabinet has a classic country look and makes the ideal place to store heirlooms. *See a photo of the hutch cabinet with its doors closed on* page 42.

CUTTING DIAGRAM FOR PINE HUTCH CABINET

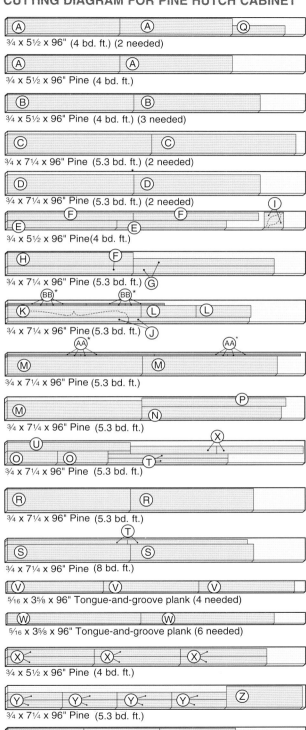

(A) (A) (Q)
¾ x 5½ x 96" (4 bd. ft.) (2 needed)

(A) (A)
¾ x 5½ x 96" Pine (4 bd. ft.)

(B) (B)
¾ x 5½ x 96" Pine (4 bd. ft.) (3 needed)

(C) (C)
¾ x 7¼ x 96" Pine (5.3 bd. ft.) (2 needed)

(D) (D)
¾ x 7¼ x 96" Pine (5.3 bd. ft.) (2 needed)

(F) (F) (I)
(E) (E)
¾ x 5½ x 96" Pine (4 bd. ft.)

(H) (F)
¾ x 7¼ x 96" Pine (5.3 bd. ft.) (G)

(BB)* (BB)*
(K) (L) (L)
¾ x 7¼ x 96" Pine (5.3 bd. ft.) (J)

(AA)* (AA)*
(M) (M)
¾ x 7¼ x 96" Pine (5.3 bd. ft.)

(M) (P)
(N)
¾ x 7¼ x 96" Pine (5.3 bd. ft.)

(U) (X)
(O) (O) (T)
¾ x 7¼ x 96" Pine (5.3 bd. ft.)

(R) (R)
¾ x 7¼ x 96" Pine (5.3 bd. ft.)

(T)
(S) (S)
¾ x 7¼ x 96" Pine (8 bd. ft.)

(V) (V) (V)
⁵⁄₁₆ x 3⅝ x 96" Tongue-and-groove plank (4 needed)

(W) (W)
⁵⁄₁₆ x 3⅝ x 96" Tongue-and-groove plank (6 needed)

(X) (X) (X)
¾ x 5½ x 96" Pine (4 bd. ft.)

(Y) (Y) (Y) (Y) (Z)
¾ x 7¼ x 96" Pine (5.3 bd. ft.)

(Z) (Z) (Z)
¾ x 7¼ x 96" Pine (5.3 bd. ft.)
*Plane or resaw to the thickness listed in the Materials List.

MATERIALS LIST FOR PINE HUTCH CABINET

PART	FINISHED SIZE			MTL.	QTY.
	T	W	L		
CARCASES					
A* base sides	¾"	15¼"	35¼"	EP	2
B* base top and bottom	¾"	14¹⁵⁄₁₆"	39¾"	EP	2
C* upper sides	¾"	12¼"	45½"	EP	2
D* upper top and bottom	¾"	11¹⁵⁄₁₆"	39¾"	EP	2
FACE FRAMES					
E base stiles	¾"	2½"	35¼"	P	2
F frame rails	¾"	2½"	40½"	P	3
G upper stiles	¾"	2½"	45½"	P	2
H upper top rail	¾"	4½"	40½"	P	1
I* brackets	¾"	5"	5"	P	2
J door stops	¾"	1½"	39"	P	2
TRIM					
K* front skirt	¾"	4"	42"	P	1
L* side skirts	¾"	4"	16¾"	P	2
M* top	¾"	17"	42½"	EP	1
N cap front	¾"	4"	45"	P	1
O* cap sides	¾"	4"	15¼"	P	2
P* crown front	¾"	2¹³⁄₁₆"	44½"	P	1
Q* crown sides	¾"	2¹³⁄₁₆"	15"	P	2
SHELVES					
R* base shelf	¾"	13"	38¾	EP	1
S* upper shelf	¾"	10"	38¾"	EP	1
T shelf trims	¾"	1½"	38¾"	P	4
BACK					
U back rail	¾"	2¾"	39¾"	P	1
V* base back	⁵⁄₁₆"	39¾"	30⅞"	PP	1
W* upper back	⁵⁄₁₆"	39¾"	43¼"	PP	1
DOORS					
X stiles	¾"	2½"	27⅞"	P	8
Y rails	¾"	2½"	17⅝"	P	8
Z* panels	¾"	13¼"	23⁹⁄₁₆"	EP	2
AA* vertical stops	¼"	⅜"	23⅝"	P	8
BB* horizontal stops	¼"	⅜"	12⅝"	P	8

*Parts initially cut oversized. See the instructions.
Materials Key: EP = Edge-joined pine; P = Pine; PP = Beaded tongue-and-groove knotty pine planking.
Supplies: 6d finish nails; #20 biscuits; ¼" perforated hardboard; #8 x 1¼" flathead wood screws; #8 x 1¼" roundhead wood screws; #8 flat washers; #17 x ¾" wire brads; #16 x 1" wire brads; #16 x 1¼" wire nails; ⅝ x 3" mending plates (2); #5 x ⅝" flathead brass wood screws; #4 x½" roundhead brass wood screws; #18 x½" brass escutcheon pins; spray adhesive; single-strength or antique glass; stain; clear finish.
Blades and bits: Stack dado set; chamfer, ⅛" round-over, and ⅜" round-over router bits.
Hardware: Brass cupboard catches (2); adjustable nonmortise partial-wrap inset hinges with screws (8); library door latches (2); brass shelf supports (package of 20).
Planking: Look for ⁵⁄₁₆ x 3⅝ x 96" beaded tongue-and-groove knotty pine planking at local lumberyards or home centers.

A look at the hutch with its cabinet door closed.

Note: *If you wish to build only the sideboard base, we've made doing that simple. Just skip any part of the instructions that are printed in red text. These sections cover making the upper cabinet.*

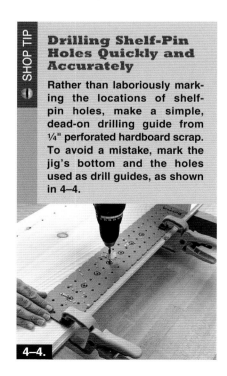

Drilling Shelf-Pin Holes Quickly and Accurately

Rather than laboriously marking the locations of shelf-pin holes, make a simple, dead-on drilling guide from ¼" perforated hardboard scrap. To avoid a mistake, mark the jig's bottom and the holes used as drill guides, as shown in 4–4.

4–4.

Edge-Join the Part Blanks

1 Select boards to edge-join into blanks for the base sides (A), base carcase top and bottom (B), upper sides (C), upper carcase top and bottom (D), top (M), base shelf (R), and upper shelf (S). Match them for grain and color, and use boards that will make blanks slightly longer and wider than the part sizes in the Materials List.

2 Joint the mating edges, and glue and clamp together the boards. Mark the part letters on the ends. Once the glue is dry, sand the blanks to 220 grit.

Make the Carcases

1 Cut the base sides (A), base carcase top and bottom (B), upper sides (C), and upper carcase top and bottom (D) to size. Cut the rabbets and dadoes across the width of the sides, and the rabbets along the sides' inside rear edges, where shown on the Carcases and Face Frames drawings in 4–6. Make sure you have mirror-image parts.

2 Glue and clamp together the base carcase (A/B) and the upper carcase (C/D). Square the assemblies, and toenail the tops and bottoms to the sides with finish nails, where shown on the Carcases, Face Frames and Toenailing drawings in 4–6.

3 Drill shelf-pin holes in the sides (A, C), where shown, using the method suggested in

4–5.

When clamping the face frames in place, make certain that the carcase bottoms protrude evenly above the bottom rails.

the Shop Tip "Drilling Shelf-Pin Holes Quickly and Accurately."

Add the Face Frames

1 Cut the base stiles (E), frame rails (F), upper stiles (G), and upper top rail (H) to the sizes listed. Install a dado blade in your tablesaw, and cut the half-laps where shown on the Carcases and Face Frames drawings in 4–6.

<u>**Sideboard base builder's note:**</u> *Make only two frame rails (F).*

2 Glue and clamp together the face frames. Then measure the diagonals to make certain the frames are square.

3 Cut a ¾ x 5¼ x 6¼" blank for the brackets (I). Make two copies of the bracket pattern in 4–16 *(page 49)*. Enlarge the patterns to 133% for full size.

4–6.

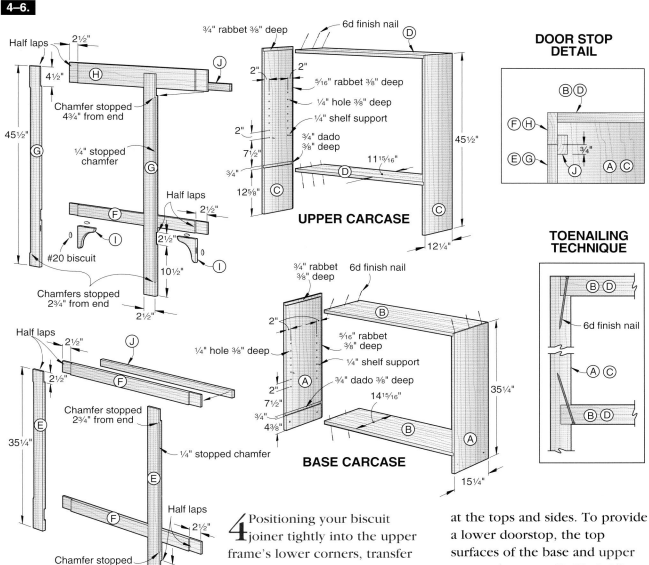

DOOR STOP DETAIL

TOENAILING TECHNIQUE

UPPER CARCASE

BASE CARCASE

FACE FRAMES

Cut the patterns to the lines, and adhere them to the blank with spray adhesive as shown on the Cutting Diagram on *page 41*. Bandsaw and sand the brackets to shape. Rout round-overs on the edges where shown.

4 Positioning your biscuit joiner tightly into the upper frame's lower corners, transfer the joiner's centering mark to the frame rail (F) and upper stiles (G). Position the brackets where shown in the Carcases and Face Frames drawings in 4–6, and transfer these locations to them. Plunge slots for #20 biscuits into the rails, stiles, and brackets. Glue, biscuit, and clamp the brackets in place.

5 Glue and clamp the face frames to the carcases, flush

at the tops and sides. To provide a lower doorstop, the top surfaces of the base and upper carcase bottoms (B, D) sit ⅜" above the top edges of the lower frame rails (F), as shown in 4–5. Sand the frames' top and side edges flush with the carcases' tops and sides.

6 Rout the ¼" stopped chamfers on the base and upper stiles (E, G), where shown on the Carcases and Face Frames drawings in 4–6.

4–7.

Bend a thin strip of wood to form a shallow arc, and draw curved lines connecting the end and center patterns.

7 Checking the inside widths of your carcases, cut the doorstops (J) to size. Glue and clamp them to the face frames, where shown on the Door Stop drawing in 4–6, on *page 43.*

Sideboard base builder's note: *Make only one doorstop (J).*

Make the Skirts and Top

1 Cut the front skirt (K) and the side skirts (L) to width, but 1" longer than the lengths listed. Set the side skirts aside.

2 Miter-cut the front skirt to finished length. Make two copies of the end pattern and one copy of the center pattern in 4–16, on *page 49*, at 133%. Cut the patterns to the lines, and use spray adhesive to adhere them to the skirt where shown in 4–8. You'll flip over the pattern for the right end and apply it face down.

3 Use a fairing strip to draw gently curving lines connecting the patterns' ends, as shown in 4–7. Bandsaw and sand the skirt to shape.

4 Rout ½" chamfers along the top edges of the front and side skirts (K, L), where shown on the Base Cabinet Exploded View drawing in 4–9. Glue and clamp the front skirt in place.

5 Miter one end of each side skirt (L), making a mirrored pair. Fit them in place, mating their miters with those on the front skirt (K). Mark the side skirts flush with the back edges of the base sides (A), and trim them to length.

6 Drill holes and slots in the base sides, where shown on the Base Cabinet Exploded View drawing in 4–9. Apply glue to the miter and front 2" of the side skirts, and clamp them in place. Using the holes and the slots' centers as guides, drill ³⁄₃₂" pilot holes in the skirts. Drive #8 x 1¼" flathead wood screws through the countersunk holes, and #8 x 1¼" roundhead wood screws fitted with #8 flat washers through the slots.

7 Retrieve the edge-joined blank for the top (M), and cut it to finished size. Round over the top's ends, then edges, as shown on the Top Partial Round-over Detail drawing in 4–9.

Now Add the Cap and Crown

1 Cut the cap front (N) to size, and miter the ends. Cut the cap sides (O) about 1" longer than the length in the Materials List, and miter one end of each. Mark the centers of the mitered ends, and plunge-cut slots for #20 biscuits.

2 Glue and clamp the cap front (N) to the top of the upper cabinet, centered side to side, and overhanging 2¼" where shown in the Upper Cabinet Exploded View, Crown and Cove, and Back Rail Rabbets drawings in 4–10, *page 46*. Align

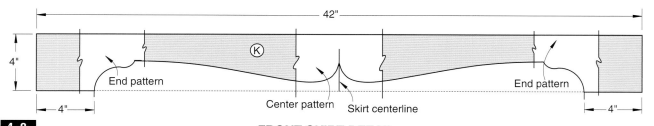

4–8.

FRONT SKIRT DETAIL

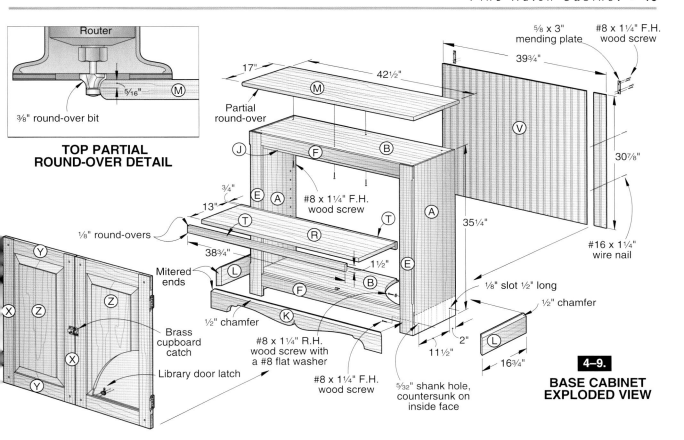

TOP PARTIAL ROUND-OVER DETAIL

Router

⅜" round-over bit

⁵⁄₁₆"

M

17"

42½"

M

Partial round-over

⅛" round-overs

13"

38¾"

J

F

B

E

A

T

R

L

F

B

K

¾"

#8 x 1¼" F.H. wood screw

1½"

T

A

E

Mitered ends

Brass cupboard catch

Library door latch

½" chamfer

#8 x 1¼" R.H. wood screw with a #8 flat washer

#8 x 1¼" F.H. wood screw

⁵⁄₃₂" shank hole, countersunk on inside face

Y

X

Z

Z

X

Y

⅝ x 3" mending plate

#8 x 1¼" F.H. wood screw

39¾"

V

30⅞"

#16 x 1¼" wire nail

35¼"

⅛" slot ½" long

½" chamfer

2"

11½"

16¾"

L

4–9.

BASE CABINET EXPLODED VIEW

the miters with the front corners of the face frame. Drill pilot and countersunk shank holes through the cap front and into the upper carcase top (D), and drive in the screws.

3 Position the cap sides (O), mark them flush with the back edges of the upper sides (C), and trim them to finished length. Drill countersunk shank holes and slots in the cap sides, where shown on the Top View Detail drawing in **4–10** (*page 46*). Apply glue only to the miters, insert the biscuits, and clamp the cap sides in place. Using the countersunk shank holes and the centers of the slots as guides, drill pilot holes into

the carcase top (D). Drive #8 x 1¼" flathead wood screws through the countersunk holes and #8 x 1¼" roundhead wood screws fitted with #8 flat washers through the slots.

4 Cut the crown front and sides (P, Q) about 2" longer than finished length. Bevel-rip their edges, where shown in the two steps in **4–11** (*page 47*). Sand away the sawblade marks.

5 Miter-cut the crown front (P) to length. Miter and crosscut the crown sides to length.

6 Glue and clamp the crown front to the upper top rail (H) and cap front (N), where shown on the Crown and

Cove drawing in **4–10**. Drill pilot and countersunk shank holes through the upper top rail and the cap front into the crown front, where shown. Drive the screws. Apply glue only to the miters and top edges of the crown sides (Q), and clamp them in place. Drill pilot and countersunk shank holes only through the cap sides into the crown sides. Drive the screws.

Make the Shelves and Fit the Backs

1 Retrieve the blanks for the base shelf (R) and upper shelf (S), and cut them to finished size. Cut the shelf trim (T) to size.

4–10.

UPPER CABINET EXPLODED VIEW

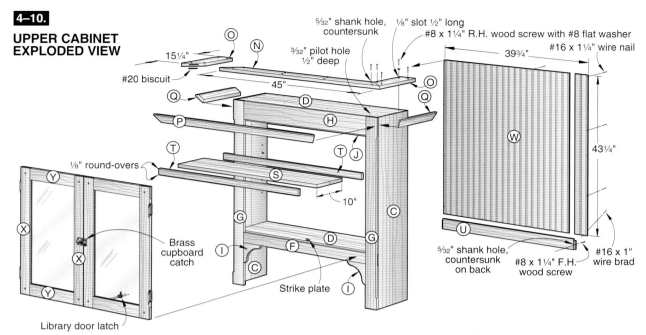

5/32" shank hole, countersunk

1/8" slot 1/2" long

#8 x 1 1/4" R.H. wood screw with #8 flat washer

#16 x 1 1/4" wire nail

15 1/4"

#20 biscuit

3/32" pilot hole 1/2" deep

45"

39 3/4"

43 1/4"

1/8" round-overs

Brass cupboard catch

Strike plate

Library door latch

5/32" shank hole, countersunk on back

#8 x 1 1/4" F.H. wood screw

#16 x 1" wire brad

BACK RAIL RABBETS

4"

2 1/4"

7/8"

1/4"

5/8"

3/4"

#8 x 1 1/4" F.H. wood scew

CROWN AND COVE

5/16" rabbet 1/2" deep

7/16"

2 3/4"

1/2"

2 1/4"

3/8" rabbet 7/16" deep

3/8"

5/16"

TOP VIEW DETAIL

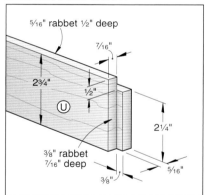

1/8" slot 1/2" long

1 1/2"

1/2"

7/8"

Location of Q

Location of P

5/32" shank holes, countersunk

1/2"

2 1/2"

7/8"

13 3/4"

2 1/2"

Glue and clamp the trim to the shelves, as shown on **4–9** and **4–10**. Sand the trim flush with the tops of the shelves. Chuck a 1/8" round-over bit in your hand-held router, and rout the shelf trim edges. Set the shelves aside.

Sideboard base builder's note:
Make only two shelf trims (T).

2 Cut the back rail (U) to size. With a dado blade in your tablesaw, rabbet the ends and one edge, where shown on the Back Rail Rabbets drawing in **4–10**. Apply glue, and clamp the rail in place flush with the bottom of the upper sides (C). Drill pilot and countersunk shank holes through the rail into the sides, and drive in the screws.

3 From 5/16"-thick, 8'-long beaded tongue-and-groove planks, cut 12 pieces each for the base back (V) and upper back (W) to the lengths listed. Lay one set of planks on your workbench, fitting the tongues and grooves together. Measure the rabbet-to-rabbet width of one carcase, and center this measurement on the assembled planks. Trim equal

4–11. MAKING THE CROWN

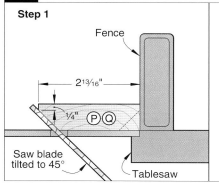

Step 1

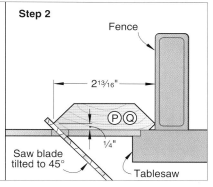

Step 2

amounts off the first and last planks of both back assemblies so they will be centered in their openings. Set the planks aside.

Next, Cut and Assemble the Doors

1 Measure the face frame openings. The length of the stiles (X) should be ⅛" less than the height of the openings. The sum of the lengths of two rails (Y) should be ¼" less than the width of the openings. Make any necessary adjustments to the lengths of the parts, and cut the stiles and rails to size. Edge-join oversize blanks for the panels (Z). Resaw and plane ¼ x ⅜" stock for the vertical stops (AA) and the horizontal stops (BB), making the parts about 1" longer than the lengths listed.

Sideboard base builder's note: *Make only four stiles (X), four rails (Y), four vertical stops (AA), and four horizontal stops (BB).*

SHOP TIP

A Simple Way to Make the Doors

Using only your tablesaw with a blade and a dado set, you can make sturdy, good-looking raised-panel or glass-insert doors for this or any project. Here's how:

1 Lay out the doorframe parts the way they will be assembled, and mark their inside back edges. Install a dado blade in your tablesaw, and cut ⅜" rabbets ½" deep along the marked edges. Then cut laps in the ends of the stiles and rails, where shown in 4–13.

2 Apply glue to the laps, and clamp the door frames. Check them for square by measuring their diagonals. Set the frames on a flat surface to dry.

3 Cut the panels (Z) to finished size. Each panel should be ⅛", narrower and 1/16" shorter than its rabbeted opening. Set up your tablesaw, as shown in Step 1 in 4–13, and cut saw kerfs around the perimeter of the face of each panel. Cut the bevels, as shown in Step 2. Install a dado blade, and rabbet the backs of the panels, as shown in Step 3. Sand the sawblade marks from the bevels and rabbets.

4 Cut the vertical and horizontal stops (AA, BB) to fit the rabbeted openings. Clip the head off a #17 x ¾" wire brad, and use it to drill pilot holes through the stops.

4–12.

A sturdy raised-panel door.

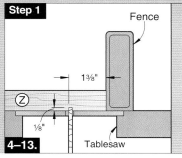

Step 1

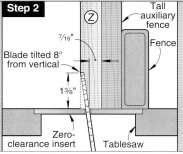

Step 2

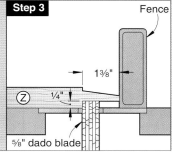

Step 3

4–13.

4–14.

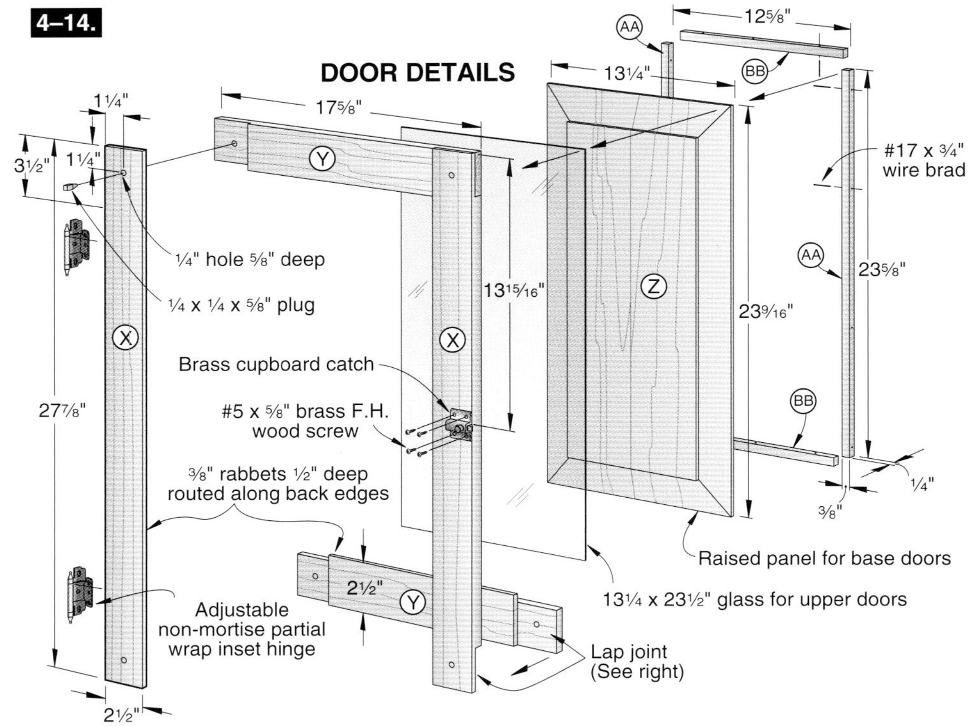
DOOR DETAILS
12⅝"
13¼"
17⅝"
1¼"
3½"
1¼"
AA
BB
Y
X
Z
#17 x ¾" wire brad
¼" hole ⅝" deep
¼ x ¼ x ⅝" plug
13¹⁵⁄₁₆"
23⁹⁄₁₆"
23⅝"
Brass cupboard catch
27⅞"
#5 x ⅝" brass F.H. wood screw
⅜" rabbets ½" deep routed along back edges
¼"
⅜"
Raised panel for base doors
2½"
13¼ x 23½" glass for upper doors
Adjustable non-mortise partial wrap inset hinge
Lap joint (See right)
2½"

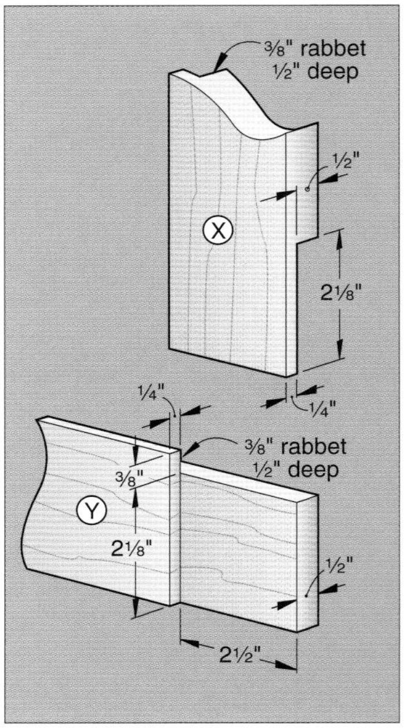
⅜" rabbet ½" deep
½"
X
2⅛"
¼"
¼"
⅜" rabbet ½" deep
⅜"
Y
2⅛"
½"
2½"

DOOR LAP JOINT DETAILS

2 Build the door frames and panels, as explained in the Shop Tip "A Simple Way to Make the Doors" on *page 47.*

3 With the doors complete, drill ¼" holes ⅝" deep in the frames' corners, where shown, and install the decorative square plugs.

4 Position and mount the hinges on the door and face frames. With the hinges mounted and the door frames in place, center and install the library door latches, where shown on the Base Cabinet Exploded view in **4–9**, **4–10,** and **4–15**. Each latch strike has one slot and one hole. Position the strike, and drill a pilot hole at the center of the slot. Secure the strike with a roundhead screw, as shown. Do not drive in the escutcheon pin at this time. Mount the cupboard catches to the doors, where shown on the Base Cabinet Exploded View drawing in **4–9**, and in **4–10** and **4–14**.

Note: *To give the bright brass cupboard catches an antique patina to better match the black hinges, soak them in a mild household ammonia solution; then scrub off and rinse.*

Apply the Finishes

1 Remove the hardware. Finish-sand all parts and assemblies to 220 grit. Set aside the planks for the backs (V, W).

2 To give the pine an antique amber glow, brush on two coats of oil-based satin polyurethane, sanding with 220-grit sandpaper between coats.

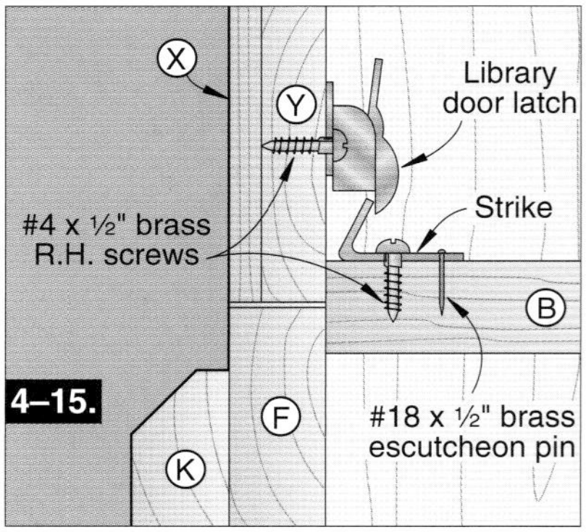
X
Y
Library door latch
Strike
#4 x ½" brass R.H. screws
B
4–15.
F
K
#18 x ½" brass escutcheon pin

BASE CABINET DOOR LATCH DETAIL

3 Retrieve the back planks, and apply a stain. We used a water-based wood stain, following the instructions on the can. To avoid discoloring the stain, brush on two coats of water-based satin polyurethane.

Ⓚ **FRONT SKIRT
END PATTERN**
(2 needed)

**FRONT SKIRT
CENTER PATTERN** Ⓚ

Center

4–16.

**Enlarge FRONT SKIRT END
PATTERN, FRONT SKIRT
CENTER PATTERN and
BRACKET PATTERN
to 133% for full size.**

5"

⅛"
round-over

**BRACKET
PATTERN**
(2 needed) Ⓛ

5"

Assembling the Cupboard

1 Install the backs (V, W) in the base and upper carcases. Use #16 x 1¼" wire nails to fasten the base back (V) planks to the base sides (A) and the base carcase top and bottom (B). Use #16 x 1¼" wire nails to fasten the upper back (W) planks to the upper sides (C) and the upper carcase top and bottom (D). Toenail the upper back planks to the back rail (U) with #16 x 1" wire brads.

2 Clamp the top (M) to the base carcase, flush at the back and centered side to side.

Drill pilot and countersunk shank holes through the base carcase top (B) into the top (M), where shown on the Base Cabinet Exploded View in **4–9**, on *page 45*. Drive in the screws.

3 Have single-strength glass cut ⅛" smaller in each dimension than the doors' rabbeted openings. Install the panels (Z) in the base door frames, and glass in the upper door frames, where shown in the Door Details in **4–14**. Nail in the stops (AA, BB) with #17 x ¾" wire brads.

4 Reattach the hinges, and hang the doors. Make sure the carcases are sitting square,

and use the hinges' slotted screw holes to align the doors. Drill pilot holes, and drive in the screws that fix the hinges in place. Reinstall the library door latches, adjust their strikes, and then drive in the escutcheon pins. Remount the cupboard door catches.

5 Center the upper cabinet on the base. Drill pilot holes, and screw the mending plates to the cabinets' backs, securing the upper cabinet to the base. Install the shelf supports and shelves.

TRADITIONAL SIDEBOARD

Looking for a handsome, versatile serving piece with plenty of storage for fine dinnerware and linens? This traditional oak beauty with three spacious cupboards and drawers and seven adjustable shelves may be just the ticket. Using straight-forward half-lap joinery for the face frame, stub tenon-and-groove construction for the doors, and super-simple locking joints for the drawers, building this unit is a snap. If you wish, you can add wine racks and/or a door to the center cupboard, as shown.

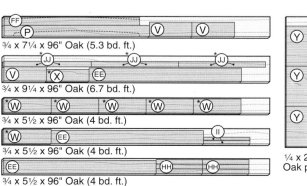

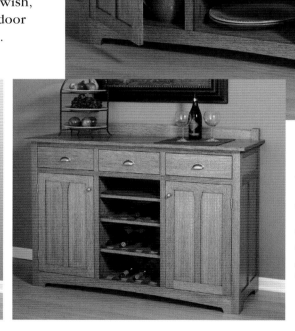

With cupboards, drawers, and shelves, this traditional sideboard has plenty of storage. Prefer the sideboard to be fully enclosed? Add a door as shown. Or store 12 of your favorite vintages by building wine racks.

CUTTING DIAGRAM FOR TRADITIONAL SIDEBOARD

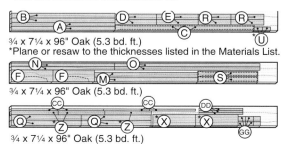

¾ x 7¼ x 96" Oak (5.3 bd. ft.)
*Plane or resaw to the thicknesses listed in the Materials List.

¾ x 7¼ x 96" Oak (5.3 bd. ft.)

¾ x 7¼ x 96" Oak (5.3 bd. ft.)

¾ x 7¼ x 96" Oak (5.3 bd. ft.)

¾ x 9¼ x 96" Oak (6.7 bd. ft.)

¾ x 5½ x 96" Oak (4 bd. ft.)

¾ x 5½ x 96" Oak (4 bd. ft.)

¾ x 5½ x 96" Oak (4 bd. ft.)

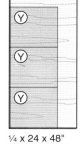

¼ x 24 x 48"
Oak plywood

CUTTING DIAGRAM (continued)

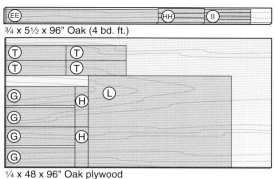

¾ x 5½ x 96" Oak (4 bd. ft.)

¼ x 48 x 96" Oak plywood

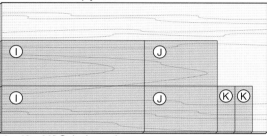

¾ x 48 x 96" Oak plywood

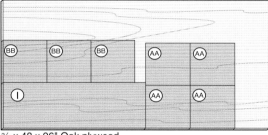

¾ x 48 x 96" Oak plywood

Begin with the Sides

1 Cut the front stiles (A), rear stiles (B), center stiles (C), top rails (D), center rails (E), bottom rails (F), lower panels (G), and upper panels (H) to the sizes in the Materials List at *right*. Save the rail cutoffs to make test tenons. For continuous grain flow from the lower to upper ¼" plywood panels (G, H), lay them out in the configuration shown on the Cutting Diagram. Sand the panels with 220-grit sandpaper.

2 Using your tablesaw, cut a ¼" groove ⁵⁄₁₆" deep centered along one edge of parts A, B, D, and F, and along both edges of parts E, where shown in **4–22**. (The grooves can be cut with a standard blade in two passes to exactly fit the thickness of the plywood panels.)

MATERIALS LIST FOR TRADITIONAL SIDEBOARD

PART	T	W	L	MTL.	QTY.
SIDE ASSEMBLIES					
A front stiles	¾"	1⅜"	37¼"	O	2
B rear stiles	¾"	1¾"	37¼"	O	2
C center stiles	¾"	2"	25⅛"	O	2
D top rails	¾"	2"	15"	O	2
E center rails	¾"	2"	15"	O	2
F bottom rails	¾"	4⅜"	15"	O	2
G lower panels	¼"	7⅛"	25⅛"	OP	4
H upper panels	¼"	15"	4¾"	OP	2
CASE					
I top, center shelf, and bottom	¾"	17"	51½"	OP	3
J lower dividers	¾"	17"	26⅜"	OP	2
K upper dividers	¾"	17"	6⅜"	OP	2
L back	¼"	34"	51¾"	OP	1
FACE FRAME					
M outer stiles	¾"	1¾"	37¼"	O	2
N inner stile blanks	¾"	1¼"	37¼"	O	2
O top and center rails	¾"	1¼"	52½"	O	2
P bottom rail	¾"	4"	52½"	O	1
DOORS (TWO)					
Q stiles	¾"	2"	25¼"	O	4
R rails	¾"	2"	11⅞"	O	4
S center stiles	¾"	2"	21¾"	O	2
T panels	¼"	5⁹⁄₁₆"	21¾"	OP	4
U mounting blocks	½"	1¼"	3"	O	2
DRAWERS (THREE)					
V fronts	¾"	5¼"	15⅜"	O	3
W sides	½"	5¼"	17⅛"	O	6
X backs	½"	4¼"	15⅜"	O	3
Y bottoms	¼"	14⅞"	17⅛"	OP	3
Z drawer-slide spacers	⁷⁄₁₆"	1½"	16⅞"	O	3
SHELVES					
AA outside shelves	¾"	16"	16⅝"	OP	4
BB inside shelves	¾"	16"	15⅞"	OP	3
CC outside shelf edging	¾"	¾"	16⅝"	O	4
DD inside shelf edging	¾"	¾"	15⅞"	O	3
TOP ASSEMBLY					
EE* top	¾"	19¼"	55"	EO	1
FF crest	¾"	3"	49"	O	1
GG* end trim	1½"	1¾"	2¾"	LO	2
WINE RACKS (OPTIONAL)					
HH center supports	¾"	1¾"	16¾"	O	9
II outer supports	¾"	1¼"	16¾"	O	6
JJ rails	⅜"	2"	15¾"	O	6

*Parts initially cut oversized. See the instructions.
Materials Key: O = Oak; OP = Oak plywood; EO = Edge-joined oak; LO = Laminated oak.
Supplies: Spray adhesive; #8 x 1¼" panhead screws (6); #8 flat washers (6); #8 x 1¼" flathead wood screws (5); #10 biscuits (2); #17 x 1" wire nails. For optional face-nailing of the face frame to the case: 6d finish nails; stainable wood putty.
Blades and Bits: Dado-blade set; 45° chamfer and drawer-lock router bits (½"-diameter shank).
Hardware: Includes 2¼" full-wrap inset hinges (4); 25mm knobs (2); drawer pulls (3); 1¼" spring catches with strikes (2); 17" center-mount drawer slides with plastic-headed glide tacks and screws (3); ¼" shelf supports, 2 packages of 20.
Hardware for Sideboard and Optional Center Door: All hardware listed above plus 2¼" partial-wrap inset hinges (2); an additional 25mm knob; an additional 1¼" spring catch with strike.

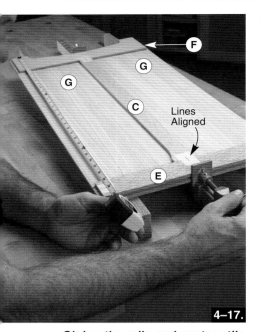

4–17.

Gluing the rails and center stile.
With the lines on the center stile
(C) and center and bottom rails
(E, F) aligned, check for equal 31"
measurements on each side of
the assembly to verify square.

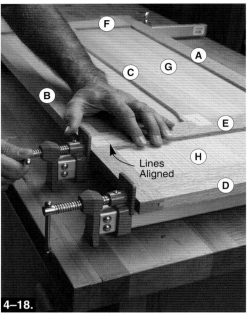

4–18.

Completing the side assembly. With the
lines on the center rail (E) and the front and
rear stiles (A, B) aligned and the top rail (D)
and bottom rail (F) flush with the stiles' ends,
clamp the side assembly together.

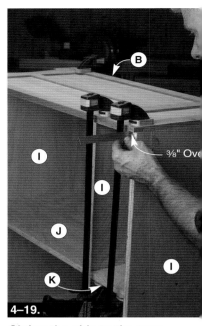

4–19.

Gluing the side to the case.
Position the side assembly so that
it overhangs the case's front edge
by ⅜" while the rabbeted edge of
the rear stile (B) is flush with the
case's back edge.

Then, cut a ¼" groove ¹¹⁄₁₆" deep, centered along both edges of the center stiles (C).

3 To form tenons on the ends of parts C, D, E, and F, where dimensioned in **4–23** (*page 54*), first fit your tablesaw with a dado blade. Then, cut a test tenon on the end of one of the rail cutoffs. Check the tenon's fit in a stile's groove. If necessary, adjust your setup and recheck the fit. When satisfied, cut the tenons on the parts' ends.

4 Make four copies of the center stile end-pattern in **4–32** on *page 59* at 200%. (If you plan to make the sideboard's optional

center door, make five copies of the pattern.) Spray-adhere a pattern to one end of each center stile (C), aligning the pattern with the tenon's shoulder. Set the remaining patterns aside. Extend straight lines from the pattern lines to the stiles' opposite ends. Then, bandsaw and sand to the lines. Remove the patterns.

5 Make six copies of the combined side assembly and face frame bottom-rail pattern in **4–32** on *page 59* at 200%. Then, draw a centerline across the width of the bottom rails (F). Spray-adhere two patterns to each rail, aligning them with the marked centerline. (You'll need

to flip over one of the patterns on each rail to complete the contour.) Set aside the remaining patterns. Now, bandsaw and sand the bottom rails to shape. Remove the patterns.

6 Dry-assemble parts A through H to form the two side assemblies, centering the center stiles (C) to the center and bottom rails (E, F). Verify that the parts fit together correctly. Then, to make it easy to realign the parts, draw alignment lines across the joints between the center stiles and the center and bottom rails, and between the center rails and the front and rear stiles (A, B). Disassemble the parts.

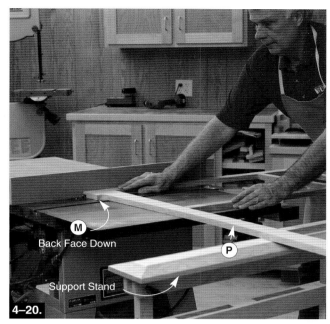

Rabbeting the face frame. *Keeping the face frame (M/N/O/P) tight against the saw's rip fence, and supporting the frame with a stand, rabbet the back edges of the outer stiles (M).*

Attaching the face frame. *Clamp the face frame (M/N/O/P) to the case around the perimeter and on the inside to ensure that it is securely attached to the lower and upper dividers (J, K).*

7 Glue and clamp the center stiles (C) between the center and bottom rails (E, F). Insert the lower panels (G) in place, without glue, to help square each assembly. Check for square, as shown in **4–17**. When the glue dries, complete the side assemblies by gluing and clamping together the front and rear stiles (A, B), lower and upper panels (G, H), and top rails (D), as shown in **4–18**.

8 Using your tablesaw and a dado blade adjusted to the thickness of your ¾" plywood for the top, center shelf, and bottom (I), cut ¼"-deep dadoes and rabbets on the inside face of each side assembly, where

dimensioned on the Case drawing in **4–24**. Then, adjust your dado blade to the thickness of your ¼" plywood for the back (L), and cut a ⅜"-deep rabbet along the back inside edge of the rear stile (B) on both assemblies, where shown in **4–22**. Now, sand the assemblies smooth with 220-grit sandpaper.

Making the Case

Note: *The plywood top, center shelf, and bottom (I) are located in the dadoes and rabbets in the side assemblies. Because the thickness of plywood varies slightly, you may need to adjust the depth of the dadoes in parts*

I so that the lower dividers (J) and upper dividers (K) will fit snugly between them. Measure the thickness of your plywood. If it's less than ¾", adjust the dadoes' depths as needed.

1 From ¾" plywood, cut the top, center shelf, and bottom (I); lower dividers (J); and upper dividers (K) to the sizes listed. From ¼" plywood, cut the back (L) to size. Sand the back smooth, and set it aside. Using your dado blade adjusted to the ¾" plywood's thickness, cut ¼"-deep dadoes on the inside faces of the top and bottom (I) and on both faces of the center shelf (I), where dimensioned on the Case Detail drawing in **4–24**.

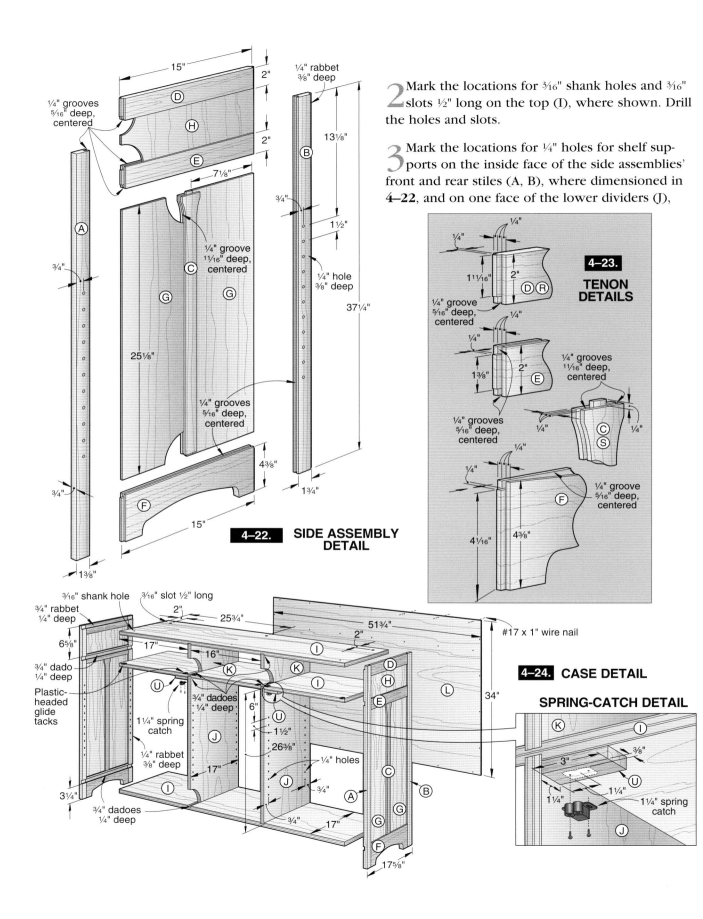

2 Mark the locations for 3⁄16" shank holes and 3⁄16" slots 1⁄2" long on the top (I), where shown. Drill the holes and slots.

3 Mark the locations for 1⁄4" holes for shelf supports on the inside face of the side assemblies' front and rear stiles (A, B), where dimensioned in **4–22**, and on one face of the lower dividers (J),

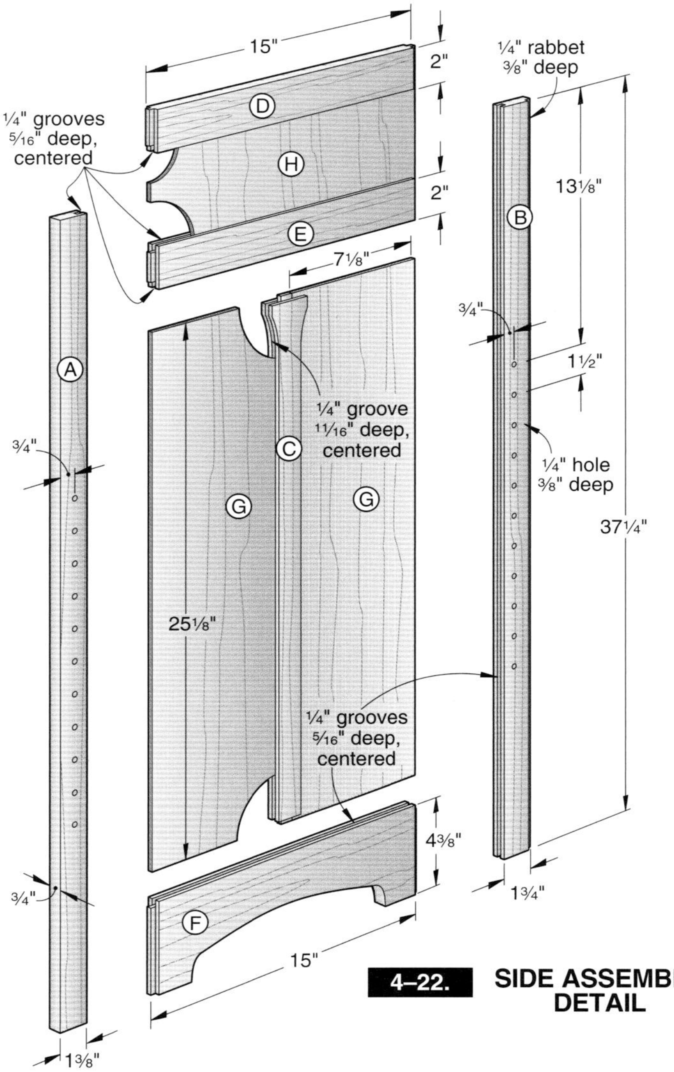

15"
2"
2"
1⁄4" rabbet 3⁄8" deep
1⁄4" grooves 5⁄16" deep, centered
D
H
E
B
13 1⁄8"
7 1⁄8"
3⁄4"
1 1⁄2"
A
1⁄4" groove 11⁄16" deep, centered
C
1⁄4" hole 3⁄8" deep
G
G
37 1⁄4"
25 1⁄8"
1⁄4" grooves 5⁄16" deep, centered
4 3⁄8"
1 3⁄4"
F
15"
1 3⁄8"

4–22. SIDE ASSEMBLY DETAIL

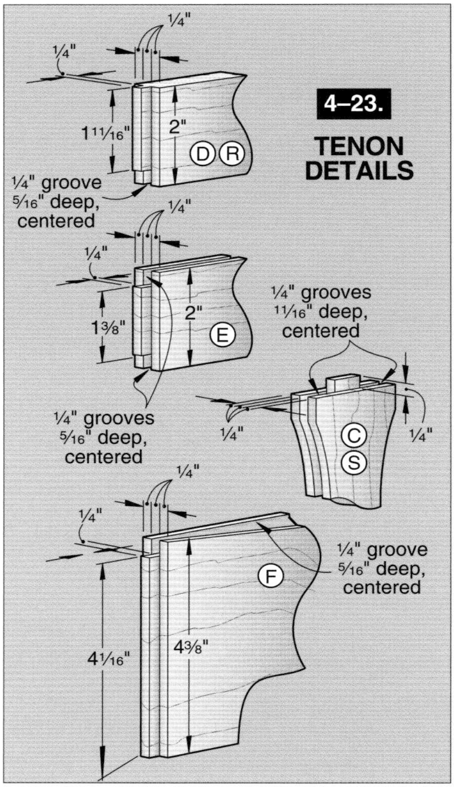

1⁄4"
1⁄4"
1 11⁄16"
2"
D R
1⁄4" groove 5⁄16" deep, centered
1⁄4"
1⁄4"
1 3⁄8"
2"
E
1⁄4" grooves 11⁄16" deep, centered
1⁄4" grooves 5⁄16" deep, centered
1⁄4"
1⁄4"
C
S
1⁄4"
1⁄4"
1⁄4" groove 5⁄16" deep, centered
F
4 1⁄16"
4 3⁄8"

4–23. TENON DETAILS

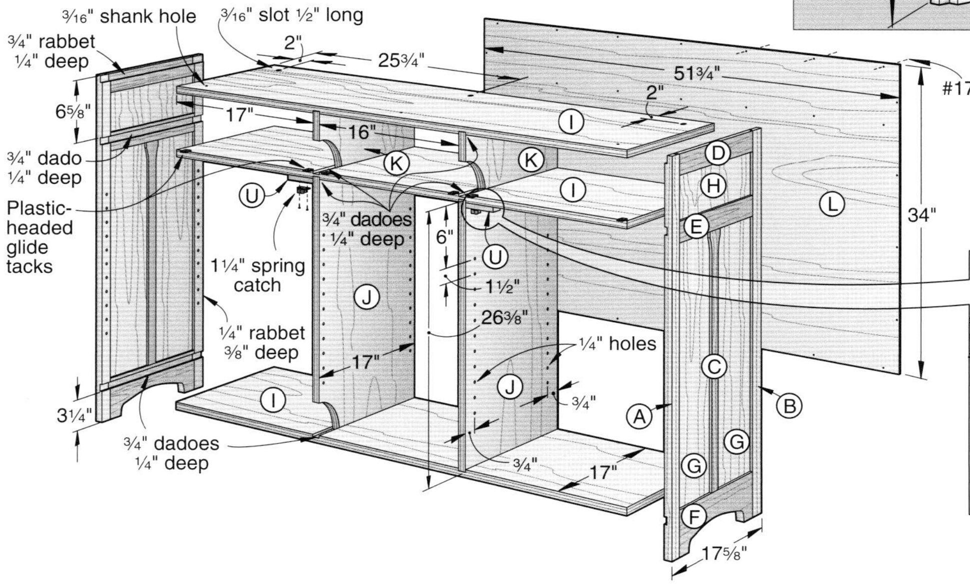

3⁄16" shank hole
3⁄16" slot 1⁄2" long
3⁄4" rabbet 1⁄4" deep
2"
25 3⁄4"
51 3⁄4"
#17 x 1" wire nail
6 5⁄8"
17"
2"
16"
I
3⁄4" dado 1⁄4" deep
K
K
D
U
I
H
Plastic-headed glide tacks
3⁄4" dadoes 1⁄4" deep
E
L
6"
34"
U
1 1⁄4" spring catch
J
1 1⁄2"
1⁄4" rabbet 3⁄8" deep
26 3⁄8"
1⁄4" holes
17"
C
J
3⁄4"
I
A
B
3 1⁄4"
3⁄4" dadoes 1⁄4" deep
G
G
3⁄4"
17"
F
17 5⁄8"

4–24. CASE DETAIL

SPRING-CATCH DETAIL

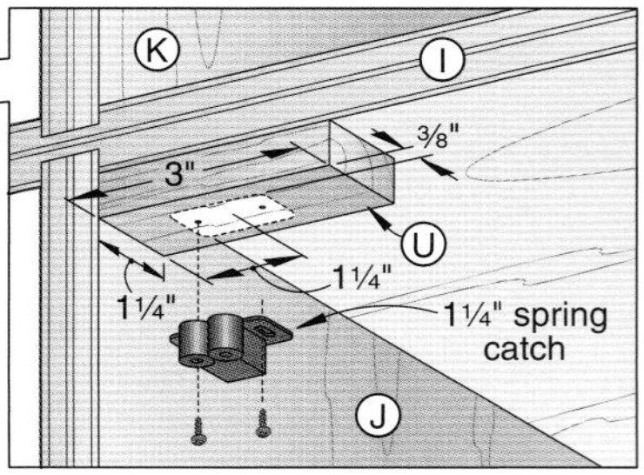

K
I
3⁄8"
3"
U
1 1⁄4"
1 1⁄4"
1 1⁄4" spring catch
J

where dimensioned on the Case drawing in **4–24**. Then, drill the holes ⅜" deep in the stiles and through the dividers.

4 To assemble the case, first glue and clamp the lower dividers (J) between the bottom and center shelf (I) on a flat surface, checking for square. When the glue dries, glue and clamp to this assembly the upper dividers (K) and top (I), again verifying square. Now, glue and clamp the side assemblies to the case, as shown in **4–19,** on *page 52.* You can avoid using extra-long clamps by clamping the side assemblies to the dividers, as shown.

Add the Face Frame

1 Cut the outer stiles (M), inner stile blanks (N), top and center rails (O), and bottom rail (P) to the sizes listed in the Materials List, saving the cutoffs.

2 Lay out the half-lap joints on the parts, where dimensioned in **4–25**. Using a dado blade in your tablesaw, cut half-laps in two of the cutoffs. Put the pieces together, and check for a flush-fitting joint. Adjust your setup and retest as needed. When the fit is acceptable, cut the half-laps.

3 Retrieve the two copies of the face frame bottom-rail pattern in **4–32** (*page 59*). Spray-adhere them to the ends of the bottom rail (P), aligning them with the half-laps' shoulders. To complete the rail's contour,

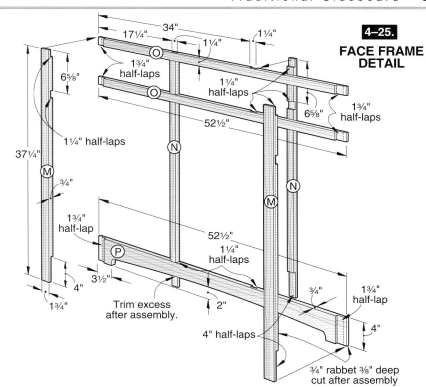

4–25.
FACE FRAME DETAIL

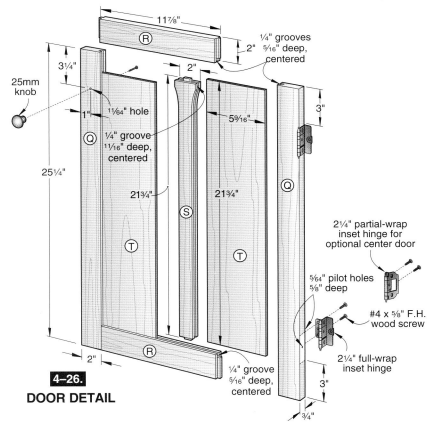

4–26.
DOOR DETAIL

4–27.

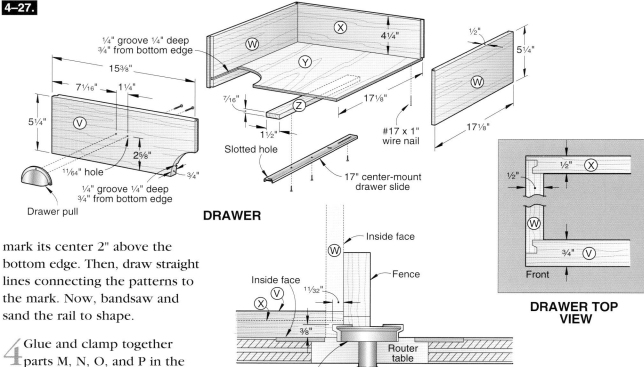

¼" groove ¼" deep
¾" from bottom edge

15⅜"

7¹⁄₁₆"   1¼"

5¼"

Ⓥ

2⅝"

¹¹⁄₆₄" hole

¼" groove ¼" deep
¾" from bottom edge

Drawer pull

¾"

4¼"

Ⓦ   Ⓧ

Ⓨ

Ⓩ

1½"

Slotted hole

⁷⁄₁₆"

17⅛"

#17 x 1"
wire nail

17" center-mount
drawer slide

½"

5¼"

Ⓦ

17⅛"

½"

½"   Ⓧ

Ⓦ

¾"   Ⓥ

Front

**DRAWER TOP
VIEW**

DRAWER

mark its center 2" above the
bottom edge. Then, draw straight
lines connecting the patterns to
the mark. Now, bandsaw and
sand the rail to shape.

4 Glue and clamp together
parts M, N, O, and P in the
arrangement shown. When the
glue dries, trim the bottom of
the inner stile blanks (N) flush
with the contoured edge of the
bottom rail (P) using a jigsaw.
Then, using your tablesaw with
a dado blade, cut a ¾" rabbet
⅜" deep along the back outside
edge of the outer stiles (M)
where shown in **4–20** (*page 53*)
and detailed in **4–25** (*page 55*).

5 Glue and clamp the face
frame to the front of the
case, as shown in **4–21** (*page
53*), ensuring the edges of the
outer stiles (M) are flush with
the outside faces of the front
stiles (A). You will need about
twenty 24"-long (minimum)
clamps to secure the frame. As
an alternative to using clamps,
you can face-nail the frame to
the case using 6d finish nails.

Inside face

Ⓦ

Inside face

Ⓥ

¹¹⁄₃₂"

Ⓧ

⅜"

Fence

Router
table

Drawer-lock
router bit

DRAWER-LOCK JOINT

When the glue dries, sand the
frame smooth.

Make the Doors

*Note: The Materials List shows
the quantities of parts for two
doors. If you wish to add the
optional center door, increase
the quantities of parts Q
through U accordingly.*

1 Cut the stiles (Q), rails (R),
center stiles (S), panels (T),
and mounting blocks (U) to the
sizes in the Materials List. Sand
the ¼" plywood panels smooth.
As you did for the side assemblies, cut a ¼" groove (sized to
fit the panels) ⁵⁄₁₆" deep, centered

*Mounting the cabinet slide. Using
a small awl or nail, make pilot holes
for mounting the cabinet slide
member. Drive the screws using
a short screwdriver.*

4–28.

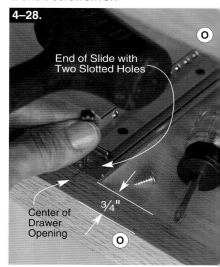

Ⓞ

End of Slide with
Two Slotted Holes

Center of
Drawer
Opening

¾"

Ⓞ

along one edge of parts Q and R, where shown in **4–26**. Then, cut a ¼" groove ¹¹⁄₁₆" deep centered along both edges of parts S. Now, form tenons on the ends of parts R and S, where dimensioned in **4–23**.

2 Copy the center stile (S) end patterns in **4–32** (on *page 59*) at 200%. Spray-adhere them to the ends of the center stiles. As before, extend the pattern lines. Then, bandsaw and sand the stiles to shape. Next, remove the patterns.

3 Dry-assemble the doors to ensure that the parts fit together correctly. Center the center stiles (S), and draw marks across their joints with the rails (R) for realignment. Then, glue and clamp the doors together with the stiles centered, and check for square. When the glue dries, sand the doors smooth.

4 Identify the doors' best sides to face out. Then, drill an ¹¹⁄₆₄" screw hole for a 25mm knob through the inner stile (Q) of each door, where dimensioned in **4–26**. (You can hinge the optional center door to open from the right or left, so locate the knob screw hole where appropriate.) Using a hacksaw, trim the 1¼"-long machine screws (supplied with the knobs) to 1" long. Mount the knobs.

5 Mark the locations for the 2¼" inset hinges on the outer stiles' edges, where dimensioned in **4–26**. (The outer doors use full-wrap hinges, and the optional center door uses partial-wrap

hinges.) While holding the hinges in position, mark the screw-hole locations on the edge and back face of the stiles using an awl. Then, drill pilot holes, and screw the hinges in place.

6 Position a door, centered vertically, in the face-frame opening. (For an easy way to support the door in the opening, see the Shop Tip "Using a Steel Rule When Hanging Cabinet Doors.") Mark the centers of the hinges' vertical screw adjustment slots on the face-frame edge. Remove the door. Then, drill pilot holes, and mount the door to the face frame without snagging the screws. Repeat for the other door(s).

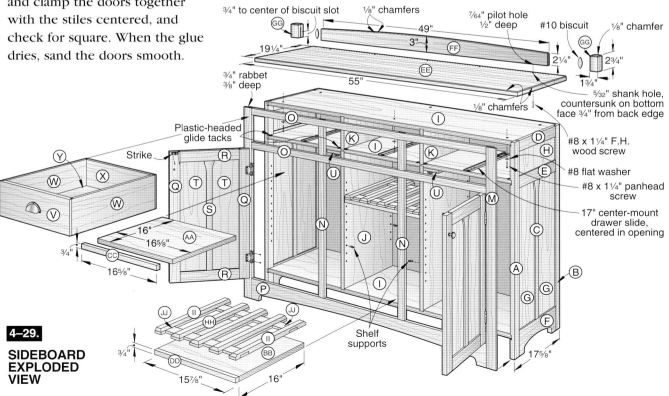

¾" to center of biscuit slot
⅛" chamfers
49"
3"
⁷⁄₆₄" pilot hole ½" deep
#10 biscuit
⅛" chamfer
19¼"
2¼"
2¾"
1¾"
¾" rabbet ⅜" deep
55"
⅛" chamfers
⁵⁄₃₂" shank hole, countersunk on bottom face ¾" from back edge
Plastic-headed glide tacks
Strike
#8 x 1¼" F.H. wood screw
#8 flat washer
#8 x 1¼" panhead screw
17" center-mount drawer slide, centered in opening
16"
16⅝"
¾"
16⅝"
Shelf supports
4–29.
SIDEBOARD EXPLODED VIEW
¾"
15⅞"
16"
17⅝"

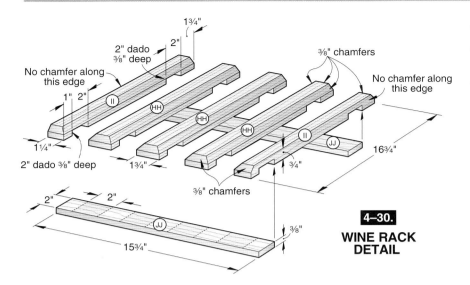

4-30.
WINE RACK DETAIL

7 Adjust the doors for an equal reveal at the top and bottom. (It should be ¹⁄₁₆", the same as the door-hinge reveal.) Then, tighten the screws. For the outer doors, drill pilot holes centered in the screw holes in the hinges' wraparound leaves into the face frame's back side, and drive in the screws. Now, check for an equal reveal on the side of the doors opposite the hinges. If necessary, plane the edge of the stiles (Q) to match the reveal.

8 Glue the mounting blocks (U) in position, where shown in 4–24 (page 54), tight against the dividers (J) and the face frame's back face.

9 Position 1¼" spring catches on the mounting blocks, where dimensioned on the Spring Catch Detail drawing in 4–24. Drill pilot holes, and fasten the catches using the supplied screws. Engage the strikes in the catches. Then, close the doors

and press on them to mark the strikes' locations. (The strikes have barbs on their back sides.) Now, open the doors, and align the strikes with the indentations. Drill pilot holes, and screw the strikes in place.

Make the Drawers

1 Cut the fronts (V), sides (W), backs (X), bottoms (Y), and drawer-slide spacers (Z) to the sizes in the Materials List (page 51). Center the fronts in the face-frame openings, and check for a ¹⁄₁₆" reveal all around that matches the doors' reveal. If necessary, trim the fronts, and adjust the size of the sides, backs, and bottoms accordingly.

2 Mark centerpoints on the fronts (V) for the drawer-pull screw holes, where dimensioned on the Drawer drawing in 4–27 (page 56). Then, drill ¹¹⁄₆₄" holes through the fronts at the marked locations.

Note: As an alternative to forming lock joints using a drawer-lock router bit, you can join the drawers together using rabbet joints cut with your tablesaw or dovetails.

3 Chuck a drawer-lock bit in your table-mounted router. Set the bit height, and position the router fence where shown on the Drawer Top view drawing in 4–27. Then, rout the ends on the inside faces of the fronts (V), backs (X), and sides (W) where shown on the Drawer Top View drawing in 4–27, positioning the parts on the table and against the fence in the orientations shown on the Drawer-Lock Joint drawing in 4–27.

4 Using your tablesaw, cut a ¼" groove ¼" deep and ¾" from the bottom edge of the fronts (V) and sides (W) for the ¼" plywood bottoms (Y), where shown in the Drawer drawing in 4–27. Then, glue and clamp the fronts, sides, and backs (X) together, checking for square. When the glue dries, slide the bottoms (Y) into place, and nail them to the bottom of the backs, where shown. Now, glue and clamp the drawer-slide spacers (Z) to the bottoms, centered from side to side and tight against the fronts. Sand the drawers smooth.

5 Draw centerlines along the length of the spacers (Z). Separate the 17" center-mount drawer slides. Then, center the smaller drawer-slide members

Using a Steel Rule When Hanging Cabinet Doors

Holding a cabinet door in position while marking the hinge mounting-hole locations on the face frame can be tricky. When mounting a door that uses hinges with vertical adjustment slots, such as the inset hinges used for the sideboard's doors, here's an easy way to support the door approximately centered in the cabinet opening. Simply clamp a steel rule from an adjustable square to the cabinet bottom, and set the door on the rule, as shown at *right*. (The rule measures approximately ³⁄₃₂" thick—close to the desired ¹⁄₁₆" reveal for the side-

board.) While holding the door vertically at the top with one hand, use your other hand to mark the center of the hinges' slotted holes on the face frame. Then, drill the holes and mount the door, adjusting it as needed to equalize the top and bottom reveal before fully tightening the screws (**4–31**).

on the spacers' marked center-lines with the slides' slotted-hole ends tight against the fronts (V). Drill pilot holes, and drive the supplied screws, where shown on the Drawer drawing in **4–27**.

6 Mark the center of the drawer openings in the face frame. Aligning a framing square with the marks, draw lines across the width of the center shelf (I). Then, center the larger cabinet-slide members on the lines with the slides' front ends (the ends with two slotted holes) located ¾" back from the outside face of the face frame. Now, mount the slides, as shown in **4–28** (*page 56*). (The rear mounting brackets supplied by the manufacturer with the slides are not used.)

7 To prevent the drawers from rocking, install plastic-headed glide tacks (supplied with the slides), where shown in **4–29** (*page 57*). Using a hammer, drive the tacks into the joint between the face frame and center shelf (I). Then, mount the drawer pulls, install the drawers, and verify that they operate smoothly. If you need to adjust a drawer, loosen the

cabinet slide's screws, reposition the slide, and tighten the screws.

Make the Shelves and Top

1 Cut the outside shelves (AA), inside shelves (BB), outside shelf edging (CC), and inside shelf edging (DD) to the sizes in the Materials List (*page 51*). Glue and clamp the edging to the shelves, where shown in **4–29**, keeping the edging flush with the shelves' faces and ends. When the glue dries, sand the shelves smooth, and then set them aside.

2 Edge-join enough ¾"-thick boards to make a 20 x 56" workpiece for the top (EE). When the glue dries, crosscut and then rip the top to the finished size. To secure the crest (FF) later, where shown, drill countersunk shank holes in the bottom face of the top along its back edge.

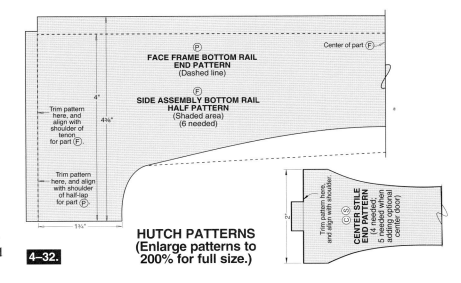

4–32.

HUTCH PATTERNS
(Enlarge patterns to 200% for full size.)

4–33.

Gluing the end trim to the crest.
Using #10 biscuits, glue and clamp the end trim (GG) to the crest (FF). When the glue dries, chisel off the exposed biscuit ends.

3 Cut the crest (FF) to size. Mark the ends and center of the arch, where dimensioned in 4–29 (*page 57*). Then, bend a fairing stick to these points, and draw the arch. Bandsaw and sand the arch to shape.

4 From ¾"-thick stock, cut two 1¾ x 8" pieces to form the end trim (GG). Laminate the pieces to make a 1½"-thick blank. Then, crosscut two 2¾"-long end-trim pieces from the blank.

5 Cut slots for #10 biscuits for joining the end trim (GG) to the crest (FF). Where shown in 4–29, first mark the slots' center-lines on the parts' faces ¾" from their bottoms. Then, adjust your biscuit-joiner fence to center the slot cutter on the ¾"-thick crest, and plunge the slots in its ends. Readjust the fence to center the cutter on the 1½"-thick end trim. With the trim pieces held in your vise, plunge the mating slots in their edges.

6 Using a 45° chamfer bit in your handheld router, rout ⅛" chamfers on the top (EE), crest (FF), and end trim (GG) where shown in 4–29. Sand the parts smooth.

7 Keeping their bottoms flush, glue and clamp the end trim (GG) to the crest (FF), as shown in 4–33. When the glue dries, glue and clamp the crest/end trim assembly to the top (EE), centering the assembly side to side and aligning the end-trim back faces flush so they are flush with the top's back edge. Then, centering on the countersunk shank holes in the top, drill pilot holes into the crest, and drive in the screws.

8 Position the top assembly (EE/FF/GG) on the case, centering the assembly side to side with the back edges of the top (EE) and rear stiles (B) flush. Then, attach the assembly with panhead screws and flat washers from inside the drawer cavities, where shown in 4–29.

Add the Wine Racks (Optional)

1 Cut the center supports (HH), outer supports (II), and rails (JJ) to size. Using your router and chamfer bit, rout ⅜" chamfers along the ends, then edges, of the supports, where shown in 4–30. Then, using your tablesaw and dado blade, cut 2" dadoes ⅜" deep in the supports' bottom faces, where dimensioned, to fit the rails.

2 From ¾"-thick scrap, cut four 2 x 4" spacers. Then, glue and clamp together the supports and rails, inserting the spacers in the center of the rack to position the supports 2" apart while keeping the outer supports (II) flush with the ends of the rails (JJ). When the glue dries, sand the racks smooth.

Add a Finish

1 Remove the drawers, doors, and hardware. Sand any areas that need it with 220-grit sandpaper, and remove the dust. If you nailed the face frame to the case, fill the nail holes with a stainable wood putty.

2 Stain the sideboard, if you wish. Then, apply three coats of a clear finish. Satin polyurethane was used on the sideboard shown on *page 50*. (The sideboard was sanded to 320 grit between coats.)

3 Remount the hardware, and install the doors and drawers. Then, position the back (L) in the rabbets in the rear stiles (B) tight against the top (EE). Nail the back to the case, where shown on the Case drawing in 4–24 (*page 54*).

4 Finally, install the inside and outside shelves where you wish using ¼" shelf supports, and place any wine racks in position. Now, move this beautiful piece to your dining room, and fill it with your finest china and special wines.

CHAPTER 5

centers for great entertainment

GATHERING AREAS, SUCH AS living and family rooms, are prone to accumulate clutter. But the right furniture and shelving can provide places to store everything, without being commonplace. When you build a cabinet to house your audiovisual equipment and accessories, you'll be doing just that.

You could opt for a ready-to-assemble unit made with engineered sheet-good parts covered in simulated wood plastic or paper veneer. But for practically the same amount of money, you could build one of the attractive pieces you'll find in this chapter. Of course, you'll have to put in some shop time (and enjoy every hour of it!).

Begin by checking out the details for making the country pine cabinet shown here. It will hold a large-screen television (32"), plus give a home to your audio equipment, and look great doing it.

Or do you just want a place to store your CDs and DVDs? You'll find it on *page 68* in the form of an Arts and Crafts-style unit with adjustable glass shelves.

Maybe you're looking for a cabinet with more potential than either of the above. If so, the entertainment center on *page 74* may be what you're seeking. Its optional side cabinets can hold books and collectibles as well as a host of audiovisual disks.

So "shop" the following pages, pick the unit that suits you, and then head for your workshop.

COUNTRY ENTERTAINMENT CENTER

This country entertainment center can be used as a storage system for your electronic components and more.

Built in pine, this sharp-looking, traditional-style cabinet can perform as a small armoire as well as a home for your audiovisual equipment. It's sized to fit a 32"-screen television.

Create the Cabinet Sides

1 Edge-join narrower stock to size to form the cabinet sides (A), bottom (B), and top (C) to the dimensions in the Materials List, plus ½" in width and 1" in length.

2 Lay out the panels for the best grain match. Mark the edges that will receive the splines. See **5–1** for reference (*page 64*).

3 Using a ¼" slotting cutter, rout ¼" slots, centered, along the marked edges of the panels. Stop the slots 2" from the ends for the top panel (C). (See the Spline Detail drawing in **5–1,** *page 64*.) The slots in the side and bottom panels go all the way through.

4 From ¼" stock (we used plywood), cut ¹⁵⁄₁₆"-wide splines to the lengths needed to fit the routed slots. Cut or sand the ends of the top-panel splines to shape.

5 Glue, spline, and clamp together the side panels (A), bottom panel (B), and top panel (C), checking that the panels remain flat. Remove excess glue.

CUTTING DIAGRAM FOR COUNTRY ENTERTAINMENT CENTER

A
B
3/4 x 11 1/4 x 96" Pine (8 bd. ft.) (2 needed)
E
D
A
3/4 x 11 1/4 x 96" Pine (8 bd. ft.)
G
F
H
A
3/4 x 11 1/4 x 96" Pine (8 bd. ft.)
C
C
3/4 x 7 1/4 x 96" Pine (5.3 bd. ft.) (2 needed)
J
L
K
M
3/4 x 11 1/4 x 96" Pine (8 bd. ft.)
*Plane or resaw to the thickness listed in the Materials List.
N
*P
*Q
O
3/4 x 5 1/2 x 96" Pine (4 bd. ft.)
R
S
2 1/2 x 96" Crown Molding
U
T
V
T
Y
3/4 x 9 1/4 x 96" Pine (6.6 bd. ft.)
W
W
3/4 x 5 1/2 x 96" Pine (4.8 bd. ft.) (3 needed)
X
X
3/4 x 9 1/4 x 96" Pine (6.6 bd. ft.) (3 needed)
I
1/4 x 48 x 96" Hardboard

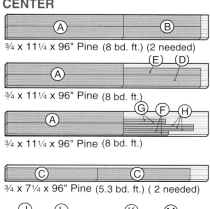

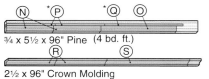

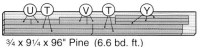

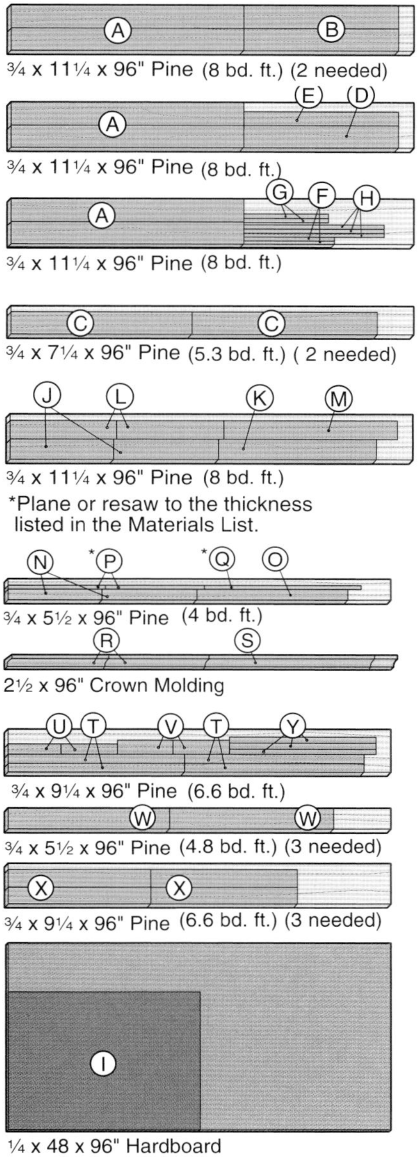

6 Rip and crosscut the panels (A, B, C) to the finished sizes in the Materials List.

7 To fit the shelf standards later, mark the locations, and cut a pair of 5/8" grooves 1/4" deep 2 1/2" from the front and back edges in the side panels.

MATERIALS LIST FOR COUNTRY ENTERTAINMENT CENTER

Part	FINISHED SIZE T	W	L	MTL.	QTY.
CABINET CARCASE					
A* sides	3/4"	21 1/8"	54 1/4"	EP	2
B* bottom	3/4"	21 1/8"	34 1/2"	EP	1
C* top	3/4"	24 7/8"	42"	EP	1
D bottom rail	3/4"	5 3/8"	36"	P	1
E top rail	3/4"	4"	36"	P	1
F cleats	3/4"	1"	21 1/8"	P	2
G cleats	3/4"	1"	20"	P	2
H cleats	3/4"	1"	33"	P	3
I back	1/4"	35 1/4"	48 7/8"	H	1
MOLDING					
J* bottom sides	3/4"	5 1/4"	22 5/8"	P	2
K* bottom front	3/4"	5 1/4"	37 1/2"	P	1
L* bottom sides	3/4"	4 5/8"	23 3/8"	P	2
M* bottom front	3/4"	4 5/8"	39"	P	1
N top sides	3/4"	2 3/4"	22 5/8"	P	2
O top front	3/4"	2 3/4"	37 1/2"	P	1
P* dentil molding	1/2"	1"	22 3/8"	P	2
Q* dentil molding	1/2"	1"	37"	P	1
R* crown molding	1 7/8"	2 1/2"	24 1/2"	P	2
S* crown molding	1 7/8"	2 1/2"	41 1/4"	P	1
DOORS					
T stiles	3/4"	2 1/2"	44 3/4"	P	4
U top rails	3/4"	2 1/2"	14"	P	2
V bottom rails	3/4"	3 3/4"	14"	P	2
W* panels	3/4"	13 7/8"	39 7/16"	EP	2
SHELVES					
X* shelves	3/4"	18"	34 3/8"	EP	3
Y* fronts	3/4"	1 1/2"	34 3/8"	P	3

*Parts initially cut oversized. See the instructions.
Materials Key: EP = Edge-joined pine; P = Pine; H = Hardboard.
Supplies: #6 x 1/2" flathead wood screws; #6 x 3/4" flathead wood screws; #8 x 1 1/4" flathead wood screws; 8' pine crown molding; cabinet top and bottom pivot hinges; cabinet middle pivot hinges; pulls; roller catches; 5/8" brown or walnut finished shelf standards (4); wood conditioner; stain; clear finish.

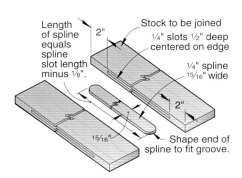

Length of spline equals spline slot length minus ⅛".

2"

Stock to be joined

¼" slots ½" deep centered on edge

¼" spline ¹⁵⁄₁₆" wide

2"

¹⁵⁄₁₆"

Shape end of spline to fit groove.

SPLINE DETAIL

Assemble the Carcase

1 Rip and crosscut the bottom front rail (D) and top front rail (E) to size from ¾"-thick pine stock.

2 Cut the cleats (F, G, H) to size. Drill and countersink the mounting holes through the cleats.

3 Position and square the side cleats (F) on the cabinet sides (A), where located on the Carcase Assembly drawing in **5–1**. Screw the cleats in place. Position and screw the top cleats (G) in place.

4 Dry-clamp the bottom and top panels (B, C) to the side panels. The back edge of the bottom and top is flush with the back edge of the sides. The top panel overhangs both side panels by 3". Check for square, and screw (without glue) the panels together.

5 Dry-clamp the rails (D, E) in place, drill countersunk screw holes, and then glue and screw these pieces to the carcase.

6 Rout a ⅜" rabbet ¼" deep along the back inside edge of the assembled cabinet, and then square up the round-routed corners with a chisel.

7 Measure the rabbeted opening, and cut the back (I) to size from ¼" hardboard. If you plan to use the cabinet for electronic components, bore ventilation and wire access holes. See the Carcase Assembly drawing in **5–1** for reference.

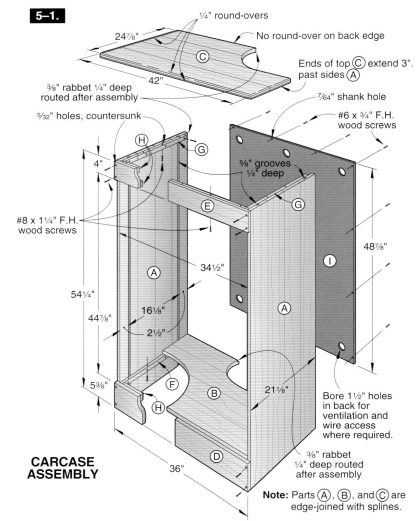

5–1.

¼" round-overs

No round-over on back edge

24⅞"

Ends of top C extend 3". past sides A

42"

⅜" rabbet ¼" deep routed after assembly

⁷⁄₆₄" shank hole

#6 x ¾" F.H. wood screws

⁵⁄₃₂" holes, countersunk

4"

⅝" grooves ¼" deep

48⅞"

#8 x 1¼" F.H. wood screws

34½"

54¼"

16⅛"

44⅞"

2½"

5⅜"

21⅛"

Bore 1½" holes in back for ventilation and wire access where required.

CARCASE ASSEMBLY

36"

⅜" rabbet ¼" deep routed after assembly

Note: Parts A, B, and C are edge-joined with splines.

Now Add the Decorative Pine Molding

1 Cut the bottom trim pieces (J, K, L, M) to the size shown in the Materials List plus 1" in length.

2 Rout a ½" cove along the top front edge of the inner trim pieces (J, K). (See the Upper and Lower Molding Detail drawings in **5–2** for reference.) Miter-cut the pieces, and screw them (without glue) to the cabinet bottom.

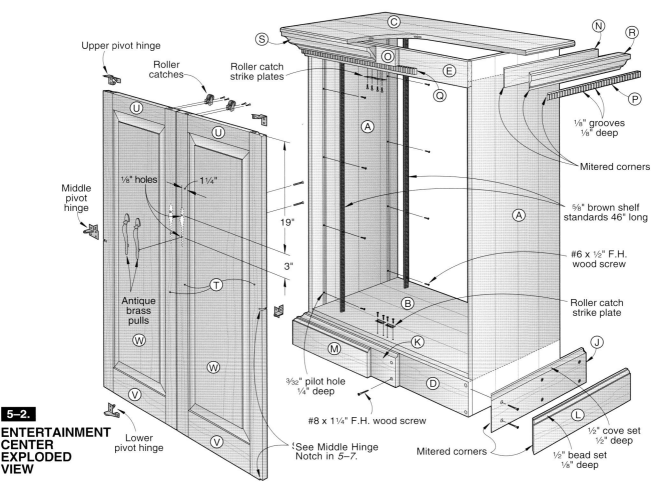

Upper pivot hinge

Roller catches

Roller catch strike plates

Middle pivot hinge

⅛" holes

1¼"

19"

3"

Antique brass pulls

Lower pivot hinge

Ⓤ Ⓤ Ⓣ Ⓦ Ⓦ Ⓥ Ⓥ

5–2.
ENTERTAINMENT CENTER EXPLODED VIEW

See Middle Hinge Notch in *5–7.*

Ⓒ Ⓢ Ⓞ Ⓔ Ⓠ Ⓐ Ⓐ Ⓑ Ⓚ Ⓜ Ⓓ

Ⓝ Ⓡ Ⓟ

⅛" grooves ⅛" deep

Mitered corners

⅝" brown shelf standards 46" long

#6 x ½" F.H. wood screw

Roller catch strike plate

Ⓙ Ⓛ

½" cove set ½" deep

½" bead set ⅛" deep

Mitered corners

3/32" pilot hole ¼" deep

#8 x 1¼" F.H. wood screw

---

3 Rout a ½" bead along the top front edge of the outer trim pieces (L, M). Miter-cut these pieces, and then glue them to the cabinet.

4 Cut the top trim pieces (N, O) to size, and screw them (without glue) to the top of the cabinet. (Refer to the Upper and Lower Molding Detail drawings in **5–2**.)

5 Cut the dentil molding pieces (P, Q) to size, plus 2" in length. Construct the jig shown in **5–3**, *page 66*. The center of the ⅛" kerf in the miter extension should be ½" from the center of the indexing pin.

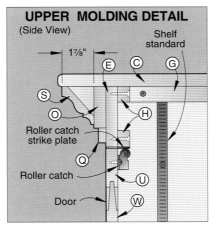

UPPER MOLDING DETAIL
(Side View)

1⅞"

Ⓔ Ⓒ Ⓖ

Shelf standard

Ⓢ Ⓞ Ⓗ

Roller catch strike plate

Ⓠ Ⓤ

Roller catch

Door Ⓦ

6 Make one kerfing cut across the end of one of the dentil molding strips. Next, position this kerf on the indexing pin, and make the second cut. Repeat the process, as shown in **5–4**, to make all the evenly spaced kerfs.

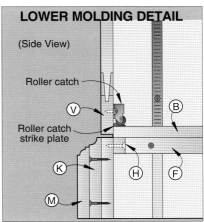

LOWER MOLDING DETAIL

(Side View)

Roller catch

Ⓥ Ⓑ

Roller catch strike plate

Ⓚ Ⓗ Ⓕ

Ⓜ

Repeat this process for each of the pieces.

7 Miter-cut the dentil molding pieces (P, Q), and glue them to the cabinet, where shown on the Exploded View drawing in **5–2**.

5-3. CUTTING THE DENTIL MOLDING

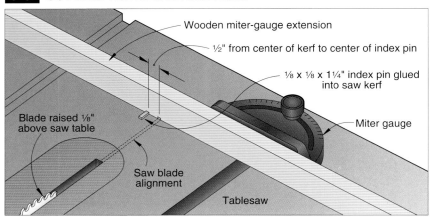

Wooden miter-gauge extension

½" from center of kerf to center of index pin

⅛ x ⅛ x 1¼" index pin glued into saw kerf

Miter gauge

Blade raised ⅛" above saw table

Saw blade alignment

Saw blade alignment

Tablesaw

5-4.

Use a wooden miter-gauge extension with a guide for cutting the dentil mold.

5-5. DOOR

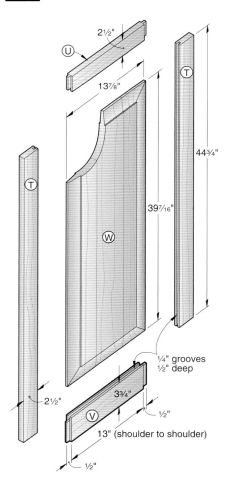

U

T

T

W

2½"

13⅞"

44¾"

39⁷⁄₁₆"

¼" grooves ½" deep

2½"

3¾"

V

½"

13" (shoulder to shoulder)

½"

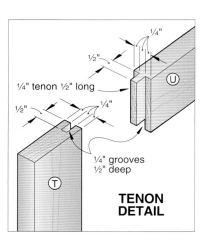

¼"

½"

¼" tenon ½" long

½"

¼"

¼"

U

¼" grooves ½" deep

T

TENON DETAIL

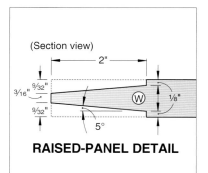

(Section view)

2"

³⁄₁₆"   ⁹⁄₃₂"

⁹⁄₃₂"

W

⅛"

5°

RAISED-PANEL DETAIL

8 To add the pine crown molding (R, S), you can do the following: Purchase an 8' piece at a local home center. Select a straight, flat 2 x 4, and glue it to the back face of the crown molding, where shown in *Step 1* of **5–6**. Now, rip the edges of the lamination, where shown in *Steps 1* and *2* of **5–6**.

9 Measure and miter-cut the front piece (S) to length, and glue it to the top front of the cabinet. Repeat for the side pieces (R).

Construct the Doors

1 Cut the door stiles (T), top rails (U), and bottom rails (V) to size.

2 Attach a ¼" dado blade to your tablesaw, and raise it ½" above the surface of the saw table. Cut a ¼" groove, centered from side to side, along one edge of each part. (First test-cut the groove using scrap stock of the same thickness as the stiles and rails to ensure it is centered.) See the Door and Tenon Detail drawings in **5–5** for reference.

5–6. RIPPING THE CROWN MOLDING

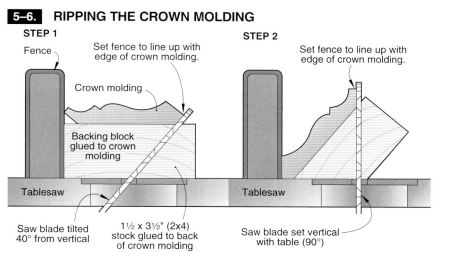

STEP 1

Fence

Set fence to line up with edge of crown molding.

Crown molding

Backing block glued to crown molding

Tablesaw

Saw blade tilted 40° from vertical

1½ x 3½" (2x4) stock glued to back of crown molding

STEP 2

Set fence to line up with edge of crown molding.

Tablesaw

Saw blade set vertical with table (90°)

5–7.

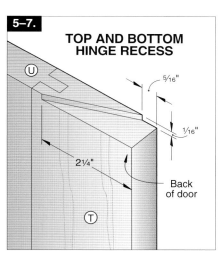

TOP AND BOTTOM HINGE RECESS

U

5⁄16"

1⁄16"

2¼"

Back of door

T

MIDDLE HINGE NOTCH

T

½"

5⁄16"

¾"

Back of door

3 To cut the stub tenons on the ends of the rails, use a miter gauge with an attached wood extension for support, and cut a ½" rabbet ¼" deep on both faces of each end of each rail.

4 For stability and flatness, edge-join narrower, straight-grained stock to form the two door panels (W) to the size in the Materials List plus 1" in length and width. Later, cut the door panels to finished size.

5 To cut the raised panels, tilt your tablesaw blade 5° from vertical, and elevate the blade 2" above the saw table. Position the rip fence, test-cut scrap stock to create the same shape shown on the Raised-Panel Detail drawing in 5–5, and cut each edge of each panel. Sand the cut areas to remove saw marks.

6 Test-fit the door pieces, and trim them if necessary. Then, finish-sand the panels and stain them. (For a more even stain application on the pine, you can apply wood conditioner before applying the stain.) Then, glue and clamp together each door, checking for square. Rest the clamped assemblies on a flat surface.

Install Pivot Hinges on the Doors and Carcase

1 Mark the upper and lower hinge recesses, where shown on the Top and Bottom Hinge Recess drawing in 5–7. Then, mark the locations for the middle notches, where shown on the Middle Hinge Notch drawing in 5–7. Follow the instructions supplied with the pivot hinges to form the top, bottom, and middle hinge recesses and notches.

2 Mount the hinges to the doors, and fasten the hinges to the cabinet. Mount the roller catches to the doors and cabinet. Drill the holes for the pulls. Attach the pulls and catches.

3 Crosscut the shelf standards, and install them in the cabinet.

Add the Shelves and a Finish

Note: The shelves are dimensioned to allow a little more than 1" of clearance between the back edge of the shelf and the front edge of the back piece (I). The gap allows passageway for the cords from your electrical components to the wire-access holes.

1 Using the same procedure you used to form the panels for the side, bottom, and top

5–8.

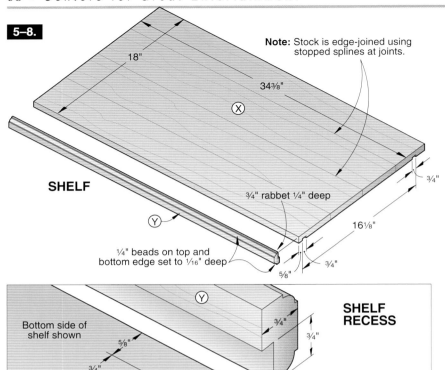

Note: Stock is edge-joined using stopped splines at joints.

18"

34⅜"

Ⓧ

¾"

SHELF

¾" rabbet ¼" deep

Ⓨ

16⅛"

¼" beads on top and bottom edge set to ¹⁄₁₆" deep

⅝"

¾"

Ⓨ

Bottom side of shelf shown

SHELF RECESS

¾"

¾"

⅝"

¾"

Ⓧ

1¹⁄₁₆"

STEP 1
Lay out hole location, and bore a ¾" hole ⅛" deep.

⅛" **STEP 2**
Chisel remaining waste from notch.

panels, edge-join and spline enough pine stock for the number of shelves (X) that you'll need.

2 Cut the shelves to fit between the shelf standards.

3 Cut the shelf fronts (Y) to size plus 1" in length. Cut a ¾" rabbet ¼" deep along the back edge of each. (See the Shelf Recess drawing in **5–8** for reference.) Glue and clamp a front to each shelf.

4 Rout ¼" beads along the front edge of each shelf front. Trim the ends of the shelf fronts flush with the ends of each shelf.

5 Fit the clips on the shelf standards. Form clip recesses on the bottom of each shelf, where dimensioned in **5–8**.

6 Remove all the hardware from the cabinet and doors. Remove the back (I) from the cabinet. Finish-sand all the pieces. Apply wood conditioner, and then stain and add a clear finish. (We used a satin polyurethane.)

7 Reattach the hardware, and then hang the doors. Screw the cabinet back in place.

SHOWTIME STORAGE

Everyone has different needs for storing CDs, DVDs, and other electronic media. With this unit, shown on the *opposite page*, you quickly can rearrange the glass shelves inside to hold a variety of your favorite sights and sounds, with room left over for those valued collectibles that need protection.

Make the Four Long, Lean Legs

1 If you can find 8/4 stock for the legs (A), you can skip the laminating process. Otherwise, rip eight ¾"-thick blanks into 1¾ x 45" strips, and glue up four pairs into leg blanks. After the glue dries, joint one edge of each blank. Rip the blank 1⁹⁄₁₆" wide, and joint it to 1½" square. Cut the legs 43¾" long, and rout a ⅛" chamfer around their bottom ends.

2 Arrange the legs (A) with the lamination lines running from front to back, as shown in **5–9** and **5–10** (*page 70*). Using a felt-tipped pen, mark the position of each leg on its top, using "LR" for left rear, for example. Referring to **5–9** and **5–10**, lay out the location of the mortises on each of the project's legs.

3 To make the mortises, follow the steps in **5–13**. For the best results, set up your drill press with a fence and a brad-point bit.

CUTTING DIAGRAM FOR SHOWTIME STORAGE

¾ x 9¼ x 96" Oak (6.6 bd. ft.)

¾ x 7¼ x 96" Oak (5.3 bd. ft.)

½ x 5½ x 72" Oak (3 bd. ft.)

½ x 5½ x 72" Oak (3 bd. ft.)

MATERIALS LIST FOR SHOWTIME STORAGE

PART	FINISHED SIZE			MTL.	QTY.
	T	W	L		
A* legs	1½"	1½"	43¾"	LO	4
B top side rails	¾"	2"	6¼"	O	2
C bottom side rails	¾"	2¼"	6¼"	O	2
D top rails, front/back	¾"	2"	12⅞"	O	2
E bottom rails, front/back	¾"	2¼"	12⅞"	O	2
F side panels	½"	3⅞"	35¼"	O	2
G* back panel	½"	10½"	35¼"	EO	1
H bottom	¾"	5¾"	11"	O	1
I* top	¾"	8⅞"	15½"	EO	1

*Parts initially cut oversized. See the instructions.
Materials Key: LO = Laminated oak; O = Oak; EO = Edge-joined oak.
Supplies: #8 x ½" flathead wood screws (8); ¼" glass shelves (4); glue; stain; finish.
Hardware: Desktop fasteners (10); ¼" spoon-style bronze shelf pins; optional curio cabinet light.

This Arts and Crafts unit has glass shelves that can be repositioned, making it easy to customize the unit to store your CDs, DVDs, or other electronic media.

4 Making an easy template will save you time when drilling the shelf-pin holes. To make this template, cut a piece of scrap hardwood ¼ x 1½ x 32", and lay out the hole centerpoints, where dimensioned in **5–9**. Use double-faced tape to position the template on the left rear leg (A), making sure the edges and the top end are flush. Illustration **5–11** (*page 71*) shows the jig in action. Drill through the template and ½" deep into the leg. After you drill the left rear leg, put the template on the right front leg. After you drill that leg, put double-faced tape on the other side of the template to position it for the other two legs.

Make the Rails

1 Rip and crosscut the rails (B, C, D, E) to the sizes in the Materials List. Save ¾"-thick scraps that are 1¼" wide to make test cuts for the tenons.

2 Referring to **5–14** (*page 71*), set up your tablesaw to cut the tenons. Raise the blade ¼" above the table, and make a cut into each face of a scrap, forming a test tenon. Check the fit of the tenon into a mortise, and make any adjustments necessary. When you're satisfied with the setup, cut the cheeks of each tenon. With the same setup, make the ¼"-deep cut at the top of rails B and D. Raise the blade

5–9. SIDE ASSEMBLY DETAIL

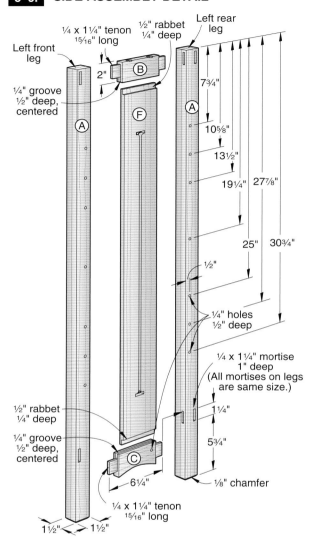

*Note: If you are installing the optional curio cabinet light, drill the mounting-screw pilot holes in the front top rail and cut the cord notch in the back top rail, where shown on **5–15** (page 72).*

4 Referring to **5–10**, mark the centerpoint of the arcs on the bottom rails (C, E). Connect that point to the bottom ends, as shown in **5–12** and described in the Shop Tip "Marking Arcs in a Pinch." Bandsaw and sand to the line.

5 Drill the shelf-pin holes in the inner faces of the bottom side rails (C), where shown on the Exploded View drawing in **5–15** (*page 72*).

6 Mark the centerpoints and drill the counterbores and pilot holes for the desktop fasteners on the top edges of the top side rails (B), where dimensioned on the Mounting Clip Detail drawing in **5–16** (*page 72*). Use a ¾" Forstner bit and a 7⁄64" twist drill in your drill press.

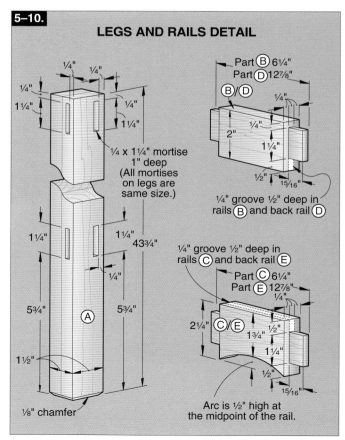

5–10. LEGS AND RAILS DETAIL

to ½" above the table, and make the top cut in the bottom rails (C, E), and the bottom cut in all the rails. Refer to **5–10** to see the layout of the tenons.

3 Install a ¼" dado blade in your tablesaw, raise it ½" above the table, and set your rip fence to cut the groove centered in the rails, where shown in **5–10**. Cut this groove in the lower edge of the top side rails (B) and the back top rail (D), and the upper edge of the bottom side rails (C) and the back bottom rail (E). The front rails (D, E) are not grooved.

Drill the left rear and right front legs with the shelf-pin template in this position. For the other legs, flip the template placing its opposite face upward.

Make the Panels, Bottom Shelf, and Top

1 From ½"-thick stock, cut the side panels (F) to size, and edge-join an oversize blank for the back panel (G). From ¾"-thick stock, cut the bottom (H) to size, and edge-join an oversize

blank for the top (I). With the glue dry, cut parts G and I to finished size.

2 Install a ½" dado blade in your tablesaw, and raise it ¼" above the table. Cut the rabbets along the inside ends of the panels (F, G).

3 Make two copies of the Side Panel Full-Size Detail Pattern in **5–18** (*page 73*). Use spray adhesive to join them to the side panels (F), 4½" from each end, as indicated on the pattern. Drill the ⅜" start and stop holes through the panels.

4 Chuck a ¼" straight bit into your table-mounted router, and clamp a fence behind the bit, 1¹⁵⁄₁₆" from its centerpoint. Put the panel against the fence, and clamp another fence flush against the other side of the panel. Refer to **5–17** (*page 72*) to see this setup. Rout the slots in both side panels (F).

5 Install a #4 blade (.035 x .015" with 18 teeth per inch) in your scrollsaw, and make the cutouts at the slots' ends.

SHOP TIP

Marking Arcs in a Pinch

You don't need fancy drafting equipment to draw a smooth arc like the one at the bottom of the bottom rails (C, E). Simply rip a wood strip to ⅛ x ¾ x 15" and pinch it in a clamp until it forms a smooth arc connecting the bottom ends of the rail.

5–12.

5–13.

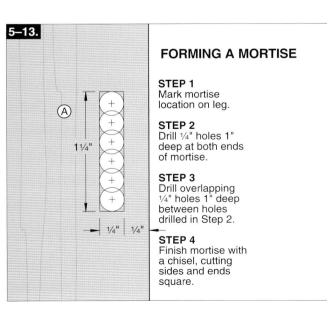

FORMING A MORTISE

STEP 1
Mark mortise location on leg.

STEP 2
Drill ¼" holes 1" deep at both ends of mortise.

STEP 3
Drill overlapping ¼" holes 1" deep between holes drilled in Step 2.

STEP 4
Finish mortise with a chisel, cutting sides and ends square.

Ⓐ 1¼" ¼" ¼"

5–14.

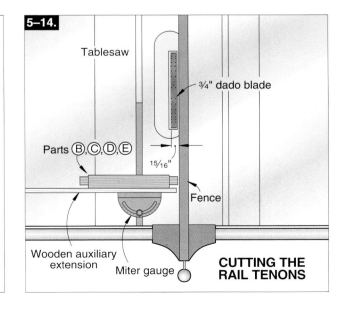

Tablesaw

¾" dado blade

Parts ⒷⒸⒹⒺ

15⁄16"

Fence

Wooden auxiliary extension

Miter gauge

CUTTING THE RAIL TENONS

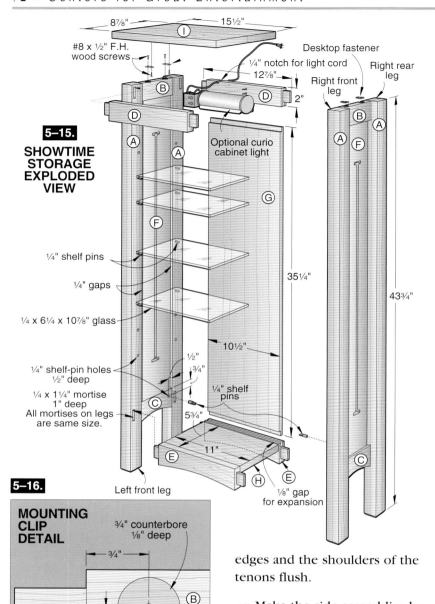

5–15.
SHOWTIME STORAGE EXPLODED VIEW

8⅞" 15½"

#8 x ½" F.H. wood screws

¼" notch for light cord
12⅞"

Desktop fastener

Right rear leg

Right front leg

2"

Optional curio cabinet light

¼" shelf pins

¼" gaps

¼ x 6¼ x 10⅞" glass

35¼"

43¾"

10½"

¼" shelf-pin holes ½" deep

½"
¾"

¼ x 1¼" mortise 1" deep
All mortises on legs are same size.

¼" shelf pins

5¾"

11"

5–16.

Left front leg

⅛" gap for expansion

5–17.

Put the bit through the side panel's start hole, and turn on the router. Move the panel to the stop hole, switch off the router, and remove the panel.

MOUNTING CLIP DETAIL

¾" counterbore ⅛" deep

¾"

¼"

⁷⁄₆₄" pilot hole ½" deep

Assemble the Project

1 Before assembly, give all of the parts a final sanding with 220-grit sandpaper, and smooth any sharp edges. Glue and clamp the front bottom rail (E) to the bottom (H), making the top edges and the shoulders of the tenons flush.

2 Make the side assemblies by gluing up two legs (A), a top side rail (B), a bottom side rail (C), and a side panel (F). Secure the panels to the rails with a single drop of glue in the center of the rails' grooves. Center the panels between the legs. This construction keeps the panels centered, but still allows them to expand and contract. Check that each assembly is square and flat.

3 With the glue dry, join the side assemblies with the top rails (D), the front bottom rail/bottom (E/H), back bottom rail (E), and the back panel (G). Assemble the back panel and rails in the same manner as the side panels and rails. To support the back edge of the bottom, insert shelf pins in the holes previously drilled in the bottom side rails (C).

4 Drive #8 x ½" flathead wood screws through the desktop fasteners into the top side rails (B). Adjust the top (I) for an equal reveal on all sides, mark the fastener locations on the top, and drill ⁷⁄₆₄" pilot holes ½" deep. Remove the top and the desktop fasteners.

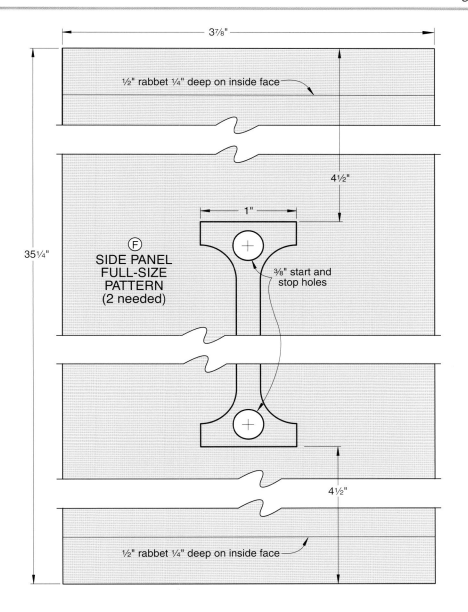

3⅞"

½" rabbet ¼" deep on inside face

4½"

1"

Ⓕ
SIDE PANEL
FULL-SIZE
PATTERN
(2 needed)

⅜" start and
stop holes

35¼"

4½"

½" rabbet ¼" deep on inside face

5–18.

Make two copies of this full-size pattern, and trim them to 3⅞" width. Then cut the patterns apart between the center break lines. Use spray adhesive to adhere the patterns to the side panels. Position the tops of the I-shape cutouts 4½" from the panels' top edges, and the bottoms of the cutouts 4½" from the panels' bottom edges, as indicated at left.

Apply a Durable Finish

1 Using a sanding block and 220-grit paper, give the completed project a quick once-over to smooth grain that was raised when wiping off glue squeeze-out.

2 After removing the dust with a tack cloth, apply a coat of stain. Then apply a coat of gloss polyurethane, followed by a coat of satin. Between coats, sand with 220-grit sandpaper.

3 With the finish dry, replace the desktop fasteners and top, and add shelf pins. Make a template for the shelves from ¼"-thick plywood. Take the template to a glass shop to ensure that your shelves will fit. Have the shelves' edges ground with a pencil edge.

***Note:** If you are installing the optional curio cabinet light, fasten it to the front rail, and lay the cord in the rear rail's notch before replacing the top.*

CABINET COMBINATION

G ive your CD sound system, TV, and VCR or DVD player a fitting home with this three-piece cabinet combination.

The main attraction, the center cabinet, offers room for a 27"-screen television. Flipper doors pull out from the interior and neatly hide the screen when not in use. Optional matching side cabinets abound with room for practically everything else.

Make the Carcase

1 Cut the sides (A), bottom (B), and top (C) to size from ¾" cherry plywood. Or, for a less expensive alternative, stain birch plywood (a gel stain is recommended) to look like cherry.

2 Cut the rabbets in the sides (A), bottom (B), top (C), and grooves in the top (C), where indicated in **5–19**, on *page 76*.

A storage system for home electronics. See the photo on the facing page *for a look at just the center cabinet.*

CUTTING DIAGRAM FOR CENTER CABINET COMBINATION

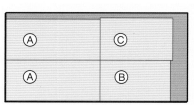

¾ x 48 x 96" Cherry plywood

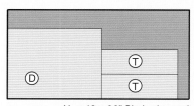

¼ x 48 x 96" Birch plywood

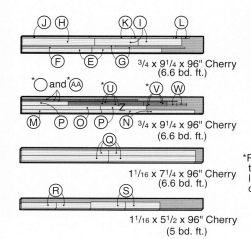

¾ x 9¼ x 96" Cherry
(6.6 bd. ft.)

¾ x 9¼ x 96" Cherry
(6.6 bd. ft.)

1¹¹⁄₁₆ x 7¼ x 96" Cherry
(6.6 bd. ft.)

1¹¹⁄₁₆ x 5½ x 96" Cherry
(5 bd. ft.)

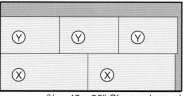

¾ x 48 x 96" Cherry plywood

*Plane or resaw to the thickness listed in the Bill of Materials.

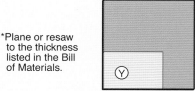

¾ x 48 x 48" Cherry plywood

MATERIALS LIST FOR CABINET COMBINATION

PART	FINISHED SIZE T	W	L	MTL.	QTY.
CENTER CABINET CARCASE					
A sides	¾"	22¼"	49⅝"	CP	2
B bottom	¾"	22¼"	38"	CP	1
C top	¾"	23"	38½"	CP	1
D back	¼"	38"	49½"	BP	1
FACE FRAME					
E top rail & cleat	¾"	2¼"	37"	C	2
F bottom rail	¾"	¾"	37"	C	2
G stiles	¾"	¾"	49¼"	C	2
BASE					
H front	¾"	4"	38½"	C	1
I sides	¾"	4"	23"	C	2
J cleat	¾"	¾"	35½"	C	1
K cleats	¾"	¾"	21½"	C	2
L cleats	¾"	¾"	4"	C	2
TOP					
M front	¾"	1¾"	42"	C	1
N sides	¾"	1¾"	24¾"	C	2
O* cove front	¾"	2⅛"	41½"	C	1
P* cove sides	¾"	2⅛"	24½"	C	2
DOORS					
Q stiles	1 1/16"	3"	46"	C	4
R top rails	1 1/16"	3"	18 5/16"	C	2
S bottom rails	1 1/16"	3½"	18 5/16"	C	2
T panels	¼"	13 1/16"	40¼"	BP	2
U muntin bars	½"	½"	39½"	C	4
V muntin bars	½"	½"	12 5/16"	C	4
W door-stops	¾"	¾"	5"	C	4
INSERT CABINET					
X sides	¾"	20"	46 3/16"	CP	2
Y shelves	¾"	20"	31¾"	CP	4
Z banding	¼"	¾"	46 3/16"	C	2
AA banding	¼"	¾"	31¼"	C	4

*Initially cut the parts oversized. Trim to finished size according to the instructions.
Materials Key: CP = Cherry plywood; BP = Birch plywood; C = Cherry.
Supplies: #6 x ½" flathead wood screws; #6 x ¾" flathead wood screws; #8 x 1¼" flathead wood screws; #8 x 2" flathead wood screws; #12 x 1½" flathead wood screws; primer; paint; clear finish.
Hardware: Heavy-duty flipper-door system; inset carrier strip and hinges.

3 Glue and screw the carcase (A, B, C) together, checking for square. Remove excess glue.

4 Measure the rabbeted opening, and cut the back (D) to size. Drill the mounting holes through the back side of the back panel and into the rabbet in the carcase.

5 Mark the oval openings on the back (D), and cut them to shape. The openings provide ventilation and wire access. Set the back panel aside; you'll attach it later.

6 From solid cherry, cut the face-frame rails and stiles (E, F, G) to size, cutting the pieces the exact width of the thickness of your plywood. Keeping the edges of the face-frame pieces flush with the surfaces of the plywood, glue and clamp them to the carcase.

7 Sand the face frame flush with the plywood, being careful not to sand through the thin veneer.

Build the Sturdy Base

Build the base so it is flush with the cabinet exterior. Do the following:

1 Cut the base front (H), sides (I), and cleats (J, K, L) to size. Measure the carcase before miter-cutting the front and sides to length. The outside surfaces of the base should be flush with the outside surfaces of the carcase.

2 Cut a radius in the front (H), where dimensioned on the Center Cabinet Exploded View drawing in **5–19**.

3 Drill countersunk pilot holes through the cleats. (You can do this on a drill press, using the fence to keep the holes centered.)

4 Tip the carcase upside down. Then, glue and screw the base pieces to the bottom of the carcase. Check that the miter joints pull tight.

Cover the Plywood Edges with Banding and Molding

1 Cut the carcase top banding (M, N) to fit around the plywood top (C). Glue the pieces in place.

2 To form the cove molding, cut the cove front (O) and sides (P) to the sizes in the

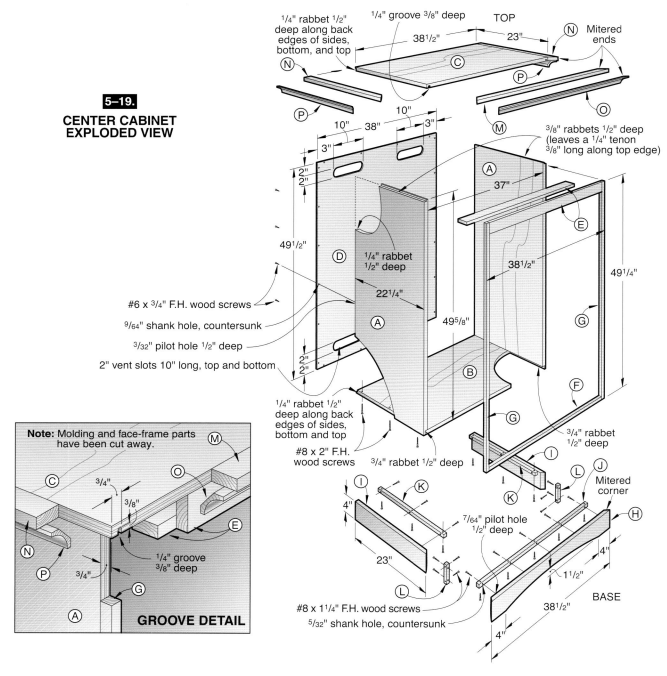

5–19.

CENTER CABINET EXPLODED VIEW

1/4" rabbet 1/2" deep along back edges of sides, bottom, and top

1/4" groove 3/8" deep

TOP

38 1/2"

23"

Mitered ends

3/8" rabbets 1/2" deep (leaves a 1/4" tenon 3/8" long along top edge)

37"

10"

10"

38"

3"

3"

2"

2"

49 1/2"

1/4" rabbet 1/2" deep

22 1/4"

#6 x 3/4" F.H. wood screws

9/64" shank hole, countersunk

3/32" pilot hole 1/2" deep

2" vent slots 10" long, top and bottom

2"

2"

1/4" rabbet 1/2" deep along back edges of sides, bottom and top

#8 x 2" F.H. wood screws

3/4" rabbet 1/2" deep

38 1/2"

49 5/8"

49 1/4"

3/4" rabbet 1/2" deep

Mitered corner

4"

23"

7/64" pilot hole 1/2" deep

4"

1 1/2"

BASE

38 1/2"

4"

#8 x 1 1/4" F.H. wood screws

5/32" shank hole, countersunk

Note: Molding and face-frame parts have been cut away.

3/4"

3/8"

1/4" groove 3/8" deep

3/4"

GROOVE DETAIL

Materials List plus 2" in length. Then, as shown in **5–21** (*page 78*), make several passes to rout the cove along one surface of each piece of stock. (You can use a crown molding bit.)

3 Bevel-rip the back edges of the cove molding at 45°, where indicated on the drawing.

4 Next, miter-cut the pieces to fit around the carcase top.

5 Glue and clamp the cove molding pieces (O, P) in place. (To do this, clamp a cleat to the carcase top. Then, use a 1 1/4"-diameter dowel and another set of clamps to pull the cove molding tight, as shown in **5–22**.)

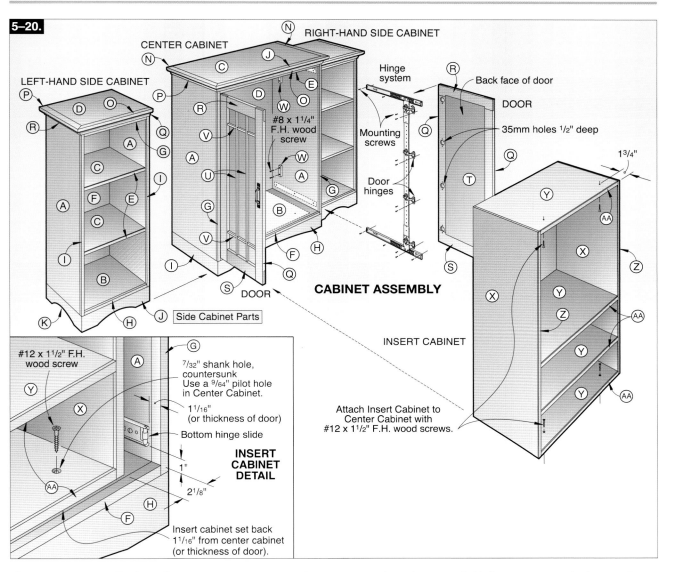

5–20.

LEFT-HAND SIDE CABINET

CENTER CABINET

RIGHT-HAND SIDE CABINET

Side Cabinet Parts

#8 x 1¹/₄" F.H. wood screw

Hinge system

Back face of door

DOOR

Mounting screws

35mm holes ¹/₂" deep

Door hinges

CABINET ASSEMBLY

DOOR

1³/₄"

INSERT CABINET

#12 x 1¹/₂" F.H. wood screw

⁷/₃₂" shank hole, countersunk Use a ⁹/₆₄" pilot hole in Center Cabinet.

1¹/₁₆" (or thickness of door)

Bottom hinge slide

1"

2¹/₈"

INSERT CABINET DETAIL

Attach Insert Cabinet to Center Cabinet with #12 x 1¹/₂" F.H. wood screws.

Insert cabinet set back 1¹/₁₆" from center cabinet (or thickness of door).

Construct a Pair of Half-Lapped Doors

1 Cut the door stiles (Q) and rails (R, S) to the sizes in the Materials List.

2 Fit your tablesaw with a dado blade, and cut mating half-laps on the ends of the stiles and rails, where shown in **5–23**. (Test-cut scrap pieces first to verify the depth of cut before cutting the stiles and rails.)

3 Glue and clamp together the door stiles and rails, measuring diagonally to check for square.

4 Sand each door smooth. Rout a ³/₈" rabbet ¹/₄" deep along the back inside edge of each door to house the door panels (T).

5 Cut the door panels (T) to fit the openings. Round the corners of the panels to match the round-routed corners. Then, mark the hole centerpoints and

drill the mounting holes so that you can screw the panels to the doorframes.

6 Cut the door muntin bars (U, V) to size. Using the dimensions in **5–23**, mark and cut the dadoes on the muntins. (You can do this on a tablesaw.)

7 Glue and clamp the muntins together, checking for square. Wipe off any excess glue with a damp cloth. (Clamp the pieces

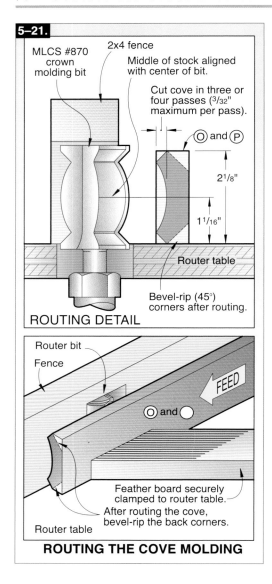

5–21.

MLCS #870 crown molding bit

2x4 fence

Middle of stock aligned with center of bit.

Cut cove in three or four passes ($3/32$" maximum per pass).

$\bigcirc$ and $\bigcirc{P}$

$2^1/8$"

$1^1/16$"

Router table

Bevel-rip (45°) corners after routing.

ROUTING DETAIL

Router bit

Fence

FEED

$\bigcirc$ and $\bigcirc$

Feather board securely clamped to router table. After routing the cove, bevel-rip the back corners.

Router table

ROUTING THE COVE MOLDING

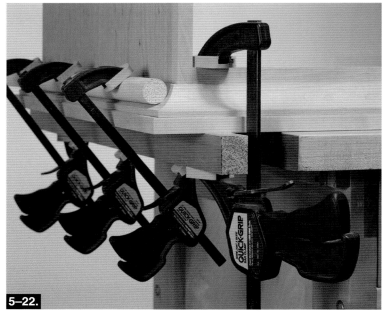

5–22.

Use a dowel and clamp block when clamping the cove molding to the top of the cabinet.

together on a piece of sheet goods to keep the muntins flat while the glue dries.)

8 Dry-assemble the door frames with the back panels (T) in place. Position the muntins (U, V) in place, and mark the hole centerpoints so that later you can screw the muntins to the door panels. Drill the countersunk mounting holes for attaching the muntins.

9 Cut the four doorstops (W) to size, and screw them to the inside face of the cabinet, where shown in **5–26** (*page 81*).

Construct the Television Insert

To construct the television insert to fit inside the center cabinet, do the following:

1 Cut to size the insert cabinet sides (X) and shelves (Y) from cherry plywood. Cut to size the front banding (Z, AA) from solid stock. The insert not only supports your electronics but also hides the flipper-door hardware.

2 Mark and cut the dadoes and rabbets, where shown in **5–24** (*page 80*). For ease of access, finish the cabinet pieces now. Then, glue and screw the insert cabinet together, checking for square. Next, glue and clamp the cherry banding to the front of the insert cabinet. Sand the pieces flush with the side and shelf edges.

Apply the Finish

Note: *Because installing the slide hardware requires precision and takes some time, you'll want to install it only once. For those reasons, finish the cabinet now, before adding the flipper-door hardware.*

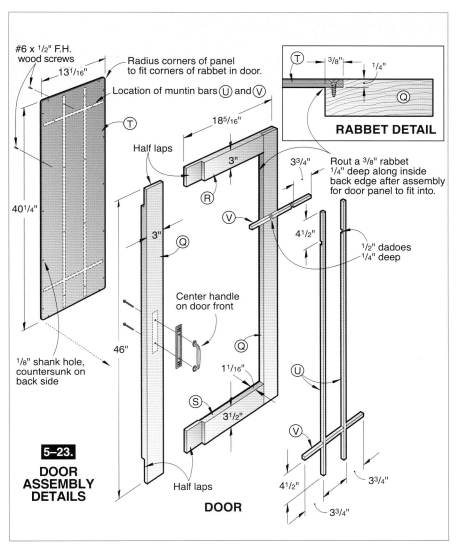

#6 x 1/2" F.H. wood screws

13 1/16"

Radius corners of panel to fit corners of rabbet in door.

Location of muntin bars (U) and (V)

(T)

18 5/16"

Half laps

3"

3 3/4"

Rout a 3/8" rabbet 1/4" deep along inside back edge after assembly for door panel to fit into.

(R)

(V)

4 1/2"

1/2" dadoes 1/4" deep

40 1/4"

3"

(Q)

(Q)

Center handle on door front

1/8" shank hole, countersunk on back side

46"

(Q)

1 1/16"

(U)

(S)

3 1/2"

(V)

4 1/2"

3 3/4"

3 3/4"

5–23.
DOOR ASSEMBLY DETAILS

Half laps

DOOR

(T) 3/8" 1/4"

(Q)

RABBET DETAIL

---

1 Finish-sand the cabinet with 220-grit sandpaper.

2 Paint the back (D) and door panels (T).

3 Screw the door panels in place; then screw the muntins to the panels.

Install the Flipper-Door Hardware

***Note:** The hardware system will come with an installation* instruction manual. *The following instructions and illustrations are meant to clarify some of the steps.*

1 Cut two spacers, one measuring 1 x 1 x 21" and the other measuring the thickness of your door by 12" long. As shown in **5–25** (*page 80*), use the 21" spacer to position the bottom slid 1" above the bottom of the carcase. Then, use the 12" spacer to position the slide at a

distance the exact thickness of your door from the front edge of the cabinet. (The door for the Cabinet Combination shown on *page 74* measured 1 1/16".) See **5–26** (*page 81*) for dimension particulars.

2 Drill the pilot holes and screw the bottom slide in place. Repeat for the other side of the cabinet.

3 Attach the top slide and hinge carrier to the bottom slide. Then, using the hinge carrier to hold the top slide parallel to the bottom slide, screw the top slide in place, as shown in **5–27**. Again, use the 12" spacer to position the top slide at a distance the thickness of your door from the front of the cabinet.

4 Cut a scrap piece of stock the same size as one of the door stiles (Q). You'll use this in *Step 6* to drill the hinge holes.

5 Mount your hinge base plates to the hinge carrer, working your way out from the center of the hinge carrier. See **5–26** for reference. Position the scrap stile along the edge of the hinge carrier. Then, place a 1/8" spacer between the scrap stile and carcase. This will provide an even reveal at the top and bottom of the door-frame. Clamp the scrap stile in place. Use a square to mark the center of each hinge onto the scrap stile, as shown in **5–28**.

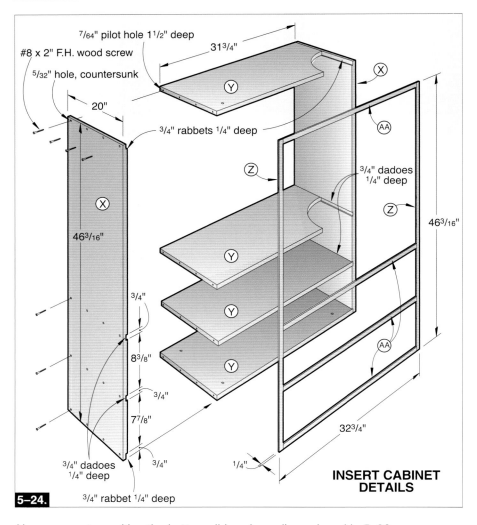

7/64" pilot hole 1¹/2" deep

#8 x 2" F.H. wood screw

5/32" hole, countersunk

31³/4"

20"

³/4" rabbets ¹/4" deep

46³/16"

³/4" dadoes ¹/4" deep

46³/16"

³/4"

8³/8"

³/4"

7⁷/8"

³/4" dadoes ¹/4" deep

³/4"

³/4" rabbet ¹/4" deep

1/4"

32³/4"

INSERT CABINET DETAILS

X   Y   Z   AA

5–24.

*Use spacers to position the bottom slide, where dimensioned in **5–26.***

5–25.

6 Do not drill the holes in the doors until you've verified the locations in the scrap stock. To do this, fit your drill press with a fence and 1⅜" Forstner bit (same size as 35mm bit). Drill the hinge hole 1" from the back edge of the scrap stile.

7 Mount the hinges to your scrap stile. Attach the four hinges to the base plates attached to the hinge carrier. As stated in the hinge instructions, adjust the hinges as necessary for an even reveal between the edge of the stile and the carcase side. (It is easier to adjust the hinge locations on the scrap stile than to do this on the assembled doors.) Once adjusted, unsnap the hinges from the hinge plates. Repeat for the other hinge assembly.

8 Install the cable blocks and then the cable system.

9 Use a square to carefully transfer the hole locations from the scrap stile to the doors. Bore the holes where marked. Remove the hinges one at a time from the scrap stile, and insert them into the 1⅜" holes in the door in the same sequence. Once you have the hinges in place, reattach the hinges to the hinge base plates. Double-check for proper alignment. Repeat for the other door.

5-26. **CENTER CABINET**

CENTER CABINET

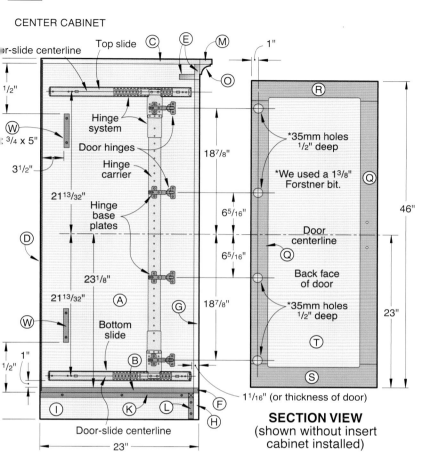

5-28.

Transfer the hinge hole centerpoints to scrap stile, and drill the holes to verify their locations before drilling them in the door stiles.

Build the Side Cabinets

1 Build the side cabinets with the same procedures used to construct the center cabinet. See the Side Cabinets' Materials List and Cutting Diagram on *page 82* for part sizes. Review **5-29** (*page 83*) for further reference. Note that the side-cabinet molding that abuts the center cabinet is cut at a 90° angle for a flush fit.

Add a Finish, Assemble the Projects, and Add Your Components

1 Finish-sand the side cabinets, and apply the finish.

5-27.

Locate the top slide's position in the cabinet, drill the mounting holes, and screw the slide in place.

CUTTING DIAGRAM FOR SIDE CABINETS

(enough for two cabinets)

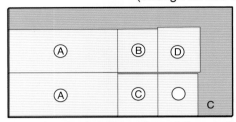
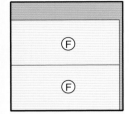

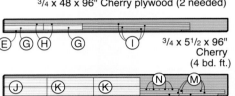

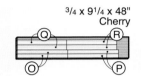

3/4 x 48 x 96" Cherry plywood (2 needed)

1/4 x 48 x 48" Birch plywood

3/4 x 5 1/2 x 96" Cherry (4 bd. ft.)

3/4 x 9 1/4 x 48" Cherry

3/4 x 9 1/4 x 96" Cherry (6.6 bd. ft.)

MATERIALS LIST FOR SIDE CABINETS

Part	FINISHED SIZE*			MTL.	QTY.
	T	W	L		
Side Cabinet Carcases					
A sides	3/4"	19 1/4"	46 5/8"	CP	4
B bottoms	3/4"	19 1/4"	17 3/4"	CP	2
C shelves	3/4"	18 3/4"	17 1/4"	CP	4
D tops	3/4"	20"	18 1/4"	CP	2
E banding	1/4"	3/4"	17 1/4"	C	4
F backs	1/4"	17 3/4"	46 1/2"	BP	2
FACE FRAMES					
G top rails	3/4"	2 1/4"	16 3/4"	C	2
H bottom rails	3/4"	3/4"	16 3/4"	C	2
I stiles	3/4"	3/4"	46 1/4"	C	4
Bases					
J fronts	3/4"	4"	18 1/4"	C	2
K sides	3/4"	4"	20"	C	4
L cleats	3/4"	3/4"	15 1/4"	C	2
M cleats	3/4"	3/4"	18 1/2"	C	4
N cleats	3/4"	3/4"	4"	C	4
Tops					
O fronts	3/4"	1 3/4"	20"	C	2
P sides	3/4"	1 3/4"	21 3/4"	C	2
Q cove fronts	3/4"	2 1/8"	19 3/4"	C	2
R cove fronts	3/4"	2 1/8"	21 1/2"	C	2

*Initially cut parts oversized. Trim to finished size according to the instructions.
Materials Key: CP = Cherry plywood; BP = Birch plywood; C = Cherry.
Supplies: #6 x 1/2" flathead wood screws; #6 x 3/4" flathead wood screws; #8 x 1 1/4" flathead wood screws; #8 x 2" flathead wood screws; #12 x 1 1/2" flathead wood screws; primer; paint; clear finish.

2 Paint the side cabinet backs (F), and screw them in place.

3 Position the side cabinets against the center cabinet. If a gap exists between the cabinets, drill mounting holes through the side cabinet sides (A) and into but not through the center cabinet sides (A). Position the holes so the screws won't be highly visible. Use wood screws to pull the cabinets tight to each other, eliminating the gap.

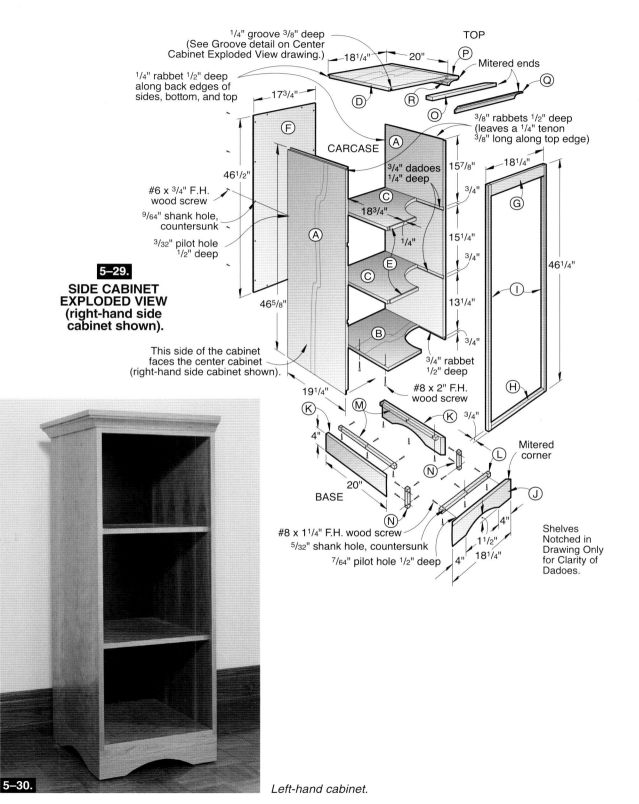

¹/₄" groove ³/₈" deep
(See Groove detail on Center
Cabinet Exploded View drawing.)

TOP

18¹/₄"   20"

P   Mitered ends

Q

¹/₄" rabbet ¹/₂" deep
along back edges of
sides, bottom, and top

17³/₄"

D   R   O

F

³/₈" rabbets ¹/₂" deep
(leaves a ¹/₄" tenon
³/₈" long along top edge)

A   CARCASE

A

³/₄" dadoes   15⁷/₈"
¹/₄" deep

18¹/₄"

46¹/₂"

³/₄"

G

#6 x ³/₄" F.H.
wood screw

⁹/₆₄" shank hole,
countersunk

³/₃₂" pilot hole
¹/₂" deep

C

18³/₄"

¹/₄"

A

E

C

15¹/₄"

³/₄"

46¹/₄"

5–29.
SIDE CABINET
EXPLODED VIEW
(right-hand side
cabinet shown).

13¹/₄"

I

³/₄"

46⁵/₈"

B

³/₄" rabbet
¹/₂" deep

This side of the cabinet
faces the center cabinet
(right-hand side cabinet shown).

#8 x 2" F.H.
wood screw

19¹/₄"

K   M

#8 x 2" F.H.
wood screw

K   ³/₄"

H

4"

20"

BASE

N

#8 x 1¹/₄" F.H. wood screw
⁵/₃₂" shank hole, countersunk
⁷/₆₄" pilot hole ¹/₂" deep

N

L   Mitered
corner

J

4"

1¹/₂"

4"   18¹/₄"

Shelves
Notched in
Drawing Only
for Clarity of
Dadoes.

5–30.

Left-hand cabinet.

6

organizing your library

YOU DON'T HAVE TO BE A BOOK collector or librarian to accumulate a great assortment of tomes. Because no one can part with—or pass by—a good book, they continue to stack up. But you really don't want them to do that literally. You naturally want books to be organized on shelves and protected from damage.

Book shelving falls into two basic categories: open and enclosed. Generally, open shelving consists of shelves that extend beyond the supports and that have no backs. Without these viewing obstructions, open shelves lend themselves well to display. This type of simple shelving was discussed in Chapter 2. Enclosed shelves, on the other hand, typically fit between two solid or closed sides and a back. Attaching a back strengthens the assembly and prevents wracking.

In this chapter, you'll find three types of enclosed shelving units. The classic barrister's bookcase is on the opposite page. It is followed by a traditional masterpiece on page 94. On page 100, you'll see how to build one bookcase in three popular styles, and each of them is a pleasure to view.

So get started with one or more of these very achievable ideas. And have fun!

BARRISTER'S BOOKCASE

Y̲ou may stack these bookcases up to five units high. With two units, as shown in the inset, your bookcase can perform as a dining room sideboard or a hall table.

Build a base, a top, and as many bookshelf cases as you wish to go in between. All the parts simply stack on top of one another and screw together. You'll make your own wood door guides, and, aside from wood screws in various sizes, the only hardware you will need are knobs.

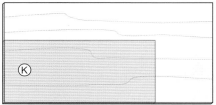

Barrister's bookcase

CUTTING DIAGRAM FOR BARRISTER'S BOOKCASE

¾ x 7¼ x 96" Quartersawn white oak (5.3 bd. ft.)

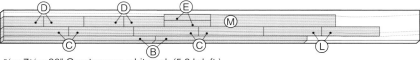

¾ x 7¼ 96" Quartersawn white oak (5.3 bd. ft.)   *Plane or resaw to the thicknesses
listed in the Materials List.

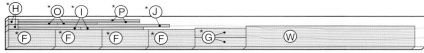

¾ x 7¼ x 96" Quartersawn white oak (5.3 bd. ft.)

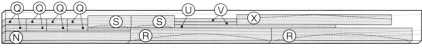

¾ x 5½ x 96" Quartersawn white oak (4 bd. ft.)

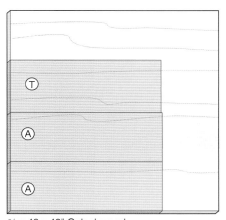

¾ x 48 x 48" Oak plywood

¼ x 24 x 48" Oak plywood

MATERIALS LIST FOR BARRISTER'S BOOKCASE

PART	FINISHED SIZE T	W	L	MTL.	QTY.
CASE					
A* upper and lower panels	¾"	11¾"	34"	OP	2
B* banding	¾"	¾"	34"	QO	2
C stiles	¾"	2¼"	15"	QO	4
D rails	¾"	2½"	9¼"	QO	4
E mullions	¾"	1½"	10¾"	QO	2
F side panels	⅜"	4⅛"	10¹¹⁄₁₆"	QO	4
G door guides	⅝"	2¼"	11¾"	QO	2
H bumper blocks	⅝"	1¼"	2⅛"	QO	2
I* side trim	⅝"	⅝"	13½"	QO	2
J* upper trim	⅝"	⅝"	34"	QO	1
K back	¼"	15"	34¾"	OP	1
DOOR					
L stiles	¾"	2¼"	13⅜"	QO	2
M upper rail	¾"	2¹³⁄₁₆"	28⅞"	QO	1
N lower rail	¾"	2¼"	28⅞"	QO	1
O vertical stops	⅜"	⅜"	9¹⁄₁₆"	QO	2
P horizontal stops	⅜"	⅜"	28⅛"	QO	2
BASE AND TOP					
Q feet	1½"	1½"	4¼"	LQO	4
R front and back rails	¾"	3"	32½"	QO	2
S side rails	¾"	3"	10"	QO	2
T base panel	¾"	12⅝"	34¾"	OP	1
U* front banding	¾"	¾"	36¼"	QO	1
V* side banding	¾"	¾"	13⅜"	QO	2
W* top	¾"	14⅝"	38¾"	EQO	1
X crest	¾"	2½"	35½"	QO	1

*Parts initially cut oversized. See the instructions.
Materials Key: OP = Oak plywood; QO = Quartersawn white oak; LQO = Laminated quarter-sawn white oak; EQO = Edge-joined quartersawn white oak.
Supplies: #20 biscuits; ½" oak dowel; #8 x 1", #8 x 1¼", #8 x 1½", and #4 x ½" flathead wood screws; #17 x ⅝" wire brads; single-strength glass; ½"-diameter tack bumpers; putty stick; paraffin wax.
Blades and Bits: Stack dado set; ½" Forstner bit; chamfer router bit; ⅜" rabbeting router bit.
Knobs: Antique brass ⅞"-diameter knobs with 1" back plates (2 per door).

Note: The Materials List and Cutting Diagram show the number of parts needed for a one stackable bookcase. Multiply the number of case parts and door parts by the number of bookshelf cases you wish to make.

Start with the Carcase

1 Cut the upper and lower panels (A) to width, but about 1" longer than indicated in the Materials List. Rip the banding (B) to width, but about 1" longer than listed. Glue and clamp the banding to the panels. With the glue dry, sand the banding flush with the panels, and cut the assemblies to length, trimming both ends.

2 With the panels oriented so their good sides will face into the case, rout ¹⁄₁₆" chamfers on the banding, where shown in **6–1**. Finish-sand the assemblies to 220 grit.

3 For the case sides, cut the stiles (C), rails (D), and mullions (E) to the sizes listed. Install a ⅜" dado blade in your tablesaw, and cut the centered grooves, where shown in **6–2**.

4 To form the tenons on the ends of the rails and mullions, switch to a ¼" dado blade. To set the tenons' length, position the fence to the right of the blade, and ⅜" from the blade's left side. Attach an auxiliary extension to your miter gauge so it just grazes the fence. After first testing your cuts in scrap, form the tenons,

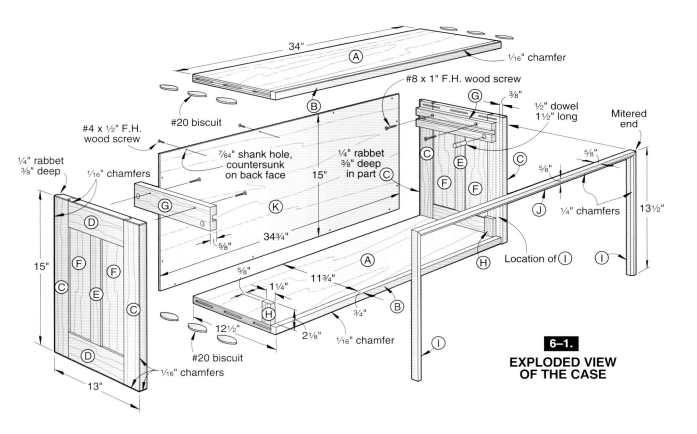

34"

Ⓐ

¹⁄₁₆" chamfer

#8 x 1" F.H. wood screw

Ⓖ

³⁄₈"

¹⁄₂" dowel 1½" long

Mitered end

Ⓑ

#20 biscuit

#4 x ½" F.H. wood screw

Ⓒ

Ⓒ

⁵⁄₈"

⁵⁄₈"

¼" rabbet ³⁄₈" deep

¹⁄₁₆" chamfers

⁷⁄₆₄" shank hole, countersunk on back face

¼" rabbet ³⁄₈" deep in part Ⓒ

15"

Ⓖ

Ⓔ

Ⓕ

Ⓕ

Ⓙ

¼" chamfers

13½"

Ⓓ

Ⓖ

Ⓚ

Ⓕ

Ⓒ

15"

Ⓒ

Ⓕ

34¾"

⁵⁄₈"

Ⓔ

Ⓒ

Ⓗ

Location of Ⓘ

Ⓓ

¹⁄₁₆" chamfers

13"

⁵⁄₈"

11¾"

1¼"

Ⓗ

12½"

2⅛"

¾"

¹⁄₁₆" chamfer

Ⓐ

Ⓑ

Ⓘ

Ⓘ

#20 biscuit

Ⓘ

6–1.

EXPLODED VIEW OF THE CASE

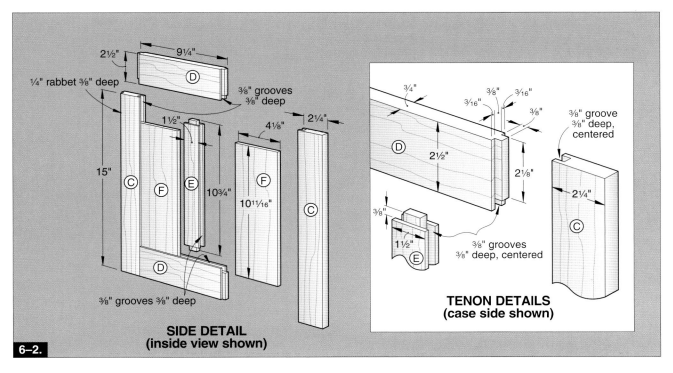

2½"

9¼"

Ⓓ

¼" rabbet ³⁄₈" deep

³⁄₈" grooves ³⁄₈" deep

2¼"

1½"

4⅛"

15"

Ⓒ

Ⓕ

Ⓔ

Ⓕ

Ⓒ

10¾"

10¹¹⁄₁₆"

Ⓓ

³⁄₈" grooves ³⁄₈" deep

SIDE DETAIL (inside view shown)

¾"

³⁄₈"

³⁄₁₆"

³⁄₁₆"

³⁄₈"

³⁄₈"

³⁄₈" groove ³⁄₈" deep, centered

Ⓓ

2½"

2⅛"

2¼"

³⁄₈"

Ⓒ

1½"

Ⓔ

³⁄₈" grooves ³⁄₈" deep, centered

TENON DETAILS (case side shown)

6–2.

where shown in **6–2**, making two passes over the blade.

5 Resaw and plane stock for the side panels (F), and cut them to size. So seasonal wood movement won't expose unstained wood after the project is complete, finish-sand the panels and apply stain.

6 Before assembling the case sides, apply pieces of masking tape to the rails (D), and mark on them the centered location of the mullions (E). Guided by the marks, glue and clamp the mullions between the rails. Add the stained side panels (F) and stiles (C), as shown in **6–3**.

7 With the glue dry, cut rabbets along the case sides' inside back edges, for the back (K). Rout ¹⁄₁₆" chamfers along the sides' outside edges, and along the front top and bottom corners of the front stiles (C), where shown in **6–1**, on *page 87.* Finish-sand the side assemblies.

8 Adjust your biscuit joiner to center a slot in the thickness of the ¾" plywood. Mark their centerlines, and plunge slots for #20 biscuits in the ends of the case top and bottom assemblies A/B. Aligning the back edges of the top and bottom assemblies with the edges of the rabbets in the case sides, transfer the biscuit centerlines to the case sides. Plunge the slots in the sides. Glue, biscuit, and clamp the case together, making certain it is square.

Masking Tape with Alignment Marks

Mullion

Side Panel

Rail

Stile

6–3.

With the mullion and rails assembled, slide in the panels without glue. Glue and clamp the stiles to the rails, keeping them flush at the top and bottom.

9 Plane stock to ⅝" thick for the door guides (G), and cut them to size. Cut the grooves on your tablesaw with a dado blade, where shown in **6–4**. Chuck a ½" Forstner bit in your drill press, and drill the holes. Drill the countersunk shank holes. Make certain you have mirror-image parts. Finish-sand the guides, and clamp them in place, where shown in **6–1**. The ends of the guides should be flush with the edge of the sides' back rabbets.

Using the shank holes as guides, drill pilot holes into the case sides, and drive the screws. Cut four 1½"-long oak dowels and glue two of them in the guides' front holes. Set aside the other two for the stops that will later be installed in the rear holes.

10 Plane stock for the bumper blocks (H), and cut them to size. Finish-sand the blocks. Glue and clamp them in place, where shown in **6–1**.

6–4. **DOOR GUIDE (inside face shown)**

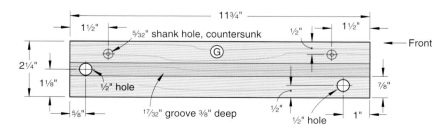

11¾"

1½"

⁵⁄₃₂" shank hole, countersunk

½"

1½"

Front

2¼"

G

1⅛"

½" hole

⅞"

⅝"

¹⁷⁄₃₂" groove ⅜" deep

½"

½" hole

1"

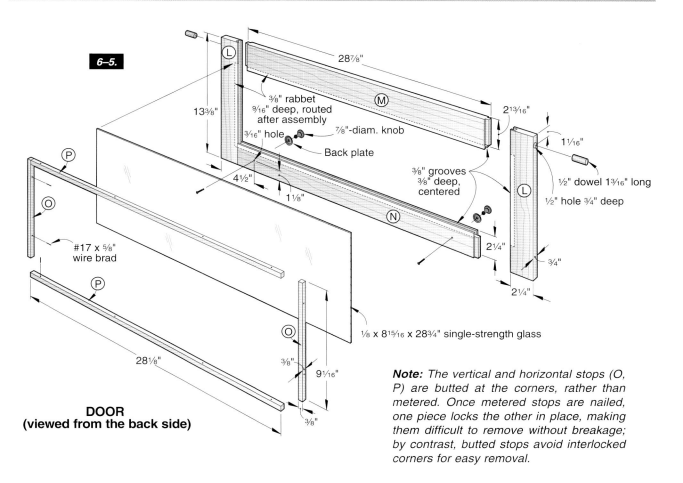

6–5.

28⅞"

13⅜"

⅜" rabbet
⁹⁄₁₆" deep, routed
after assembly

2¹³⁄₁₆"

1¹⁄₁₆"

⅜ "-diam. knob
³⁄₁₆" hole

Back plate

⅜" grooves
⅜" deep,
centered

½" dowel 1³⁄₁₆" long
½" hole ¾" deep

4½"

1⅛"

P

#17 x ⅝"
wire brad

2¼"

¾"

2¼"

O

⅛ x 8¹⁵⁄₁₆ x 28¾" single-strength glass

28⅛"

P

⅜"

9¹⁄₁₆"

O

⅜"

DOOR
(viewed from the back side)

Note: *The vertical and horizontal stops (O, P) are butted at the corners, rather than metered. Once metered stops are nailed, one piece locks the other in place, making them difficult to remove without breakage; by contrast, butted stops avoid interlocked corners for easy removal.*

11 Cut blanks for the side trim (I) and the upper trim (J) about 1" longer than the sizes in the Materials List. With a chamfer bit in your table-mounted router, rout the chamfers, where shown. Miter-cut the side trims to length. Finish-sand the trims, and glue and clamp them in place tight against the end of the door guides (G) and the front sides of the bumper blocks (H). Miter-cut the upper trim to length. Finish-sand the trim, and glue and clamp it in place, aligning it with the side trims.

12 Cut the back (K) to size, and drill countersunk shank holes, where shown in **6–1**. Finish-sand the back, and set it aside.

Build the Door

1 Cut the stiles (L), upper rail (M), and lower rail (N) to size. In the same manner as for making the case sides, cut the centered grooves, where shown in **6–5**. Drill the ½" holes in the stiles for the dowels.

2 Form the tenons on the ends of the door rails in the same manner as for making the case

sides. Glue and clamp the door frame together, making sure it is square and flat. With the glue dry, cut the ½" dowels to length, and glue them in the stiles' holes.

3 To make the rabbeted opening for the glass, chuck a ⅜" rabbeting bit in your handheld router. With the bit's pilot bearing riding on the groove's outside lip, rout away the groove's inside lip, forming a ⁹⁄₁₆"-deep rabbet. For best results, see the Shop Tip "Avoid Tear-Out with Climb-Cutting" on *page 91*. Square the corners with a chisel.

4 Mark the knob locations, where shown in **6–5**. Drill the screw holes, and finish-sand the door.

5 Resaw and plane stock for the vertical stops (O) and horizontal stops (P). Cut them to size. Clip the head off a #17 wire brad, and use it to drill pilot holes in the stops where shown. Sand the stops to 220 grit.

Make the Base and Top

1 Plane down thicker stock or laminate thinner stock for the feet (Q), and cut them to size. Rout ⅛" chamfers on their bottom edges.

2 Cut the front and back rails (R) and the side rails (S) to size. Mark the ends and centers of the arches, where shown in **6–6**. Bend a fairing stick to these points, and draw the arches. Bandsaw and sand them to shape.

3 Adjust your biscuit joiner to center a slot in the thickness of the feet. Mark the slot centerlines on the outside faces of the feet, where shown in **6–6**. Plunge the slots. Align the rails with the feet, keeping their top edges flush, and transfer the slot centerlines to the outside faces of the rails. Readjust your biscuit joiner to center a slot in the thickness of the rails, and plunge the slots. Finish-sand the feet and rails.

4 Glue, biscuit, and clamp a pair of legs to the front and back rails. With the glue dry, form a frame by gluing, biscuiting, and clamping the side rails in place. Make certain the feet/rails assembly (Q/R/S) is square and flat.

5 Cut the base panel (T) to the size in the Materials List. Rip the front banding (U) and side bandings (V) to width, but about 1" longer than listed. Miter one end of each band. Fit and mark the front band, as shown in **6–7** and **6–8**, and miter-cut it to length. With all three bands clamped in place, mark the side bands flush with the back edge of the base panel (T), and trim them to length. Glue and clamp the bands to the base panel.

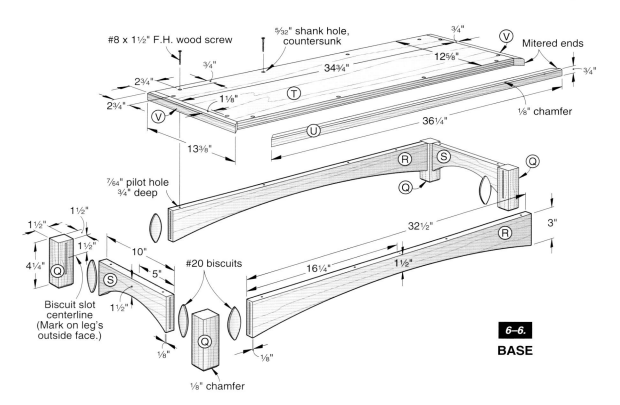

6–6.
BASE

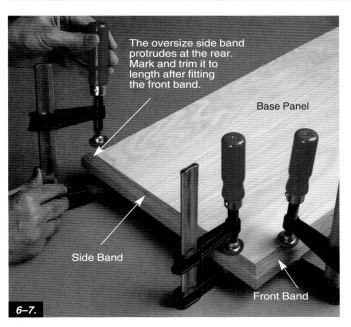

The oversize side band protrudes at the rear. Mark and trim it to length after fitting the front band.

Base Panel

Side Band

Front Band

6–7.

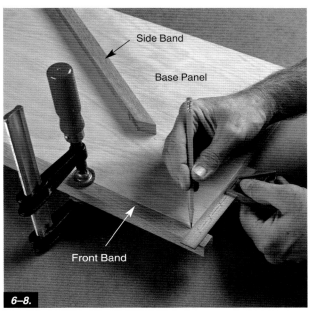

Side Band

Base Panel

Front Band

6–8.

Fit the metered ends of the side and front bands around the panel's first corner, temporarily clamping them in place.

Next, using a sharp pencil and ruler, mark the miter's heel on the front band at the panel's second corner.

SHOP TIP

Avoid Tear-Out with Climb-Cutting

When creating a rabbet for the glass by removing the door frame groove's ³⁄₁₆"-thick inside lip with a rabbeting bit, it is all too easy to tear out long splinters, ruining your frame. To avoid this, employ a routing method called "climb-cutting."

First, to provide clearance for the router bit's pilot bearing, insert scrap spacers between the frame and the workbench, as shown in 6–9. Then clamp the door frame securely to your workbench. You'll have to stop routing several times, shifting the position of your clamps as you work your way around the frame.

Holding the router firmly, ease the bit into the frame until the pilot bearing contacts the outside lip. Slowly move the router in a counterclockwise direction around the inside of the frame. You'll have to resist the bit's tendency to grab the wood and pull the router along. Because the bit's clockwise rotation pushes the wood fibers toward the frame members as it cuts rather than trying to pull them away, as in normal routing, tear-out is eliminated.

Once you've worked your way around the frame, make a second counterclockwise pass to clean up the edge.

"Climb-cutting" with a router to avoid tear-out. Although it may appear otherwise, this photo shows climb-cutting only a ³⁄₁₆"-thick by ³⁄₈"-wide lip from the door frame. Most of the material was removed earlier when a centered groove was cut in the parts.

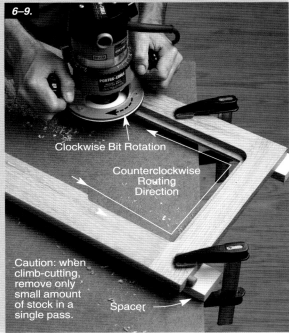

6–9.

Clockwise Bit Rotation

Counterclockwise Routing Direction

Caution: when climb-cutting, remove only small amount of stock in a single pass.

Spacer

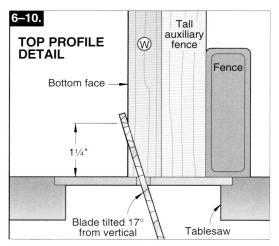

6–10.

TOP PROFILE DETAIL

Bottom face →

1¼"

Blade tilted 17° from vertical

Tall auxiliary fence

W

Fence

Tablesaw

With the glue dry, sand the bands flush with the panel, and rout chamfers, where shown. Finish-sand the base panel assembly.

6 To complete the base assembly, mark the centerpoints of the countersunk shank holes in the base panel, where shown in **6–6** (*page 90*), and drill them. Clamp the base panel assembly (T/U/V) to the feet and rails assembly (Q/R/S), flush at the back, and centered side to side. Using the shank holes in the base panel as guides, drill pilot holes into the rails, and drive the screws.

7 Edge-join an oversize blank for the top (W). Once the glue is dry, cut it to finished size. With your tablesaw set up as shown in **6–10**, cut bevels along the bottom of the top's ends, then along the front edge, where shown in **6–11**. Sand away the saw-blade marks, backing your sandpaper with a firm block to keep the bevels' edges crisp. Rout chamfers along the upper front edge and ends, where shown. Finish-sand the top.

8 Cut the crest (X) to the size listed. Make marks at the center of the top edge and 1¾" up from the bottom at the ends, where shown in **6–11**. Connect the marks with a straightedge, and draw the top profile. Draw the radii at the ends. Bandsaw and sand the crest to shape. Rout the chamfer. Then finish-sand the crest.

9 Glue and clamp the crest (X) to the top (W), centered, where shown in **6–11**. Drill pilot and countersunk shank holes through the top into the crest, and drive the screws.

Apply the Finish and Assemble the Bookcase

1 Examine all the parts and assemblies, and resand any areas that need it. If you wish, apply a stain and let it dry.

2 Apply a clear finish. To add an amber tone to the stain's color, we brushed on oil-based satin polyurethane.

3 Lay the bookshelf case on its back on your workbench. Clamp the base to it, flush at the back and centered side to side. Drill pilot and countersunk shank holes through the base panel (T) into the case's lower panel (A), where shown in **6–11**, and drive in the screws. Clamp the top assembly to the case, flush at the back and

centered side to side. Drill pilot and countersunk shank holes through the case's upper panel (A) into the top (W), where shown, and drive the screws. Stand the assembly upright.

4 Have single-strength glass cut ⅛" smaller in width and length than the door's rabbeted opening. Lay the door face down, and install the glass. Position the stops (O, P), and drive brads through the previously drilled pilot holes. Set the brads, and fill the holes with a matching color putty stick.

5 Apply wax to the grooves in the door guides (G) and their dowels. Install the door from the rear, sliding it over the door guide dowels at the front, and engaging the door's dowels in the guides' grooves. Retrieve the two door-stop dowels, and tap them into the guides' rear holes. Do not glue them in.

6 Clamp the back (K) in place. Using the previously drilled shank holes as guides, drill pilot holes into the case. Drive the screws.

7 Install the knobs. Drill pilot holes for the tack bumpers, positioning them to leave ¾" between the bumpers and the bumper blocks' front edges. Tap in the tack bumpers.

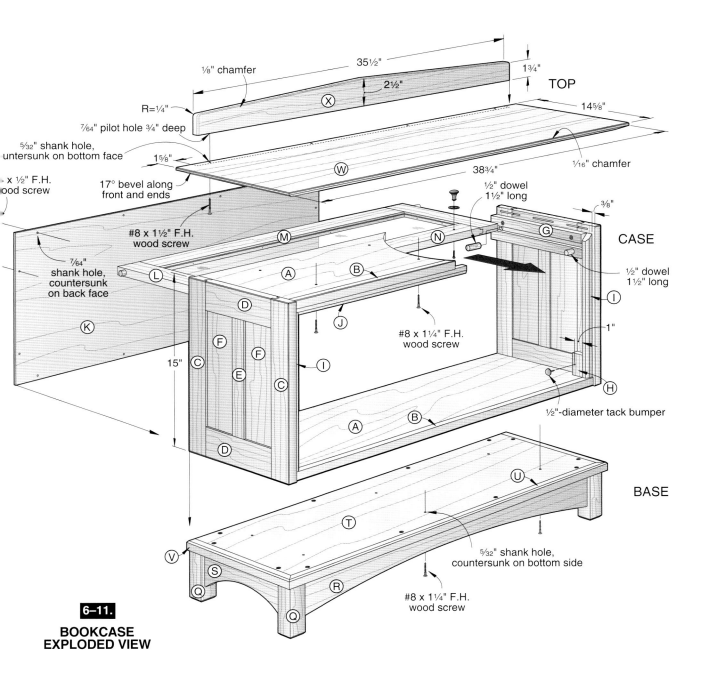

1/8" chamfer

35 1/2"

2 1/2"

1 3/4"

TOP

R=1/4"

7/64" pilot hole 3/4" deep

14 5/8"

5/32" shank hole, countersunk on bottom face

1 5/8"

1/16" chamfer

x 1/2" F.H. wood screw

17° bevel along front and ends

38 3/4"

1/2" dowel 1 1/2" long

3/8"

CASE

#8 x 1 1/2" F.H. wood screw

1/2" dowel 1 1/2" long

7/64" shank hole, countersunk on back face

1"

#8 x 1 1/4" F.H. wood screw

15"

1/2"-diameter tack bumper

BASE

5/32" shank hole, countersunk on bottom side

#8 x 1 1/4" F.H. wood screw

6–11.

BOOKCASE EXPLODED VIEW

SHELVING SHOWCASE

Fluted face-frame stiles and a richly molded top all set the style for this full-length bookcase. Featuring six shelves, five of which adjust on standards and brackets, it's the perfect accent for a home study, family room, or any other reading haunt.

Make the Basic Cabinet

1 From ¾" plywood (we used walnut), cut the sides (A) and top and bottom (B) to the sizes in the Materials List. (To support the thin veneer fibers and minimize splintering when cross-cutting the plywood, we lightly marked the cutlines with a pencil. Next, we placed masking tape next to the cutlines, made the cuts, and then removed the remaining tape.)

2 Referring to the Basic Cabinet drawing in **6–12** (*page 96*), mark the rabbet and dado locations across the top inside edge and 5¼" from the bottom edge of the sides (A). Cut or rout the rabbets and dadoes. (You can use a router fitted with a straight bit and an edge guide.)

3 Cut a ¼" rabbet ½" deep along the back inside edge of each side piece (A). (See the Back Panel Detail drawing in **6–12** for reference.) Now, cut a pair of ⅝" grooves ³⁄₁₆" deep

This full-length bookcase features six shelves, a molded top, and fluted face-frame stiles.

CUTTING DIAGRAM FOR SHELVING SHOWCASE

*Plane or resaw to the thicknesses listed in the Materials List.

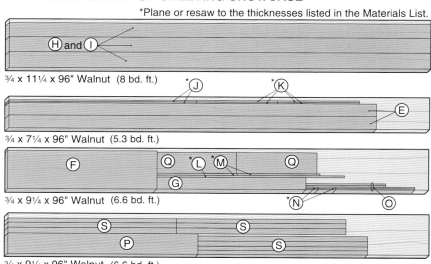

¾ x 11¼ x 96" Walnut (8 bd. ft.)

¾ x 7¼ x 96" Walnut (5.3 bd. ft.)

¾ x 9¼ x 96" Walnut (6.6 bd. ft.)

¾ x 9¼ x 96" Walnut (6.6 bd. ft.)

Cutting Diagram continues on page 95

CUTTING DIAGRAM FOR SHELVING SHOWCASE (continued)

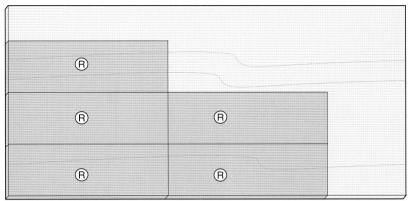

¾ x 48 x 96" Walnut plywood

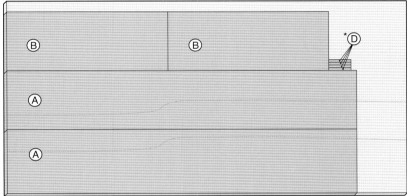

¾ x 48 x 96" Walnut plywood

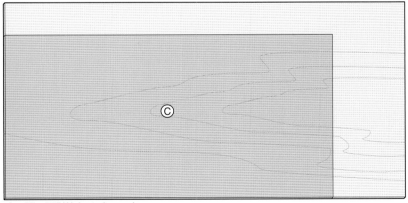

¼ x 48 x 96" Walnut plywood

MATERIALS LIST FOR SHELVING SHOWCASE

PART	FINISHED SIZE			MTL.	QTY.
	T	**W**	**L**		
BASIC CABINET					
A sides	¾"	15¼"	84"	WP	2
B top and bottom	¾"	14⅝"	39"	WP	2
C back panel	¼"	39½"	78¾"	WP	1
D filler blocks	³⁄₁₆"	⅝"	5⅛"	WP	4
E* stiles	¾"	3¹⁄₁₆"	84"	W	2
F top rail	¾"	9"	34"	W	1
G bottom rail	¾"	3"	34"	W	1
MOLDING					
H* front cove	1¹³⁄₁₆"	3"	44¼"	LW	1
I* sides	1¹³⁄₁₆"	3"	17¾"	LW	2
J* front trim	¼"	½"	41"	W	2
K* side trim	¼"	½"	16⅛"	W	4
L* front trim	¾"	⅜"	40¾"	W	1
M* side trim	¾"	⅜"	16"	W	2
N* bull-nosed trim	⅜"	¼"	3¼"	W	4
O* bull-nosed trim	⅜"	¼"	15⅞"	W	4
P* base	¾"	5"	41½"	W	1
Q* base	¾"	5"	16⅜"	W	2
SHELVES					
R* shelves	¾"	13"	38⅜"	WP	5
S* shelf edging	¾"	1¼"	38⅜"	W	10

on the inside face of each side piece for the shelf standards. (First test-cut the groove in a piece of scrap stock to verify that the standard will fit snugly into it and remain flush with the surface of the wood.)

4 Cut a ⅜" rabbet ⅜" deep along the front outside edge of each side piece to form a tongue.

5 Dry-clamp the pieces, and check for square. Measure

*Initially cut these parts oversized. Trim to finished size according to the instructions.
Materials Key: WP = Walnut plywood; W = Walnut; LW = Laminated walnut.
Supplies: ⅜" dowel pins 1½" long; #8 x 1¼" flathead wood screws; #8 x 1½" flathead wood screws; #4 finish nails; ¾ x 17 brads; ⅝ x 72" flush-mounted shelf standards (walnut finish) with mounting brads and supports; finish.

the width of the rabbeted opening in the cabinet back, and cut the back panel (C) to size from ¼" walnut plywood. The plywood back is flush with the top face of the top (B) and with the bottom face of the bottom (B).

6 Glue and clamp together the basic cabinet; check for square. Glue and nail the back panel in place. Installing the back panel now helps square up the assembly.

7 Temporarily position the shelf standards in the grooves. Measure the grooved opening above each. Then, to match the veneered cabinet interior, cut and resaw four filler blocks (D) from ¾" walnut plywood to fit. Glue the filler blocks in place; remove the standards.

Make the Walnut Face Frame

1 Cut the stiles (E), top rail (F), and bottom rail (G) to the sizes in the Material's List.

2 Cut or rout a ⅜" groove ⅜" deep along the back outside edge of both stiles (E), where shown on the Back Panel Detail drawing in **6–12**. Note that the stiles (E) extend 1⁄16" past the outside face of the sides (A). This protrusion will be routed flush later.

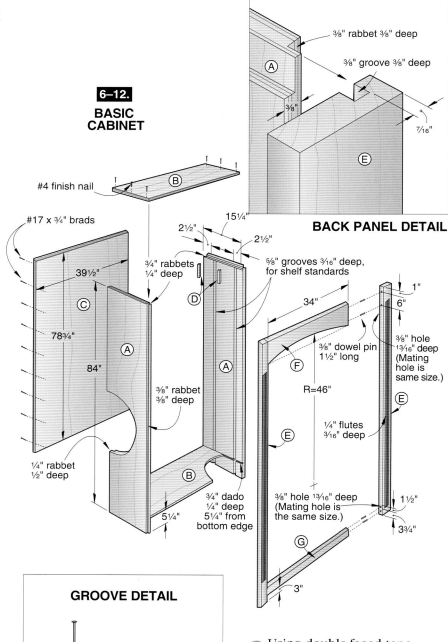

6–12.
BASIC CABINET

BACK PANEL DETAIL

GROOVE DETAIL

3 Using double-faced tape, adhere the top rail (F) so that it is flush with one end of a sheet of plywood. Using trammel points, swing a 46" arc intersecting the lower corners of the top rail along the bottom edge of the top rail. (See the Basic

6–13.

Left: *Rout ¼" flutes ³⁄₁₆" deep using a router fitted with an edge guide and stops clamped to the ends of the stile.*

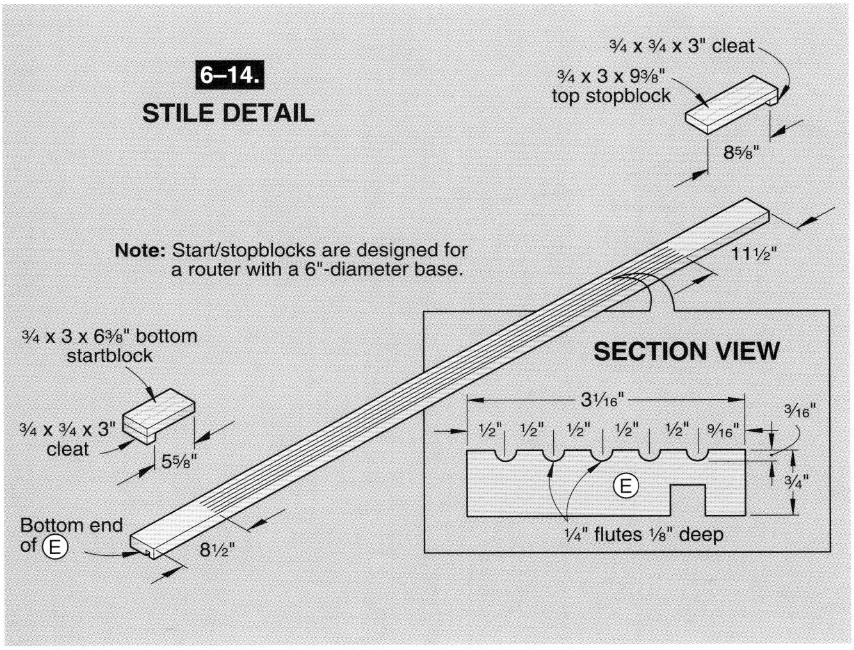
6–14.
STILE DETAIL
¾ x ¾ x 3" cleat
¾ x 3 x 9⅜" top stopblock
8⅝"
Note: Start/stopblocks are designed for a router with a 6"-diameter base.
11½"
¾ x 3 x 6⅜" bottom startblock
¾ x ¾ x 3" cleat
5⅝"
Bottom end of (E)
8½"
SECTION VIEW
3¹⁄₁₆"
½" ½" ½" ½" ½" ⁹⁄₁₆"
³⁄₁₆"
¾"
(E)
¼" flutes ⅛" deep

Cabinet drawing in **6–12** for reference.) Bandsaw the arc to shape. Sand the arc to remove the saw marks.

4 Construct a startblock and stopblock to the sizes shown in the Stile Detail drawing in **6–14**. Clamp the longer block to the top front face of the stile and the shorter block to the bottom end, where shown in the Stile Detail drawing in **6–14**.

5 Fit your router with an edge guide and a ¼" core-box bit.

6 Now, before routing the flutes, position the router against the blocks to check that the flutes will start 8½" from the bottom end of the stile and stop 11½" from the top; adjust the length of the stops if necessary. (The location of the stops will depend on the size of your router base.)

7 Set the bit to cut ³⁄₁₆" deep, and rout five flutes in the front face of both stiles, as dimensioned in the Section View drawing in **6–14**. To minimize sanding later, make a second pass on each flute (**6–13**).

8 Dry-clamp the face-frame pieces (E, F, G) to the frame, and mark dowel-hole reference lines across the front face of each, where dimensioned on the Basic Cabinet drawing in **6–12**. Remove the clamps, and drill ⅜" mating holes 1³⁄₁₆" deep where marked on the drawing.

9 Glue and clamp the face frame, checking for square. Later, remove the clamps, and sand the back surface flush for a tight fit against the front.

Attach the Face Frame and Rout the Molding Groove

1 Glue and clamp the face frame to the cabinet. (Before clamping the face frame to the cabinet, place masking tape on the walnut plywood next to the joints being glued so that any glue squeeze-out will dry on the tape. After the glue has dried, peel off the tape and excess glue. This is easier than removing the squeeze-out with a damp cloth or scraping it off after it dries.)

2 Mount a flush-trimming laminate bit into your router. Rout the ¹⁄₁₆" protruding outside edge of the stiles flush with the outside face of the cabinet sides (A). (This is more effective than trying to plane the edges flush.)

3 Mount a ¼" straight bit in your router. Clamp a straightedge (you can use a piece of plywood) to the cabinet side. Rout

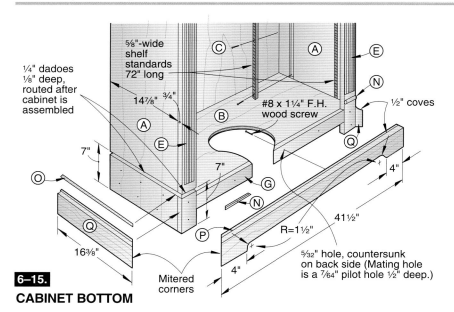

6–15.
CABINET BOTTOM

Labels on the figure: ¼" dadoes ⅛" deep, routed after cabinet is assembled; ⅝"-wide shelf standards 72" long; 14⅞"; ¾"; #8 x 1¼" F.H. wood screw; ½" coves; 7"; 7"; 4"; 41½"; R=1½"; 4"; 16⅜"; Mitered corners; 5/32" hole, countersunk on back side (Mating hole is a 7/64" pilot hole ½" deep.)

a ¼" dado ⅛" deep and 10" from the top edge of the cabinet top, where shown on the Cabinet Top drawing in **6–16**. Move the straightedge and rout the other side. Now, rout the front face. Using **6–15** for reference, rout the dado across the bottom of the cabinet.

Shape the Cove Molding for the Top

1 To form the thick top cove molding, cut three pieces of ¾"-thick stock to 3½" wide by 8' long. (This will give you enough stock for parts H and I.)

2 Glue and clamp the three pieces of stock face to face with the edges and ends flush.

3 Scrape excess glue from one edge, and then joint it flat. Rip the opposite edge on your tablesaw for a 3" finished width.

4 Resaw or plane the lamination to 1 13/16" thick. (See **6–17**.)

5 Clamp a piece of straight stock to the top of your 10" tablesaw, where shown in **6–19**. Raise the blade ⅛" above the saw table surface, and pass the workpiece over the blade. Continue to raise the blade and take light cuts (no more than ⅛" per pass) until you achieve the full ½" depth of the cove. (An 80-tooth, carbide-tipped blade produces the smoothest cuts.)

6 Next, follow the four-cut sequence in **6–18** to trim the edges of the molding to shape.

7 Now, miter-cut the front cove molding piece (H) and the two side pieces (I) to fit the front and sides of the cabinet.

BULLNOSE

⅜"; ¼"; ⅛" round-overs (¼" bullnose)

6–16. **CABINET TOP**

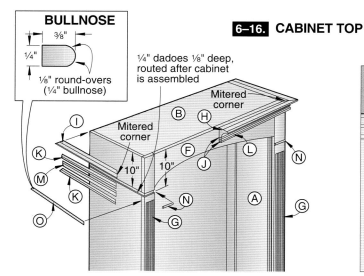

Labels: ¼" dadoes ⅛" deep, routed after cabinet is assembled; Mitered corner; Mitered corner; 10"; 10"

COVE MOLDING DETAIL

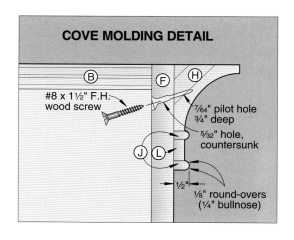

Labels: #8 x 1½" F.H. wood screw; 7/64" pilot hole ¾" deep; 5/32" hole, countersunk; ½"; ⅛" round-overs (¼" bullnose)

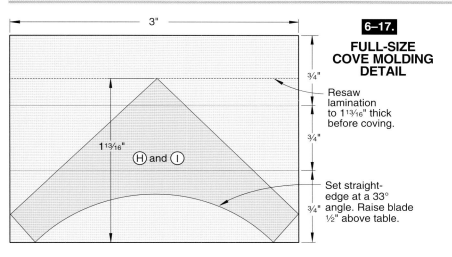

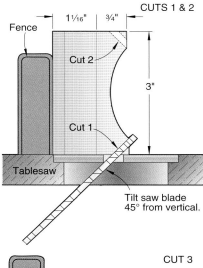

6–17.
FULL-SIZE COVE MOLDING DETAIL

3"

¾"

Resaw lamination to 1¹³⁄₁₆" thick before coving.

¾"

1¹³⁄₁₆"

H and I

¾"

Set straight-edge at a 33° angle. Raise blade ½" above table.

6–18.
BEVEL-RIPPING COVE MOLDING DETAIL

CUTS 1 & 2

Fence

1¹⁄₁₆" ¾"

Cut 2

Cut 1

3"

Tablesaw

Tilt saw blade 45° from vertical.

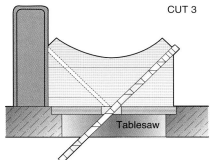

CUT 3

Tablesaw

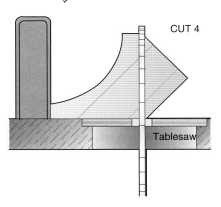

CUT 4

Tablesaw

8 Drill mounting holes through the cabinet for attaching the cove molding pieces (H, I). Glue and screw the pieces in place, flush with the top of the cabinet. (See the Cove Molding Detail drawing in **6–16**.)

Make the Rest of the Moldings

1 Cut the remaining molding pieces (J, K, L, M, N, O) to size plus 2" in length. To form the bullnose on the front edge of J and K, rout a pair of ⅛" round-overs along the front edge. (See the Bullnose drawing in **6–16**.)

2 With the back edges flush, glue part L between parts J. Repeat with the side pieces K and M. Miter-cut the ends, and then glue and clamp the trim strips J/L and K/M to the cabinet.

3 Miter-cut the bullnosed strips N and O to length for both the cabinet top and bottom. Glue them into the previously cut dadoes in the cabinet.

4 Cut the base molding pieces (P, Q) to size plus 2" in length. Rout a ½" cove along the top outside edge of each.

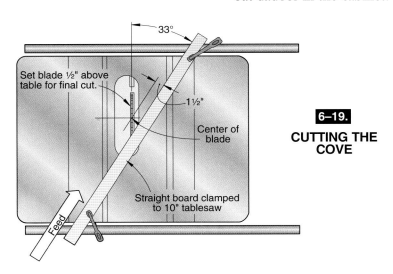

33°

Set blade ½" above table for final cut.

1½"

Center of blade

Straight board clamped to 10" tablesaw

Feed

6–19.
CUTTING THE COVE

6–20.

SHELF

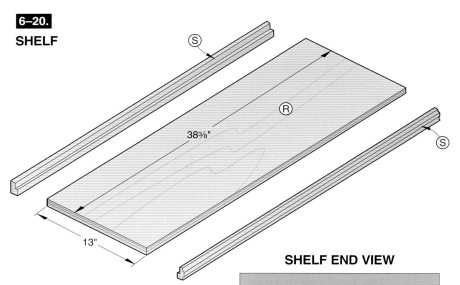

38⅜"

13"

SHELF END VIEW

1¼"

Ⓡ

Ⓢ

Front edge of shelf

¾" rabbets ¼" deep   ¼" coves

Ⓡ

Ⓢ

Front edge of shelf

Using **6–15** for reference, miter-cut the pieces to length, mark the radii on the front piece, and cut it to shape. Drill mounting holes through the cabinet and into the back side of the base molding pieces. Glue and screw the pieces to the cabinet bottom.

Cut and Edge the Shelves, Then Finish the Cabinet

1 Cut the walnut plywood shelves (R) and front and back strips (S) to size plus 1" in length.

2 Cut or rout ¾" rabbets ¼" deep in each strip, where shown in the Shelf drawing in **6–20**. Next, rout ¼" coves along the front edge, where shown in the Shelf End View drawings in **6–20**.

3 Glue the strips to the front and back of the shelf. Later,

crosscut both ends to trim the shelves to finished length. Sand smooth. (Wrap sandpaper around a ½" piece of dowel to sand the coves.)

4 Finish the cabinet. (A good suggestion is to apply one coat of dark walnut oil finish, followed by five coats of natural oil finish.)

Nail the shelf standards in the grooves, checking that the numbers on the standards are right-side up. Add brackets to support the shelves.

ONE BOOKCASE, THREE WAYS

Here's a masterpiece you can build that will showcase your treasured tomes for years to come. Simply build the basic case in the wood of your choice, and then add the traditional, country, or Shaker top and bottom trim. The bookcase, which measures 33¾" wide by 13" deep by approximately 6½' high, has one fixed shelf and three adjustable shelves to hold loads of books or display items. Oak and oak plywood were the primary materials used for the traditional bookcase shown on the *facing page*, cherry and cherry plywood were used for the Shaker unit, and knotty pine and knotty-pine plywood were used for the country look. But you can use less-expensive materials, such as solid poplar with birch plywood—particularly if you plan to paint the unit.

Build the Case

1 Cut the sides (A) to the size in the Materials List. As explained in the Materials Key, choose the plywood species that suits your bookcase style.

2 Using a dado-blade set adjusted to the thickness of your ¾" plywood, cut ¼"-deep rabbets on the inside face of the sides (A) at their ends, where shown on the Side drawing in **6–21,** on *page 103*. Then, cut a ¼"-deep dado near the center, where

Traditional

Country

Shaker

This bookcase can be built in three styles: traditional, country, or Shaker.

CUTTING DIAGRAM FOR ONE BOOKCASE, THREE WAYS

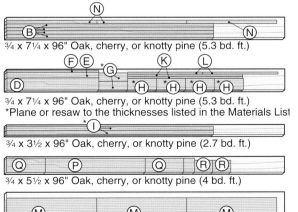

N

B   N

¾ x 7¼ x 96" Oak, cherry, or knotty pine (5.3 bd. ft.)

F E *G   K   L

D   *H *H *H *H

¾ x 7¼ x 96" Oak, cherry, or knotty pine (5.3 bd. ft.)
*Plane or resaw to the thicknesses listed in the Materials List

*I

¾ x 3½ x 96" Oak, cherry, or knotty pine (2.7 bd. ft.)

Q   P   Q   R R

¾ x 5½ x 96" Oak, cherry, or knotty pine (4 bd. ft.)

M   M   M

C   C   C

A

A

¾ x 48 x 96" Oak, cherry, or knotty-pine plywood

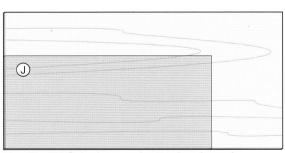

J

¼ x 48 x 96" Oak, cherry, or knotty-pine plywood

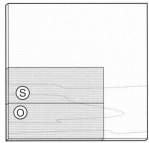

S

O

¾ x 48 x 48" Birch plywood

The Cutting Diagram continues on page 102 with diagrams for the traditional top, country top, and Shaker top.

CUTTING DIAGRAM (continued)

Traditional Top Cutting Diagram

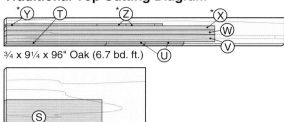

¾ x 9¼ x 96" Oak (6.7 bd. ft.)

¾ x 24 x 48" Birch plywood

Country Top Cutting Diagram

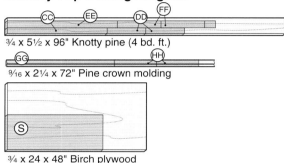

¾ x 5½ x 96" Knotty pine (4 bd. ft.)

⁹⁄₁₆ x 2¼ x 72" Pine crown molding

¾ x 24 x 48" Birch plywood

Shaker Top Cutting Diagram

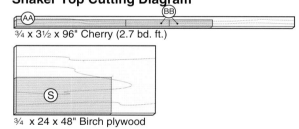

¾ x 3½ x 96" Cherry (2.7 bd. ft.)

¾ x 24 x 48" Birch plywood

dimensioned. Now, on the outside face of the sides, drill countersunk shank holes centered on the width of the rabbets and dadoes.

3 To drill the ¹⁹⁄₆₄" holes on the inside face of the sides (A) for the shelf paddle-support sleeves, where dimensioned on the Side and Shelf Support Detail drawings in **6–21** and **6–22**, first mark centerlines for the holes on masking tape along the sides' inside faces. Mark near one edge first, and then transfer the marks to the opposite edge using a framing square. (See the Shop Tip "Using Shelf Supports with Metal Sleeves," *page 104,*

MATERIALS LIST FOR ONE BOOKSHELF, THREE WAYS

PART	FINISHED SIZE			MTL.	QTY.
	T	W	L		
CASE					
A sides	¾"	11¾"	71½"	CP	2
B front stiles	1½"	1¼"	71½"	CL	2
C top, fixed shelf, and bottom	¾"	11¾"	31¾"	CP	3
D top front rail	¾"	†	31¾"	CS	1
E fixed-shelf front rail	¾"	2"	31¾"	CS	1
F bottom front rail	¾"	¾"	31¾"	CS	1
G top side rails	¼"	3"	10"	CS	2
H middle and bottom side rails	¼"	4"	10"	CS	4
I back stiles	½"	1½"	71½"	CS	2
J back	¼"	32¾"	71½"	CP	1
K upper fillers	¾"	¾"	††	CS	2
L lower fillers	¾"	¾"	26"	CS	2
M adjustable shelves	¾"	10¾"	31⅛"	CP	3
N shelf trim	¾"	1¼"	31⅛"	CS	3
BASE					
O bottom panel	¾"	12⅝"	33"	BP	1
P* front trim	¾"	5"	34½"	CS	1
Q* side trim	¾"	5"	13⅜"	CS	2
R corner blocks	¾"	4¼"	6¼"	CS	2
TRADITIONAL TOP					
S top panel	¾"	12⅝"	33"	BP	1
T front banding	¾"	¾"	34½"	O	1
U side banding	¾"	¾"	13⅜"	O	2
V band blank	¾"	2½"	72"	O	1
W cap blank	¾"	1¾"	72"	O	1
X* cove blank	⅝"	⅝"	72"	O	1
Y* front dentil molding	¼"	¾"	31¼"	O	1
Z* side dentil molding	¼"	¾"	10"	O	2
SHAKER TOP					
S top panel	¾"	12⅝"	33"	BP	1
AA front edging	¾"	2⅜"	37¾"	C	1
BB side edging	¾"	2⅜"	15"	C	2
COUNTRY TOP					
S top panel	¾"	12⅝"	33"	BP	1
CC front banding	¾"	2"	34½"	KP	1
DD side banding	¾"	2"	13⅜"	KP	2
EE* front cap	¾"	2½"	38"	KP	1
FF* side caps	¾"	2½"	15⅛"	KP	2
GG front crown molding	⁹⁄₁₆"	2¼"	37"	P	1
HH side crown molding	⁹⁄₁₆"	2¼"	14⅝"	P	2

*Parts initially cut oversize. See the instructions.
†**For traditional and Shaker bookcases**, width of part D is 3".
For country bookcase, width of part D is 4¼".
††**For traditional and Shaker bookcases**, length of part K is 39¾".
For country bookcase, length of part K is 38½".
Materials Key: CP = Choose plywood species; CL = Choose laminated solid stock species; CS = Choose solid stock species; BP = Birch plywood; O = Oak; C = Cherry; KP = Knotty pine; P = Pine. For items CP, CL, and CS, use oak for the traditional bookcase, cherry for the Shaker bookcase, and knotty pine for the country bookcase.
Supplies: Spray adhesive; #6 x ¾", #8 x 1¼", and #8 x 1½" flathead wood screws; #20 biscuits.
Blades and Bits: Dado-blade set; ¹⁹⁄₆₄" brad-point drill bit. **For the country bookcase**, chamfer router bit. **For the Shaker bookcase**, ¼" round-over router bit. **For the traditional bookcase**, chamfer, ¼" and ½" cove router bits.
Hardware: Brass paddle supports (package of 20); brass sleeves, five packages of 20 each.

6–21.

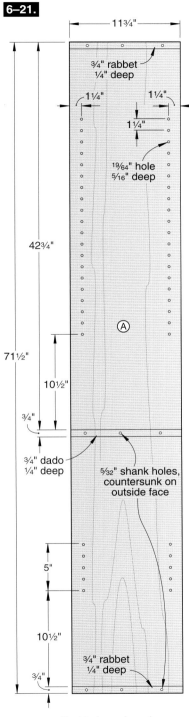

11¾"

¾" rabbet
¼" deep

1¼" 1¼"

1¼"

19⁄64" hole
5⁄16" deep

42¾"

Ⓐ

71½"

10½"

¾"

¾" dado
¼" deep

5⁄32" shank holes,
countersunk on
outside face

5"

10½"

¾" rabbet
¼" deep

¾"

(Inside face shown)

SIDE

6–22.

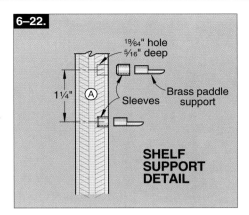

19⁄64" hole
5⁄16" deep

1¼" Ⓐ

Sleeves

Brass paddle
support

**SHELF
SUPPORT
DETAIL**

6–23.

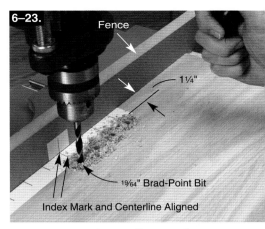

Fence

1¼"

19⁄64" Brad-Point Bit

Index Mark and Centerline Aligned

*With the marked centerlines on the
tape aligned with the drill-press fence's
index mark, drill 19⁄64" holes 5⁄16" deep
in the sides (A).*

for more information on the shelf
support and sleeve hardware.)

4 Next, chuck a 19⁄64" brad-point
bit in your drill press, and
position the fence 1¼" back
from the bit's center. Make an
index mark on the fence centered with the bit. Then, aligning the marked centerlines with
the index mark, drill 5⁄16"-deep
holes in the sides, as shown in
6–23. Now, sand the sides with
220-grit sandpaper.

5 From ¾"-thick stock, cut four
1¼ x 71½" pieces to form
the front stiles (B). Laminate the
pieces to make a pair of 1½"-
thick stiles.

6 Using the same dado-blade
stack as before, cut a ¾" rabbet ½" deep along the back face
of the stiles, where shown in
Step 1 in **6–24**, to receive the
sides (A). Then, glue and clamp
the stiles to the front edge of the
sides, where shown in the
Exploded View drawing in
6–26. When the glue dries,
adjust the dado set to match
your ¾"-thick stock, and cut a
¼"-deep groove along the inside

face of the stiles, where shown
in *Step 2* in **6–24**.

7 Cut the top, fixed shelf, and
bottom (C) and their accompanying rails (D, E, F) to size.

8 For a Shaker bookcase, lay
out the curve on the top
front rail (D), where dimensioned
in **6–29** (*page 106*). Then,
band-saw and sand the rail to
shape.

9 For a country bookcase, make
four copies of **6–34** (*page
110*) at 200%. Next, draw a centerline across the width of the
top front rail (D). Spray-adhere
two copies to the rail, aligning
them with the marked centerline,
where shown on the Country
Top Front Rail and Base Trim
drawing in **6–29**. (You'll need to
trim one copy and flip it over to
complete the contour.) Set aside
the remaining copies. Now, bandsaw and sand the rail to shape,
and remove the patterns.

6–24.

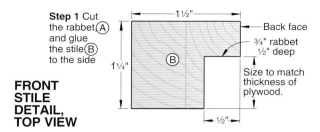

Step 1 Cut the rabbet Ⓐ and glue the stile Ⓑ to the side

FRONT STILE DETAIL, TOP VIEW

1½"
1¼"
½"
Back face
¾" rabbet ½" deep
Size to match thickness of plywood.
Ⓑ

Step 2 Cut a groove in the stile/side assembly.

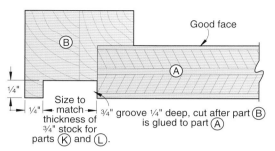

Good face
Ⓑ
Ⓐ
¼"
¼"
Size to match thickness of ¾" stock for parts Ⓚ and Ⓛ.
¾" groove ¼" deep, cut after part Ⓑ is glued to part Ⓐ

10 Glue and clamp the top, fixed-shelf, and bottom front rails (D, E, F) to the top, fixed shelf, and bottom (C), where shown on the Exploded View drawing in **6–26**, keeping the rails' and panels' ends flush and the rails' top edge even with the panels' top face. Position the top panel's best face down and the fixed shelf and bottom panels' best face up. When the glue dries, sand the assemblies smooth.

11 Assemble the case by gluing, screwing, and clamping the side assemblies (A/B) to the top, fixed-shelf, and bottom assemblies (C/D, C/E, C/F). Check the case for square.

Complete the Case

1 Cut the top side rails (G), middle and bottom side rails (H), and back stiles (I) to size. Sand the parts smooth. To avoid glue squeeze-out when mounting these parts, see the Shop Tip "Dealing with Glue Squeeze-Out" on *page 105*.

2 Glue and clamp the top side rails (G) and bottom side rails (H) to the sides (A), flush with their top and bottom edges,

where shown in the Exploded View drawing in **6–26**. Then, when the glue dries, glue and clamp the middle side rails (H) to the sides, as shown in **6–28**.

3 Glue and clamp the back stiles (I) to the sides (A), flush with their ends and tight against the side rails (G, H). The stiles overhang the sides' back edges by ¼".

4 Cut to size the ¼" plywood back (J). Then, on the rear of the back, drill countersunk shank holes, where shown on

the Exploded View drawing in **6–26**. Now, position the back on the case, drill pilot holes using the shank holes as guides, and drive the screws.

5 Cut the upper and lower fillers (K, L) to size to fit the ¾"-wide grooves in the front stiles (B). For traditional and Shaker bookcases, cut the upper filler (K) 39¾" long. For a country bookcase, cut the upper filler (K) 38½" long. Glue and clamp the fillers in place.

SHOP TIP

Using Shelf Supports with Metal Sleeves

Have you ever been frustrated by shelf supports that won't stay in their holes, sag over time, or require pliers to remove? Holes that are worn or were drilled slightly oversize to prevent binding cause the first two problems, and holes that are swollen by moisture or were drilled slightly undersize to resist loosening cause the third problem. Here's a simple way to prevent these irritations. Use brass paddle supports with mating sleeves, shown in **6–25**. The sleeves protect the holes from wear, and they provide a consistent fit with the supports so they're always easy to insert and remove. There is another plus: The sleeves hide the hole walls, which can be unsightly, particularly in plywood.

To ensure that the ⁵⁄₁₆"-diameter sleeves stay snug in their holes, drill the holes using a ¹⁹⁄₆₄" brad-point bit. To install the sleeves, insert their beveled ends in the holes, and tap them in with a hammer.

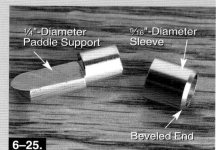

¼"-Diameter Paddle Support
⁵⁄₁₆"-Diameter Sleeve
Beveled End

6–25.

6 Cut the adjustable shelves (M) and shelf trim (N) to size. Then, glue and clamp the trim to the shelves, flush with their ends and top faces. Sand the shelves smooth.

SHOP TIP

6–27.

Dealing with Glue Squeeze-Out

Removing excess glue when assembling parts is messy and risky. If you leave the slightest residue, it can seal the wood and block stain penetration, resulting in a blotchy finish. Here's a simple way to avoid the problem. Cut ⅛" grooves ⅛" deep and ⅛" from a part's edges on its glue surface, where shown in 6–27. Then, apply glue to the area between the grooves, and clamp the part in place. The grooves will capture the excess glue, preventing it from oozing beyond the part's edges.

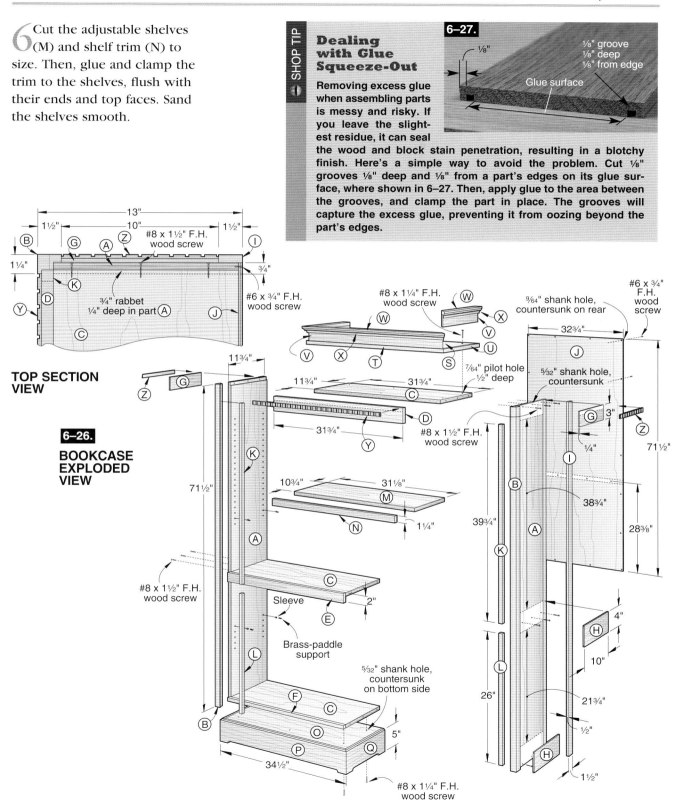

TOP SECTION VIEW

6–26.

BOOKCASE EXPLODED VIEW

6–28.

Using 21¾"-long spacers to position the middle side rail (H) above the bottom side rail, glue and clamp the rail to the side (A).

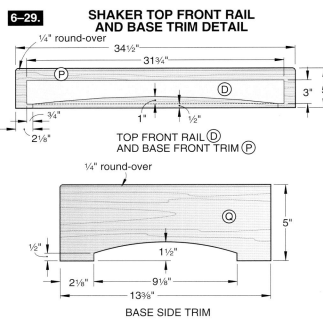

6–29.

SHAKER TOP FRONT RAIL AND BASE TRIM DETAIL

TOP FRONT RAIL (D) AND BASE FRONT TRIM (P)

BASE SIDE TRIM

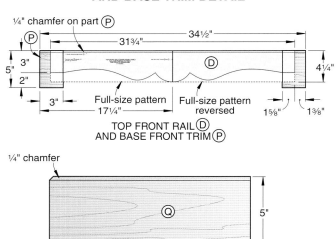

COUNTRY TOP FRONT RAIL DETAIL AND BASE TRIM DETAIL

TOP FRONT RAIL (D) AND BASE FRONT TRIM (P)

BASE SIDE TRIM

Add the Base

1 Cut the bottom panel (O) to size. Next, to form the front trim (P) and side trim (Q), cut a 5 x 65" workpiece from ¾"-thick stock. Then, rout the applicable profile along an edge of the workpiece. For a Shaker bookcase, rout a ¼" round-over, where shown on the Shaker Top Front Rail and Base Trim drawing in **6–29**. For a country bookcase, rout a ¼" chamfer, where shown on the Country Top Front Rail and Base Trim drawing in **6–29**. For a traditional bookcase, rout a ¼" cove, where shown in **6–30**.

2 Miter-cut the trim (P, Q) to length to fit the bottom panel. For the best appearance, maintain a continuous grain flow across the trim pieces, as laid out on the Cutting Diagram.

3 Lay out the applicable contour on the trim. For a Shaker bookcase, lay out the curve on the front and side trim (P, Q), where dimensioned on the Shaker Top Front Rail and Base Trim drawing in **6–29**. For a country bookcase, adhere the remaining two copies of the Base Front Trim Pattern in **6–34** (*page 110*) to the front trim (P), as you did for the top front rail (D), where shown on the Country Top Front Rail and Base Trim drawing in **6–29**. (The country base's side trim [Q] does not have a contour.) For a traditional base, lay out the

contour on the front and side trim (P, Q), where dimensioned in **6–30**.

4 Bandsaw the trim to shape, cutting just outside the lines, and then sand to the lines.

5 Cut the corner blocks (R) to size, angle-cutting one end, where dimensioned in **6–30**.

6 Mark centerlines for #20 biscuits on the bottom panel (O), trim (P, Q), and corner blocks (R), where shown in **6–30**. Then, position your biscuit-joiner fence to center the slot cutter on the thickness of the bottom panel. Plunge all of the slots except the ones in the trim's mitered ends. For these, reposition the fence to offset the slot 1/8" from the trim's inside face. Do this to ensure the slot cutter does not go through the outside face. Now, plunge the slots in the mitered ends.

7 Assemble the bottom panel, trim, and corner blocks, as shown in **6–31**. When the glue dries, sand the assembly smooth.

8 Using a helper, set the bookcase on its back on your workbench. Then, position and clamp the base assembly (O/P/Q/R) tight against the bookcase's bottom, flush with the back and centered side to side. Drill countersunk mounting holes through the bottom panel (O) and 1/2" into the bottom (C), where shown in the Exploded View drawing in **6–26** and **6–30**, and drive the screws. Now, with the instructions in one of the three following sections, add a traditional, Shaker, or country top to the bookcase.

Now Add a Traditional Top

1 Cut the plywood top panel (S) to size. Then, miter-cut the front and side edging (T, U) to length to fit the panel, where shown in the Traditional Top drawing in **6–33**. Now, glue and clamp the edging to the panel.

2 To form the top trim assembly, cut the band, cap, and cove blanks (V, W, X) to the sizes in the Materials List, except cut the cove blank (X) to a width of 1½". (The cove blank is extra wide for safety when routing.) Rout a 1/4" chamfer along an edge of the cap blank (W) and a 1/2" cove along an edge of the cove blank (X), where shown. Now, rip the cove blank to a width of 5/8".

3 Glue and clamp the blanks together in the arrangement shown in the Traditional Top and Side Section Detail drawings in **6–33**. When the glue dries, miter-cut the assembly so that the back (short) edge measures 12¼" for the sides and 32¼" for the front.

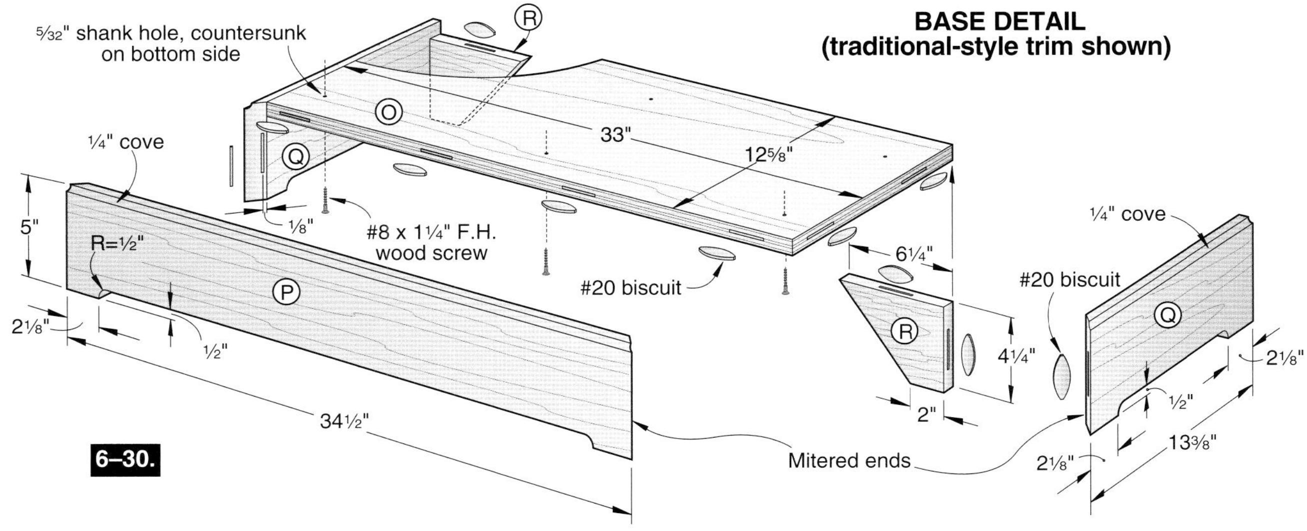

BASE DETAIL
(traditional-style trim shown)
5/32" shank hole, countersunk on bottom side
R
O
Q
1/4" cove
33"
12 5/8"
5"
R=1/2"
1/8"
#8 x 1 1/4" F.H. wood screw
P
#20 biscuit
6 1/4"
1/4" cove
#20 biscuit
R
Q
2 1/8"
1/2"
4 1/4"
2 1/8"
1/2"
2"
34 1/2"
Mitered ends
2 1/8"
13 3/8"

6–30.

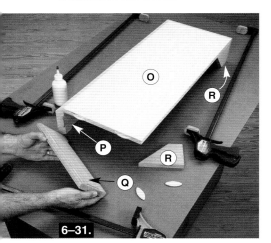

6–31.

With glue applied in the biscuit slots, assemble the bottom panel (O), trim (P, Q), and corner blocks (R) with #20 biscuits, and clamp the assembly together.

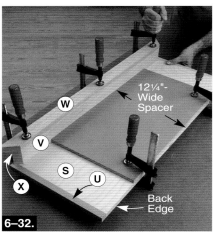

12¼"-Wide Spacer

Back Edge

6–32.

Using a 12¼"-wide scrap spacer to position the front trim (V/W/X) from the back edge of the top panel (S), and centering the assembly side to side, glue and clamp it to the panel.

4 Glue the front trim piece to the top panel (S), as shown in **6–32**. Then, glue and clamp the side trim pieces in place.

5 With the bookcase on its back, position and clamp the top panel/trim assembly (S through X) tight against the bookcase's top, flush with the back, and centered side to side. Drill mounting holes through the top panel (S) and into the top (C), where shown in **6–26** and the Traditional Top drawing in **6–33**, and drive the screws.

6 To form the front and side dentil moldings (Y, Z) shown in **6–26**, cut a ¾ x 54" workpiece from ¼"-thick oak. Mark the locations for ¼" dadoes spaced ¾" apart along the length of the workpiece, where dimensioned in the Dentil Molding Detail drawing in **6–33**. Now, using a dado blade, cut the dadoes ⅛" deep.

7 Cut the molding to the listed lengths, leaving ¼"-wide recesses at the ends of the front dentil molding (Y) and ⅛" wide recesses at the ends of the side dentil molding (Z), where shown. Now, glue the front molding to the top front rail (D) and the side molding to the top side rails (G), tight against the top-panel edging (T, U), where shown in the Exploded View (**6–26**).

Add a Shaker Top

1 Cut the plywood top panel (S) to size. Then, miter-cut the front and side edging (AA, BB) to length to fit the panel, where shown on the Shaker Top drawing in **6–33**. Now, glue and clamp the edging to the panel.

2 Tilt your tablesaw's blade to 17° from vertical. Now, using a tall auxiliary fence attached to your rip fence for support,

bevel-rip the edging, where dimensioned on the Side Section Detail drawing in **6–33**, cutting the side edging first and then the front edging. Sand the bevels smooth.

3 With the bookcase on its back, position and clamp the top panel/trim assembly (S/AA/BB) tight against the book-case's top, flush with the back, and centered side to side. Drill mounting holes through the top panel (S) and into the top (C), where shown on the Exploded View drawing in **6–26** and the Shaker Top drawing in **6–33**, and drive the screws.

Try a Country Top

1 Cut the plywood top panel (S) to size. Then, miter-cut the front and side bands (CC, DD) to length to fit the panel, where shown on the Country Top and Side Section Detail drawings in **6–33**. Now, glue and clamp the bands to the panel.

2 From ¾"-thick knotty pine, cut a 2½ x 72" workpiece to form the front and side caps (EE, FF). Then, rout a ¼" chamfer along an edge of the workpiece, where shown. Miter-cut the caps to length to fit on top of the bands (CC, DD). Now, glue and clamp the caps in place, keeping their back edge flush with the bands' back face.

3 Cut the front and side crown molding (GG, HH) to the lengths listed. (One option is

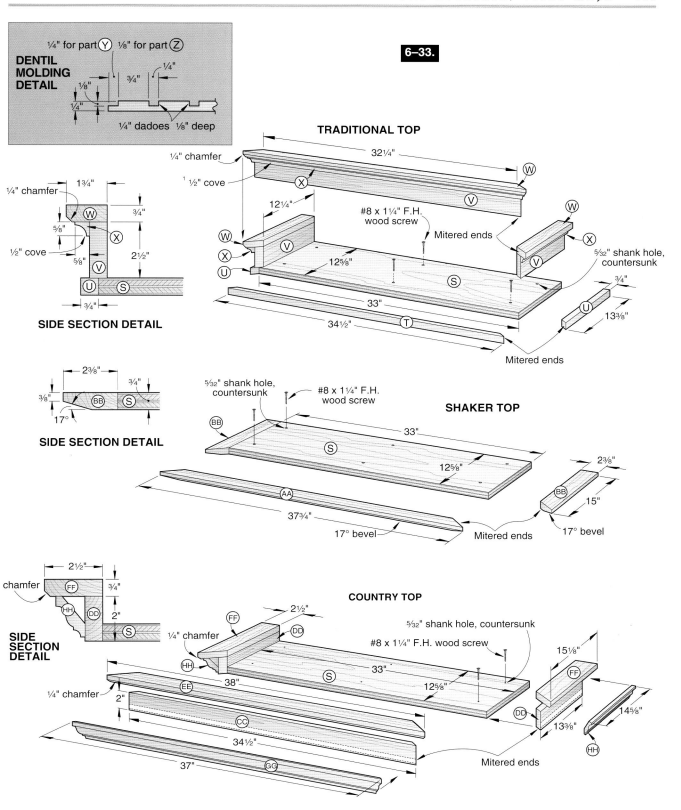

DENTIL MOLDING DETAIL

¼" for part Y   ⅛" for part Z
⅛"   ¾"   ¼"
⅛"
¼"
¼" dadoes   ⅛" deep

6–33.

TRADITIONAL TOP

32¼"   W
¼" chamfer
1½" cove   X   V
12¼"
#8 x 1¼" F.H. wood screw   Mitered ends   W   X   V
W
X
U
12⅝"   S
⅝/32" shank hole, countersunk
¾"
33"   U   13⅜"
34½"   T
Mitered ends

SIDE SECTION DETAIL

¼" chamfer   1¾"
¾"
W
⅝"   X
½" cove   V
⅝"
U   S
¾"
2½"

SIDE SECTION DETAIL

2⅜"   ¾"
⅜"   BB   S
17°

SHAKER TOP

⁵/32" shank hole, countersunk   #8 x 1¼" F.H. wood screw
BB
33"   S
12⅝"
2⅜"
BB   15"
AA
37¾"
17° bevel   Mitered ends   17° bevel

SIDE SECTION DETAIL

2½"
chamfer   FF   ¾"
HH   DD   2"
S

COUNTRY TOP

2½"   FF   DD
¼" chamfer
⁵/32" shank hole, countersunk
#8 x 1¼" F.H. wood screw
HH
33"   S
12⅝"
EE   38"
¼" chamfer   2"
CC
34½"
37"   GG
15⅛"   FF
DD
13⅜"   HH   14⅝"
Mitered ends

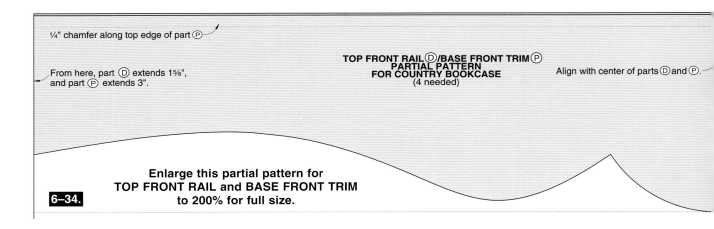

¼" chamfer along top edge of part Ⓟ

From here, part Ⓓ extends 1⅝", and part Ⓟ extends 3".

TOP FRONT RAIL Ⓓ/BASE FRONT TRIM Ⓟ
PARTIAL PATTERN
FOR COUNTRY BOOKCASE
(4 needed)

Align with center of parts Ⓓ and Ⓟ.

Enlarge this partial pattern for
TOP FRONT RAIL and BASE FRONT TRIM
to 200% for full size.

6–34.

to use architectural pine wood molding, available at home centers.) Then, glue the molding to the bands (CC, DD) and caps (EE, FF), where shown.

Apply a Finish

1 Sand any areas that need it with 220-grit sandpaper, and remove the dust.

2 Finish the bookcase as you wish. For the finish on the traditional bookcase shown on *page 101*, apply an oil-based stain and two coats of water-based clear satin polyurethane. Sand the bookcase to 320 grit between coats.

For the finish on the Shaker bookcase, *page 101*, do not use a stain, but apply two coats of satin lacquer. Sand it to 320 grit between coats.

For the finish on the country bookcase on *page 101*, apply a wood conditioner to help the knotty pine absorb the stain evenly. (While doing this, keep the wood wet until it stops soaking in the conditioner before wiping off the excess.) Then, apply a pine-colored oil-based stain. After the stain dries, finish

with two coats of fast-drying polyurethane, sanding to 220 grit between coats.

3 Finally, install the sleeves (beveled end in first) for the paddle supports in all of the holes in the sides (A). Then, with your helper, place the bookcase where you wish, and install the paddle supports and shelves (M/N).

Now, start filling this lofty library with your favorite books.

7

storage
solutions for
your homework

NO MATTER HOW OLD WE BECOME, HOMEWORK still builds up. This is not necessarily the kind of homework teachers assigned back in high school and college, but the records of daily activity.

If your utility bills, credit card statements, insurance premium notices, and other papers are still piling up on your dining table or kitchen counter, then you'll welcome the comforting, clutter-reducing projects in this chapter.

None of the three projects on the following pages are designed for full-blown home offices that require lots of tabletop space, but each will help you get and stay organized, and look good doing it. And if you do happen to bring paperwork work home from time to time, two of them offer you a place to do it. They are tidy, space-saving units that provide lots of specialized storage.

The drop-front writing desk, shown on page 112, *will make an attractive addition to practically any room in your home. If you don't have time to clean up the desktop before company drops by, simply close the front!*

On page 119, *you'll find another neat homework station that lends itself more to computer components. The final piece, on* page 128, *is an eye-catching versatile storage unit for anything from computer disks to CDs and DVDs.*

1 Glue up boards to make the necessary panels and shelves (A, B, C, D, Q). Then scrape off any dried glue squeeze-out, and sand the joints smooth.

2 Cut the desktop (A), the floorboard (B), and the side panels (C) to the sizes shown in the Carcase Parts drawing in 7–4 (*page 114*). Mark the "slant front" layout lines at the upper front corners of the side panels, but don't cut them yet.

Drop-front writing desk.

DROP-FRONT WRITING DESK

The best traditional desk designs have always offered a way to organize your paperwork, and just as important, to keep clutter out of sight when you're not working. This unit excels at both tasks. The version shown *above* is built of pine, colorfully stained, and has a decidedly country flair. But you can employ a hardwood like oak for a different look.

Make the Edge-Glued Panels for the Larger Parts

Note: This project involves a number of wide panels and shelves made from solid pine (see the Materials List). Before machining any individual parts, you'll want to glue up boards for these panels. If stock is already thicknessed to ¾", the edge joints must be aligned closely.

MATERIALS LIST FOR DROP-FRONT WRITING DESK

PART		FINISHED SIZE			MTL.	QTY.
		T	W	L		
A	desktop	¾"	12"	34"	EP	1
B	floorboard	¾"	17½"	34"	EP	1
C	side panels	¾"	17"	36¼"	EP	2
D	shelves	¾"	15⅞"	32"	EP	2
E	filler strip	¾"	2"	31½"	P	1
F	back panel	¼"	32¼"	36¼"	Ply	1
G	foot halves	¾"	4"	4"	P	8
H	corner blocks	¾"	2¾"	2¾"	P	4
I	glue blocks	¾"	¾"	3¼"	P	4
J	top/bottom panels	¾"	10¾"	31½"	P	2
K	uprights	½"	10¾"	6"	P	5
L	drawer shelves	¾"	10¾"	12½"	P	2
M	drawer fronts	¾"	2³⁄₁₆"	12⅜"	P	4
N	drawer sides	½"	2³⁄₁₆"	10½"	P	8
O	drawer backs	½"	1⁹⁄₁₆"	11⅞"	P	4
P	drawer bottoms	¼"	9⅞"	11⅞"	Ply	4
Q	drop-leaf panel	¾"	12"	27⅛"	EP	1
R	end caps	¾"	2½"	12"	P	2
S	door stiles	¾"	2½"	22⅝"	P	4
T	door upper rails	¾"	2½"	11¹¹⁄₁₆"	P	2
U	door lower rails	¾"	3"	11¹¹⁄₁₆"	P	2
V	door panels	½"	11½"	18¹⁄₁₆"	EP	2

Materials Key: EP = Edge-glued pine; P = Pine; Ply = Pine/fir plywood.
Supplies: #6 x ¾" flathead wood screws; #8 x 1¼" flathead wood screws; #8 x 1½" flathead wood screws; #10 x 1¼" flathead wood screws; #17 x 1" wire brads; brass-plated hinge/support (1 pair); ½" porcelain knobs (4); ¾" porcelain knobs (3); no-mortise hinges (2 pair), magnetic catches (2).

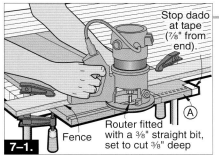

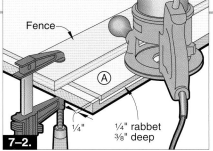

7–1. Fence / Router fitted with a ⅜" straight bit, set to cut ⅜" deep / Stop dado at tape (⅞" from end). / Ⓐ

Routing the ⅜"-wide stopped dadoes in the underside of the desktop and the upper face of the floorboard.

7–2. Fence / Ⓐ / ¼" / ¼" rabbet ⅜" deep

Routing the rabbets along the rear edges of those same panels.

Rout the Dadoes and Rabbets

1 Rout the ⅜"-wide stopped dadoes in the underside of the desktop and the upper face of the floorboard (**7–1**). Next, use the same straight bit to rout the rabbets along the rear edges of those same panels (**7–2**).

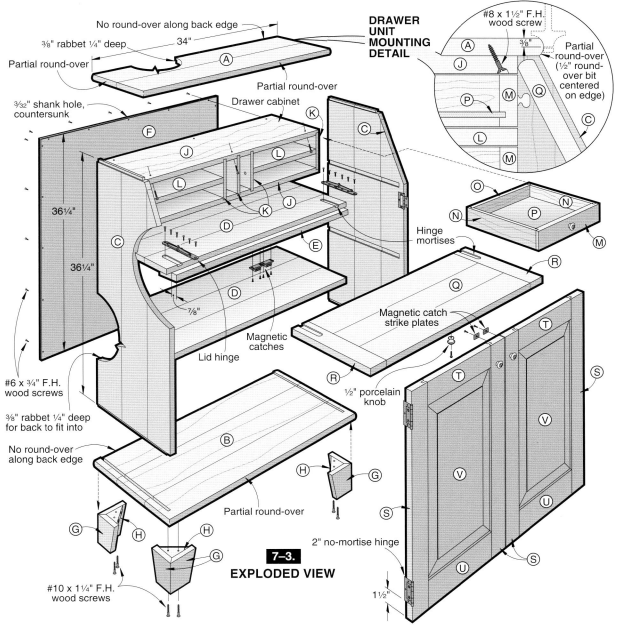

DRAWER UNIT MOUNTING DETAIL

#8 x 1½" F.H. wood screw / Ⓐ / ⅜" / Partial round-over (½" round-over bit centered on edge) / Ⓙ / Ⓟ / Ⓜ / Ⓠ / Ⓛ / Ⓒ / Ⓜ

No round-over along back edge
⅜" rabbet ¼" deep / 34"
Partial round-over
Ⓐ
Partial round-over
Drawer cabinet
³⁄₃₂" shank hole, countersunk
Drawer cabinet
Ⓕ / Ⓚ / Ⓒ / Ⓙ / Ⓛ / Ⓛ / Ⓚ / Ⓙ / Ⓓ / Ⓒ / Ⓔ / Ⓓ
36¼"
36¼"
⅞"
Hinge mortises
Ⓞ / Ⓝ / Ⓟ / Ⓝ / Ⓜ
Magnetic catches
Lid hinge
Magnetic catch strike plates
Ⓠ / Ⓡ
#6 x ¾" F.H. wood screws
⅜" rabbet ¼" deep for back to fit into
No round-over along back edge
½" porcelain knob
Ⓡ / Ⓣ / Ⓣ / Ⓢ / Ⓥ / Ⓥ / Ⓤ / Ⓢ / Ⓢ / Ⓤ
Ⓑ
Ⓗ / Ⓖ
Partial round-over
Ⓢ
Ⓖ / Ⓗ / Ⓗ / Ⓖ
2" no-mortise hinge
1½"
7–3.
EXPLODED VIEW
#10 x 1¼" F.H. wood screws

Note that the rabbet on each panel should extend only to the dado locations, not all the way to the ends.

2 Using a ½"-radius round-over bit in your router table, rout the thumbnail profile on the front and end edges of the desktop and floorboard. (See the example in the inset drawing in **7–3**.)

3 Clamp the side panels together, and jigsaw close to your layout line to create the slant front angle. Then clamp a straightedge on the line and true up the edges with a router and a flush-trim bit. (Separate the panels if your flush-trim bit isn't long enough to cut both edges at once.)

4 Install a ⅜" dado blade and a wood auxiliary fence on your tablesaw, and cut the tongue along the top and bottom edges of each side panel. (See the Tongue Detail drawing in **7–4**.) Make two passes (with alternate faces down on the saw table) so that the tongue is centered on each edge. Use a handsaw and a chisel to cut the tongues just shy of the front edge, where indicated.

5 Designate the side panels as "left" and "right" so you can do the layout marking for the stopped dadoes to make mirror images. With their inside faces marked, clamp a straightedge guide in place and rout the dadoes. (This is similar to the technique shown in **7–1**, on *page 113*.) Use a chisel to square up the stopped ends of each dado.

6 Making sure you have them oriented correctly, rout (or saw) the full-length rabbet along the inside rear edge of each side panel (C).

Make the Shelves and Assemble the Carcase

1 If you haven't done so already, trim the edge-glued panels for the upper and lower shelves (D) to size. These two parts measure the same size, but you'll mortise only the upper shelf for the drop-leaf hinges. (See the Hinge Mortise detail drawing in **7–4**.)

2 Clamp a straightedge guide and a stopblock near one end of the upper shelf, and use a

7–4. CARCASE PARTS

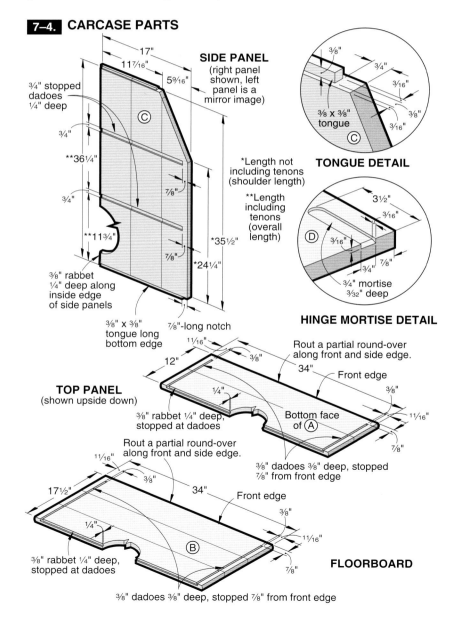

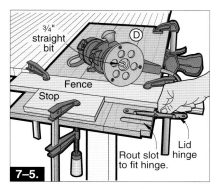

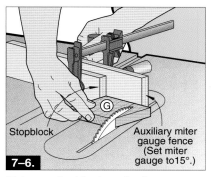

Routing the mortise for the hinge.

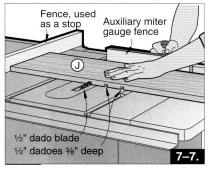

Using a stopblock and miter gauge to cut a 15° taper.

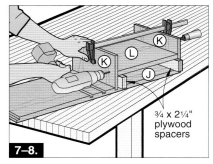

Cutting dadoes in the inside faces of the panels.

Fastening drawer shelves to uprights.

¾" straight bit to rout the mortise for the hinge. (See the Hinge Mortise detail in **7–4** and **7–5**.) Use a chisel to bevel the very edge of the mortise, creating clearance for the hinge knuckle. Repeat the same sequence for the other hinge and make sure they both fit properly, but don't install them yet.

3 After a quick test fit, glue and clamp the shelves (D) into the dadoes in the side panels. Lay the assembly (back edges down) on your workbench.

4 Next, glue and clamp the desktop (A) and the floorboard (B) to the side panels (C), fitting the tongues into their corresponding dadoes. Check for equal diagonal measurements to make sure the assembly is squared up; then let the glue dry.

Turn to the Carcase Details

1 Cut the filler strip (E), and glue it in place on the underside of the upper shelf, offset ⅞" from the front edge.

2 Cut the back panel (F) from ¼" plywood, and drill countersunk holes for the mounting screws. Temporarily fasten the panel with #6 x ¾" screws.

3 Cut eight 4"-square blocks of ¾" stock for the desk feet (G). These are actually halves that get glued up in pairs. (See **7–9**.) Then cut a 45° bevel on one edge of each half, for a miter joint.

7–9. FOOT DETAIL

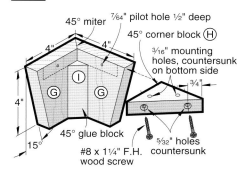

4 Before gluing up the feet, cut the 15° taper on the non-beveled edge of each half. You can use a stopblock attached to your tablesaw's miter gauge to make these cuts (**7–6**).

5 Cut the corner blocks (H) and glue blocks (I) for the foot assemblies, and drill the countersunk screw holes in the corner blocks, as shown in **7–9**. Both of these pieces help reinforce the feet.

6 Glue and screw the parts together to make up the four foot assemblies. Then fasten them to the underside of the floorboard (B), ½" in from each corner edge.

Build the Drawer Unit Assembly

1 From ¾" stock, cut the top and bottom panels (J) for the drawer storage assembly. Cut the drawer shelves (L) to the same width, but leave them ½" longer than the final dimension.

2 Install a ½" dado blade in your tablesaw to cut dadoes in the inside faces of the panels

7–10.

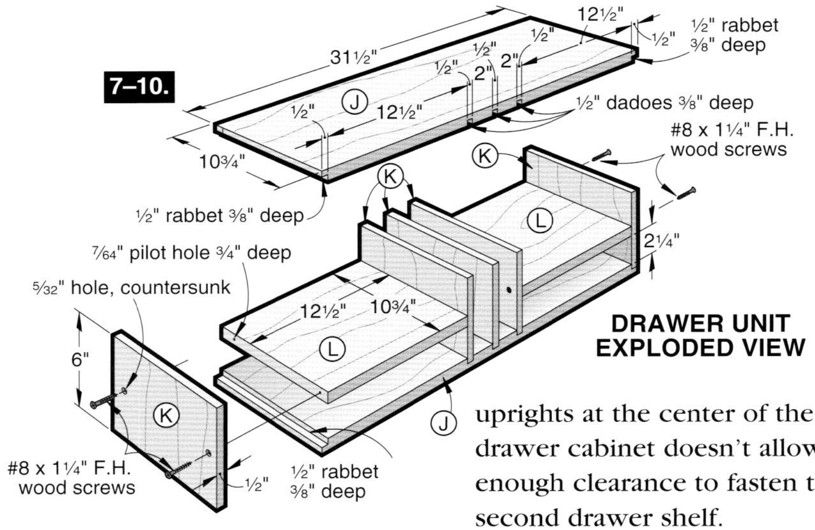
31½"
12½"
½"
½"
½"
2"
2"
½"
½" rabbet
⅜" deep
J
12½"
½" dadoes ⅜" deep
#8 x 1¼" F.H.
wood screws
10¾"
K
K
½" rabbet ⅜" deep
L
2¼"
7⁄64" pilot hole ¾" deep
5⁄32" hole, countersunk
12½"
10¾"
6"
L
K
J
#8 x 1¼" F.H.
wood screws
½"
½" rabbet
⅜" deep
DRAWER UNIT
EXPLODED VIEW

(J). Center the first dado in each; then reset the rip fence as an end stop for the two outside dadoes (**7–7**, *page 115*). Finally, shift the fence closer, and add an auxiliary wood fence to cut the end rabbets on each panel.

3 Now mill the ½" stock you'll need for the five uprights (K), and cut these parts to size.

4 Trim the drawer shelves (L) so their length matches the distance between the end rabbets and the "outside" dadoes in the panels (J).

5 Cut a pair of 2¼"-wide spacer blocks, and use them to support the drawer shelves while you fasten each one to a pair of uprights (**7–8**, *page 115*). Dry-fit the uprights for this step so you can temporarily remove the subassembly after the drawer shelf (L) is secured. This step is necessary because, if the other section is already in place, the tight spacing between the uprights at the center of the drawer cabinet doesn't allow enough clearance to fasten the second drawer shelf.

6 Apply glue to the dadoes and rabbets and put together the drawer storage assembly. Secure everything with clamps and check for square. After the glue sets up, drill countersunk screw holes along the front and rear edges of the top panel (one at the center and one near each end), and fasten the cabinet to the desk carcase. (See the Drawer Unit Mounting Detail drawing in **7–3**, *page 113*.)

Craft the Drawers to Fit

1 Cut the eight ½"-thick drawer sides (N) and four drawer backs (O); then you can turn immediately to the drawer fronts (M) and the plywood drawer bottoms (P).

7–11.

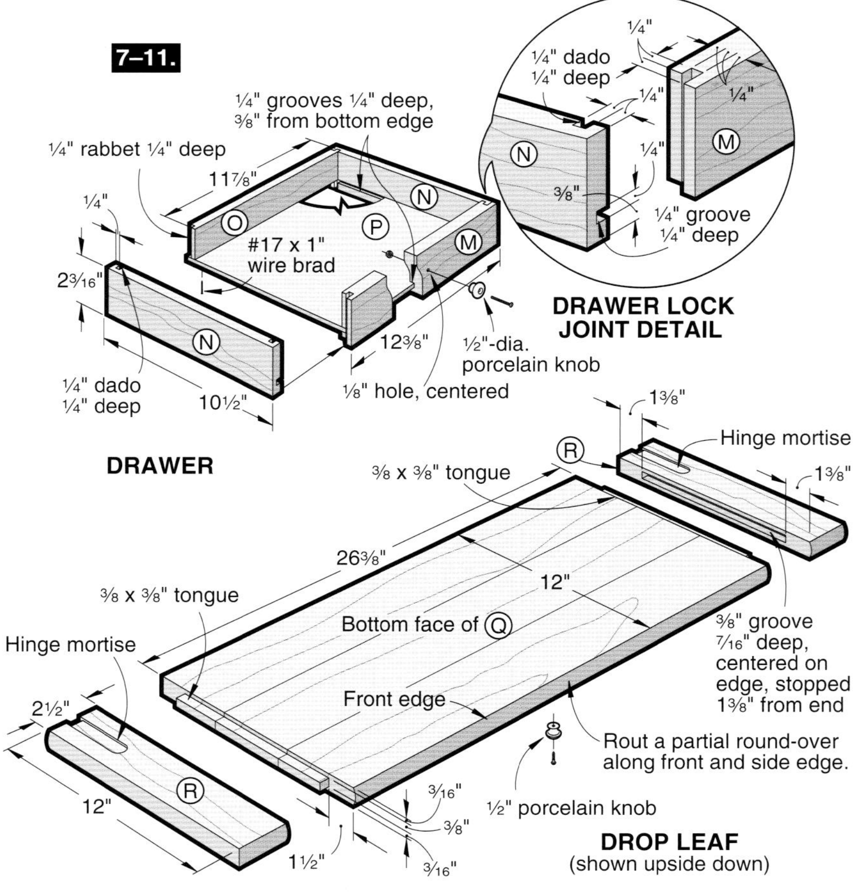
¼" grooves ¼" deep,
⅜" from bottom edge
¼" rabbet ¼" deep
11⅞"
¼"
O
N
P
M
#17 x 1"
wire brad
2³⁄16"
N
¼" dado
¼" deep
10½"
12⅜"
½"-dia.
porcelain knob
⅛" hole, centered
DRAWER
¼"
¼" dado
¼" deep
¼"
¼"
¼"
N
M
⅜"
¼" groove
¼" deep
DRAWER LOCK
JOINT DETAIL
1⅜"
R
Hinge mortise
1⅜"
⅜ x ⅜" tongue
26⅜"
12"
⅜ x ⅜" tongue
Bottom face of Q
Hinge mortise
⅜" groove
7⁄16" deep,
centered on
edge, stopped
1⅜" from end
Front edge
2½"
Rout a partial round-over
along front and side edge.
R
12"
3⁄16"
⅜"
3⁄16"
1½"
½" porcelain knob
DROP LEAF
(shown upside down)

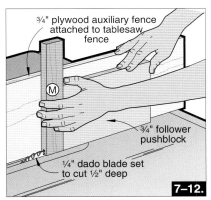

Cutting dadoes in the ends of a drawer front.

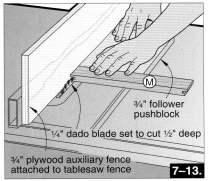

Cutting away part of the inside tongue on the end of the drawer front.

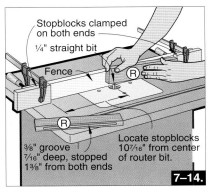

Making the first pass.

2 Cut the drawer fronts (M) from ¾" solid stock; then install a ¼" dado blade on your tablesaw to cut the joinery for the drawer parts.

3 Mount a tall wood auxiliary fence on your tablesaw's rip fence, and with a follower block for support, cut the ½"-deep dadoes in the ends of each drawer front, as shown in **7–12**. This cut leaves two ¼"-thick tongues, both the same length, at each end.

4 Reset the auxiliary fence directly against the dado blade, but leave the blade height setting intact. Then guide the drawer front (face up) past the blade to cut away ¼" of the inside tongue on each end (**7–13**). With that done, drill holes for the knobs, and set aside the drawer fronts.

5 Lower the blade height to ¼", and cut the rabbets at the ends of the drawer backs (O). (Note that this joint differs slightly from that on the drawer fronts.) Remove the auxiliary fence, adjust the rip fence, and cut the lock joint dadoes in the drawer sides (N).

6 Shift the rip fence again to cut the grooves for the drawer bottoms. You want this detail in the drawer sides (N) and fronts (M), but not the backs (O). (The backs are cut narrower to sit atop the drawer bottoms.)

7 Dry-assemble a drawer to confirm the size of the plywood drawer bottoms (P). Cut those parts; then glue the drawers together, and fasten the drawer bottoms with 1" wire brads.

Make the Drop Leaf

Note: *The last component for the top section of the desk is the drop-leaf panel (Q). Like the other large carcase pieces, this panel gets glued up from narrower boards, but it has an additional feature to keep it stable and flat. Two end caps (R) are fitted to the drop leaf (one at each end), a method sometimes called "breadboard" construction. (See the Drop Leaf drawing in 7–11.) Grooves in the caps house a wide tenon or tongue from the center panel, which resists cupping but can still move relatively freely in response to seasonal changes in humidity.*

1 Cut the drop-leaf panel (Q) and the caps (R) to size; then set up a ¼" straight bit in your router table. Adjust the fence for a ³⁄₁₆" offset from the bit. The closer you get to an exact setting the better, but cutting the groove in two passes (alternating faces against the fence) will ensure that it ends up dead-center on your stock.

2 Clamp stopblocks to the fence to index the ends of the drop-leaf caps, and adjust the cutter height to about half the finished depth. Lower each cap onto the cutter for the first pass (**7–14**). Make another pass with the opposite face against the fence; then adjust the bit to full depth and repeat the process with each cap.

3 Use a dado blade on your tablesaw to cut the tongues on the ends of the drop-leaf panel (Q). Fine-tune the cutting depth so that two passes (with alternating faces down) create a snug fit between these tongues and the end cap grooves.

4 Trim the tongues back 1½" from the edge of the panel, as shown. Do a dry test-fit first; then glue and clamp the end caps to the drop leaf panel. (Apply glue to only the first 3" of the joint at the hinge edge of the panel to allow some "floating" of the wood.)

5 After the glue dries, clamp the drop leaf in place temporarily (in the open position), and transfer the locations of the hinge mortises in the top shelf (D) to the drop-leaf end caps (R). Rout and chisel the mortises as before; then install the hinges and check the fit. When closed, the drop leaf should just clear the front edge of the desktop (A) and rest against the drawer cabinet. Make any necessary adjustments, and install the knob.

Construct the Doors for the Lower Half

Because a drop-leaf design creates leg room while you're working at the desk, there's no need for the kneehole feature common to fixed-top desks. The design for this desk uses that valuable space for enclosed storage, tucked away neatly behind a pair of raised-panel doors. (See the Door Assembly and Panel Detail drawings in **7–15**.)

You can make them easily with just a tablesaw.

1 Cut the stiles (S), upper rails (T), and lower rails (U) to size.

2 Install a ¼" dado blade and cut the centered grooves in the inside edges of the stiles and rails.

3 Using the rip fence as an end stop, and the miter gauge to guide the stock, cut the tenons on the ends of the top and bottom rails. (See the Tenon Detail drawing in **7–15**.)

4 Plane additional stock to ½" thick, and edge-glue boards for the door panels (V). After the

glue joints are dry and sanded smooth, cut the two panels to finished size.

5 To bevel the door panels, first mount a tall auxiliary fence and a feather-board setup to steady the panels. Then tilt your sawblade to 7°, as shown in the Panel Detail drawing in **7–15**. Cut the bevels with the panel on edge, doing the ends first to prevent tear-out; then sand off the saw marks.

6 After a dry test to fit the parts, glue up the door assemblies. Like the drop-leaf panels, the raised panels need room to shrink and expand within their frames, so apply glue to only the center of each

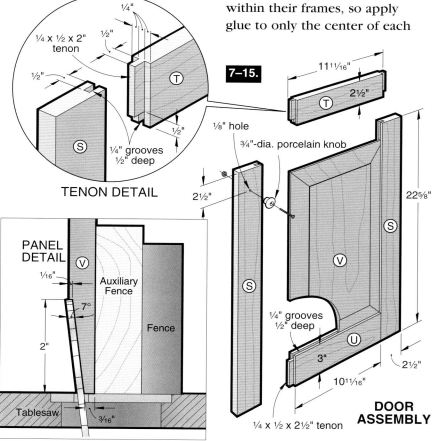

7–15.

TENON DETAIL

PANEL DETAIL

DOOR ASSEMBLY

panel end. Make sure each door is square and flat before you set it aside for the glue to dry.

7 Install the hardware for the doors. This includes the knobs; no-mortise hinges; and, after the doors are hung, the magnetic catches.

Finally, Finish the Drop-Front Writing Desk

1 Remove the hardware from the doors and the drop leaf, and also the screws that are holding the drawer cabinet and the carcase back panel in place. Finish-sand all of these components along with the desk carcase.

2 If you choose to apply the finish used on the desk shown on *page 112*, first apply a stain conditioner to prevent blotching of the pine. Next, use a water-based antique red stain for the carcase, drop leaf, and doors. The drawer cabinet and drawers for the desk shown on *page 112* do not necessarily take a stain, but you can apply one to determine the look you want.

The antique red stain requires about four to six hours of drying time. Follow this up with two coats of satin polyurethane on the entire project. After allowing 24 hours of drying time for the second coat, reinstall all the hardware, and reassemble the desk.

A cherry cabinet that serves as a computer workstation. See additional views on page 120.

See additional views on page 120.

HIDEAWAY HOME OFFICE

Does a computer workstation look out of place in your traditional furnishing scheme? Hide its clutter behind the frame-and-panel front of this handsome cherry cabinet. The three-panel drop leaf gives you instant access to your equipment and a spacious worktop. There's a pigeonhole to store your keyboard and mouse, and a shelf that holds a monitor up to 17¾" tall. The doors below hide a pair of file drawers and provide plenty of storage for your computer and other supplies.

Start with the Carcase Parts

1 Referring to the Cutting Diagram on *page 120*, cut the plywood parts A through I to the sizes in the Materials List on *page 121*.

2 Cut four strips of banding (J) to the size listed. From these lengths, cut bands for each of the parts A through E, and G through I. Glue and clamp the

Above right: *A look at the cabinet with its doors open reveals plenty of storage space within.*

Above left: *The computer workstation has a pigeonhole to store your keyboard and mouse, and a shelf that holds a monitor up to 17¾" tall.*

Right: *The bottom doors hide file drawers and storage for your computer supplies.*

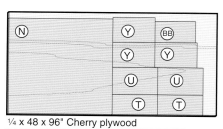

CUTTING DIAGRAM FOR HIDEAWAY HOME OFFICE

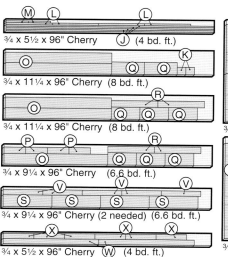

Ⓜ Ⓛ Ⓛ

¾ x 5½ x 96" Cherry Ⓙ (4 bd. ft.)

Ⓞ Ⓠ Ⓠ Ⓚ

¾ x 11¼ x 96" Cherry (8 bd. ft.)

Ⓞ Ⓡ Ⓠ Ⓠ Ⓠ

¾ x 11¼ x 96" Cherry (8 bd. ft.)

Ⓟ Ⓟ Ⓡ Ⓞ Ⓠ Ⓠ Ⓠ

¾ x 9¼ x 96" Cherry (6.6 bd. ft.)

Ⓥ Ⓥ Ⓥ Ⓢ Ⓢ Ⓢ Ⓢ

¾ x 9¼ x 96" Cherry (2 needed) (6.6 bd. ft.)

Ⓧ Ⓧ Ⓧ

¾ x 5½ x 96" Cherry Ⓦ (4 bd. ft.)

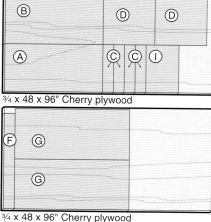

Ⓑ Ⓓ Ⓓ Ⓐ Ⓒ Ⓒ Ⓘ

¾ x 48 x 96" Cherry plywood

Ⓕ Ⓖ Ⓖ

¾ x 48 x 96" Cherry plywood

Ⓝ Ⓨ Ⓑ Ⓑ Ⓨ Ⓨ Ⓤ Ⓤ Ⓣ Ⓣ

¼ x 48 x 96" Cherry plywood

Ⓐ Ⓐ Ⓩ Ⓐ Ⓐ Ⓩ Ⓐ Ⓐ Ⓩ Ⓑ Ⓑ Ⓑ Ⓑ

¼ x 48 x 48" Cherry plywood

Ⓗ Ⓔ

¾ x 48 x 48" Cherry plywood

Note: *For all parts, the length is always the dimension of the wood parallel to the grain.*

MATERIALS LIST FOR HIDEAWAY HOME OFFICE

PART		FINISHED SIZE			MTL.	QTY.
		T	W	L		
CARCASE						
A	fixed shelf	3/4"	21½"	44¼"	CP	1
B	drawer shelf	3/4"	22½"	44¼"	CP	1
C	upper dividers	3/4"	21½"	4"	CP	4
D	lower dividers	3/4"	22½"	22⅞"	CP	2
E	bottom	3/4"	22½"	44¼"	CP	1
F	front skirt	3/4"	44¼"	4"	CP	1
G	sides	3/4"	22¾"	52"	CP	2
H	carcase top	3/4"	22½"	44¼"	CP	1
I	adjustable shelf	3/4"	21½"	14⅛"	CP	1
J	banding	½"	3/4"	96"	C	4
K	skirt blocks	3/4"	3½"	4"	C	2
L	drawer slides	3/4"	15/16"	21¼"	C	4
M	trim	3/4"	7/8"	10⅛"	C	2
N	back	¼"	45¼"	48"	CP	1
O*	top	3/4"	24¼"	47¾"	EC	1
DRAWERS						
P	pencil drawer fronts/backs	3/4"	3"	10"	C	4
Q*	file drawer fronts/backs	3/4"	10¾"	13¼"	EC	4
R*	pencil drawer sides	½"	3"	21½"	C	4
S*	file drawer sides	½"	10¼"	21½"	EC	4
T	pencil drawer bottoms	¼"	9½"	21"	CP	2
U	file drawer bottoms	¼"	12¾"	21"	CP	2
DROP LEAF AND DOORS						
V	stiles	3/4"	2½"	18¼"	C	10
W	drop-leaf rails	3/4"	2½"	44⅛"	C	2
X	door rails	3/4"	2½"	14⅛"	C	6
Y	drop-leaf panels	¼"	11⅞"	18¼"	CP	3
Z	door panels	¼"	9⅝"	18¼"	CP	3
AA*	drop-leaf liners	¼"	11⅜"	17¾"	CP	3
BB	door liners	¼"	9⅛"	17¾"	CP	3

*Parts initially cut oversized. See the instructions.
Materials Key: CP = Cherry plywood; C = Cherry;
EC = Edge-joined cherry.
Supplies: #8 x ¾" panhead screws (16); #8 x 1¼" panhead screws
(6); 3/16" flat washers (6); #8 x 1" flathead wood screws (18);
#20 biscuits; glue; 24 x 48" plastic laminate; contact cement; finish.
Hardware: 2½" no-mortise hinges w/screws (9); shelf supports (4);
22" full-extension drawer slides w/screws (2 pairs); magnetic catches
w/screws (5); flap stays w/screws (2), knobs (4); levelers with
brackets (4); hanging-file rails (4 x 2').

bands to the panels so they are flush at the edges and ends. The skirt (F) does not get banded. With the glue dry, sand the bands flush with the panels. Set the adjustable shelf (I) aside.

Adjust your biscuit joiner to cut a slot centered in the thickness of your ¾" plywood. Mark the biscuit locations in the edges of parts B through F, and H, where indicated in **7–16** (*page 122*). Plunge the slots. Mark the biscuit locations in the ends of the bottom face of the fixed shelf (A), the top of the drawer shelf (B), and the tops of the inside faces of the sides (G). Plunge the slots.

Note: *Where three biscuits are shown, locate a biscuit 3" from each edge, and center the third one. Where two biscuits are shown, locate them at the one-third points.*

4 Set your biscuit joiner fence for vertical plunging. Using a straightedge as a guide, offset from the biscuit centerlines and clamped to the workpiece, plunge the rest of the biscuit slots. The biscuit slots are centered 1⅜" from the front edges in the underside of the bottom (E) and the inside face of the sides (G) for the attachment of the front skirt (F), as shown in **7–18** (*page 122*). When marking the locations of the biscuits that secure the upper dividers (C) to the drawer shelf (B), remember that the dividers are 1" narrower than the shelf.

5 Drill the 1½" wire-access holes in the fixed shelf (A), drawer shelf (B), and bottom (E), where shown on part B in **7–16** (*page 122*). Drill the ¼" leveler adjustment holes in the bottom's corners, where shown. Drill the holes and slots in the carcase top (H) for the screws that will fasten the top (O) to the carcase, where shown in **7–17** (*page 122*).

6 Install a dado blade in your tablesaw, and cut a ¼" rabbet ½" deep for the back (N) in the rear inside edges of the sides (G). Position the leveler brackets on the sides, where shown in **7–18**, and drill the screw pilot holes.

7 Mark the locations and drill ¼" holes for the shelf supports in the lower dividers (D), where shown in **7–16**. See the Shop Tip "A Jig That Won't Wear Out" on *page 123*.

8 Finish-sand the carcase parts to 220 grit. Take care not to round the edge bands. To keep your joints tight, smooth out the sharp edges with a sanding block after you assemble the carcase.

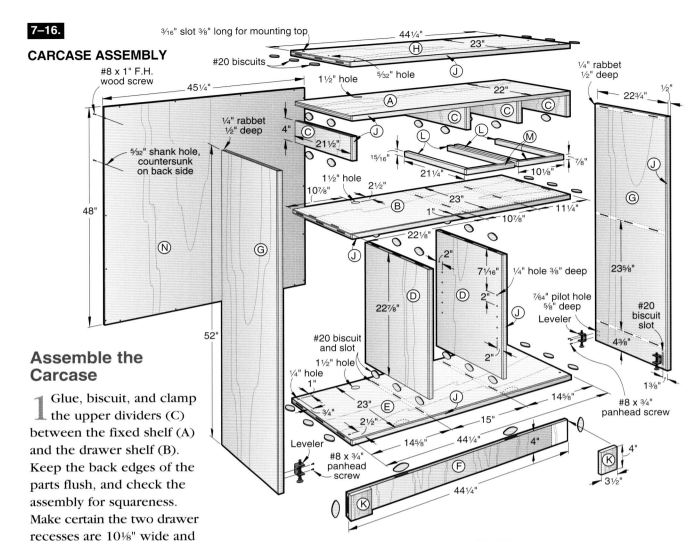

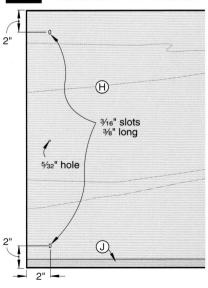

7–16.

CARCASE ASSEMBLY

³⁄₁₆" slot ⅜" long for mounting top

#20 biscuits

44¼"

23"

H

J

⁵⁄₃₂" hole

¼" rabbet ½" deep

#8 x 1" F.H. wood screw

45¼"

1½" hole

22"

A

22¾"

½"

¼" rabbet ½" deep

4"

C

J

C

C

C

⁵⁄₃₂" shank hole, countersunk on back side

21½"

L

L

M

J

15⁄16"

7⁄8"

48"

1½" hole

10⅞"

2½"

21¼"

10⅛"

G

B

23"

23⅝"

N

G

1"

10⅞"

11¼"

22⅛"

J

2"

D

22⅞"

D

7¹⁄₁₆"

¼" hole ⅜" deep

2"

⁷⁄₆₄" pilot hole ⅝" deep

Leveler

52"

#20 biscuit slot

#20 biscuit and slot

J

2"

4⅜"

1½" hole

¼" hole

1"

23"

E

J

14⅝"

1⅜"

#8 x ¾" panhead screw

Assemble the Carcase

1 Glue, biscuit, and clamp the upper dividers (C) between the fixed shelf (A) and the drawer shelf (B). Keep the back edges of the parts flush, and check the assembly for squareness. Make certain the two drawer recesses are 10⅛" wide and uniform from front to back. Set this assembly aside until the glue dries.

2 With their back edges resting on your workbench, glue, biscuit, and clamp the lower dividers (D) between assembly A/B/C and the bottom (E). Once again, keep the back edges of all the parts flush, and check the assembly for square. Make certain the spacing from the ends of parts B and E to the dividers (D) and between the dividers is equal and uniform front to back. Let the glue dry.

3 Glue, biscuit, and clamp the skirt (F) to the bottom (E). Keep the skirt and the bottom perpendicular to each other and their ends flush. Let the glue dry.

4 Screw the leveler brackets to the sides (G). Apply glue to one end upper divider (C), then glue, biscuit, and clamp the first side to the assembly A/B/C/D/E, and the carcase top (H) to the side, as shown in **7–20**. Keep the side's front edge flush with the edges of parts B, E, and H. Let

¾"

2½"

15"

14⅝"

44¼"

4"

K

4"

Leveler

#8 x ¾" panhead screw

F

K

44¼"

3½"

7–17. **CARCASE TOP DETAIL**

2"

0

2"

H

³⁄₁₆" slots ⅜" long

⁵⁄₃₂" hole

2"

0

J

2"

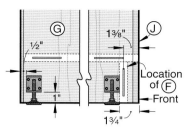

7–18. **LEVELER DETAIL**

the glue dry. Glue, biscuit, and clamp the second side in place.

5 Cut the skirt blocks (K) to size, and finish-sand them to 220 grit. Glue and clamp them to the skirt (F), where shown in **7–16**.

6 Cut the drawer slides (L) and the drawer trim (M) to size. Glue and clamp them into the pencil drawer recesses, where shown on **7–16**. The faces of the drawer trim are flush with the ends of the upper dividers (C/J), as shown on the Flap Stay drawing in **7–28**, on *page 129*. The drawer slides will protrude ¹⁄₁₆" above the trim.

7 Measure the carcase for the back (N). The back covers the rear edges of parts E and H, and fits into the rabbets in the sides. Cut the back to size, clamp it to the carcase, and drill pilot and countersunk shank holes. Remove the back, finish-sand it to 220 grit, and set it aside for finishing later.

8 Edge-join solid stock to make a 25 x 49" blank for the top (O). Trim it to finished size, and finish-sand it to 220 grit. Set the top aside.

A Jig That Won't Wear Out

Making a hardboard guide for drilling shelf support holes is common practice. The drawback is that the same ¼" bit is used to drill the holes in both the guide and the cabinet part. Repeated use enlarges the guide's holes, leading to inaccurate hole placement and wobbly shelves. Solve this problem by drilling ⅜" holes in the guide and using a ¼" self-centering bit to drill the shelf support holes, as shown in **7–19**. This **7–19.** way, the bit's retractable centering sleeve, rather than the ¼" drill bit, contacts the guide hole, eliminating wear on the drilling guide. Self-centering bits are available from most woodworking supply catalogs.

Make the Sturdy Drawers

1 Check the critical dimensions of your drawer openings. The width of the pencil drawer fronts/backs (P) and pencil drawer sides (R) must be ¹⁄₁₆" less than the dimension from the top of the pencil drawer guides (L) to the bottom of the fixed shelf (A). The length of parts P must be ⅛" less than the width of the pencil drawer openings. To accommodate the drawer slides (L), the length of the file drawer fronts/backs (Q) must be 1" less than the width of the file drawer opening. Edge-join blanks about 1" oversize in length and width for the file drawer fronts/ backs (Q) and the file drawer sides (S). Cut parts P, R, and S to size. Cut parts Q to length, but make them 10⅞" wide.

Note: Set aside scraps of drawer front and side stock for testing your tablesaw setup when cutting the lock-rabbet joints.

2 To accommodate the hanging-file rails, the file drawer fronts and backs (Q) are ½" wider than the sides. Rip ½" strips off the tops of the file drawer fronts/backs, where shown on the Drawers drawing in **7–21** (*page 124*). Mark these strips so they can be glued to their mating parts after the lock-rabbet joints are formed.

3 Install a ¼" dado blade in your tablesaw, and attach a 6"-high auxiliary fence to your rip fence. Following the four steps in **7–22**, cut the lock rab-

7–20.

A 90° plywood clamping bracket keeps the carcase top and side perpendicular.

7–21. **DRAWERS**

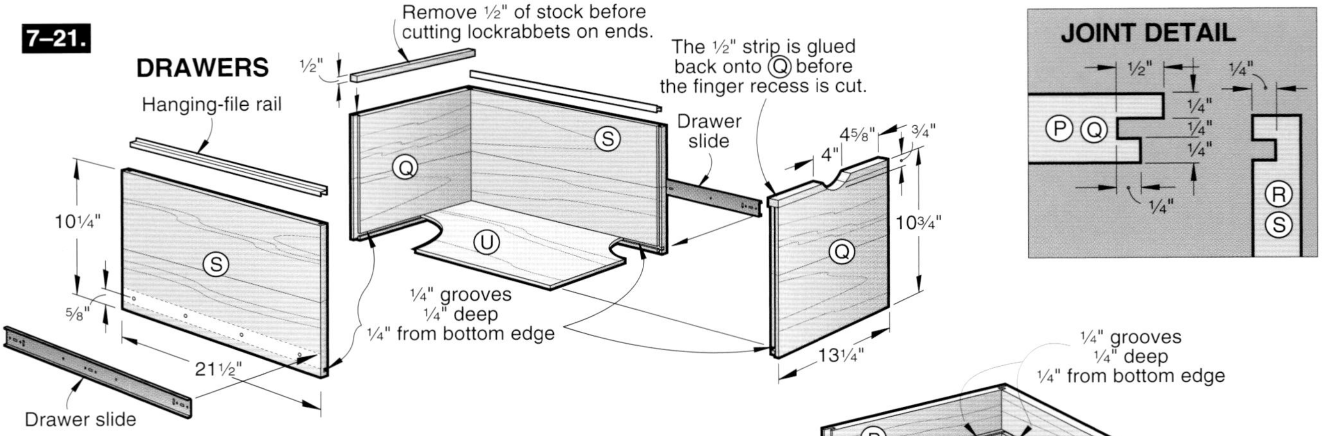

Remove ½" of stock before cutting lockrabbets on ends.
½"
Hanging-file rail
The ½" strip is glued back onto Q before the finger recess is cut.
Drawer slide
4⅝"
¾"
4"
10¼"
10¾"
S
Q
S
U
Q
⅝"
¼" grooves ¼" deep ¼" from bottom edge
21½"
13¼"
Drawer slide
JOINT DETAIL
½"
¼"
¼"
¼"
¼"
¼"
P Q
R S

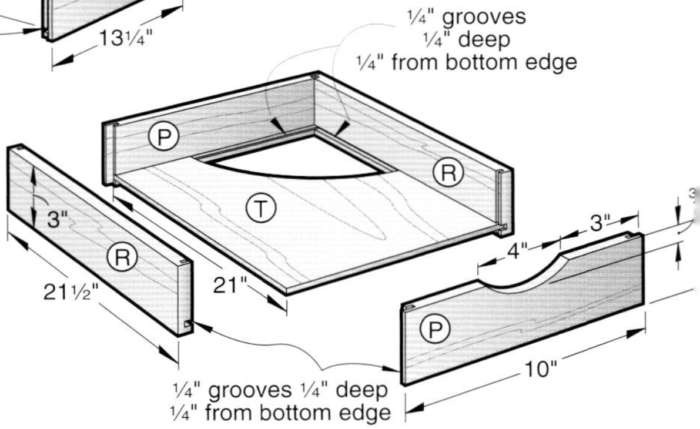

¼" grooves ¼" deep ¼" from bottom edge
P
R
T
3"
R
21½"
21"
4"
3"
P
10"
¼" grooves ¼" deep ¼" from bottom edge

bets shown on **7–21** and the bottom grooves in the drawer parts P, Q, R, and S. Use a follower block to eliminate chip-out and to steady the narrow pencil drawer parts while making the cuts.

4 Retrieve the ½" strips cut from the file drawer fronts and backs (Q). Glue and clamp them to their respective parts. With the glue dry, sand the joints flush.

5 Draw the finger recesses on the pencil and file drawer fronts (P, Q), where shown on the Drawer drawing in **7–21**. Bandsaw, and then sand the recesses.

6 Cut the drawer bottoms (T, U) to size. Glue and clamp the drawers together. Make sure they are square and flat. With the glue dry, sand the corner joints flush.

Build the Drop Leaf and Doors

1 Cut the stiles (V), drop-leaf rails (W), and door rails (X) to size. Set aside some scraps of this stock to test your stub tenon and groove cuts.

2 With your regular tablesaw blade, cut ¼"-deep, centered grooves for the ¼"-plywood panels in the edges of the rails and stiles. To get perfectly sized centered grooves, position the fence to roughly center your scrap stock

7–22. **MACHINING THE DOOR PARTS**

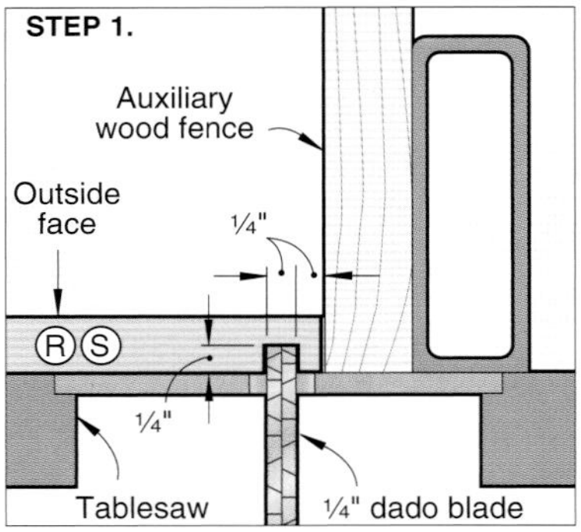

STEP 1.
Auxiliary wood fence
Outside face
¼"
R S
¼"
Tablesaw
¼" dado blade

To make the drawer-side half of the lock-rabbet joint, cut dadoes across the drawer sides' ends.

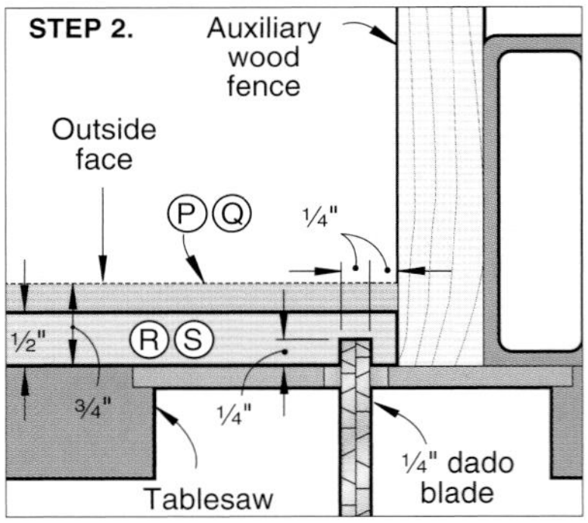

STEP 2.
Auxiliary wood fence
Outside face
P Q
¼"
½"
R S
¾"
¼"
Tablesaw
¼" dado blade

Without moving the blade or fence, cut the drawer-bottom grooves in the fronts and sides.

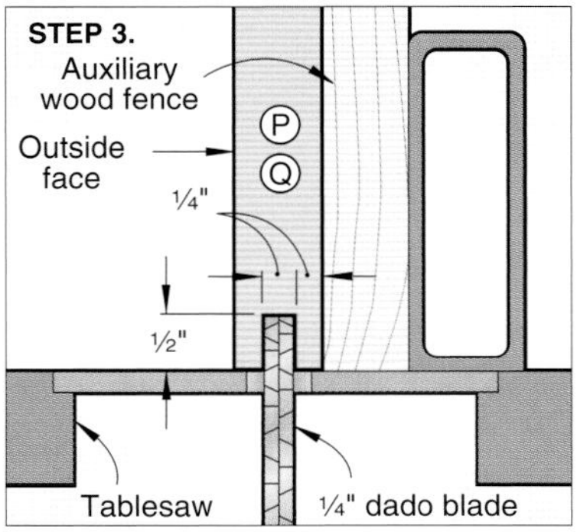

STEP 3.
Auxiliary wood fence
Outside face
P
Q
¼"
½"
Tablesaw
¼" dado blade

To make the drawer-front half of the joint, raise the dado blade and cut grooves in the fronts' ends.

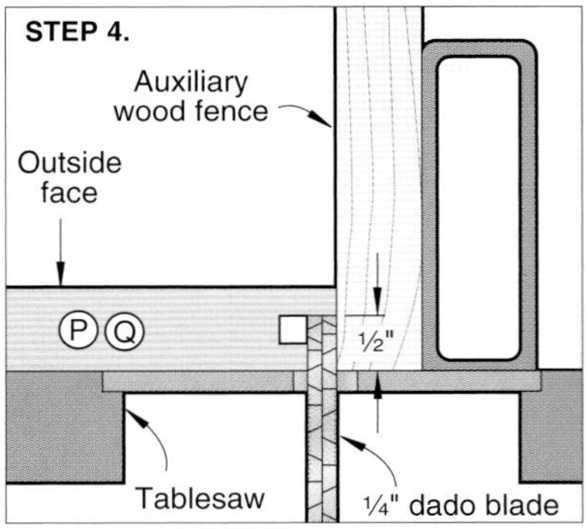

STEP 4.
Auxiliary wood fence
Outside face
P Q
½"
Tablesaw
¼" dado blade

Reposition the fence, and finish the joint by cutting away part of the groove's inside lip.

7–23.

To help align the no-mortise hinges while drilling, push them, knuckle up, against a small scrap block.

on the blade. Make two passes over the blade, turning the scrap around end for end between passes. Test the fit of your plywood. If necessary, nudge the fence toward the blade, and make two passes. Repeat this procedure until a good fit is achieved. Now cut all the grooves in the rails and stiles, where shown in **7–24**. Note that the two center stiles (V) in the drop leaf get grooves along both edges.

3 To form the stub tenons on the ends of the stiles, shown on the Stub Tenon and Groove drawing in **7–24**, install a ¼" dado blade in your tablesaw, and attach an auxiliary extension to your miter gauge. Cut stub tenons, as shown in **7–26**. To ensure a good fit of the tenons in the grooves, first test the blade and stopblock positions with your scrap stock.

4 Cut the drop-leaf panels (Y) and door panels (Z) to size. The panels are an exact fit in their respective frames, so dry-assemble the drop leaf and doors to make sure the parts go

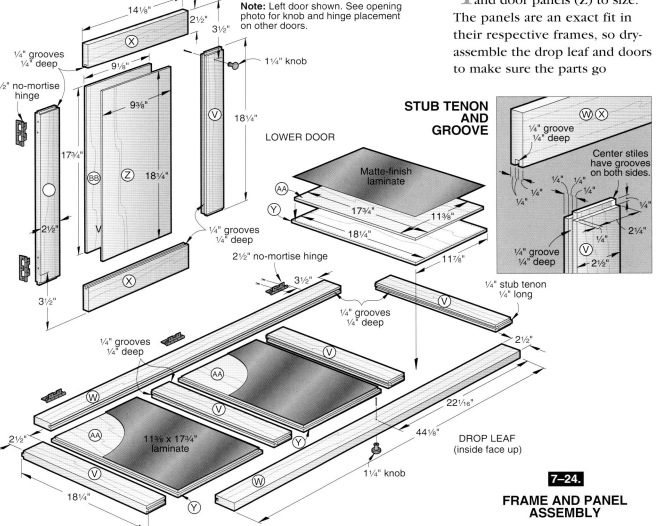

Note: Left door shown. See opening photo for knob and hinge placement on other doors.

STUB TENON AND GROOVE

7–24.

FRAME AND PANEL ASSEMBLY

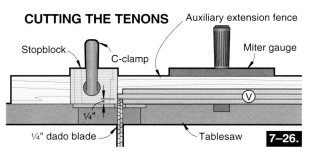

CUTTING THE TENONS

Stopblock · C-clamp · Auxiliary extension fence · Miter gauge · ¼" dado blade · ¼" · Tablesaw · **7–26.**

Left: *Using wedges to hold the doors in place, mark the hinge locations on masking tape adhered to the carcase.* **7–25.**

together properly. Glue and clamp together the drop leaf and doors, check that they are square, and set them on a flat surface to dry.

5 Cut three ¼ x 12⅜ x 18¾" plywood blanks for the drop-leaf liners (AA), and three 12⅛ x 18½" pieces of plastic laminate. (Black matte-finish laminate was used for the computer workstation shown on *pages 119* and *120*.) Adhere the laminate to the liners with contact adhesive, keeping the laminate's edges inside the liners' edges. Check the stile-to-stile and rail-to-rail dimensions of the drop leaf's inside face, and trim the liners to fit, cutting through both the laminate and the plywood. Set the drop-leaf liners aside. Measure the doors for the door liners (BB), and cut them to fit. Glue and clamp the liners to the doors' inside faces.

6 Mark the knob locations, centered on the drop-leaf rail and door stiles, where shown on the Frame and Panel Assembly drawing in **7–24**. Drill the holes. Locate the hinges, and

attach them to the drop leaf and doors, as shown in **7–23**.

7 Transfer the hinge locations from the doors to the carcase, as shown in **7–25**. Position an unmounted hinge on the marks, and use it as a guide to drill the screw pilot holes. Repeat with the drop leaf.

Note: *Before fitting the doors, make sure the carcase is not wracked. If necessary, adjust the levelers until the carcase openings are square.*

Apply the Finish and Assemble the Project

1 Remove the hinges from the drop leaf and doors. Finish-sand all the parts and assemblies to 220 grit. You do not need to sand the inside surfaces of the drop leaf's panels or the backs of the drop-leaf liners. Smooth off any sharp edges with a sanding block.

2 Apply two coats of clear finish, lightly sanding with 220-grit sandpaper between coats. We used gloss polyurethane

for the first coat and satin polyurethane for the second. Do not finish the inside surfaces of the drop leaf's panels or the backs of the drop-leaf liners.

3 Glue and clamp the drop-leaf liners in place. Use plywood scraps to evenly distribute the clamping pressure.

4 Place the top (O) on the carcase, flush at the back and centered side to side, and clamp it in place. Using the holes and slots in the carcase top as guides, drill pilot holes, and secure the top with panhead screws and washers, as shown on the Final Assembly drawing in **7–28**. Remove the clamps.

5 Screw the hinges to the doors, and hang the doors in their openings. Install the magnetic catches, where shown on the Final Assembly drawing in **7–28**. Screw the strike plates to the doors. Mount the knobs.

6 Drill pilot holes, and screw the carcase members of the full-extension drawer slides to

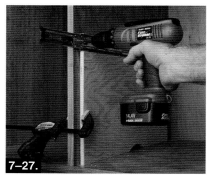

7–27.

To easily and accurately position the drawer slides, clamp an 11¼"-wide plywood spacer to the carcase.

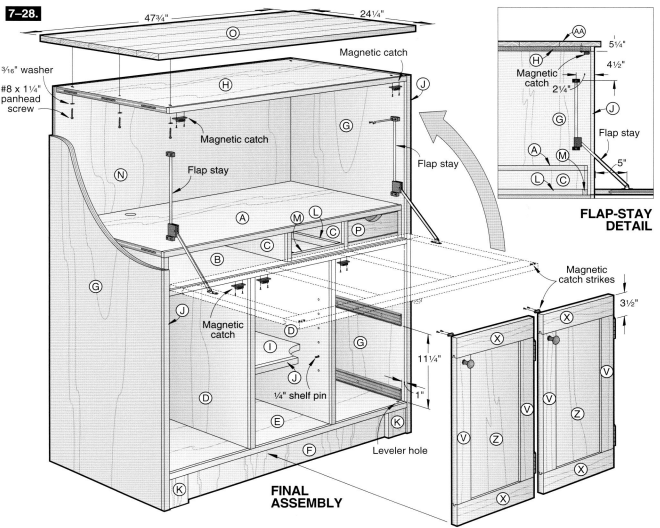

7–28.

47¾" 24¼"

O

³⁄₁₆" washer
#8 x 1¼"
panhead
screw

Magnetic catch

H

J

Magnetic catch

G

Flap stay

N

Flap stay

A   M L

G   C P

B   C

G

J

Magnetic
catch

D

I

G

J

11¼"

¼" shelf pin

D

1"

E

K

Leveler hole

F

K

**FINAL
ASSEMBLY**

AA

5¼"

H

4½"

Magnetic
catch

2¼"

J

G

Flap stay

A   M

5"

L   C

**FLAP-STAY
DETAIL**

Magnetic
catch strikes

3½"

X

X

V

V   V

Z

V

V   Z

X

X

the carcase, where shown on the Final Assembly drawing in **7–28**. The slides' front edges should be 1" back from the carcase's front edge. To position the upper slides, use an 11¼"-wide spacer, as shown in **7–27**. The lower slides sit directly on the bottom (E). Mark pilot hole centerlines ⅝" up from the drawer sides' lower edges. Clamp the slides' drawer members to the drawers, flush at the front. Using the holes in the drawer members as guides, drill pilot holes along the centerlines, and screw the drawer members in place.

Cut the plastic hanging-file rail into 20½" lengths, and slip them over the file drawer sides. Install the drawers

7 Screw the hinges to the drop leaf, and mount the drop leaf on the carcase. Open the doors to support the drop leaf, inserting scrap blocks to hold it horizontal. Mount the flap stays, where shown on the Flap-Stay Detail drawing in **7–28**. Install the knob, and mount the magnetic catches and strikes.

***Note:** The flap stays come with mounting screws. The drop-leaf*

foot is reversible, so you can make a right-hand and a left-hand pair. To speed up opening the drop-leaf, turn in the adjustment screw; to slow opening, back the screw out.

8 Slide the pencil drawers in place. Install the shelf pins and shelf. After you move your computer center to its location, use the levelers to level and true the carcase extra space. To plug in all the components locate a surge suppressor outlet strip in the left-hand cabinet.

STORAGE CABINET

This good-looking unit can neatly accommodate 160 CDs or DVDs in closed drawers.

Building the Drawers

1 Plane stock to ½" thickness, then cut the drawer fronts (A), drawer sides (B), and drawer backs (C) to the sizes in the Materials List. Make one extra drawer side to use later when positioning the drawer guide dadoes in the sides (G).

2 Lay out the drawer sides, and mark the inside surfaces right and left. Install a ½" dado blade in your tablesaw, and cut the dadoes for the backs, where shown on **7–32** (*page 130*). Use a follower block to prevent tearout.

Attach a wood auxiliary fence to your tablesaw rip fence, and position it so the dado blade just grazes its surface. Now, cut the rabbets in the edges of the drawer fronts, once again using a follower block. Drill the counterbored holes for the pulls.

3 Change to a ¼" dado blade, and cut the dadoes for the dividers first, then the grooves for the drawer bottoms in the fronts, sides, and backs. Shim the dado blade to ⁹⁄₃₂", and then cut the drawer guide grooves in the outside surfaces of the drawer sides.

4 Cut the drawer bottoms (D) to the size in the Materials List. Dry-assemble one drawer to check the fit of the drawer bottom, and make any necessary adjustments. Glue and clamp the drawer backs into the dadoes in the sides, slide the drawer bottoms into their grooves, and then glue and clamp the fronts in place. Check the drawers for square, and place them on a flat surface while the glue dries.

5 Check the dado-to-dado lengths for the dividers (E, F), then cut them to size. Chuck a ¼" straight bit in your table-mounted router, and rout the slots in the dividers, as shown in **7–29**, on *page 130*. Interlock the two dividers, and slide them into the mating dadoes in the drawers for compartmentalized storage.

Make a Carcase to Fit the Drawers

1 Cut the sides (G) to an oversize width of 11¾", and the top and base (H) to an oversize width of 12¼"—both to the length shown in the Materials List. Chuck a chamfer bit in your router. Then rout ⅜" chamfers on the front inside edges of the sides and both ends and front edges of the top and base, as shown on the Exploded View drawing in **7–35** (*page 132*).

This attractive storage cabinet is designed to keep your CD collection organized behind closed drawers.

2 Rip off the chamfered edges of the sides (G) to the width listed for the side molding (I), and those of the top and base (H) to the width listed for the top and base molding (J). Mark the mating pieces for reassembly later, as shown in **7–30**.

With the edges just ripped against your tablesaw fence, cut parts (G) and (H) to their final width.

3 Install a ¼" dado blade in your tablesaw, and cut dadoes for the sides in the top and base (H), where shown on the Parts View drawing in **7–34** (*page 131*).

Note: Measure the outside width of your drawers. The dimension between the dadoes in the top and base (H) must be ⅛" greater. Make any necessary adjustments to the location of the dadoes for a good fit.

Cut the rabbets for the back (N) in the inside back edges of the sides (G). Next, cut the rabbets on the ends of the sides so they fit snugly into the dadoes in the top and base. Finally, rout a stopped rabbet between the side dadoes in the top and base. See the Top and Parts View drawings in **7–34**.

4 Prepare to cut the drawer guide dadoes in the sides (G) by making an indexing strip ⅜" wide

MATERIALS LIST FOR STORAGE CABINET

PART		FINISHED SIZE			MTL.	QTY.
		T	W	L		
A	drawer fronts	½"	6½"	11½"	O	5
B	drawer sides	½"	6½"	10½"	O	10
C	drawer backs	½"	6½"	11"	O	5
D	drawer bottoms	¼"	8¼"	11"	H	5
E	dividers	¼"	6"	11"	H	5
F	dividers	¼"	6"	8¼"	H	5
G*	sides	¾"	10⅞"	37⅜"	EO	2
H*	top/base	¾"	10⅞"	14⅛"	EO	2
I**	side molding	¾"	⅝"	36⅞"	O	2
J**	top/base molding	¾"	1⅛"	14⅛"	O	2
K	drawer guides	¼"	½"	10½"	O	10
L	front	¾"	4"	11⅝"	O	1
M	cleats	¾"	¾"	4"	O	2
N	back	¼"	12⅛"	37⅞"	H	1

*Parts initially cut oversized; see instructions.
**Parts cut from oversize parts (G, H).
Materials Key: O = Red oak; H = Tempered hardboard;
EO = Edge-joined oak.
Supplies: #8 x 1¼" flathead wood screws (8); #6 x ¾" flathead
wood screws (18); pulls (5); stain; finish.

CUTTING DIAGRAM FOR STORAGE CABINET

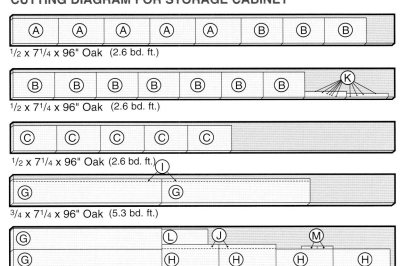

½ x 7¼ x 96" Oak (2.6 bd. ft.)

½ x 7¼ x 96" Oak (2.6 bd. ft.)

½ x 7¼ x 96" Oak (2.6 bd. ft.)

¾ x 7¼ x 96" Oak (5.3 bd. ft.)

¾ x 11¼ x 96" Oak (8 bd. ft.)

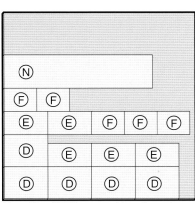

¼ x 48 x 48" Tempered hardboard

7-29.

Center the bit between the two fences that capture the dividers. A stopblock controls the length of the slot.

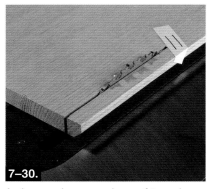

7-30.

Index marks on a piece of tape in the path of the cut ensure proper reassembly later on.

7-31.

To prevent tear-out when making a dado cut, back your workpiece with a scrap softwood follower block.

and 10½" long that fits snugly in a ¼" dado and a 3⁵⁄₁₆" long spacer block. Install a ¼" dado blade in your tablesaw, and adjust it to cut ¼" deep. Position the rip fence 3⁹⁄₁₆" to the right of the blade. Fit your miter gauge with an auxiliary fence to support the workpiece and reduce tear-out. Using the rip fence as a stop, cut the top drawer guide dado in each side.

5 Fit the indexing strip in one of the dadoes you just cut, and place the extra drawer side over the strip, engaging the groove in the drawer side. Push the drawer side toward the bottom end of the side (G) to take up the ¹⁄₃₂" play in the groove, and clamp it in place. Position the 3⁵⁄₁₆" spacer against the bot-

tom of the drawer side, and mark the top of the next drawer-guide dado, as shown in **7-33**.

Use the marked side to reposition the rip fence, and cut the second dado in both sides. Now, repeat this process until you have cut all the drawer-guide dadoes.

6 Align the index marks on the side moldings (I) with those on the sides (G), mark

SHOP TIP

A Tip for Building the Storage Unit Cabinet

To prevent tear-out when making a dado cut, back your workpiece with a scrap softwood follower block as shown in 7-31.

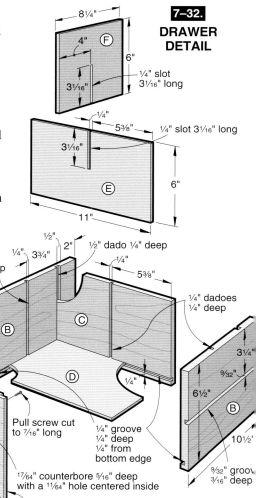

7-32.
DRAWER DETAIL

8¼"
4"
F
6"
¼" slot 3¹⁄₁₆" long
3¹⁄₁₆"

¼"
5⅜"
¼" slot 3¹⁄₁₆" long
3¹⁄₁₆"
6"
E
11"

½"
2"
½" dado ¼" deep
¼"
3¾"
¼"
5⅜"
¼" dado ¼" deep
⁹⁄₃₂" groove ³⁄₁₆" deep
½" rabbet ¼" deep
B
C
¼" dadoes ¼" deep
5⅝"
¼"
D
3¼"
6½"
A
¼"
⁹⁄₃₂"
3"
Pull screw cut to ⁷⁄₁₆" long
¼" groove ¼" deep ¼" from bottom edge
6½"
B
4¼"
3"
¹⁷⁄₆₄" counterbore ⁵⁄₁₆" deep with a ¹¹⁄₆₄" hole centered inside
10½"
11½"
⁹⁄₃₂" groove ³⁄₁₆" deep
3" brass pull
½" rabbet ¼" deep
¼" groove ¼" deep ¼" from bottom edge

7–33.

Use a craft or utility knife to mark the location of the top of the next dado in the carcase side.

trim lines at the shoulders of the top and bottom rabbets in the sides, and trim the moldings to length. Glue and clamp the side moldings to the sides, and the top and base moldings (J) to the top and base (H).

7 Cut the drawer guides (K) to size, as shown on the Exploded View drawing in **7–35**. Chamfer one end of each, and glue and clamp them in the side dadoes, centered front to back.

Note: *To allow for seasonal wood movement, the guides should be ⅛" shorter than the sides. Glue only 1" at the center of each guide.*

8 Glue the tongues on the ends of the sides into the dadoes in the top and base. Clamp the assembly, check it for square, and place it on a flat surface to dry.

9 To check the width of the front (L), slide the bottom

drawer into place. Measure the distance from the bottom of the drawer front to the top of the base (H). Subtract ¹⁄₁₆" from this dimension for the width of (L). Cut the front to size, and rout the rabbet in the ends and bottom, as shown on the Exploded View drawing in **7–35**. Remove the drawer, and set it aside.

10 Cut the cleats (M) to size. The length of the cleats should be the same as the width of the front. Drill the countersunk shank holes in the cleats. Using the shank holes as guides, drill pilot holes into the front,

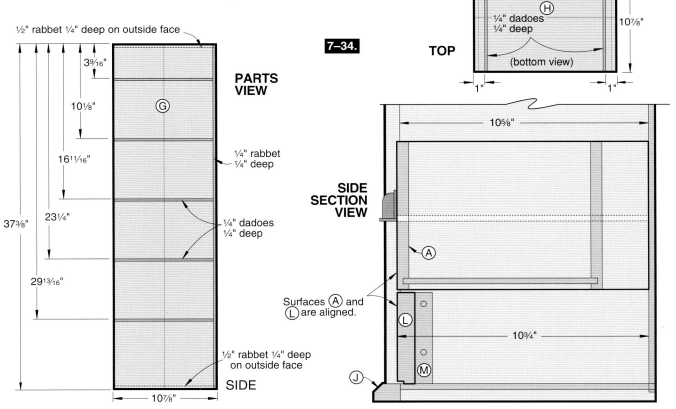

7–34.

and screw the cleats to the front. Again, using the shank holes as guides, drill pilot holes into the sides, and screw the front to the sides, where shown on the Side Section View drawing in **7–34** (*page 131*).

Measure the rabbeted opening, and cut the back (N) to size. With the back in place, drill pilot and countersunk shank holes. Now, screw the back firmly in place.

Applying a Finish and Final Assembly

1 Remove the dividers from the drawers. Finish-sand all surfaces and edges through 220-grit. Remove sanding dust and apply stain, following the manufacturers directions.

2 When the stain is dry, apply two coats of satin polyurethane, sanding with 220-grit sandpaper between coats.

3 Let the finish dry for 24 hours, trim the screws, and install the pulls. (Your local home center will sell pulls.) Reinstall the dividers, and slide the drawers in place.

4 Fill the drawers with CDs. Store eight in each compartment for easy retrieval. Now, place the cabinet in a convenient spot and enjoy a happy tune.

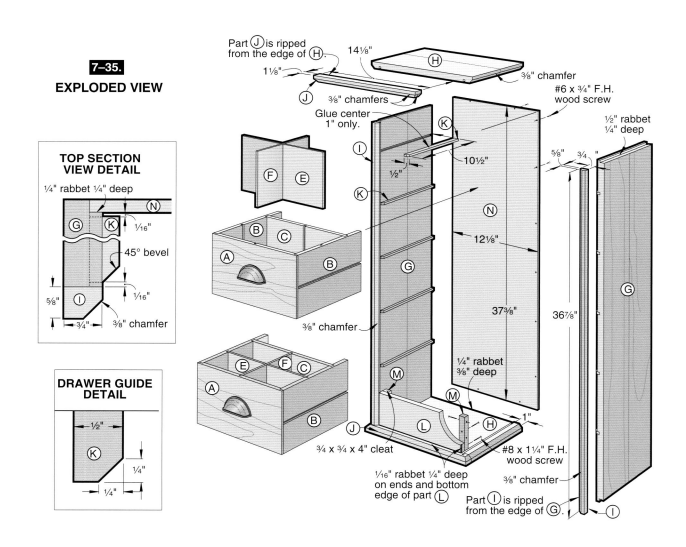

7–35.

EXPLODED VIEW

CHAPTER 8

showcases for collectibles

 *COLLECTIONS ARE AS NUMEROUS AND varied as the people who do the collecting, and each type requires housing. Of course, certain types of collections, such as mounted butterflies, benefit from complete enclosure in drawers or chests. Exposure to light would dim the specimens' hues. Other collections are meant to be seen or even touched for full appreciation—and that's the form of collection that's addressed by the projects in this chapter.*

The first project, shown on page 134, is a wonderful cherry, glass-fronted collector's cabinet. Its mirrored back reflects the details of the items enclosed, and it has a handy, concealed storage compartment. What's more, it's easy to build.

If you've been seeking the perfect display for Grandma's floral chinaware, turn to page 139 for the country-style plate rack. It has down-home charm and places cups, plates, and serving pieces on display. (For a different look, you might opt to build it in a fine hardwood, such as walnut.)

Finally, for those with a grand collection to show off, turn to the freestanding lighted showcase on page 144. Its spacious dimensions and glass shelves offer plenty of room to arrange your precious pieces. And its traditional style will do justice to whatever you choose to place inside.

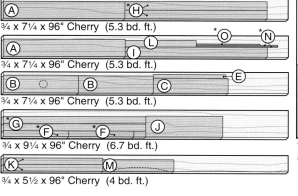

As shown in the insert, a drop-down panel, masquerading as three small drawers, conceals a storage compartment in this collector's cabinet.

MATERIALS LIST FOR COLLECTOR'S CABINET

PART	FINISHED SIZE			MTL.	QTY.
	T	W	L		
CASE					
A sides	¾"	6"	41"	C	2
B top and bottom	¾"	6"	25¼"	C	2
C shelf	¾"	5¼"	25¼"	C	1
D back	¼"	25¼"	40¼"	BP	1
E shelf rail	¾"	1¼"	24½"	C	1
F hanging cleats	½"	2"	21½"	C	2
MOLDING					
G cove blanks	⅝"	2½"	48"	C	2
H round-over blanks	½"	3"	48"	C	2
I bevel blank	¾"	3⅜"	48"	C	1
PANEL AND DOOR					
J drawer panel	¾"	7¼"	26"	C	1
K stiles	¾"	2¼"	33½"	C	2
L lower rail	¾"	2¼"	24"	C	1
M upper rail	¾"	4"	24"	C	1
N vertical stops	¼"	⅜"	27½"	C	2
O horizontal stop	¼"	⅜"	21½"	C	1

Materials Key: C = Cherry; BP = Birch plywood.
Supplies: #8 x 1" and #8 x 1½" flathead wood screws; #0 biscuits; #17 x ¾" brads; ⅛ x 24 x 30" mirror; 21⅞" x 28⅞" single-strength glass; ¼ x 5 x 24¼" glass shelves (3); mirror adhesive; #8 x 2" flathead wood screws or hollow wall anchors to fasten the hanging cleat to the wall.
Blades and Bits: Stack dado set; ½" cove, ⅜" round-over, ¼" rabbeting, and chamfer router bits.
Hardware: Statuary bronze 2½" nonmortise hinges (4); press-in magnetic catches with strikes (4); 1⅛" pewter-finish brass knobs (4); shelf supports (12); recessed canister light fixture.

COLLECTOR'S CABINET

Give your favorite collectibles maximum visibility while keeping them safely stored behind glass. Made of dark-stained cherry, this design features easy-to-make built-up crown and base moldings; a mirrored back; built-in lighting;

CUTTING DIAGRAM FOR COLLECTOR'S CABINET

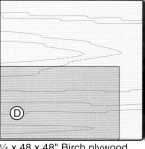

Ⓐ　　　　*Ⓗ
¾ x 7¼ x 96" Cherry (5.3 bd. ft.)

Ⓐ　Ⓛ　*Ⓞ　*Ⓝ
　　Ⓘ
¾ x 7¼ x 96" Cherry (5.3 bd. ft.)

Ⓑ　Ⓑ　Ⓒ　Ⓔ
¾ x 7¼ x 96" Cherry (5.3 bd. ft.)

*Ⓖ　*Ⓕ　*Ⓕ　Ⓙ
¾ x 9¼ x 96" Cherry (6.7 bd. ft.)

Ⓚ　Ⓜ
¾ x 5½ x 96" Cherry (4 bd. ft.)

Ⓓ

¼ x 48 x 48" Birch plywood

*Plane or resaw to the thicknesses listed in the Materials List.

and onboard storage behind a drop-down "drawer" panel. And when you're ready to hang your cabinet, interlocking cabinet and wall cleats make dead-level, rock-solid mounting a snap.

Make the Case First

1 Cut the sides (A), top and bottom (B), and shelf (C) to the sizes in the Materials List. With a dado blade, cut the rabbets and dadoes in the sides, where shown in **8–1**. Then cut the grooves for the back in the sides, top, and bottom, where shown in **8–1, 8–2,** and **8–3**. Form

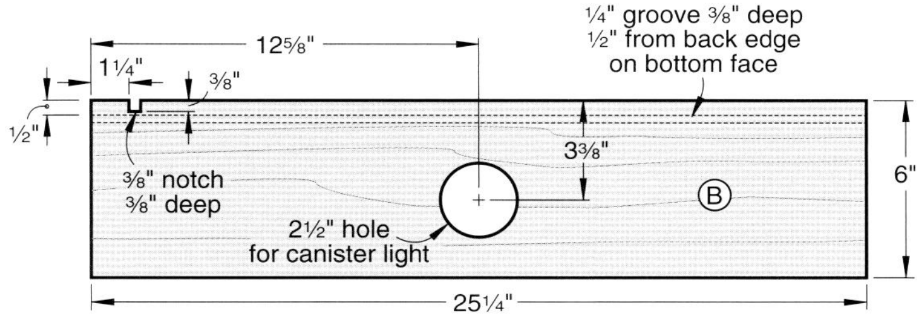
12⅝"
1¼"
⅜"
½"
¼" groove ⅜" deep
½" from back edge
on bottom face
3⅜"
6"
⅜" notch
⅜" deep
2½" hole
for canister light
B
25¼"

8–2. TOP

8–3. COLLECTOR'S CABINET EXPLODED VIEW

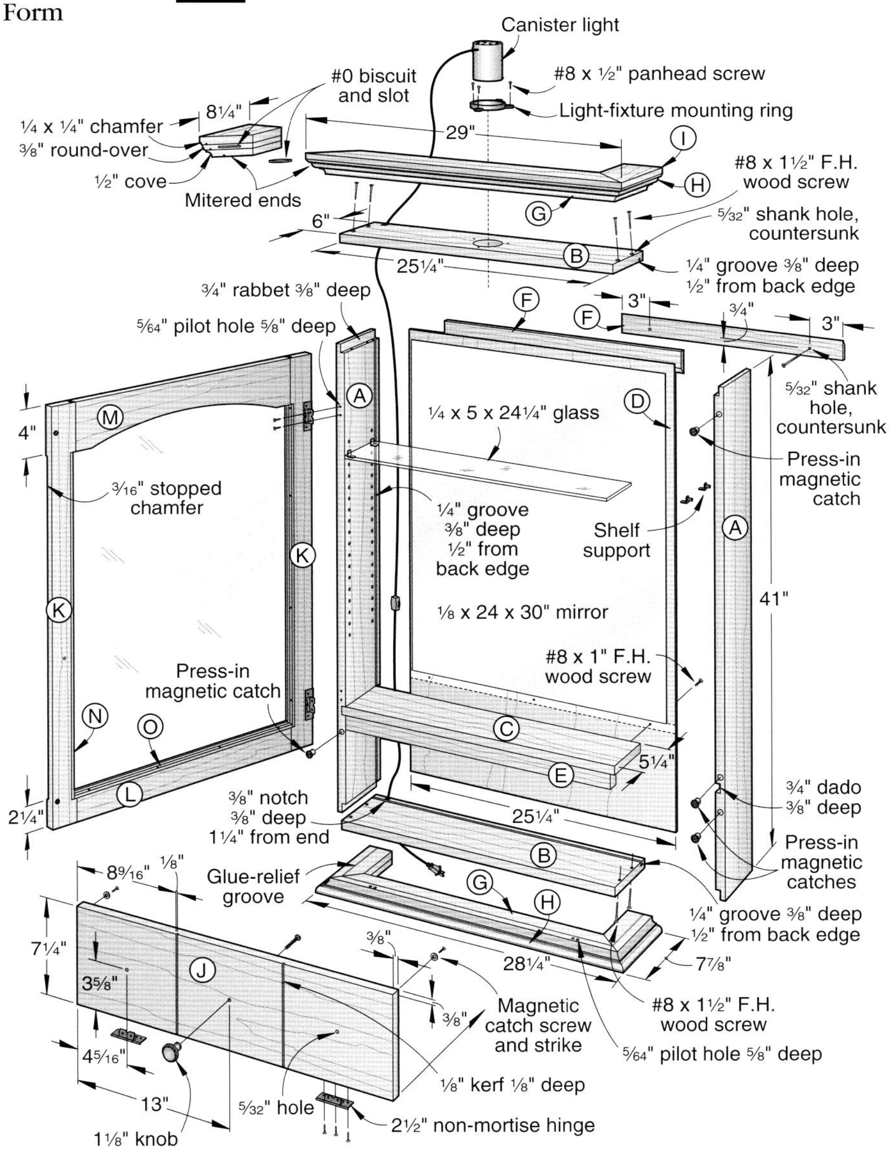
Canister light
#0 biscuit
and slot
#8 x ½" panhead screw
Light-fixture mounting ring
8¼"
¼ x ¼" chamfer
⅜" round-over
½" cove
Mitered ends
29"
I
H
#8 x 1½" F.H.
wood screw
G
6"
⁵⁄₃₂" shank hole,
countersunk
25¼"
B
¼" groove ⅜" deep
½" from back edge
¾" rabbet ⅜" deep
F
F
3"
¾"
3"
⁵⁄₆₄" pilot hole ⅝" deep
⁵⁄₃₂" shank
hole,
countersunk
4"
M
A
¼ x 5 x 24¼" glass
D
Press-in
magnetic
catch
³⁄₁₆" stopped
chamfer
¼" groove
⅜" deep
½" from
back edge
Shelf
support
K
A
K
41"
⅛ x 24 x 30" mirror
#8 x 1" F.H.
wood screw
Press-in
magnetic catch
N
O
C
5¼"
E
L
2¼"
⅜" notch
⅜" deep
1¼" from end
25¼"
¾" dado
⅜" deep
B
Press-in
magnetic
catches
8⁹⁄₁₆"
⅛"
Glue-relief
groove
G
H
¼" groove ⅜" deep
½" from back edge
7¼"
⅜"
28¼"
7⅞"
3⅝"
J
⅜"
Magnetic
catch screw
and strike
#8 x 1½" F.H.
wood screw
4⁵⁄₁₆"
⁵⁄₆₄" pilot hole ⅝" deep
⅛" kerf ⅛" deep
13"
⁵⁄₃₂" hole
2½" non-mortise hinge
1⅛" knob

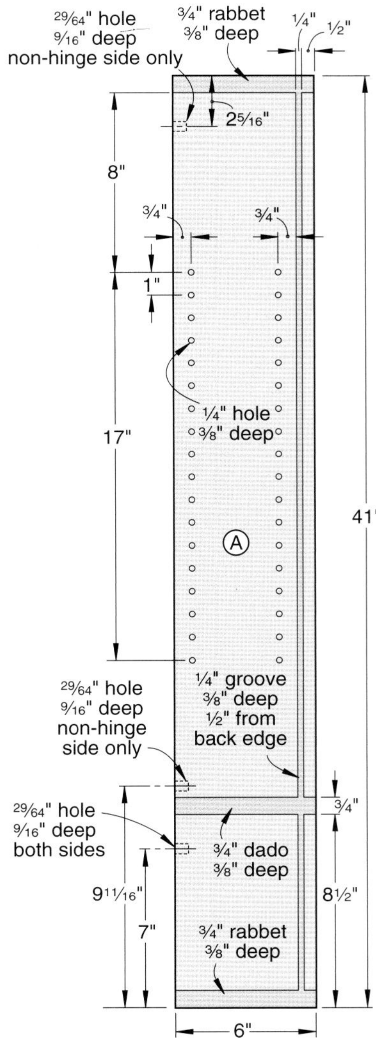
²⁹⁄₆₄" hole
⁹⁄₁₆" deep
non-hinge side only
¾" rabbet
⅜" deep
¼"
½"
2⁵⁄₁₆"
8"
¾"
¾"
1"
¼" hole
⅜" deep
17"
A
41"
²⁹⁄₆₄" hole
⁹⁄₁₆" deep
non-hinge
side only
¼" groove
⅜" deep
½" from
back edge
¾"
²⁹⁄₆₄" hole
⁹⁄₁₆" deep
both sides
¾" dado
⅜" deep
9¹¹⁄₁₆"
8½"
7"
¾" rabbet
⅜" deep
6"

8–1. SIDE SECTION

lamp cord notches in the top and bottom. Use a Forstner bit or a holesaw to bore a 2½" hole in the top (B) for the recessed canister light.

Note: Depending on the location of the nearest electrical outlet, you may wish to cut the cord notches near the opposite ends of the top and bottom. Also, the hole in the top (B) is for installing a self-ventilating light fixture. If you use a different fixture, check its hole size, and whether or not you have to vent the cabinet to avoid heat buildup.

2 With a ²⁹⁄₆₄" bit in your drill press, drill holes for the press-in magnetic catches in the

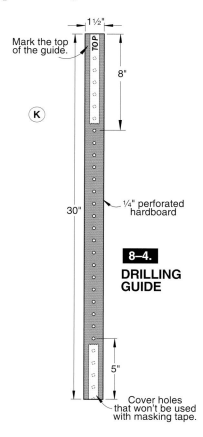

Mark the top of the guide.

TOP

1½"

8"

K

30"

¼" perforated hardboard

8–4.
DRILLING GUIDE

5"

Cover holes that won't be used with masking tape.

8–5. **HANGING CLEATS**

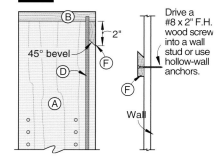

B

2"

45° bevel

F

D

A

F

Wall

Drive a #8 x 2" F.H. wood screw into a wall stud or use hollow-wall anchors.

8–6. **BUILT-UP MOLDINGS**

CROWN

3⅜"

¾"

I

¼" chamfer

2¾"

⅛" saw kerfs ⅛" deep

3"

½"

H

2¼"

⅜" round-over

2½"

⅝"

G

⅞"

½" cove

BASE (See dimensions above.)

G

H

sides' front edges, (dimensioned on **8–1**, *page 135*). There are three catches in the right-hand side and one in the left-hand side.

3 Attach a stop collar to your drill bit, and drill the shelf-support holes in the sides (A). To do this quickly and accurately, make the drilling guide shown in **8–4**. Mark the guide's top, where shown. Align the top of the guide with the top rabbets' shoulder. When drilling the front rows of holes, align the guide's edge with the sides' front edges. For the rear rows, align the guide with the

front edge of the groove for the back.

4 Cut the back (D) to size. Capturing the back in the grooves in the top, bottom, and sides, and inserting the shelf (C), glue and clamp the case together, checking it for square. With the glue dry, drill angled countersunk screw holes through the top and bottom and into the sides, and straight countersunk screw holes through the back and into the shelf. Drive the screws.

5 Cut the shelf rail (E) to size. Glue and clamp it to the shelf, where shown in **8–3**.

6 Cut the hanging cleats (F) to size, and bevel-rip them, where shown in **8–5**. Glue and

Crown molding

Base molding

8–7.

Glue and clamp the crown molding assembly (G/H/I) and base molding assembly (G/H) to the case, centered side to side and flush with the case's back.

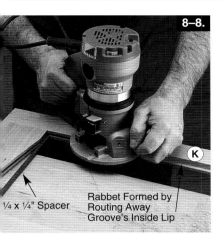

When routing away the groove's inside lip, cut a ¼ x ¼" spacer to friction-fit between the stiles (K). The bit's pilot bearing contacts the spacer, stopping the bit before it cuts into the upper rail (M).

clamp one cleat, centered side to side, to the cabinet's back.

Note: *To clear a cord notch located at either end of the top (B), the hanging cleat must be shorter than the back's width.*

Cut the Crown and Base

1 Cut the molding blanks (G, H, I) to the sizes listed. With the appropriate bits in your table-mounted router, form the edge profiles shown in **8–6**. Then, to prevent glue from squeezing out at the front when laminating the crown and base blanks, cut ⅛ x ⅛" saw kerfs. Glue and clamp the crown and base blanks together, keeping their ends and back edges flush.

2 Miter-cut the glued-up crown and base blanks to the lengths shown in **8–3** (*page 135*). Now cut slots for #0 biscuits, centered

in the thicknesses of the blanks and the lengths of the miters, and glue, biscuit, and clamp the mitered parts together. With the glue dry, sand the moldings to 220 grit.

3 Glue and clamp the completed molding assemblies to the cabinet case, as shown in **8–7**.

Add a Hinged Panel

1 Cut the drawer panel (J) to size. Then make the two saw kerfs and drill the knob holes where shown in **8–3**, in *page 135*.

2 With their knuckles against the front of the panel (J), position the hinges' large leaves on the bottom edge of the panel, where shown in **8–9**. Drill ⁵⁄₆₄" pilot holes, and drive the supplied screws. Then draw lines on the cove molding (G)

½" away from and parallel to the front edge of the bottom (B), where shown. Clamp scrap cleats to the sides (A) to keep the panel's ends flush with the sides. Now, with the panel captured between the cleats, align the holes in the hinges' small leaves with the marked lines on the cove molding (G), drill pilot holes, and drive the screws.

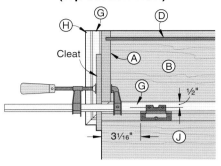

8–9. **PANEL HINGE LOCATION**
(top section view)

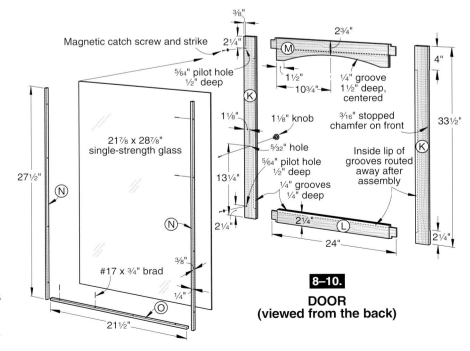

8–10.

DOOR
(viewed from the back)

Next, Build the Door

1 Cut the stiles (K), lower rail (L), and upper rail (M) to the sizes indicated in the Materials List. With a dado blade, cut the centered ¼" grooves ¼" deep in the stiles and lower rail, where shown on **8–10** (*page 137*). Then raise the blade, and cut the 1½"-deep groove in the upper rail.

2 To form the mortises centered in the stiles' grooves, chuck a ¼" brad-point bit in your drill press and drill overlapping holes, where shown in **8–11**. Then clean up the mortises' sides, and square the ends with a chisel.

3 With a dado blade in your tablesaw, and an auxiliary extension attached to your miter gauge, cut the tenons shown in **8–11** on the rails (L, M). Form the tenons' faces first, and then turn the rails on edge and cut

the haunches. For consistent cuts, clamp a stopblock to the auxiliary extension.

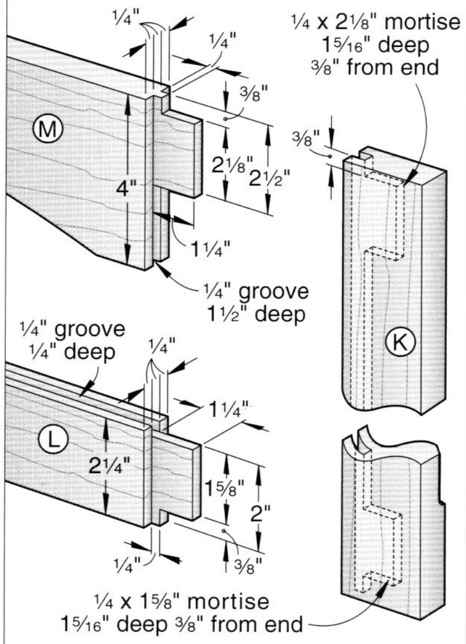

4 Mark the ends and center of the arch on the upper rail (M). Bend a fairing stick to connect the points, and draw the curve. Bandsaw and sand the arch.

5 Glue and clamp the door, checking for square. Once the glue is dry, sand the joints smooth.

6 Create a rabbet on the door to accept the glass by chucking a ¼" rabbeting bit in your handheld router, and routing away the ¼" groove's inside lip on the stiles (K) and lower rail (L). To avoid routing into the upper rail (M), insert a spacer, as shown in **8–8** (*page 137*). Avoid chip-out by removing the lip in several shallow passes, or by climb-cutting. Square the rabbet's corners with a chisel.

7 To rout the stopped chamfers on the door's outside face, cut a pair of ½ x ¾" stopblocks, one 4⅛" long for the top and one 2⅜" long for the bottom. Clamp them to the door's edge, flush at the top and bottom, and rout the chamfers, as shown in **8–12**. Repeat on the door's other edge.

8 Cut and fit the vertical stops (N) and horizontal stop (O). Cut the head off a #17 x ¾" brad, and use it to drill pilot holes in the stops, where shown in **8–10** (*page 137*).

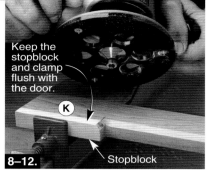

Keep the stopblock and clamp flush with the door.

K

8–12.   Stopblock

Stopblocks that are ½ x ¾" are clamped to the door's edges to stop the chamfer bit's pilot bearing, and also to prevent chip-out. The 4⅛"-long top stopblock is shown here.

9 To install the door hinges, first place them with their knuckles against the case side, where shown in **8–13**. The countersunk holes in the small leaves should face down. Drill the pilot holes. Now place the hinges on the door with their knuckles against the door's edge, as shown. The countersunk holes in the large leaves should face up.

8–11.
MORTISE AND TENON DETAILS

¼"

¼"   ¼ x 2⅛" mortise 1⁵⁄₁₆" deep ⅜" from end

⅜"

M   ⅜"

4"   2⅛"   2½"

1¼"

¼" groove 1½" deep

¼" groove ¼" deep   ¼"

K

L   1¼"

2¼"   1⅝"   2"

¼"   ⅜"

¼ x 1⅝" mortise 1⁵⁄₁₆" deep ⅜" from end

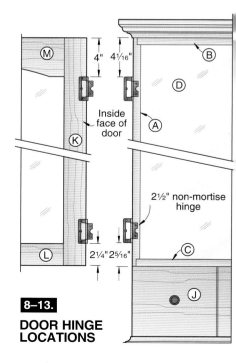

M   4"   4¹⁄₁₆"   B

D

Inside face of door

K   A

2½" non-mortise hinge

L   2¼"   2⁵⁄₁₆"   C

J

8–13.
DOOR HINGE LOCATIONS

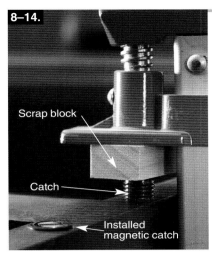

8–14.

Scrap block

Catch

Installed
magnetic catch

Press the magnetic catches into place using a clamp. Insert a small block of wood between the catch and the clamp's jaw to protect the catch and the case's finish.

Drill the pilot holes. Drill the knob screw hole, where shown in **8–10** (*page 137*).

Apply the Finish and Install the Hardware

1 Remove the drawer panel's hinges, and sand all the parts to 220 grit. Apply the finish. (To get the finish on the cabinet shown on *page 134*, apply a dark mahogany oil-based stain, and then spray on three coats of satin lacquer, sanding between coats with 320-grit sandpaper.)

2 Have the mirror, door glass, and glass shelves cut to size. (Specify a polished pencil edge on all edges of the shelves, and have the mirror's sharp edges removed.) Lay the cabinet on its back, apply mirror adhesive (available at your local glass shop or at hardware stores and home centers), and install the mirror. Push the mirror snug

against the shelf (C), and center it side to side. Let the adhesive cure for 48 hours.

3 Press the magnetic catches into their holes, as shown in **8–14**. Position the door glass, and nail in the stops. Fill the brad holes with a matching color putty stick. Screw the hinges to the panel and the door, and then screw the hinges to the case. Fasten the knobs. Drill pilot holes and mount the magnetic catch-strike plates. (If the flat-head screws provided do not sit flush with the strikes' surfaces, countersink them more deeply.)

4 Drill pilot holes, and screw the canister light's mounting ring to the top of the top (B). Slide the canister into the ring so that its top is even with the top of the crown, and tighten the clamping screw.

5 Drill countersunk holes through the wall hanging cleat. Making sure it is level, fasten the cleat to the wall, either screwing into the wall framing or using hollow wall anchors. Hang the cabinet, interlocking its cleat with the one on the wall, and placing the cord in the top and bottom notches. Install the shelf supports and shelves. Arrange your items, close the door, and switch on the light. Now step back, and admire your collection and your craftsmanship.

COUNTRY PLATE RACK

If your tastes lean toward country, this great-looking plate rack offers practicality, plus timeless charm. It's big enough to easily house a service for twelve. You can paint it in classic colors, as shown on *page 140*, or finish it to match your own decorating theme.

Make the Plate Rack Sides

1 Cut the sides (A) to the size given in the Materials List from ¾" stock. (Kiln-dried pine was used for the plate rack shown on *page 140*.) Poplar is another good choice.

2 On a 12 x 14" piece of paper, lay out the gridded side pattern (A) in **8–21** (*page 144*). Adhere the pattern to the bottom end of one side piece.

3 Using double-faced tape, adhere the two side pieces face to face, with the edges and ends flush. Cut to shape the bottom end of the taped-together pieces. (A jigsaw can be used). Now, sand the contoured edges flush.

4 Referring to the Section View drawing in **8–16** (*page 142*), mark outlines for the locations of parts D, E, and F. Mark the six centerpoints, and drill ¹⁄₁₆" guide holes (you'll drill them to exact size later), which you'll use for securing parts D, E, and F later

*This country plate rack offers practicality plus charm. It measures 53"
from top to bottom and just over 4' wide, and will easily store a setting
for twelve. You can paint it in classic colors, as shown here, or finish it
to match your own decorating theme.*

on. Use a wooden wedge to separate the pieces, being careful
not to mar the soft wood. Remove the tape. Drill a counterbored
mounting hole centered over each ¹⁄₁₆" guide hole on the outside
face of each side piece. (See the Screw Hole detail in **8–15** for
reference.)

5 Cut ¾" dadoes and rabbets ¼" deep across the inside face of
the side pieces, where dimensioned on the Section View
drawing in **8–16** (*page 142*). Now, rout a ½" rabbet ⅜" deep
along the back inside edge of each side piece, terminating the
rabbet at the bottom dado. Then chisel the bottom end of the
rabbet square.

Make the Shelves, Dividers, Rails, and Back Boards

1 Cut the shelves and top (B), dividers (C), top front rail (D),
bottom back rail (E), and back top rail (F) to the sizes in
the Materials List.

2 For housing the dividers (C), cut a pair of ¾" dadoes ¼"
deep in the two middle shelves (B). (See the Exploded View
drawing in **8–15** and **8–18**, *page 143*, for reference.)

MATERIALS LIST FOR COUNTRY PLATE RACK

PART	FINISHED SIZE T	W	L	MTL.	QTY.
A sides	¾"	11¼"	53"	P	2
B shelves & top	¾"	10¾"	47"	P	4
C dividers	¾"	10¾"	12⅞"	P	2
D top front rail	¾"	4½"	46½"	P	1
E bottom back rail	¾"	3"	46½"	P	1
F top back rail	¾"	3"	46½"	P	1
G back boards	½"	5⅞"	44"	P	8
H front crown molding	3¼" wide		*	P	1
I side crown molding	3¼" wide		*	P	2
J dowel-mount strips	⅜"	¾"	25⅝"	P	4
K divider dowels	⅜" dia.		12⅜"	BD	30
L pin rail	⅜"	¾"	39"	P	1
M shelves	¾"	10½"	9⅞"	P	2

*Length depends on actual width of pine crown
molding (width may vary between manufacturers).
Materials Key: P = Pine; BD = Birch dowel.
Supplies: #8 x 1½" flathead wood screws;
1" brads; #8 x 1½ nails; 1¼" solid-brass cup
hooks (8); latex paint; stain; clear finish; spindles
and shelf clips; 1½" spindles with ¼" tenons (13);
¼"-diameter brass-plated shelf pins (8).

CUTTING DIAGRAM FOR COUNTRY PLATE RACK

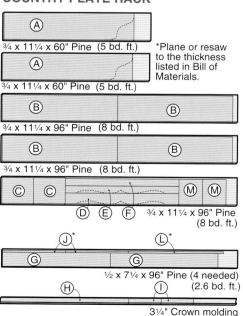

Ⓐ
¾ x 11¼ x 60" Pine (5 bd. ft.)

Ⓐ
¾ x 11¼ x 60" Pine (5 bd. ft.)

*Plane or resaw
to the thickness
listed in Bill of
Materials.

Ⓑ   Ⓑ
¾ x 11¼ x 96" Pine (8 bd. ft.)

Ⓑ   Ⓑ
¾ x 11¼ x 96" Pine (8 bd. ft.)

Ⓒ Ⓒ   Ⓜ Ⓜ
Ⓓ Ⓔ Ⓕ ¾ x 11¼ x 96" Pine (8 bd. ft.)

Ⓙ*   Ⓛ*
Ⓖ   Ⓖ
½ x 7¼ x 96" Pine (4 needed) (2.6 bd. ft.)

Ⓗ   Ⓘ
3¼" Crown molding

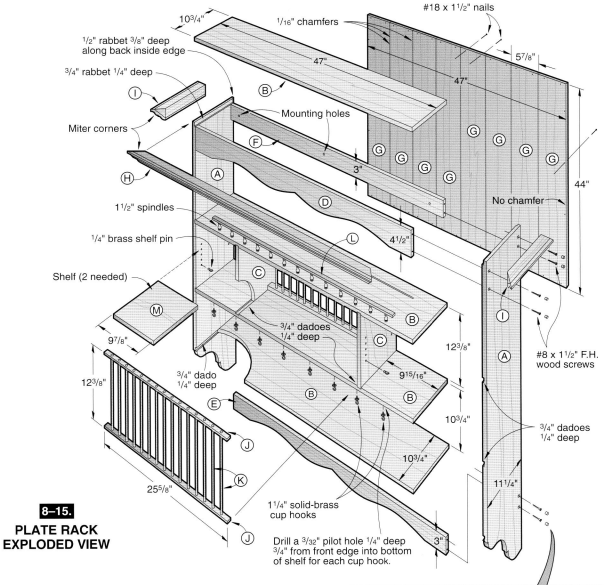

1/16" chamfers

#18 x 1 1/2" nails

10 3/4"

1/2" rabbet 3/8" deep
along back inside edge

47"

47"

5 7/8"

3/4" rabbet 1/4" deep

Miter corners

Mounting holes

44"

No chamfer

1 1/2" spindles

3"

1/4" brass shelf pin

4 1/2"

Shelf (2 needed)

3/4" dadoes
1/4" deep

12 3/8"

#8 x 1 1/2" F.H.
wood screws

9 7/8"

3/4" dado
1/4" deep

9 15/16"

3/4" dadoes
1/4" deep

12 3/8"

10 3/4"

11 1/4"

10 3/4"

1 1/4" solid-brass
cup hooks

25 5/8"

3"

8–15.

**PLATE RACK
EXPLODED VIEW**

Drill a 3/32" pilot hole 1/4" deep
3/4" from front edge into bottom
of shelf for each cup hook.

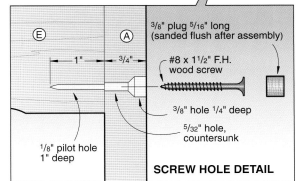

E   A

3/8" plug 5/16" long
(sanded flush after assembly)

1"   3/4"

#8 x 1 1/2" F.H.
wood screw

3/8" hole 1/4" deep

5/32" hole,
countersunk

1/8" pilot hole
1" deep

SCREW HOLE DETAIL

3 Make a shelf-hole template, as shown in the Shelf-
Hole Template drawing in **8–16**, on *page 142*.
Use the template and a portable drill fitted with a
brad-point bit to drill 1/4" holes 3/8" deep on the inside
face of the dividers (C). Trim 1/4" off the bottom end
of the template. Now, as shown in **8–17**, clamp the
template in place and drill 1/4" holes 3/8" deep on
the inside face of the side pieces (A), where shown
on the Section View drawing in **8–16**.

8–16.

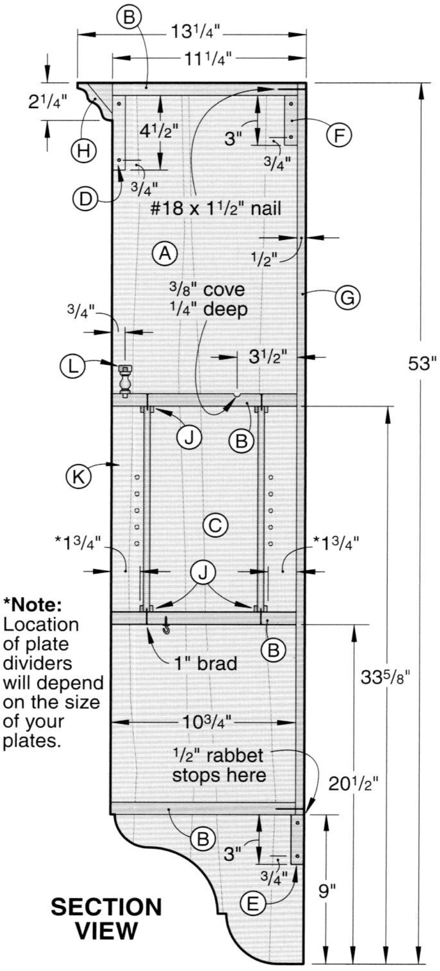
B
13 1/4"
11 1/4"
2 1/4"
H
4 1/2"
3"
3/4"
F
D
3/4"
#18 x 1 1/2" nail
A
1/2"
3/8" cove
1/4" deep
G
3/4"
L
3 1/2"
53"
J
B
K
C
*1 3/4"
*1 3/4"
J
*Note:
Location of plate dividers will depend on the size of your plates.
1" brad
B
33 5/8"
10 3/4"
1/2" rabbet stops here
20 1/2"
B
3"
3/4"
E
9"
SECTION VIEW

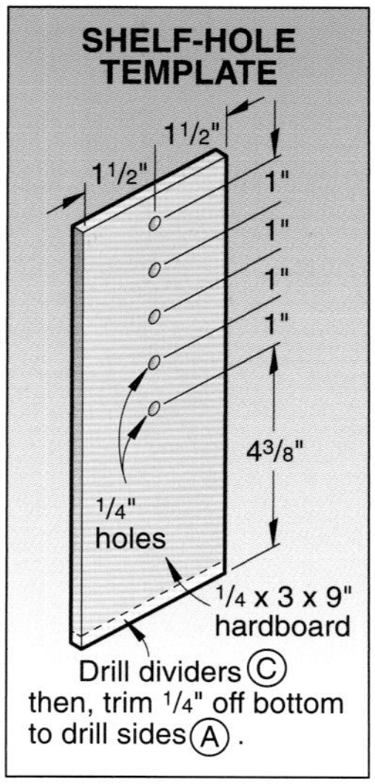
SHELF-HOLE TEMPLATE
1 1/2"
1 1/2"
1"
1"
1"
1"
4 3/8"
1/4" holes
1/4 x 3 x 9" hardboard
Drill dividers C
then, trim 1/4" off bottom
to drill sides A.

4 Mark spindle-location centerlines on the top surface of one shelf, dimensioned in **8–18**. Drill the holes, but do not erase the marked centerlines yet. (To allow for just a bit of free play when attaching the spindles later, use a 17/64" drill bit. Test-drill the holes first to determine the size of bit you'll need. Tenon size on spindles varies slightly.)

5 For making the plate groove in the top shelf (B), mount a 3/8" core-box bit to your table-mounted router. Position the fence, and clamp stops to the fence. (You may have to attach an auxiliary wooden fence to your regular router-table fence for one long enough to clamp stops to.) Rout a 3/8" groove 1/4" deep and 3 1/2" from the back edge of the top shelf, shown in **8–18**. Terminate the plate groove 2" from each end.

6 Enlarge the gridded Bottom Back Rail half-pattern shown in **8–21** and lay it out on a 5 x 48" piece of paper. Fold the pattern in half and cut the pattern to shape. Adhere it to the bottom front edge of the top-rail blank (D). Cut and sand the piece to shape, using it as a template to transfer the pattern to the bottom back rail (E). Cut and sand to shape.

7 Glue and clamp the shelves and dividers (B, C) between the sides (A). Slide the rails (D, E, F) in place, and drive the screws. Check for square. Make sure the back edges of the shelves don't protrude into the rabbets cut in the back inside edges of the side pieces. You'll fit the back boards (G) into these rabbets next.

8 Cut the 1/2"-thick back boards (G) to size. Check their fit in the rabbeted back of the plate rack. Allow 1/8" clearance at the two outside edges for expansion. Cut a 1/16" chamfer along the front edge of each, where shown on **8–15** (*page 141*). Do not install the back boards yet.

Add the Decorative Crown Molding

1 To add the pine crown molding (H, I) to the rack, purchase a 3 1/4"-wide by 8'-long piece at a local home center. Select a straight, dry 2 x 4, and glue it to the back of the crown molding, where shown in *Step 1* of **8–19**. Rip the edges, where shown in *Steps 1* and *2*.

For equally spaced holes and level shelves, make a template and drill 1/4" holes for the shelf pins.

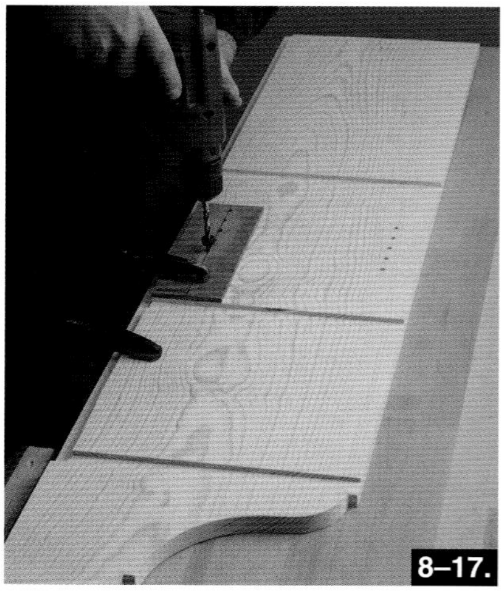

8–17.

8–18.

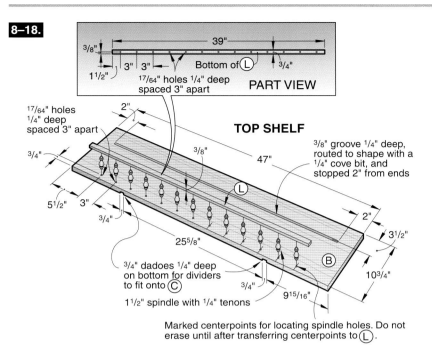

PART VIEW

3/8" · 39" · 3/8"
1 1/2" · 3" · 3" · Bottom of (L) · 3/4"
17/64" holes 1/4" deep spaced 3" apart

TOP SHELF

17/64" holes 1/4" deep spaced 3" apart

3/4"

2"

3/8"

47"

3/8" groove 1/4" deep, routed to shape with a 1/4" cove bit, and stopped 2" from ends

(L)

5 1/2"

3"

3/4"

25 5/8"

2"

3 1/2"

(B)

10 3/4"

3/4" dadoes 1/4" deep on bottom for dividers to fit onto (C)

3/4"

9 15/16"

1 1/2" spindle with 1/4" tenons

Marked centerpoints for locating spindle holes. Do not erase until after transferring centerpoints to (L).

8–19.

RIPPING THE CROWN MOLDING

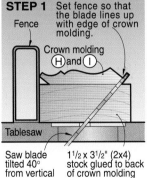

STEP 1 Set fence so that the blade lines up with edge of crown molding.

Fence

Crown molding (H) and (I)

Tablesaw

Saw blade tilted 40° from vertical

1 1/2 x 3 1/2" (2x4) stock glued to back of crown molding

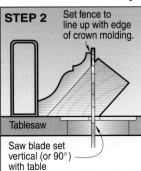

STEP 2 Set fence to line up with edge of crown molding.

Tablesaw

Saw blade set vertical (or 90°) with table

4 Assemble (without glue) the plate dividers (J, K), and check their fit in the plate rack. You want the assemblies to slide in easily now because they will tighten after the project has been painted. Trim the dowels if necessary.

5 Cut the pin rail (L) to size. Center it end to end against the front edge of the top shelf (B), and use a square to transfer the marked centerlines on the top shelf to the pin rail. Use your drill press, fitted with a fence and stop, to drill the holes in the pin rail where marked. Now, erase or sand off the marked centerlines from both the pin rail (L) and the top shelf.

6 Glue the spindles into the holes in the pin rail. Then, fit (without glue) the bottom ends of the spindles into their mating holes in the top shelf and let the

2 Measure and miter-cut the front piece (H) to length, and glue it to the top front of the plate rack. Repeat for the sides (I).

Cut and Install the Plate-Divider and Pin-Rail Assemblies

1 Cut the four dowel-mount strips (J) to size. Tape them together face to face, with the edges flush.

2 Mark the hole centerpoints on the top piece, where dimensioned in **8–20**. Mount a fence to your drill-press table to keep the holes centered edge to edge, and drill the ⅜" holes through all four taped-together pieces.

3 From ⅜" birch or maple dowel stock, crosscut the 30 plate divider dowels (K) to length.

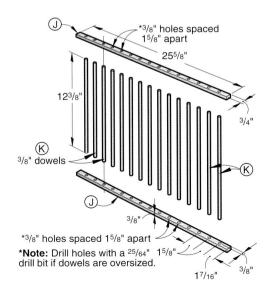

(J)

*3/8" holes spaced 1 5/8" apart

25 5/8"

12 3/8"

3/4"

(K)

3/8" dowels

(K)

(J)

3/8"

*3/8" holes spaced 1 5/8" apart

Note: Drill holes with a 25/64" drill bit if dowels are oversized.

1 5/8"

3/8"

1 7/16"

8–20. **PLATE DIVIDER (two needed)**

 **Gridded patterns for the TOP FRONT RAIL, BOTTOM BACK RAIL, and the SIDES**

1 square equals 1 inch

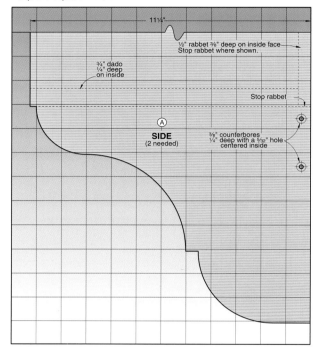

glue dry. This step aligns the spindles so you can glue them in place in the top shelf later on.

7 Cut the shelves (M) to size. Put shelf pins in the holes, and then test-fit the shelves.

Paint and Stain for a Contrasting Finish

1 Cut ⅜" plugs ⁵⁄₁₆" long, and glue one into each counter-bored hole. Sand the plugs flush.

2 Finish-sand all the parts, sanding through 320-grit.

3 Paint the plate rack, as shown on *page 140*. Stain the remaining pieces (G, K, J, L) and the spindles. (For an even

stain, apply wood conditioner to the pieces according to the directions on the can, stain the pieces with an Early American stain, and finish-coat them with a fast-drying satin polyurethane.)

4 Mark the cup-hook center-points on the bottom side of the second shelf (B). Drill pilot holes, and screw the hooks in place. Nail the back boards (G) in place with #18 x 1½" nails. Using 1" brads, nail the plate dividers and spindle assembly in place.

LIGHTED SHOWCASE

This spacious cabinet, measuring 18 x 37 x 83", includes a full-view sliding glass door; an easy-to-make built-up crown, and halogen accent lights with three output levels. Of course, there's a lot of glass in this project, and it will run you a little more than $200. Lights and hardware will add approximately $80. Although the one shown on the facing page is built from mahogany, you could use any number of less expensive woods, including oak. But keep in mind that a comparable store-bought piece will cost you $1,500 to $2,200. Savings aside, no amount of money can replace the satisfaction you'll get by building this beauty yourself.

***Note:** The following instructions describe how to build the curio cabinet with a right-sliding door. To build it with a left-sliding door, switch the positions of the wide and narrow stiles (A, B) at the front of the cabinet; reverse the orientation of the cabinet's full-extension slides; and attach the door edge (DD), shown in **8–33** (page 152), on the opposite side of the door.*

Start with the Sides

1 Cut the wide stiles (A), narrow stile (B), top rails (C), middle rails (D), and bottom rails (E) to the sizes indicated in the Materials List.

Display your collectibles and craftsmanship with this lighted cabinet. A sliding door makes access easy.

2 Cut a ¼" groove ¼" deep, centered along one edge of the stiles (A, B) and bottom rails (E), and on both edges of the middle rails (D), where shown in **8–22** and **8–23** (*pages 147* and *148*). Raise the blade to 1¼", and cut a groove centered along one edge of the top rails (C).

3 Using a 2"-wide scrap, cut and test-fit a ¼" tenon in a stile's groove. When satisfied, cut the tenons on the ends of the rails (C, D, E), where dimensioned in **8–23**.

4 Make four full-size copies of the end pattern in **8–38** (*page 154*). Cut out the shaded part of the patterns for the top rails (C). Using spray adhesive,

CUTTING DIAGRAM FOR LIGHTED SHOWCASE

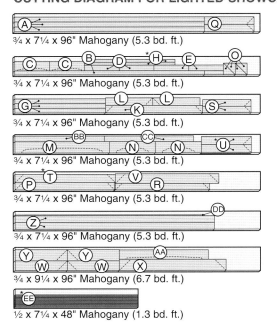

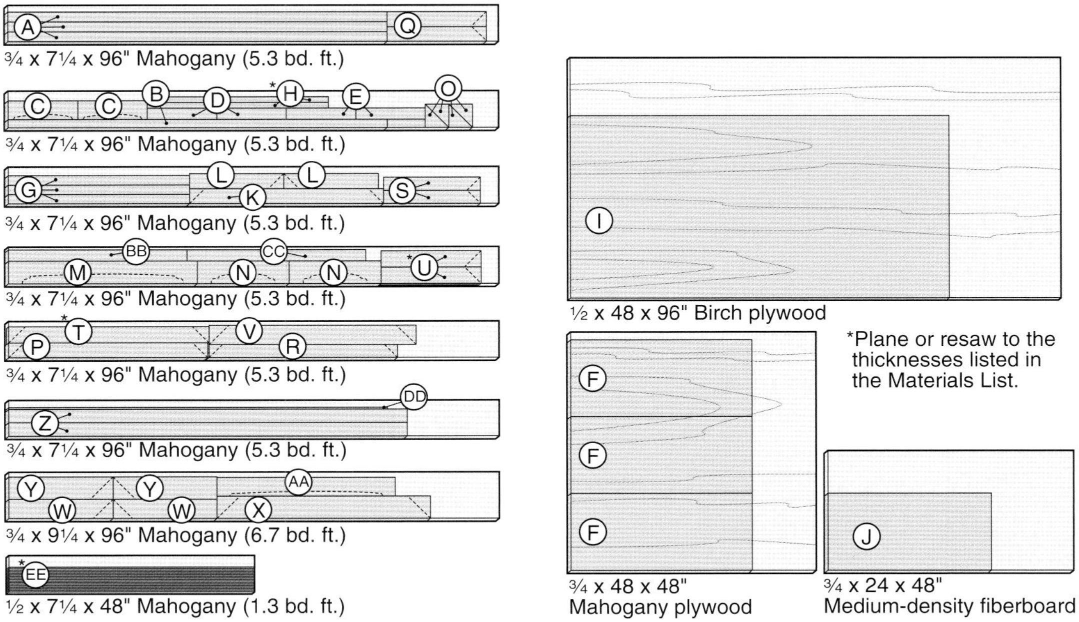

Ⓐ ————————————— Ⓠ
¾ x 7¼ x 96" Mahogany (5.3 bd. ft.)

Ⓒ   Ⓒ   Ⓑ   Ⓓ   *Ⓗ   Ⓔ   Ⓞ
¾ x 7¼ x 96" Mahogany (5.3 bd. ft.)

Ⓖ   Ⓛ   Ⓚ   Ⓛ   Ⓢ
¾ x 7¼ x 96" Mahogany (5.3 bd. ft.)

Ⓜ   ⒷⒷ   ⒸⒸ   Ⓝ   Ⓝ   Ⓤ
¾ x 7¼ x 96" Mahogany (5.3 bd. ft.)

Ⓟ   Ⓣ*   Ⓥ   Ⓡ
¾ x 7¼ x 96" Mahogany (5.3 bd. ft.)

Ⓩ   ⒹⒹ
¾ x 7¼ x 96" Mahogany (5.3 bd. ft.)

Ⓨ   Ⓦ   Ⓨ   Ⓦ   Ⓧ   ⒶⒶ
¾ x 9¼ x 96" Mahogany (6.7 bd. ft.)

*ⒺⒺ
½ x 7¼ x 48" Mahogany (1.3 bd. ft.)

Ⓘ
½ x 48 x 96" Birch plywood

*Plane or resaw to the thicknesses listed in the Materials List.

Ⓕ
Ⓕ
Ⓕ
¾ x 48 x 48"
Mahogany plywood

Ⓙ
¾ x 24 x 48"
Medium-density fiberboard

MATERIALS LIST FOR LIGHTED SHOWCASE

PART		FINISHED SIZE			MTL.	QTY.
		T	W	L		
CABINET						
A	wide stiles	¾"	2"	74¼"	M	3
B	narrow stile	¾"	1⅝"	74¼"	M	1
C	top rails	¾"	3¾"	13⅝"	M	2
D	middle rails	¾"	2¼"	13⅝"	M	2
E	bottom rails	¾"	2¼"	13⅝"	M	2
F	shelves	¾"	15½"	35½"	MP	3
G	shelf edging	¾"	1⅞"	35½"	M	3
H	shelf trim	¼"	1⅛"	35½"	M	2
I	back	½"	36½"	74¼"	BP	1
BASE						
J	base panel	¾"	15½"	32"	MDF	1
K	front trim	¾"	3"	38"	M	1
L	side trim	¾"	3"	18½"	M	2
M	front skirt	¾"	4½"	37"	M	1
N	side skirts	¾"	4½"	18"	M	2
O	corner blocks	¾"	4½"	4½"	M	4
CROWN						
P*	bullnose front	¾"	3"	38"	M	1
Q*	bullnose sides	¾"	3"	18½"	M	2
R*	flat front	¾"	2⁹⁄₁₆"	37⅛"	M	1
S*	flat sides	¾"	2⁹⁄₁₆"	18¹⁄₁₆"	M	2
T*	middle front	½"	3³⁄₁₆"	38⅜"	M	1
U*	middle sides	½"	3³⁄₁₆"	18¹¹⁄₁₆"	M	2
V*	cove front	¾"	3⅞"	39¾"	M	1
W*	cove sides	¾"	3⅞"	19⅜"	M	2
X*	cap front	¾"	4½"	41"	M	1
Y*	cap sides	¾"	4½"	20"	M	2
DOOR						
Z*	stiles	¾"	2¾"	74⅛"	M	2
AA	top rail	¾"	3¾"	35"	M	1
BB	middle rail	¾"	2¼"	35"	M	1
CC	bottom rail	¾"	2¼"	35"	M	1
DD	door edge	⅜"	¾"	74⅛"	M	1
EE*	glass stop blanks	¼"	⅜"	48"	M	16

*Parts initially cut oversized. See the instructions.
Materials Key: M = Mahogany; MP = Mahogany plywood;
BP = Birch plywood; MDF = Medium-density fiberboard.
Supplies: Spray adhesive; #20 biscuits; #8 x 1¼", #8 x 1½", and
#8 x 1¾" flathead wood screws; #4 x ½" and #4 x ¾" panhead
screws; #16 x ¾" brads; mirror mastic; ⅛ x 13½ x 28⅝" glass (2);
⅛ x 13½ x 39⅛" glass (2); ⅛ x 31⅞ x 28½" glass (1); ⅛ x 31⅞ x
39⅛" glass (1); ⅛ x 35⅜ x 29⅛" mirror (1); ⅛ x 35⅜ x 40⅞" mirror
(1); 16 x 35⅛" glass for shelves (3), ¼", ⅜", or ½" thick to suit load-
support needs; cloth-backed, double-faced tape.
Blades and Bits: Dado-blade set; ¼" and ½" rabbeting; ⅜" and ½"
round-over, ¼" roundnose, and ½" cove router bits; ¼" brad-point drill bit.
Hardware: Halogen light set with four 20-watt lights with brass finish,
transformer, and two power blocks; three-level touch pad dimmer; 2'
dual connector cable; ¼" shelf supports, polished brass, white-vinyl
coated (12); 28" full-extension slides (3).

attach the patterns to the ends of the rails, aligning
them with the tenons' shoulders. (Flip over the
pattern at one end of each rail.) Using a ⅛"-thick
wood fairing strip 16" long, lay out the rails' curved
bottom, where dimensioned, connecting the
patterns. Bandsaw and sand to the lines.

5 Mark the location of the middle rails (D) on the
stiles (A, B), where dimensioned in **8–22**. Glue
and clamp the stiles and rails (C, D, E) together,
checking for square. When the glue dries, sand the
side assemblies to 220 grit.

6 Form ¼" rabbets ½" deep for the glass and glass
stops (EE) in the side assemblies, where shown
in **8–22** and **8–25** (*page 148*), by removing the
inside lip of the assemblies' ¼ x ¼" grooves. Climb-
cut the lip to eliminate tearout. To stop the rabbets
below the top rails (C), cut a ¼ x ¼" stopblock to
fit between the stiles. Clamp the stopblock to each
top rail and rout, as shown in **8–24** (*page 148*).
Square the rabbets' corners with a chisel.

7 Cut a ½" rabbet ½" deep along the back inside
edge of each side's rear stile (A) to receive the
back (I), where shown in **8–22** and **8–25**.

Add the Shelves and Back

1 Cut the shelves (F) to size. Mark centerlines
on the top of the ¾"-thick shelves for the #20
biscuit slots centered in the shelves' ends, where
dimensioned. Now, plunge-cut the slots.

2 Cut the shelf edging (G) to size. Now, glue and
clamp the edging to the shelves, aligning their
top edges and ends. In the top shelf, drill ½" holes
for wires, where dimensioned in **8–22**.

3 From ¼"-thick stock, cut the shelf trim (H) to
size. Next, glue the trim to the top of the center
and bottom shelves' edging (G), aligning their back
edges so the trim overhangs the edgings' front by ⅜".

4 Mark lines across the length of each side
assembly's rails (C, D, E), where dimensioned in
8–22, to locate the horizontal centers of the mating
biscuit slots. Mark the vertical centerlines
of the biscuits across these lines along the same

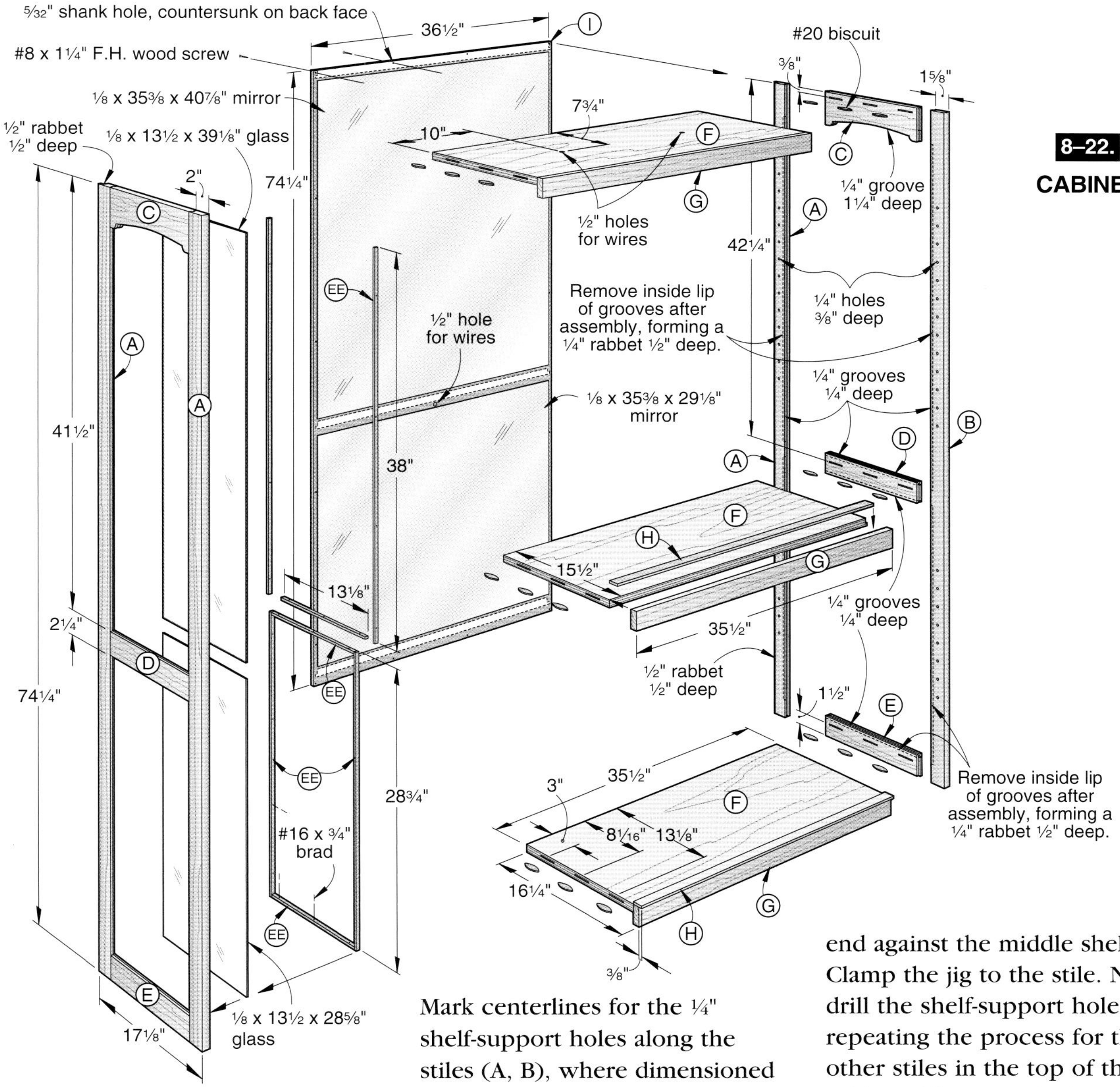
5⁄32" shank hole, countersunk on back face
#8 x 1¼" F.H. wood screw
36½"
I
⅛ x 35⅜ x 40⅞" mirror
½" rabbet
½" deep
⅛ x 13½ x 39⅛" glass
2"
74¼"
C
A
A
41½"
2¼"
D
74¼"
E
17⅛"
⅛ x 13½ x 28⅝" glass
EE
13⅛"
EE
EE
#16 x ¾" brad
EE
28¾"
38"
½" hole
for wires
10"
7¾"
F
G
½" holes
for wires
Remove inside lip
of grooves after
assembly, forming a
¼" rabbet ½" deep.
⅛ x 35⅜ x 29⅛"
mirror
#20 biscuit
⅜"
1⅝"
C
¼" groove
1¼" deep
A
42¼"
¼" holes
⅜" deep
¼" grooves
¼" deep
B
D
A
F
H
G
15½"
35½"
¼" grooves
¼" deep
½" rabbet
½" deep
1½"
E
Remove inside lip
of grooves after
assembly, forming a
¼" rabbet ½" deep.
3"
35½"
F
8 1⁄16"
13⅛"
16¼"
G
H
⅜"

8–22.
CABINET

dimensions as for the shelves, measuring from the rabbeted edge of the rear stiles (A). Plunge-cut the slots.

5 Glue, biscuit, and clamp the side and shelving assemblies together, checking for square.

6 Set the cabinet on its side on a large, flat surface. Mark centerlines for the ¼" shelf-support holes along the stiles (A, B), where dimensioned in **8–25** (*page 148*) and the Exploded View drawing in **8–28** (*page 149*).

7 Make a hole-drilling jig, as shown in the Shop Tip "Drilling with Perforated Hardboard Jigs." Center the jig's holes over one shelf-support centerline in the top of the cabinet, and position its bottom end against the middle shelf (F). Clamp the jig to the stile. Now drill the shelf-support holes, repeating the process for the other stiles in the top of the cabinet. Then cut the jig where shown, and drill the holes in the bottom of the cabinet.

8 Position the cabinet face down on your work surface. Cut the back (I) to fit into the rabbeted opening. Drill mounting holes through the back, where shown in **8–22**. Locate the holes ⅜" from the

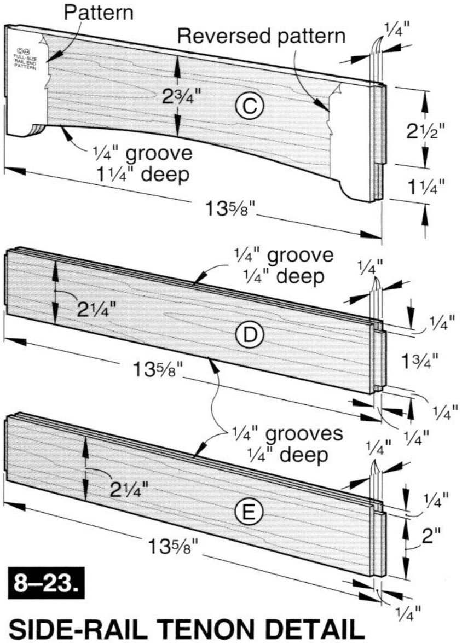
Pattern
Reversed pattern
1/4"
2 3/4"
C
2 1/2"
1/4" groove
1 1/4" deep
1 1/4"
13 5/8"
1/4" groove
1/4" deep
1/4"
2 1/4"
D
1/4"
1 3/4"
13 5/8"
1/4"
1/4" grooves
1/4" deep
1/4"
1/4"
2 1/4"
E
1/4"
2"
13 5/8"
1/4"

8–23.

SIDE-RAIL TENON DETAIL

8–25. **RIGHT SIDE ASSEMBLY**

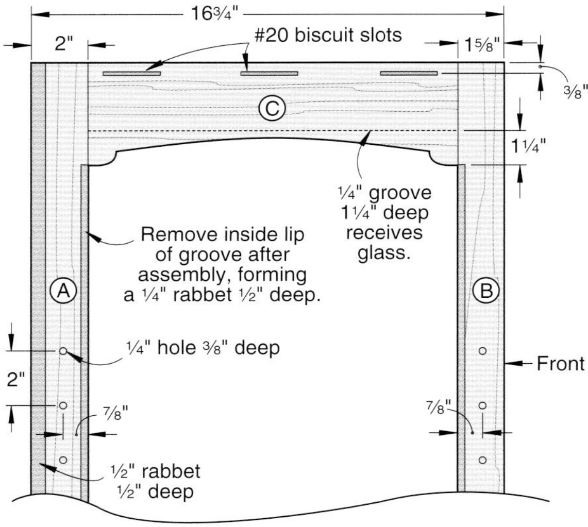
16 3/4"
#20 biscuit slots
2"
1 5/8"
3/8"
C
1 1/4"
1/4" groove
1 1/4" deep
receives
glass.
Remove inside lip
of groove after
assembly, forming
a 1/4" rabbet 1/2" deep.
A
B
1/4" hole 3/8" deep
Front
2"
7/8"
7/8"
1/2" rabbet
1/2" deep

back's top and bottom edges and 1/4" from its sides. Drive the screws. Drill a 1/2" hole for wires through the back where shown, countersinking its edges.

Build a Sturdy Base

1 Cut and miter-cut the base panel (J), front trim (K), and side trim (L) to size, where shown in **8–29**, on *page 150*.

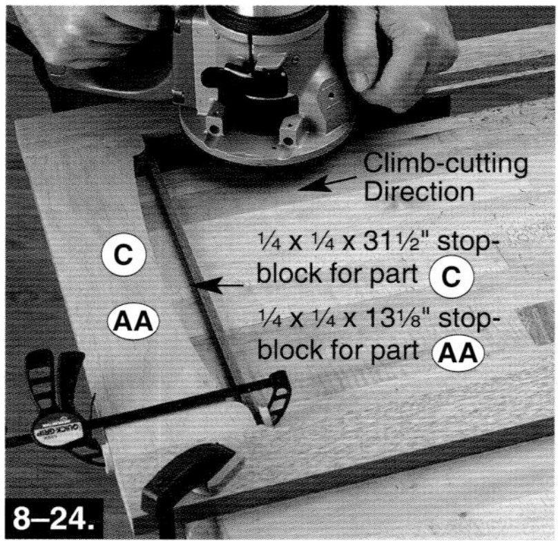
Climb-cutting
Direction
C
AA
1/4 x 1/4 x 31 1/2" stop-
block for part C
1/4 x 1/4 x 13 1/8" stop-
block for part AA

8–24.

A 1/4 x 1/4" stopblock clamped against the outside lip of the top rail's groove stops the rabbeting bit below the rail.

2 Rout a 3/4" bullnose along the outside edge of the trim pieces, where shown. (This can be done by routing a pair of round-overs using a 3/8" round-over bit.)

3 Mark a centerline across the trims' miter joints for the #20 biscuit slots. Plunge-cut the slots, centering them on the trims' thickness.

4 Glue and clamp the trim to the base panel, inserting the biscuits in the slots in the trim's miter joints. Sand the trim flush to the panel. Now, drill mounting holes through the top and bottom of the trim, where dimensioned on the Base-Section Detail drawing in **8–28** and **8–29**.

5 Cut the front skirt (M) and side skirts (N) to size, miter-cutting their ends, where shown in **8–29**. Make six copies of the

SHOP TIP

Drilling with Perforated Hardboard Jigs

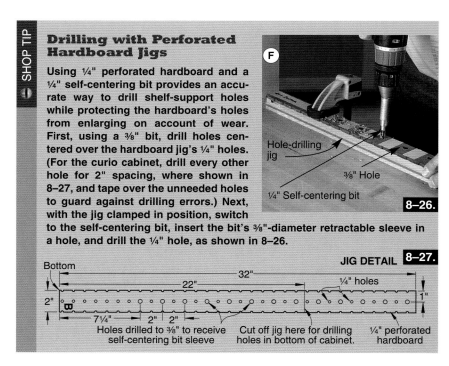

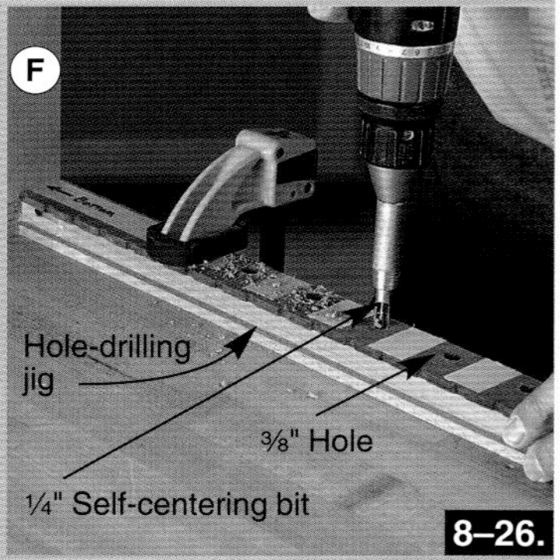
F
Hole-drilling
jig
3/8" Hole
1/4" Self-centering bit

8–26.

Using 1/4" perforated hardboard and a 1/4" self-centering bit provides an accurate way to drill shelf-support holes while protecting the hardboard's holes from enlarging on account of wear. First, using a 3/8" bit, drill holes centered over the hardboard jig's 1/4" holes. (For the curio cabinet, drill every other hole for 2" spacing, where shown in 8–27, and tape over the unneeded holes to guard against drilling errors.) Next, with the jig clamped in position, switch to the self-centering bit, insert the bit's 3/8"-diameter retractable sleeve in a hole, and drill the 1/4" hole, as shown in 8–26.

JIG DETAIL **8–27.**

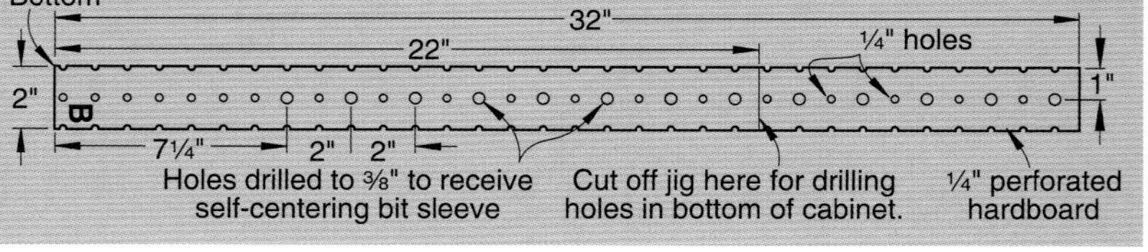
Bottom
32"
22"
1/4" holes
2"
B
1"
7 1/4"
2"
2"
Holes drilled to 3/8" to receive
self-centering bit sleeve
Cut off jig here for drilling
holes in bottom of cabinet.
1/4" perforated
hardboard

end pattern in **8–38** (*page 154*), but do not cut off the patterns' shaded area. Attach the patterns to the skirts' ends. Lay out the curve on each skirt's bottom, where dimensioned in **8–29**, connecting the patterns. band-saw and sand the curves to the lines.

6 Mark centerlines on the outside face of the skirts at the mitered corners for #20 biscuit slots. Plunge the slots in the skirts' ends, where shown, offsetting them toward the skirts' inside face to ensure the slot cutter does not go through the outside face.

7 Glue and biscuit the skirts together. Then, glue and clamp the skirt assembly to the base panel/trim assembly (J/K/L), aligning their back edges and centering the skirt assembly end to end. Using the shank holes in the trim as guides, drill pilot holes into the skirts. Drive the screws.

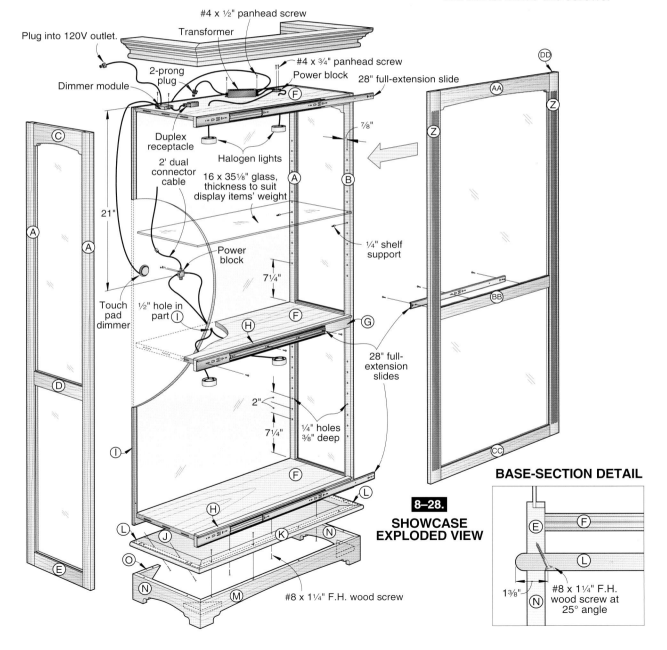

Plug into 120V outlet.

#4 x ½" panhead screw

Transformer

2-prong plug

Dimmer module

#4 x ¾" panhead screw

Power block

28" full-extension slide

Duplex receptacle

Halogen lights

2' dual connector cable

16 x 35⅛" glass, thickness to suit display items' weight

21"

¼" shelf support

Power block

7¼"

Touch pad dimmer

½" hole in part I

28" full-extension slides

2"

¼" holes ⅜" deep

7¼"

8–28.

SHOWCASE EXPLODED VIEW

#8 x 1¼" F.H. wood screw

BASE-SECTION DETAIL

1⅜"

#8 x 1¼" F.H. wood screw at 25° angle

8–29.

BASE DETAIL

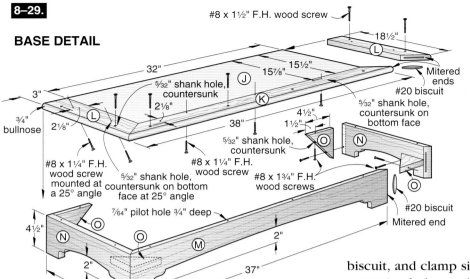

#8 x 1½" F.H. wood screw

18½"

32"

15⅞" 15½"

3"

⁵⁄₃₂" shank hole, countersunk

2⅛"

Mitered ends

#20 biscuit

⁵⁄₃₂" shank hole, countersunk on bottom face

¾" bullnose

2⅛"

38"

4½"

1½"

#8 x 1¼" F.H. wood screw mounted at a 25° angle

⁵⁄₃₂" shank hole, countersunk on bottom face at 25° angle

⁵⁄₃₂" shank hole, countersunk

#8 x 1¼" F.H. wood screw

#8 x 1¾" F.H. wood screws

#20 biscuit

Mitered end

4½"

⁷⁄₆₄" pilot hole ¾" deep

2"

2"

18"

37"

Referring to **8–29**, cut four triangular corner blocks (O) to the size shown. Drill mounting holes through the blocks, where dimensioned. Glue, clamp, and screw the blocks to the skirts and base panel (J), where shown, centering the front blocks on the skirts' width.

Place the cabinet on its back. Attach the base assembly to the cabinet, as shown in **8–30**.

Add a Crown to the Cabinet

Cut the crown parts (P through Y) to size, but 1" longer than given in the Materials List.

Using your router table, rout the ¾" bullnose on parts P and Q; the ½" round-over on parts T, U, X, and Y; and the ½" cove on parts V and W, where shown in **8–31**.

Miter-cut the ends of the parts to the dimensions shown, making sure you have left and right (mirror image) pieces for the side parts. Cut the front parts P, R, T, V, and X so their back (short) edges measure exactly 32" in length. Cut the side parts Q, S, U, W, and Y so their back edges measure exactly 15½".

Lay out the parts, and mark centerlines across the mitered joints for #20 biscuit slots. Plunge the slots, adjusting your biscuit joiner's fence as needed to center the slot on the part's thickness.

Glue and clamp part P to the cabinet's top, centering it end to end and placing it 15½" from the cabinet's back. Drill mounting holes, where shown in **8–31**, and drive the screws. Glue, biscuit, and clamp side parts Q to the top. Drill the mounting holes, and drive the screws.

Using the same method, install the remaining crown parts R through Y, as shown in **8–32**.

Construct a Door with a View

Cut the stiles (Z) to size but 4" longer than indicated in the Materials List. Mark the face of each stile 4¼" from the bottom and 5⅞" from the top to identify the flutes' length. Now, chuck a ¼"

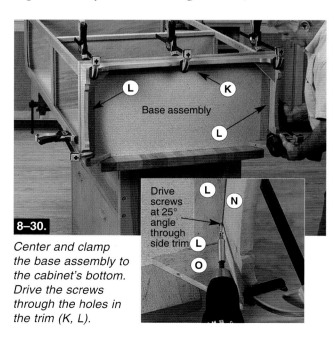

Base assembly

Drive screws at 25° angle through side trim

8–30.

Center and clamp the base assembly to the cabinet's bottom. Drive the screws through the holes in the trim (K, L).

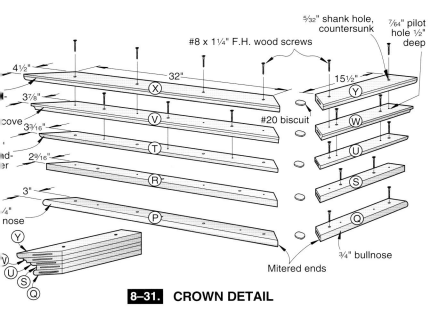

5/32" shank hole, countersunk

7/64" pilot hole 1/2" deep

#8 x 1¼" F.H. wood screws

4½"

3⅞"

cove

3³⁄₁₆"

nd-
er

2⁹⁄₁₆"

3"

¼"
nose

32"

15½"

#20 biscuit

¾" bullnose

Mitered ends

8–31. **CROWN DETAIL**

roundnose bit in your handheld router. Attach an edge guide to the router. Clamp stopblocks to the ends of the stiles where appropriate for your router to stop the flutes at the marks.

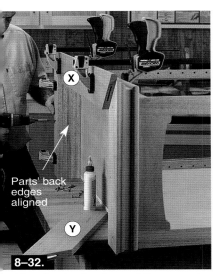

Parts' back edges aligned

8–32.

Align the back edges of the crown's parts as you assemble it. Offset each part's screw locations to avoid striking the screws below.

2 Adjust the router bit to cut a ¹⁄₁₆"-deep flute. Adjust the edge guide as needed, and cut the flutes, where dimensioned on the Fluting Detail drawing in **8–33** (*page 152*).

3 Trim the bottom of each stile (Z) 2¼" below the ends of the flutes. Then, trim the top of the stiles to their finished length of 74⅛".

4 Cut the top, middle, and bottom rails (AA, BB, CC) to size. Next, cut ¼" grooves in the rails and stiles (Z), where shown on the Door Detail drawing in **8–33** and in **8–34**.

5 In the grooves in stiles (Z), lay out the ¼" mortises 1¹³⁄₁₆" deep. Drill out the mortises using a ¼" brad-point bit in your drill press. Square the ends of the mortises and straighten their sides with a chisel.

6 Cut the ¼" tenons on the ends of the rails (AA, BB, CC), where dimensioned on **8–34**. Note that the tenons for the top rail (AA) and bottom rail (CC) are haunched (notched).

7 Make two copies of the end pattern in **8–38** (*page 154*), and cut out the shaded part. Attach them to the ends of the top rail (AA). Mark the arch on the rail where dimensioned. Bandsaw and sand to the line.

8 Dry-assemble the stiles (Z) and rails (AA, BB, CC). When the parts fit together correctly, glue and clamp them together, checking for square. Later, sand the assembled door smooth.

9 As shown in **8–24**, rout ¼" rabbets ½" deep for the glass in the door's back, where shown on the Door Detail drawing in **8–33**, by removing the inside lip of its ¼ x ¼" grooves. Square the rabbets' corners.

10 Cut the door edge (DD) to size. Glue and clamp it to the back of the door, where shown, flush with the outside edge of the stile (Z).

Install the Door

1 Using a helper, place the cabinet face up on saw-horses. Separate the cabinet slide and matching door slide parts of the full-extension slides by pressing the slide release tab shown in **8–36**. Screw the cabinet slides (the larger pieces) to the shelf edging (G), where

8–33. DOOR DETAIL

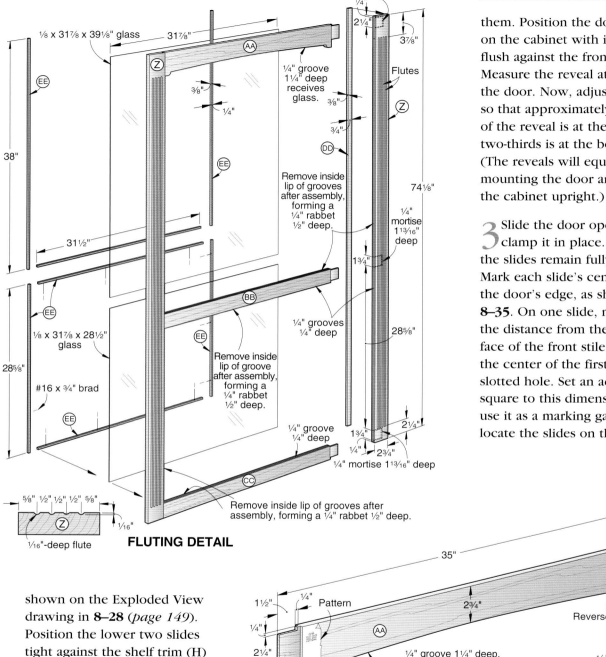

¼" mortise 1¹³⁄₁₆" deep

⅛ x 31⅞ x 39⅛" glass

31⅞"

¼"

2¼"

3⅞"

Flutes

Z

AA

EE

Z

¼" groove 1¼" deep receives glass.

⅜"

⅜"

¼"

¾"

DD

38"

74⅛"

Remove inside lip of grooves after assembly, forming a ¼" rabbet ½" deep.

¼" mortise 1¹³⁄₁₆" deep

EE

31½"

1¾"

BB

¼" grooves ¼" deep

28⅝"

EE

⅛ x 31⅞ x 28½" glass

28⅝"

EE

Remove inside lip of groove after assembly, forming a ¼" rabbet ½" deep.

#16 x ¾" brad

EE

¼" groove ¼" deep

1¾"

2¼"

¼"

2¾"

¼" mortise 1¹³⁄₁₆" deep

⅝" ½" ½" ½" ⅝"

Z

¹⁄₁₆"

CC

Remove inside lip of grooves after assembly, forming a ¼" rabbet ½" deep.

¹⁄₁₆"-deep flute

FLUTING DETAIL

---

them. Position the door face up on the cabinet with its bottom flush against the front trim (K). Measure the reveal at the top of the door. Now, adjust the door so that approximately one-third of the reveal is at the top and two-thirds is at the bottom. (The reveals will equalize after mounting the door and setting the cabinet upright.)

3 Slide the door open 4", and clamp it in place. Make sure the slides remain fully closed. Mark each slide's centerline on the door's edge, as shown in **8–35**. On one slide, measure the distance from the outside face of the front stile (A) to the center of the first vertical slotted hole. Set an adjustable square to this dimension. You'll use it as a marking gauge to locate the slides on the door.

---

shown on the Exploded View drawing in **8–28** (*page 149*). Position the lower two slides tight against the shelf trim (H) and front stile (A). Position the top slide flush with the bottom edge of the shelf edging and tight against the front stile.

2 To locate the door slides, reassemble them to the cabinet slides, and fully close

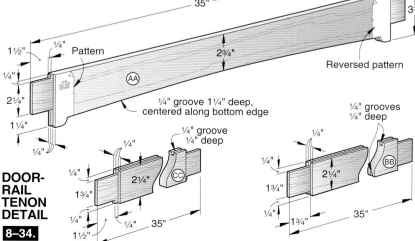

35"

3¾"

1½"

¼"

Pattern

2¾"

Reversed pattern

¼"

2¼"

AA

¼" groove 1¼" deep, centered along bottom edge

1¼"

¼"

DOOR-RAIL TENON DETAIL

8–34.

¼" groove ¼" deep

¼"

¼"

CC

2¼"

1¾"

¼"

¼"

35"

1½"

¼" grooves ¼" deep

¼"

¼"

2¼"

BB

1¾"

¼"

1¾"

35"

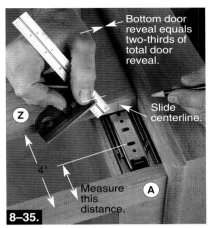

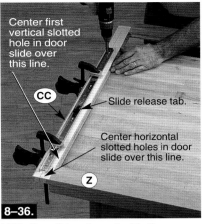

Mark the center of the slide's horizontal slotted hole on the door's edge on masking tape. Measure the distance to the first vertical slotted hole.

With the slide aligned with the marked lines, drill pilot holes through the slide's horizontal slotted holes using a self-centering bit. Drive the screws.

holes to permanently secure the slides. Remove the slides and the masking tape from the door.

8 To make the glass stop blanks (EE), plane a ½ x 7¼ x 48" piece of stock to ⅜" thickness. On your tablesaw, rip sixteen ⁵⁄₁₆"-wide strips from the stock. Plane the strips' width to ¼". Cut the glass stops to fit the openings in the cabinet's sides and door, where dimensioned on **8–22** (*page 147*) and the Door Detail drawing in **8–33**. Set aside the stops.

Put on a Finish

1 Sand any areas on the cabinet and door that need it. Remove the dust.

2 Apply a stain if you wish. (A dark mahogany oil-based wood stain was used on the showcase shown on *page 145*.) To ensure adequate adhesion of the mirrors, stain (and finish)

4 Next, place the door inside face up on your workbench. To mark the locations of the door slides, apply 2"-wide masking tape across the width of the door, aligning the tape with the top edges of the rails (AA, BB, CC). Position the preset adjustable square against the door's marked edge, and draw a line parallel to the edge across the tape on each rail.

5 Position the square against the door's bottom, and set it to the bottom slide's centerline marked on the door's edge. Transfer the centerline across the tape on the bottom rail (CC). Repeat this process to mark the centerline on the top rail (AA). To mark the middle rail (BB), measure the distance from the door's bottom to the middle slide's centerline on the door's edge. Mark this dimension on the middle rail at both ends, and

draw the centerline. (This ensures that the center slide will be parallel to the top and bottom slides.)

6 Separate the door slides from the cabinet slides. Align the slides on the door, drill pilot holes, and drive the supplied screws, as shown in **8–36**. Install the door, as shown in **8–37**.

7 Stand the cabinet upright. Check that the door opens and closes smoothly. To adjust a slide, loosen its mounting screws, reposition it as needed, and tighten the screws. When you're satisfied with the door's operation, place the cabinet face up on the sawhorses. Remove the door, and place it inside face up on your workbench. Drill pilot holes centered in the slides' round holes. One by one, transfer the screws from the slotted holes to the round

Using a helper, align the door and cabinet's slides, and slide the door in place.

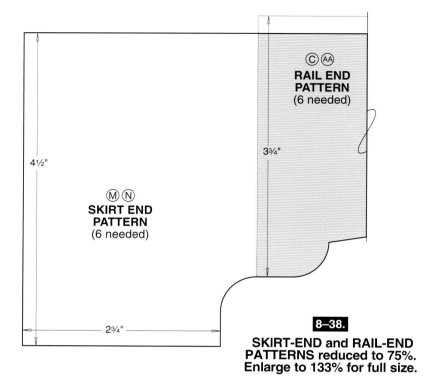

RAIL END
PATTERN
(6 needed)

3¾"

4½"

M N
SKIRT END
PATTERN
(6 needed)

2¾"

8–38.
SKIRT-END and RAIL-END
PATTERNS reduced to 75%.
Enlarge to 133% for full size.

only a 1½"-wide strip around the mirror-mounting areas on the cabinet's back (I).

3 Apply three coats of a clear finish, sanding to 320 grit between coats and removing the dust. (A clear satin lacquer was used on the cabinet shown on *page 145*.)

Install the lighting

1 Surface-mount a pair of halogen lights under the top and middle shelves (F) as directed by the manufacturer's instructions. Route the wires from the upper lights through the ½" holes in the top shelf. Feed the wires from the lower lights through the ½" hole in the back (I).

2 Referring to the Exploded View drawing in **8–28** (*page 149*), screw the transformer, dimmer module, and a power block to the top of the cabinet. On the back side of the cabinet, screw another power block to the center of the back (I) 21" from the cabinet's top. Connect the lights' and transformer's wires to the power blocks where shown.

3 Plug the wire from the touch pad dimmer into the dimmer module. Using cloth-backed double-faced tape, mount the pad in a convenient place, such as on the cabinet's back or inside the cabinet under the middle shelf.

4 Trim the transformer's power cord, attach its plug, and insert it into the dimmer module's receptacle, as directed by the manufacturer's instructions.

Install the Glass

1 Place the cabinet on its back. Apply mirror mastic (from your local glass shop) to the back of the mirrors, and press them onto the cabinet's back (I). Let the mastic cure for 24 hours.

2 Install the glass and glass stops (EE) in the cabinet's sides and door. Attach the stops with #16 x ¾" brads. To prevent splitting the stops, drill holes in them using a brad with its head snipped off.

3 Reinstall the door slides and the door. Set the cabinet upright, and move it to its final location. Install shelf supports and glass shelves. Use a suitable glass thickness to safely support your display items. For the 35⅛" span of the shelves, the maximum load ratings per square foot are as follows: 5.3 pounds for ¼" glass, 17.5 pounds for ⅜" glass, and 32.6 pounds for ½" glass.

4 Plug the module's power cord into a 120V outlet. Place your collectibles on the shelves, press the three-level touch pad dimmer to set the desired light level, and enjoy the beautiful display.

stowaway storage

TRUNKS AND CHESTS HAVE BEEN A favorite mode of storage for centuries. Settlers and immigrants loaded their belongings in them to take aboard ship for voyages to new lands (thus, the frequently used name "steamer" trunks). Because a chest or trunk was basically rectangular in shape, it could be neatly packed in the back of a wagon for long-distance land travel. Because of its ease in packing and transport, this type of storage unit was even relied on by traveling vaudevillians and circus performers.

Once a chest or trunk arrived at its destination, it was easily converted into parlor seating just as it was. For more comfort, a top pad could be added. Many old chests became heirlooms—they and their treasured contents have been passed down through the generations.

In this chapter you'll find two examples of this storage type. The hall seat on page 156 uses a design that evolved from a trunk, because under its seat (lid) you'll find plenty of room to stow hats, scarves, and other gear. Plans for a more traditional chest style begin on page 163. The chest has all the makings of a family heirloom and will look wonderful wherever you place it. So, why not give both of these great projects a try?

COUNTRY HALL SEAT

Liven up an entry or hallway with this classic, dual-purpose bench. Take a seat when pulling off your boots; then use it as handy storage for mittens, scarves, hats, and other outerwear. You can stain it to match your woodwork, or give it a stain and paint treatment for a colorful accent to your home's existing palette.

Make the Front, Back, and End Panels

***Note:** This sturdy piece was designed to function as a typical deacon's bench. If you plan to use it for toy storage or in a place where children will be opening and closing it, you must add lid supports to prevent the heavy edge-joined seat from falling shut and possibly pinching small hands and fingers.*

1 From 1¹⁄₁₆" stock (commonly called five-quarter stock), cut the base frame rails and stiles (A, B, C, D), shown on the Exploded View drawing in **9–1** (*page 158*), to the sizes given in the Materials List. (Birch was used for the Country Hall Seat shown on this page.)

2 Mount a ½" dado blade to your tablesaw. Raise the blade ½" above the surface of the saw table. Cut a groove in a piece of 1¹⁄₁₆" stock, and check

This country hall seat serves dual purposes. It is helpful for taking off your boots and for storing outerwear, and it will liven up entryways or hallways.

that a piece of ½" plywood fits in the groove. Adjust if necessary. Cut a ½" groove ½" deep, centered along the inside edge of each stile and rail, where shown on the Panels drawing in **9–2** (*page 159*).

3 Using a miter-gauge extension and a stop, cut rabbets to form tenons on the ends of the rails (A, C) to the sizes shown on the Tenon Detail drawing in **9–2**.

4 Mark the cutlines for the bevels on the bottom inside edge of the stiles (B, D), as dimensioned on the Panels drawing in **9–2**.

5 Cut eight ½ x ½ x 2" filler blocks. With the bottom

ends of the filler blocks flush with the bottom ends of the stiles (B, D), glue and clamp one block into the groove in each stile. Cut just outside the marked cutline on each stile. Then, sand the bevel-cut stile and filler block.

6 From ½" birch plywood, cut the front and back panels (E) and end panels (F) to size. Dry-clamp the four frame-and-panel assemblies to check the fit. Then, glue and clamp the assemblies, checking for square.

7 With the outside edges and top and bottom ends flush, glue and clamp the four frame-and-panel assemblies together in the configuration shown on the Exploded View drawing in **9–1** (*page 158*).

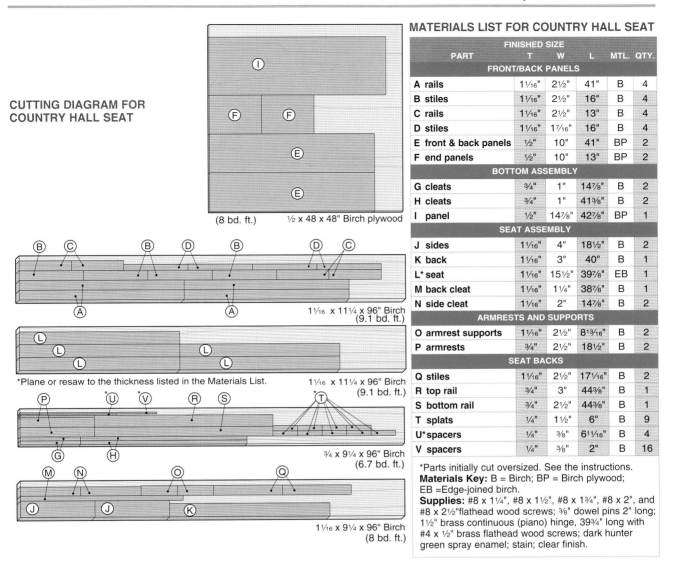

CUTTING DIAGRAM FOR COUNTRY HALL SEAT

(8 bd. ft.)   ½ x 48 x 48" Birch plywood

1¹⁄₁₆ x 11¼ x 96" Birch
(9.1 bd. ft.)

*Plane or resaw to the thickness listed in the Materials List.   1¹⁄₁₆ x 11¼ x 96" Birch
(9.1 bd. ft.)

¾ x 9¼ x 96" Birch
(6.7 bd. ft.)

1¹⁄₁₆ x 9¼ x 96" Birch
(8 bd. ft.)

MATERIALS LIST FOR COUNTRY HALL SEAT

PART	FINISHED SIZE			MTL.	QTY.
	T	W	L		
FRONT/BACK PANELS					
A rails	1¹⁄₁₆"	2½"	41"	B	4
B stiles	1¹⁄₁₆"	2½"	16"	B	4
C rails	1¹⁄₁₆"	2½"	13"	B	4
D stiles	1¹⁄₁₆"	1⁷⁄₁₆"	16"	B	4
E front & back panels	½"	10"	41"	BP	2
F end panels	½"	10"	13"	BP	2
BOTTOM ASSEMBLY					
G cleats	¾"	1"	14⁷⁄₈"	B	2
H cleats	¾"	1"	41⅜"	B	2
I panel	½"	14⁷⁄₈"	42⁷⁄₈"	BP	1
SEAT ASSEMBLY					
J sides	1¹⁄₁₆"	4"	18½"	B	2
K back	1¹⁄₁₆"	3"	40"	B	1
L* seat	1¹⁄₁₆"	15½"	39⅞"	EB	1
M back cleat	1¹⁄₁₆"	1¼"	38⅞"	B	1
N side cleat	1¹⁄₁₆"	2"	14⁷⁄₈"	B	2
ARMRESTS AND SUPPORTS					
O armrest supports	1¹⁄₁₆"	2½"	8¹³⁄₁₆"	B	2
P armrests	¾"	2½"	18½"	B	2
SEAT BACKS					
Q stiles	1¹⁄₁₆"	2½"	17¹⁄₁₆"	B	2
R top rail	¾"	3"	44⅜"	B	1
S bottom rail	¾"	2½"	44⅜"	B	1
T splats	¼"	1½"	6"	B	9
U* spacers	¼"	⅜"	6¹¹⁄₁₆"	B	4
V spacers	¼"	⅜"	2"	B	16

*Parts initially cut oversized. See the instructions.
Materials Key: B = Birch; BP = Birch plywood;
EB =Edge-joined birch.
Supplies: #8 x 1¼", #8 x 1½", #8 x 1¾", #8 x 2", and
#8 x 2½"flathead wood screws; ⅜" dowel pins 2" long;
1½" brass continuous (piano) hinge, 39¾" long with
#4 x ½" brass flathead wood screws; dark hunter
green spray enamel; stain; clear finish.

Make a Bottom for the Base

1 Cut the cleats (G, H) to size. Drill countersunk screw holes through two adjoining surfaces of each cleat.

2 Next, with the bottom edges of the cleats flush with the bottom edges of the bottom rails (A, C), screw the cleats in place.

3 Measure the opening, and cut the bottom panel (I) to size from ½" plywood. Working from the bottom side of the base, glue and screw the bottom panel in place.

Build the Seat Frame

1 Cut the seat frame parts (J, K) to size from 1¹⁄₁₆"-thick stock.

2 Using the Dowel Hole Detail drawing in **9–1**, drill a pair of dowel holes at each mating joint joining the frame parts (J, K).

3 Glue, dowel, and clamp the seat back frame member (K) between the side pieces (J). (To help keep the assembly square when clamping, cut a temporary spacer the same length as part K. Clamp the spacer between the front ends of parts J

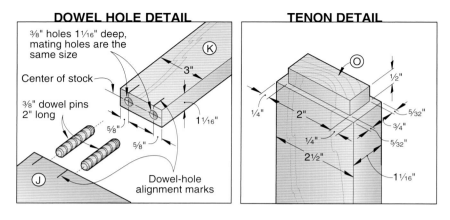

DOWEL HOLE DETAIL

3/8" holes 1 1/16" deep, mating holes are the same size

Center of stock

3/8" dowel pins 2" long

5/8"

5/8"

3"

1 1/16"

K

J

Dowel-hole alignment marks

TENON DETAIL

O

1/2"

5/32"

1/4"

2"

3/4"

1/4"

5/32"

2 1/2"

1 1/16"

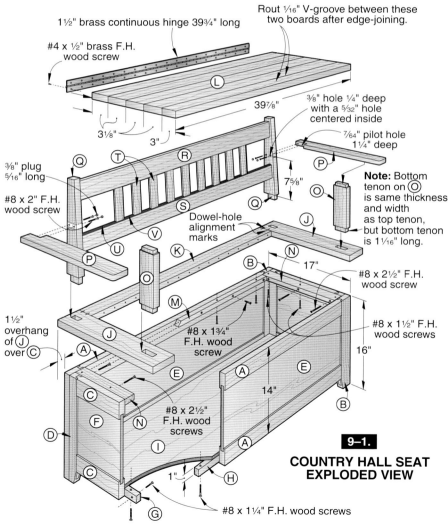

1 1/2" brass continuous hinge 39 3/4" long

Rout 1/16" V-groove between these two boards after edge-joining.

#4 x 1/2" brass F.H. wood screw

L

39 7/8"

3 1/8"

3"

3/8" hole 1/4" deep with a 5/32" hole centered inside

7/64" pilot hole 1 1/4" deep

3/8" plug 5/16" long

#8 x 2" F.H. wood screw

Q

T

R

P

O

7 5/8"

S

Q

Note: Bottom tenon on O is same thickness and width as top tenon, but bottom tenon is 1 1/16" long.

V

U

Dowel-hole alignment marks

J

P

K

O

N

B

17"

#8 x 2 1/2" F.H. wood screw

1 1/2" overhang of J over C

A

M

J

#8 x 1 3/4" F.H. wood screw

E

A

E

#8 x 1 1/2" F.H. wood screws

16"

C

14"

F

N

#8 x 2 1/2" F.H. wood screws

A

B

D

I

A

9–1.

COUNTRY HALL SEAT EXPLODED VIEW

C

1"

H

G

#8 x 1 1/4" F.H. wood screws

when gluing K in place between the back ends.) Check for square and ensure that the pieces lie flat.

4 Edge-join stock to form the 15 1/2"-wide seat (L). (Make sure the stock forms a seat blank that measures 41" long.) For ease in aligning the strips, consider dowel or biscuit joints. Later, trim the seat to finished length.

5 Rout a 1/16"-deep V-groove in the top of the seat panel (L) 3" from the front edge of the seat and centered along the joint line.

6 Cut the cleats (M, N) to size. Drill the countersunk mounting holes, and screw the cleats to the inside of the hall seat's base assembly.

Make the Supports and Armrests

1 Cut the armrest supports (O) to size. Then, referring to the Tenon Detail drawing in **9–1,** cut a 1/2"-long tenon on the top end and a 1 1/16"-long tenon on the bottom end of each armrest support.

2 Using **9–4** on *page 160*, for reference, cut the armrests (P) to size. Cut a notch in the back inside corner of each. Then cut a 1/2" radius on each of the three remaining armrest corners.

3 Carefully mark the locations and cut a 1/2"-deep mortise into the bottom side

9–2. PANELS

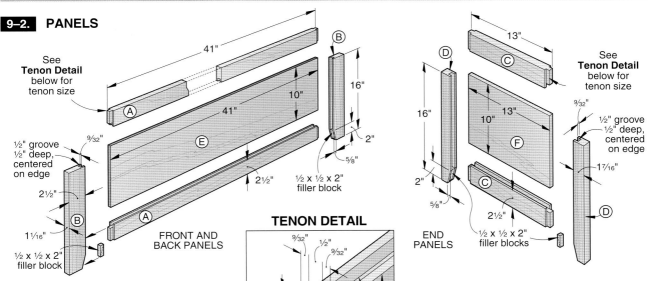

FRONT AND
BACK PANELS

TENON DETAIL

END
PANELS

of each armrest. (One way to form the mortises is to chuck a ⅝" flat-bottomed bit into your drill press, set the stop for consistent ½"-deep holes, drill out most of the waste inside each marked mortise, and then chisel away the rest.)

Add the Seat-Back Assembly for Support

1 Cut the seat-back stile blanks (Q) to the size shown in the Materials List. Fit your tablesaw with a dado blade, and form a 1¹⁄₁₆"-long tenon at the bottom end of each stile (Q) to the dimensions shown on the Tenon Detail drawing in **9–5** *(page 160)*.

2 Cut the seat-back stiles (Q) to shape, angling the front edge of each, where shown on the Seat Back Stile drawing in **9–5**. You can use a taper jig for cutting this part, or mark the cutline, cut it on a bandsaw, and sand it smooth.

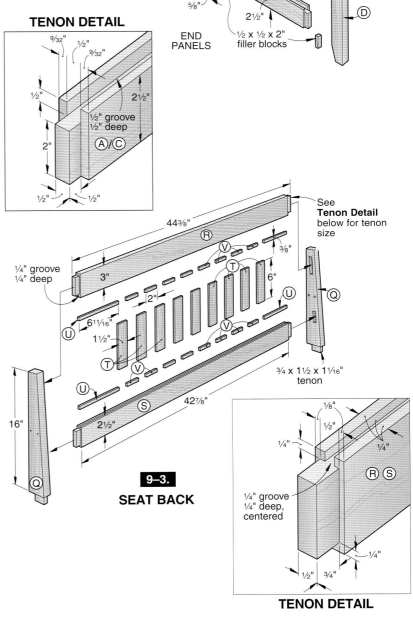

9–3.
SEAT BACK

TENON DETAIL

9–4. **PARTS VIEW**

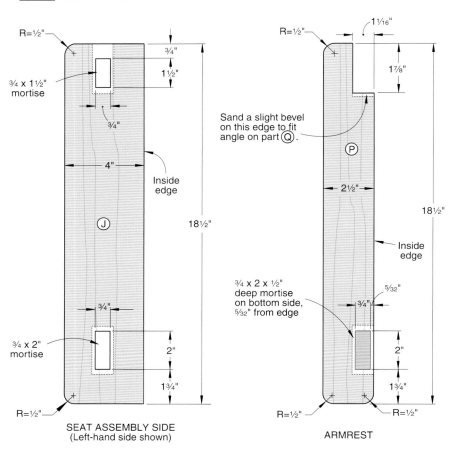

SEAT ASSEMBLY SIDE
(Left-hand side shown)

R=½"

¾ x 1½"
mortise

¾ x 2"
mortise

R=½"

¾"

¾"

4"

18½"

2"

1¾"

Inside
edge

Ⓙ

Sand a slight bevel
on this edge to fit
angle on part Ⓠ.

¾ x 2 x ½"
deep mortise
on bottom side,
5/32" from edge

R=½"

1 1/16"

1⅞"

2½"

18½"

Inside
edge

¾"

5/32"

2"

1¾"

R=½"

R=½"

Ⓟ

ARMREST

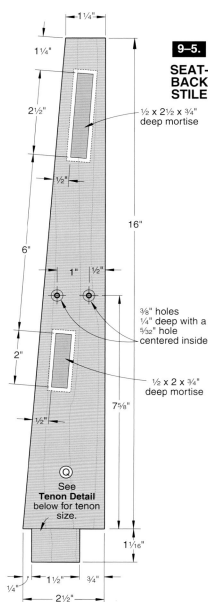

9–5.

**SEAT-
BACK
STILE**

½ x 2½ x ¾"
deep mortise

⅜" holes
¼" deep with a
5/32" hole
centered inside

½ x 2 x ¾"
deep mortise

See
Tenon Detail
below for tenon
size.

Ⓠ

1¼"

1¼"

2½"

½"

6"

16"

1"

½"

2"

7⅝"

½"

¼"

1½"

¾"

2½"

1 1/16"

3 Mark the locations and form
a pair of ¾"-deep mortises on
the inside face of each stile (Q),
where shown on the Seat-Back
Stile drawing in **9–5**. Then, mark
the locations, and drill a pair of
counterbored screw holes for
securing the armrests (P) to the
stiles later on.

4 Cut the top and bottom seat-
back rails (R, S) to size. Cut
a ¼" groove ¼" deep along one
edge of each, where shown in
9–3. Using the same drawing

and detail for reference, form a
tenon on each end of each rail.

5 Cut the ¼"-thick splats (T)
to size. Cut the spacers (U)
to size plus ½" in length. Cut the
spacers (V) to size. Dry-clamp
the seat-back assembly to check
the fit. Check for square and
trim the spacers (U) to finished
length. Glue and clamp the seat
back together, checking for
square, as shown in **9–6**.

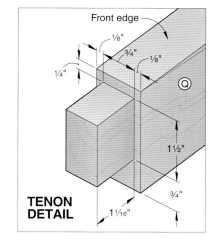

Front edge

Ⓠ

⅛"

¾"

⅛"

¼"

1½"

¾"

1 1/16"

**TENON
DETAIL**

9-6.

Immediately after clamping, check the seat-back assembly for square, and adjust the clamps as necessary.

Assemble the Country Hall Seat

Note: *Precutting the mortises in the seat sides (J) and hoping that the seat-back and armrest assemblies fit perfectly can be risky. It is much more accurate to build the seat-back assembly, and then transfer the tenon lines to the seat sides (J) to locate the mortise. Forming the mortises in the seat sides and then assembling the seat-back assembly allows absolutely no room for error regarding the fit of the tenons into the mortises.*

1 Working on a flat surface, lay the seat-back assembly against the back edge of the seat frame. Then, center the seat-back stiles

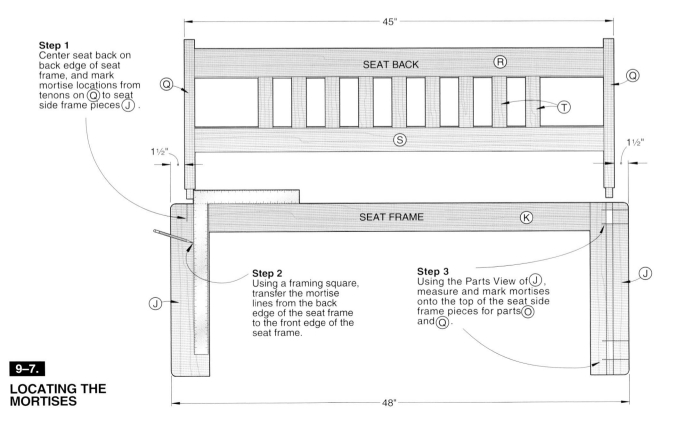

Step 1
Center seat back on back edge of seat frame, and mark mortise locations from tenons on Ⓠ to seat side frame pieces Ⓙ.

45"

SEAT BACK Ⓡ

Ⓠ

Ⓠ

Ⓣ

Ⓢ

1½"

1½"

SEAT FRAME Ⓚ

Ⓙ

Step 2
Using a framing square, transfer the mortise lines from the back edge of the seat frame to the front edge of the seat frame.

Step 3
Using the Parts View of Ⓙ, measure and mark mortises onto the top of the seat side frame pieces for parts Ⓞ and Ⓠ.

Ⓙ

Ⓙ

9-7.

LOCATING THE MORTISES

48"

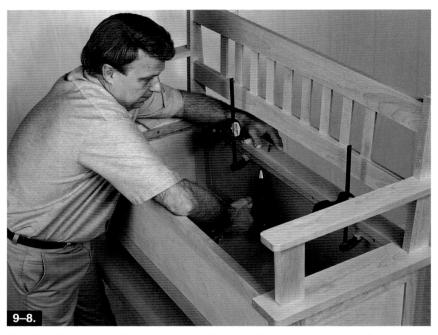

9–8.

Working from inside the base, screw through the cleats to secure the seat-frame/seat-back assembly to the base.

(Q) against the seat side frame pieces (J), where shown in **9–7**.

2 Follow the three steps in **9–7** to accurately locate the mortise on the seat side frame pieces.

3 Drill holes inside the marked mortise lines on the seat sides (J) to remove some of the waste. Next, use a sharp chisel to finish forming the mortises. Screw the seat frame to the bench base.

4 Next, glue the seat-back assembly stiles (Q) into the mortises in the seat sides (J).

5 Glue the armrest supports (O) into the mortises in the front end of the seat frame sides (J).

6 Glue and screw the armrests (P) to the seat-back stiles (Q),

and then glue them to the top ends of the armrest supports (O). While the glue is still wet, use clamps to snug-up the armrest supports between the armrests and seat-frame ends. Do the same for a tight joint between the seat-back stiles and the seat-frame sides (J).

7 Cut plugs and plug the four counterbored screw holes on the inside face of each seat-back stile (Q). Sand the plugs flush.

8 Centering it from side to side and with the back edges flush, screw the seat-frame/seat-back assembly to the cleats (M, N), as shown in **9–8**.

9 Drill pilot holes, and attach the continuous hinge to the back edge of the seat (L) and

the front edge of the seat-frame back member (K). Check that the front edge of the seat is flush with the front ends of the seat-frame sides (J). Trim if necessary. Remove the hinge for the time being.

Apply a Showroom-Quality Finish

1 Finish-sand the assembled bench and seat. (Birch needs careful attention when sanding to remove mill marks. Inadequate sanding can result in blotches when stained.)

2 Next, stain the entire bench; then apply two coats of clear finish to the entire bench as well.

3 Mask the unpainted areas of the hall seat shown on *page 156*, and spray-paint the remaining areas. (The base of the hall seat was sprayed with hunter green spray enamel, but the painted surfaces turned out to be too bright and shiny. To make them less shiny and to produce a slightly worn look, 220-grit sandpaper was wrapped around a sanding block and the edges were lightly sanded just through the paint until the underlying stained area was exposed. Then, #00 steel wool was used to lightly dull the finish.) Reattach the continuous hinge.

CEDAR-LINED HEIRLOOM CHEST

There's nothing like the fragrance of cedar. And no wood matches the overall durability and look of oak. Both woods were used in the construction of this mortise-and-tenon-framed storage chest. Follow the instructions to create an heirloom sturdy enough to hold precious memories for years to come.

Construct the Frame

1 Cut the front and back frame members—rails (A and B), stiles (C), and mullions (D)—to the sizes given in the Materials List. Note that the back frame does not have the two center mullions (D).

2 Cut the side frame members—stiles (E) and rails (F, G)—to size.

3 Lay out and cut the mortises and tenons in the frame members, where indicated in 9–9 and 9–10 (*page 165*).

4 Glue and clamp the front frame together, checking for square and adjusting if necessary. Repeat the procedure with the other frames. After the glue dries, scrape off the hardened excess and sand the joints smooth on both sides.

5 Fit your router with a rabbeting bit, and rout ½" rabbets

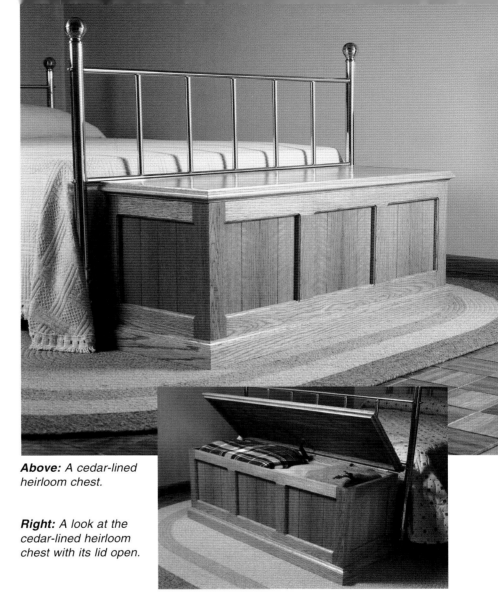

Above: *A cedar-lined heirloom chest.*

Right: *A look at the cedar-lined heirloom chest with its lid open.*

¼" deep along the inside edges of all four frames (see the Exploded View drawing in **9–11**, on *page 165*). (You can use a scrap of ¼" oak plywood to check the depth.) Square the rounded corners with a chisel. The rabbets will later house the oak plywood panels.

6 Turn the frames over, and rout a ¼" bead along the inside edges of all four frames, where shown on the Exploded View drawing in **9–11**.

7 Install a dado blade in your tablesaw, and cut a ½" groove ¼" deep, 2½" up from the bottom of each of the four frames for the chest bottom, where shown in **9–12** on *page 166*.

8 Cut a ⅜" rabbet ⅜" deep along each end of each frame, where shown on the Corner Detail (Chest) drawing in **9–11**.

9 Cut the side panels (H), the front panels (I), and the rear panel (J) to size from ¼" oak plywood.

CUTTING DIAGRAM FOR CEDAR-LINED HEIRLOOM CHEST

B
A
A
¾ x 9¼ x 96" Oak (6.7 bd. ft.)
F
G
G
C
C
E
E
¾ x 9¼ x 96" Oak (6.7 bd. ft.)
S
U
P
T
O
D
S
R
Q
R
¾ x 9¼ x 96" Oak (6.7 bd. ft.)
J
W
K
I
I
I
H
H
¼ x 48 x 96" Oak plywood
L
V
N
N
M
M
¼ x 48 x 96" Cedar plywood

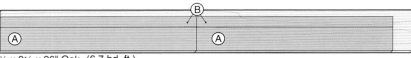

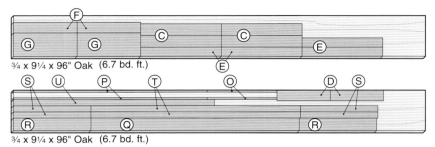

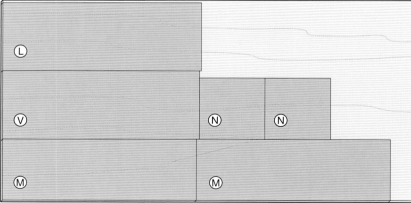

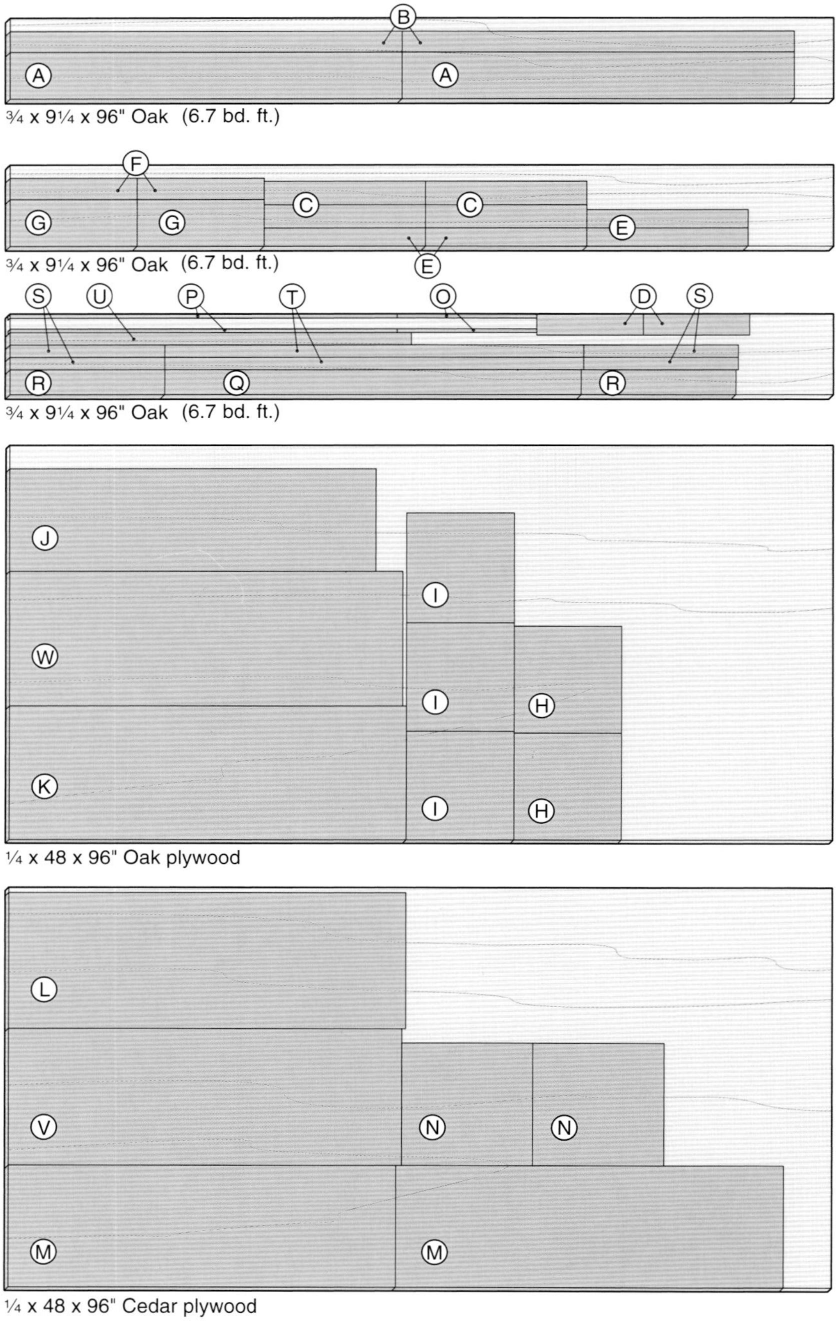

MATERIALS LIST FOR CEDAR-LINED HEIRLOOM CHEST

PART	FINISHED SIZE * T	W	L	MTL.	QTY.
A bottom rails	¾"	5½"	44"	O	2
B top rails	¾"	2½"	44"	O	2
C stiles	¾"	2½"	18½"	O	4
D mullions	¾"	2¼"	12½"	O	2
E side stiles	¾"	2⅛"	18½"	O	4
F side top rails	¾"	2½"	14¼"	O	2
G side bottom rails	¾"	5½"	14¼"	O	2
H side panels	¼"	13¼"	11½"	OP	2
I front panels	¼"	13½"	11½"	OP	3
J rear panel	¼"	11½"	43"	OP	1
K* bottom panel	¼"	16 3/16"	45 15/16"	OP	1
L* bottom liner	¼"	16 3/16"	45 15/16"	CP	1
M front/back liners	¼"	14"	45½"	CP	2
N side liners	¼"	14"	15¼"	CP	2
O* side molding	¼"	¼"	15¾"	O	2
P* front/back molding	¼"	¼"	45½"	O	2
Q* front/back base molding	¾"	3"	48½"	O	1
R* side base molding	¾"	3"	18"	O	2
S Side lid molding	1½"	1½"	18"	LO	2
T* front lid molding	1½"	1½"	48½"	LO	1
U back lid trim	¾"	1½"	46½"	O	1
V* lid liner	¼"	16¾"	46½"	CP	1
W* lid panel	¼"	16¾"	46½"	OP	1

*Parts initially cut oversized. See the instructions.
Materials Key: O = Oak; OP = Oak plywood; CP = Cedar plywood; LO = Laminated oak.
Supplies: Counterbalanced lid support; #8 x 1¼" brass flathead wood screws; 1½ x 2½" brass butt hinges (3); ½" brads; stain; finish; 0000 steel wool; contact cement.
Bits: ⅛" high-speed steel veining router bit.

10 To mark the veins on the front and side panels, first locate the vertical centerline on each panel. Next, mark lines 3⅛" apart on each side of the centerline. Now, set up a straightedge, and rout three ⅛" veins 1/16" deep in each panel.

11 Glue panels H, I, and J in the rabbeted openings in the framework. Remove any glue squeeze-out on the face of the panels with a damp rag immediately after clamping.

9–9.

FRONT FRAME

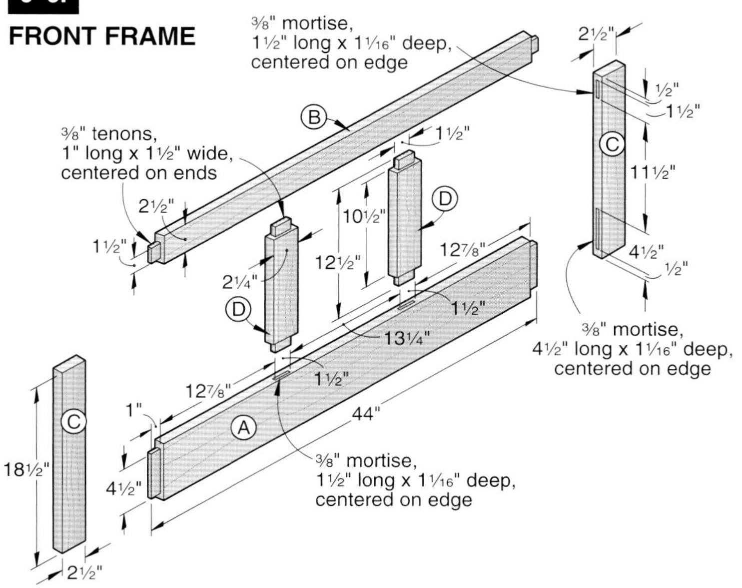
3/8" mortise,
1 1/2" long x 1 1/16" deep,
centered on edge
2 1/2"
1/2"
1 1/2"
3/8" tenons,
1" long x 1 1/2" wide,
centered on ends
1 1/2"
11 1/2"
10 1/2"
2 1/2"
1 1/2"
12 1/2"
12 7/8"
2 1/4"
4 1/2"
1/2"
1 1/2"
13 1/4"
3/8" mortise,
4 1/2" long x 1 1/16" deep,
centered on edge
12 7/8"
1 1/2"
1"
44"
18 1/2"
4 1/2"
3/8" mortise,
1 1/2" long x 1 1/16" deep,
centered on edge
2 1/2"
A
B
C
D

9–10.

SIDE FRAME

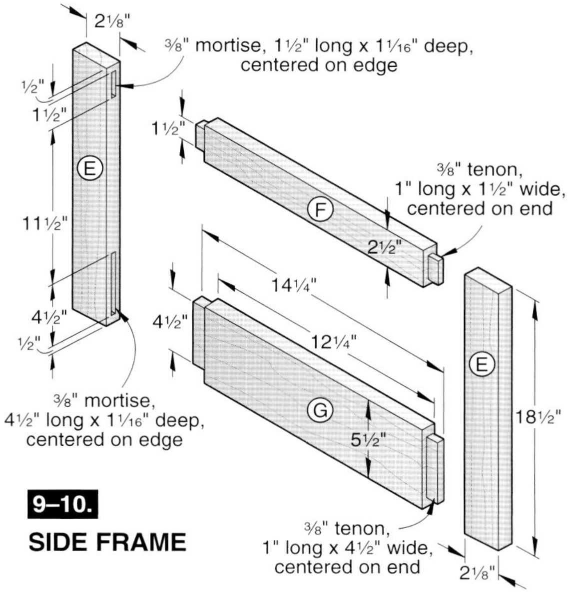
2 1/8"
3/8" mortise, 1 1/2" long x 1 1/16" deep,
centered on edge
1/2"
1 1/2"
1 1/2"
3/8" tenon,
1" long x 1 1/2" wide,
centered on end
11 1/2"
2 1/2"
14 1/4"
4 1/2"
4 1/2"
1/2"
12 1/4"
3/8" mortise,
4 1/2" long x 1 1/16" deep,
centered on edge
18 1/2"
5 1/2"
3/8" tenon,
1" long x 4 1/2" wide,
centered on end
2 1/8"
E
F
G

9–11.

HEIRLOOM CHEST EXPLODED VIEW

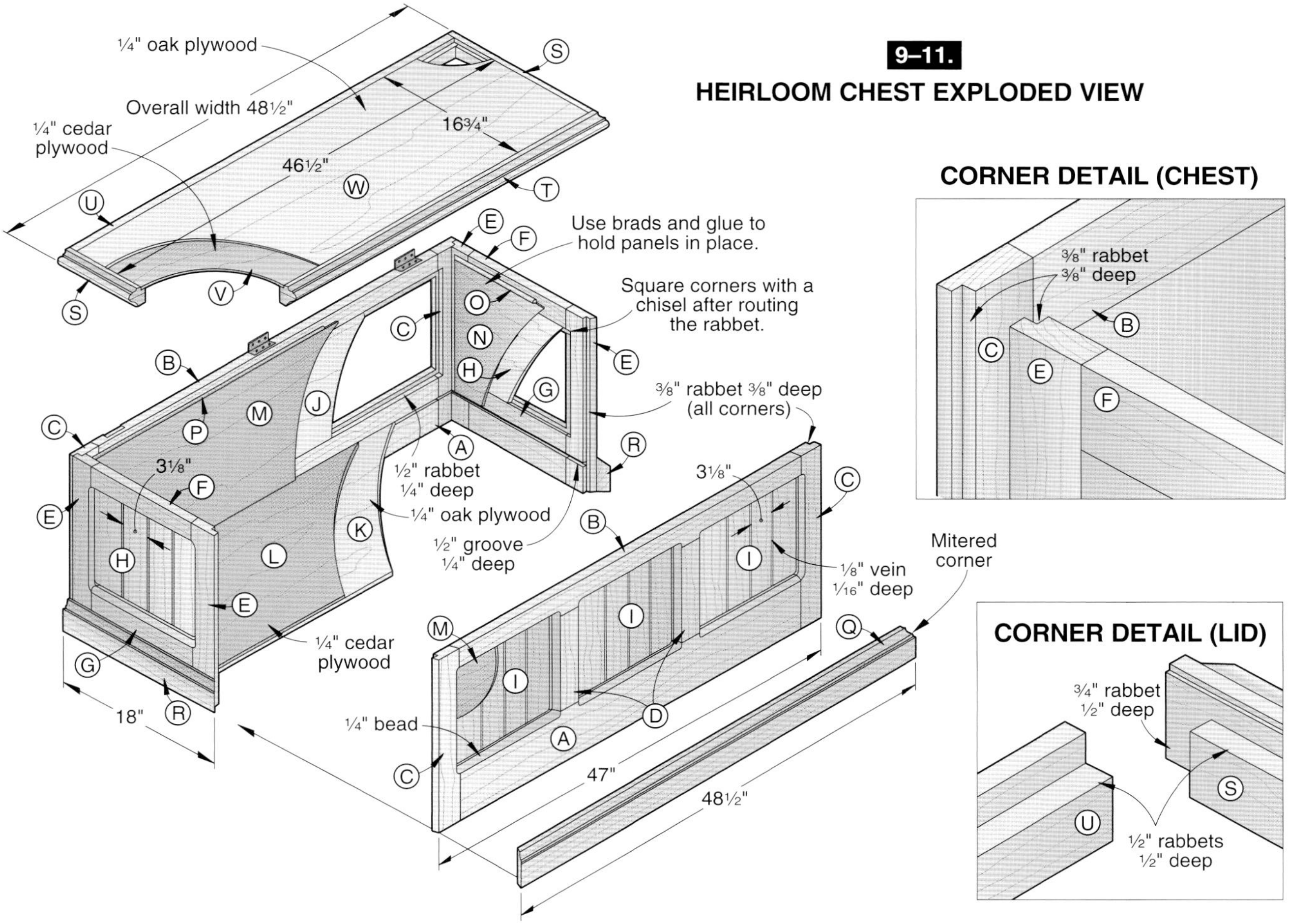
1/4" oak plywood
Overall width 48 1/2"
1/4" cedar plywood
16 3/4"
46 1/2"
Use brads and glue to hold panels in place.
Square corners with a chisel after routing the rabbet.
3/8" rabbet 3/8" deep (all corners)
1/2" rabbet 1/4" deep
1/4" oak plywood
1/2" groove 1/4" deep
3 1/8"
3 1/8"
1/8" vein 1/16" deep
Mitered corner
1/4" cedar plywood
18"
1/4" bead
47"
48 1/2"
CORNER DETAIL (CHEST)
3/8" rabbet 3/8" deep
CORNER DETAIL (LID)
3/4" rabbet 1/2" deep
1/2" rabbets 1/2" deep

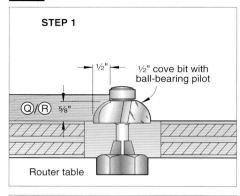

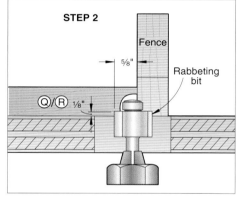

9–14. ROUTING THE BASE MOLDING

STEP 1

½" cove bit with ball-bearing pilot

½"

Q/R ⅝"

Router table

STEP 2

Fence

⅝"

Rabbeting bit

Q/R ⅛"

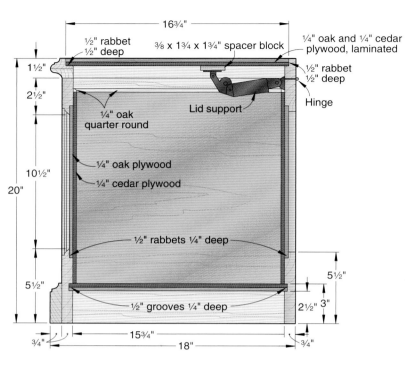

16¾"

½" rabbet ½" deep

⅜ x 1¾ x 1¾" spacer block

¼" oak and ¼" cedar plywood, laminated

½" rabbet ½" deep

1½"

2½"

¼" oak quarter round

Lid support

Hinge

10½"

¼" oak plywood

¼" cedar plywood

20"

½" rabbets ¼" deep

5½"

5½"

½" grooves ¼" deep

2½" 3"

¾"

15¾"

18"

¾"

9–12. SIDE SECTION

12 To fashion the bottom, cut the oak plywood panel (K) and cedar plywood liner (L) to size plus ½" on all sides. Then, laminate the two plywood pieces with contact cement. Finally, trim the laminated panel to finished size (16³⁄₁₆ x 45¹⁵⁄₁₆") with a tablesaw or with a circular saw and a straightedge. (Cut the laminated panel ⅛" shorter in length and width than the dadoed opening to allow for contraction of the framework.)

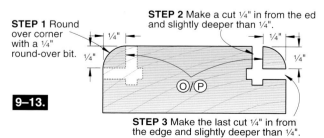

STEP 1 Round over corner with a ¼" round-over bit.

STEP 2 Make a cut ¼" in from the ed and slightly deeper than ¼".

¼"

¼"

¼"

¼"

O/P

9–13.

STEP 3 Make the last cut ¼" in from the edge and slightly deeper than ¼".

CUTTING THE QUARTER ROUND (FULL SIZE)

13 Dry-clamp the chest framework, making sure that the bottom (K/ L) doesn't prevent the rabbeted corner joints from fitting snugly. Once the framework fits together correctly, glue and clamp it, checking for square and making sure that the top edges of the four frames are flush.

14 Scrape off the excess glue after it dries. Then, sand all surfaces smooth.

Line the Chest

1 Cut the front and back lining pieces (M) to size from ¼" cedar plywood, keeping the grain direction horizontal. Then, check the fit of the pieces in the chest, but do not glue them in position yet. Cut the side liners (N) to size and dry-fit them, trimming if necessary.

2 Glue and brad the front and back liners in place, and then the side liners.

9–15 ROUTING THE LID MOLDING

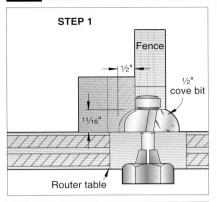

STEP 1

Fence

1/2"

1/2" cove bit

1 11/16"

Router table

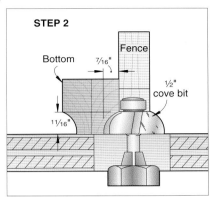

STEP 2

Bottom 7/16" Fence

1/2" cove bit

1 11/16"

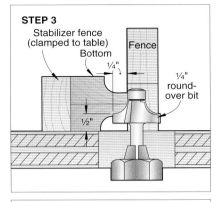

STEP 3

Stabilizer fence (clamped to table)

Bottom 1/4" Fence

1/4" round-over bit

1/2"

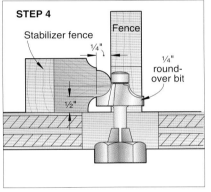

STEP 4

Stabilizer fence Fence

1/4"

1/4" round-over bit

1/2"

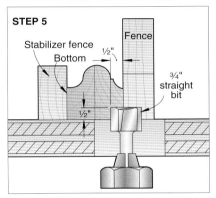

STEP 5

Stabilizer fence Fence

Bottom 1/2"

3/4" straight bit

1/2"

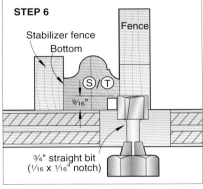

STEP 6

Stabilizer fence Fence

Bottom

(S)/(T)

9/16"

3/4" straight bit
(1/16 x 1/16" notch)

---

3 Cap the top edge of the liner material with quarter-round molding (O, P). To make these pieces, cut a piece of 3/4" oak 2" wide and 62" long. (For safety's sake and ease of cutting the pieces on a tablesaw, use a 2"-wide board.) Rout a 1/4" round-over on two edges, where shown in *Step 1* of **9–13**. Then, follow *Steps 2* and *3* to rip the two quarter-round pieces from the oak strip. The thin strips may have a tendency to kick back when the cut is completed. To be safe, use a pushblock and don't stand directly behind the piece being cut.

4 Miter-cut the side molding strips (O) and dry-clamp them above the 1/4" cedar liners. Miter-cut the front and back strips (P) to fit. Glue and brad the molding strips in position, and sand them flush with the cedar-plywood lining.

Rout the Base and Lid Molding

1 Cut the base molding pieces (Q, R) to size plus 2" in length.

2 Follow the two-step procedure in **9–14** to rout the decorative contours on the three molding pieces.

3 Miter-cut both ends of the front piece and the front end of each side molding. Then, glue and clamp the pieces to the chest.

4 To form the lid molding, start by cutting four pieces of 3/4" oak to 1 3/4 x 20" for the sides (S) and two pieces of 1 3/4 x 50" for the front (T). Laminate the four 20"-long pieces into two blocks that measure 1 1/2 x 1 3/4 x 20". Do the same to the two 50"-long pieces. (Form a scrap lamination about 12" in length to use for making test cuts. Then position the router bits as shown in **9–15**, test-cut the scrap, and readjust the bits as necessary before routing the finished pieces to

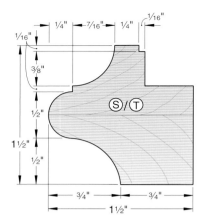

9–16. LID MOLDING DETAIL

match the profile shown in **9–16**. Scrape off excess glue, and rip all three laminated pieces to 1½" finished width. Also, cut the lid's back trim piece (U) to finished size.

5 Follow *Steps 1* through *6* in **9–15** to rout the decorative molding (S, T). Now, go back and rout a ½" rabbet ½" deep along the top inside edge of the back trim piece (U), following *Step 5* of **9–15**.

6 Cut the lid pieces V and W to size plus ½" on all sides.

Then laminate the two pieces with contact cement, and trim the panel to finished size.

7 Glue and clamp the back trim piece to the laminated panel (V,W), keeping the ends flush.

8 Next, cut a ¾" rabbet ½" deep in the back end of each side molding piece (S), where shown on the Corner Detail (Lid) drawing in **9–11**, *page 165*.

9 Miter-cut the side molding pieces (S) and front molding piece (T) to length. Now, glue and clamp them to the lid assembly, being careful not to mar the routed edge. (When clamping, you can use scrap spacers with the clamps for uniform pressure and to prevent marring the oak veneer plywood.)

Add a Finish and the Hardware

1 Mortise the back rail (B) and back trim piece (U) for the hinges. Note that the middle hinge is centered, whereas

the other two are positioned 4" in from each end.

2 Sand the chest smooth— especially the cedar lining, which will remain unfinished. Use masking tape and newspaper to mask the lining, and apply the finish of your choice. (To produce the finish shown on the chest on *page 165*, stain it first and then apply several coats of polyurethane, using steel wool between coats.) Remove the tape and newspaper.

2 Install the hinges. Then attach the lid support and spacer block, where shown on **9–12**.

Note: Cedar slowly loses its aroma over time. You can revive the fragrance by lightly sanding it with 220-grit sandpaper. You also can plane a solid piece of cedar, put the shavings in a nylon or sock, and place it in the chest for use as a pomander.

10

super shelves and storage centers

AS YOU HAVE LEARNED BY NOW, HOME storage comes in many forms and styles. So far in this book you have seen cabinets, a hutch, sideboards, entertainment and computer centers, desks, bookcases, display cases, chests, and other items. So you might be thinking, "How much more can there be?"

Actually, plenty. In fact, there are so many storage types that it would take a book twice the size of this one even to attempt to cover storage completely. This chapter contains two storage projects that didn't quite fit into any of the preceding ones.

The first, on page 170, is a unit with shelves, boxes with doors, and drawers. You can shape the unit to be and do anything you want. You'll note that it's also quite a handsome project that will look perfect in your den, living room, or wherever you choose to locate it.

The second unit, on page 180, is for one of the most commonly disorganized places in the home—the laundry room. By following the laundry center design and the complete building instructions, you will find a way to organize that room. So try it out!

KNOCKDOWN CABINET SYSTEM

This sleek, versatile cabinet system lends itself to any number of furniture pieces that easily assemble and disassemble. The following instructions show you how to build the components, detailed *above*; you decide what your needs are, and build the furniture to suit. The key to the system lies in the cam-lock knockdown hardware, which lets you alter your furniture as your needs change or grow. If you don't require the knockdown feature, you can join the parts by conventional methods, such as screws or biscuits.

Assemble the components in four ways. As shown in the examples, you can build a bookshelf or display shelf, sideboard, buffet cabinet, chest of drawers, or any combination of these elements— tall or short, wide or narrow. Because the shelf unit looks the same from both sides, and the door and drawer boxes have finished backs, as shown at right, *this project can be positioned away from a wall, acting as a room divider.*

MATERIALS LIST FOR KNOCKDOWN CABINET SYSTEM

PART		FINISHED SIZE			MTL.	QTY.
		T	W	L		
CARCASE						
A	sides (tall)	¾"	13¼"	61¾"	MP	2
A	sides (short)	¾"	13¼"	31¼"	MP	2
B	shelves (tall)	¾"	13¼"	28"	MP	5
B	shelves (short)	¾"	13¼"	28"	MP	3
C*	side banding (tall)	¾"	¾"	61¾"	M	4
C*	side banding (short)	¾"	¾"	31¼"	M	4
D*	bottom banding	¾"	¾"	28"	M	2
E*	shelf edging (tall)	¾"	1⅛"	28"	M	8
E*	shelf edging (short)	¾"	1⅛"	28"	M	4
BASE AND TOP						
F	base stretchers (single)	¾"	3"	29½"	MY	2
F	base stretchers (double)	¾"	3"	59"	MY	2
G	base sides	¾"	3"	14¾"	MY	2
H*	feet (single unit)	3"	3"	2¼"	LMY	4
H*	feet (double unit)	3"	3"	2¼"	LMY	6
I	reveal stretchers (single)	¾"	2¾"	29"	MY	2
I	reveal stretchers (double)	¾"	2¾"	58½"	MY	2
J	reveal sides	¾"	2¾"	14¼"	MY	2
K*	top (single)	¾"	15¾"	30½"	EM	1
K*	top (double)	¾"	15¾"	60"	EM	1
BOXES						
L	sides	¾"	12½"	14"	MP	2
M	top/bottom	¾"	12½"	12½"	MP	2
N	drawer shelf	¾"	12½"	12½"	MP	1
O*	side banding	¾"	¾"	14"	M	4
P*	top/bottom banding	¾"	¾"	12½"	M	4
Q*	drawer shelf banding	¾"	¾"	12½"	M	2
R	back	¼"	13"	13"	MP	1
DOOR						
S	stiles	¾"	2"	13⅞"	M	2
T	rails	¾"	2"	10⅜"	M	2
U	panel	¾"	10⅜"	10⅜"	MP	1
DRAWERS						
V	fronts/backs	½"	5⅜"	11¾"	M	4
W	sides	½"	5⅜"	13"	M	4
X	bottoms	¼"	11¾"	12½"	MP	2
Y*	slide cleats	¼"	2½"	12"	M	2
Z	faces	¾"	6⅞"	13⅞"	M	2
AA	glides	⅜"	¾"	1½"	M	4

*Parts initially cut oversized. See the instructions.
Materials Key: MP = Maple plywood; M = Maple; MY = Mahogany;
LMY = Laminated mahogany; EM = Edge-joined maple.
Supplies: #8 x ¾" flathead wood screws; #8 x 1¼" flathead wood screws;
#8 x 1½" flathead wood screws; #8 x 2" flathead wood screws; 8-32 x 1½"
roundhead machine screws.
Hardware:
• Each pair of *tall sides* (A) requires 20 cam housings and screw studs.
• Each pair of *short sides* (A) requires 12 cam housings and screw studs.
• Each door box requires eight cam housings and screw studs, two hinges
and hinge plates, one knob, and four bumpers.
• Each drawer box requires 12 cam housings and screw studs, two under-
mount drawer slides, eight 1" washer-head screws, two knobs with 1½"-
long knob screws, and four bumpers.
Drill Bits: ¼-inch drill bit; 1-inch carbide-tipped Forstner bit; 1½-inch
Forstner bit.

CUTTING DIAGRAM FOR KNOCKDOWN CABINET SYSTEM

TALL SHELF UNIT CUTTING DIAGRAM

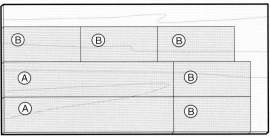

¾ x 48 x 96" Maple plywood

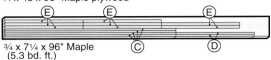

¾ x 7¼ x 96" Maple
(5.3 bd. ft.)

SHORT SHELF UNIT CUTTING DIAGRAM

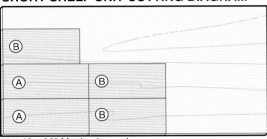

¾ x 48 x 96" Maple plywood

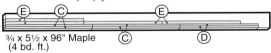

¾ x 5½ x 96" Maple
(4 bd. ft.)

DOUBLE BASE AND TOP CUTTING DIAGRAM

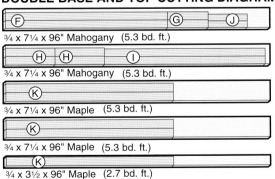

¾ x 7¼ x 96" Mahogany (5.3 bd. ft.)

¾ x 7¼ x 96" Mahogany (5.3 bd. ft.)

¾ x 7¼ x 96" Maple (5.3 bd. ft.)

¾ x 7¼ x 96" Maple (5.3 bd. ft.)

¾ x 3½ x 96" Maple (2.7 bd. ft.)

SINGLE BASE AND TOP CUTTING DIAGRAM

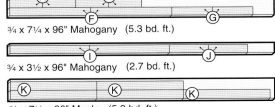

¾ x 7¼ x 96" Mahogany (5.3 bd. ft.)

¾ x 3½ x 96" Mahogany (2.7 bd. ft.)

¾ x 7¼ x 96" Maple (5.3 bd. ft.)

Cutting Diagram continues on the following page

CUTTING DIAGRAM (continued)

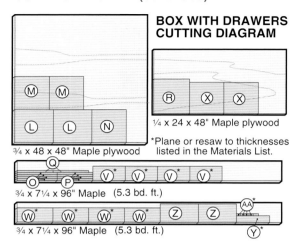

BOX WITH DRAWERS CUTTING DIAGRAM

¾ x 48 x 48" Maple plywood

M M
L L N

R X X

¼ x 24 x 48" Maple plywood

*Plane or resaw to thicknesses listed in the Materials List.

Q
O P V* V* V* V*
¾ x 7¼ x 96" Maple   (5.3 bd. ft.)

W* W* W* W* Z Z AA*
Y*
¾ x 7¼ x 96" Maple   (5.3 bd. ft.)

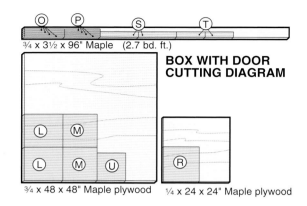

O P S T
¾ x 3½ x 96" Maple   (2.7 bd. ft.)

BOX WITH DOOR CUTTING DIAGRAM

L M
L M U
¾ x 48 x 48" Maple plywood

R
¼ x 24 x 24" Maple plywood

Plan Your Project

The Materials List and the Cutting Diagrams show parts for a pair of long and short sides, a single and double base and top, one door box (add the drawer shelf to make a drawer box), one door, and two drawers. To develop a cutting list for the configuration you want to build, draw your design on paper, then count how many components you'll need.

For example, the unit shown in the large photo on *page 170* consists of two pairs of tall sides, ten shelves (two of which are bottom shelves), one double base, one double top, six boxes with four drawer shelves, two doors, and four pairs of drawers. The chest of drawers is made up of one pair of short sides, three shelves (one of which is a bottom shelf), a single base, single top, four boxes with four drawer shelves, and four pairs of drawers.

Build the Carcase

1 From ¾" plywood, cut the sides (A) and shelves (B) to the sizes shown in the Materials List. You'll need five shelves for a tall unit and three for a short unit.

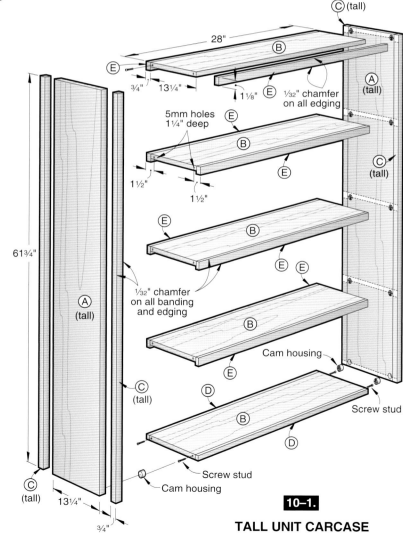

28"
C (tall)
B
E
¾" 13¼"
1⅛" E 1/32" chamfer on all edging
A (tall)
5mm holes 1¼" deep
E
B
C (tall)
1½" E
1½"
E
B
E E
1/32" chamfer on all banding and edging
A (tall)
E
B
Cam housing
Screw stud
C (tall)
D
B
D
61¾"
Screw stud
Cam housing
C (tall) 13¼"
¾"

10–1.

TALL UNIT CARCASE

10–2.

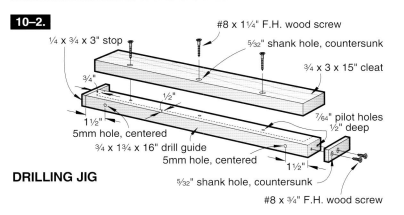

¼ x ¾ x 3" stop

#8 x 1¼" F.H. wood screw

⁵⁄₃₂" shank hole, countersunk

¾"

½"

¾ x 3 x 15" cleat

1½"

5mm hole, centered

⁷⁄₆₄" pilot holes
½" deep

¾ x 1¾ x 16" drill guide

5mm hole, centered

1½"

DRILLING JIG

⁵⁄₃₂" shank hole, countersunk

#8 x ¾" F.H. wood screw

2 Rip the side banding (C), bottom banding (D), and shelf edging (E) to width, and cut them about ½" longer than their mating plywood panels. Glue and clamp the banding to the sides and bottom shelf. Glue and clamp the edging to the remaining shelves, where indicated in **10–1**. See the Shop Tip "Reducing Sanding Time When Applying Banding" for a time-saving method for applying the banding.

3 With the glue dry, sand the banding flush with the faces of the sides and the bottom shelf. Sand the edging flush with the shelves' top faces. Trim the banding and edging ends flush with their respective panels' ends.

4 Mark the bottom end of each side (A/C). Lay out the locations of the 25mm holes for the knockdown fitting cam housings on the sides (A/C), where shown on **10–5** (*page 174*). Measure the locations for the top pair of 1" holes from the top end. Measure all the other vertical locations from the bottom end, as indicated on the drawing. See the Shop Tip "Fast, Foolproof Marking" for a good marking method.

5 Chuck a 25mm Forstner bit in your drill press, set the fence 1½" from the bit's center, and adjust the depth stop to drill ½" deep. Drill the cam-housing holes at their marked locations.

6 To drill the pilot holes in the ends of the shelves for the knockdown fitting screw studs, build the jig shown in **10–2**. When drilling the ¼" guide holes in the drill guide, use your drill press and a fence fitted with a stopblock for maximum accuracy. Clamp the jig to the shelves with their top faces up. Chuck a ¼" bit in your drill so it protrudes 3" from the chuck. Slip a #10 flat washer over the bit, and drill the stud pilot holes, as shown in **10–4**. The chuck acts as a depth stop, and the washer protects the jig from the chuck's jaws.

7 Rout a ¹⁄₃₂" chamfer on all the banding and edging, where shown on **10–1**. Finish-sand the

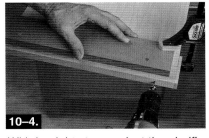

10–4.

With its right stop against the shelf's right edge, clamp the drilling jig in place, and drill the first hole. Unclamp, shift the jig so its left stop is against the shelf's left edge, and drill the second hole.

SHOP TIP

Reducing Sanding Time When Applying Banding

To reduce sanding time when applying banding, carefully plane your banding stock to one paper-thickness thicker than your plywood. Lay your panel and banding across your bar clamps, as shown in 10–3. Apply white glue for longer working time. Starting at one end and working down the panel's length, first clamp the banding flush with the panel using a pair of quick-action clamps, then draw it tight with a bar clamp.

With the glue dry, make a couple of passes with a cabinet scraper followed by a couple of swipes with a sanding block to create flush edges.

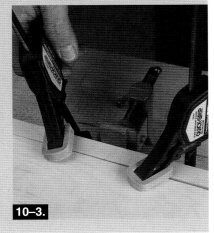

10–3.

10–5. SIDES

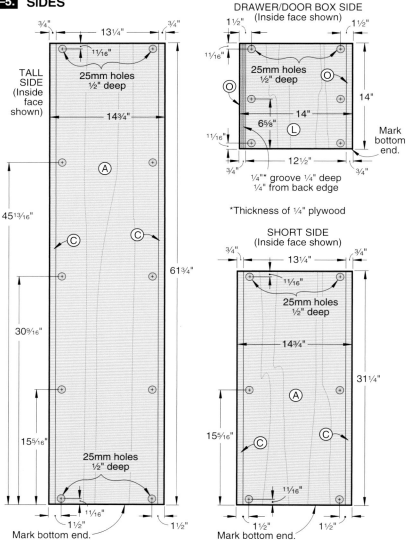

TALL SIDE (Inside face shown)

¾" 13¼" ¾"

¹¹⁄₁₆"

25mm holes ½" deep

14¾"

45¹³⁄₁₆"

Ⓐ

Ⓒ Ⓒ

61¾"

30⁹⁄₁₆"

15⁵⁄₁₆"

25mm holes ½" deep

¹¹⁄₁₆"

1½" 1½"

Mark bottom end.

DRAWER/DOOR BOX SIDE (Inside face shown)

1½" 1½"

¹¹⁄₁₆"

25mm holes ½" deep

Ⓞ Ⓞ

14"

14"

6⅝" Ⓛ

¹¹⁄₁₆"

Mark bottom end.

12½"

¾" ¾"

¼"* groove ¼" deep ¼" from back edge

*Thickness of ¼" plywood

SHORT SIDE (Inside face shown)

¾" 13¼" ¾"

¹¹⁄₁₆"

25mm holes ½" deep

14¾"

31¼"

Ⓐ

15⁵⁄₁₆"

Ⓒ Ⓒ

¹¹⁄₁₆"

1½" 1½"

Mark bottom end.

sides and shelves to 220 grit. Apply two coats of satin polyurethane, sanding lightly with 220-grit sandpaper between coats.

8 Press the cam housings into their holes so they are flush with the surface. Engage the end of your combination square in the housings' slots to rotate them into alignment. Orient the stud holes to the sides' top,

except for the bottom pairs. These stud holes should be oriented toward the bottom.

9 Drive the studs with a screw-driver until the stud's flange seats on the shelf's end.

Adding a Base and Top

1 Miter-cut the single- or double-unit base stretchers (F)

and base sides (G) to size. Glue and clamp them into a rectangular frame, as shown in **10–7**.

2 To make the six feet (H) for a double-wide unit, cut four ¾ x 3⅛ x 18" mahogany boards and laminate them into a 3"-thick blank. To make the four feet for a single-wide unit, use four ¾ x 3⅛ x 12" boards. With the glue dry, joint and plane the blank to 3" wide, and then cross-cut the 2¼"-long legs. Rout a ⅛" chamfer around the bottom of each leg.

3 Clamp the legs to the base frame with their edges flush with the edges of the base stretchers (F) and base sides (G), where shown on **10–7**. Drill pilot and countersunk shank holes, and glue and screw the legs to the frame. Sand the mating edges smooth.

SHOP TIP

Fast, Foolproof Marking

To speed the repetitive layout of the cam-housing holes, mark the desired measurements on a piece of masking tape applied to your tape measure blade. The masking tape will not interfere with the operation of your tape measure. As long as you always measure from the bottom edge of the workpiece, you won't accidentally mismark the location of a hole.

10–6.

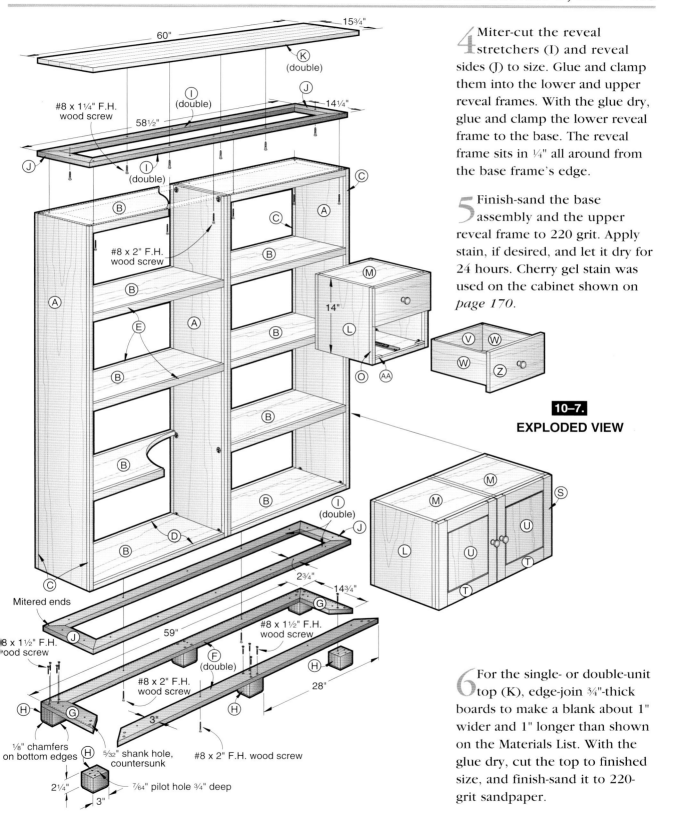

15¾"
60"
K (double)

#8 x 1¼" F.H. wood screw

I (double)
J

58½"
14¼"

J
I (double)

C
B
A
C

#8 x 2" F.H. wood screw

B
B
A
E
A
B
M
14"
L
B
O AA
B
V W
W Z
B
I (double)
J

D
B
C

Mitered ends

8 x 1½" wood screw
J
59"
2¾"
14¾"
G

#8 x 1½" F.H. wood screw

#8 x 2" F.H. wood screw
F (double)
H
28"
H

⅛" chamfers on bottom edges
H
5/32" shank hole, countersunk
#8 x 2" F.H. wood screw
G
3"
H

2¼"
3"
7/64" pilot hole ¾" deep

M
M
S
U
L
U
T
T

10–7.
EXPLODED VIEW

4 Miter-cut the reveal stretchers (I) and reveal sides (J) to size. Glue and clamp them into the lower and upper reveal frames. With the glue dry, glue and clamp the lower reveal frame to the base. The reveal frame sits in ¼" all around from the base frame's edge.

5 Finish-sand the base assembly and the upper reveal frame to 220 grit. Apply stain, if desired, and let it dry for 24 hours. Cherry gel stain was used on the cabinet shown on *page 170.*

6 For the single- or double-unit top (K), edge-join ¾"-thick boards to make a blank about 1" wider and 1" longer than shown on the Materials List. With the glue dry, cut the top to finished size, and finish-sand it to 220-grit sandpaper.

10–8.

Insert the shelf studs in the cam-housing sockets. Turn the cams with a Phillips screwdriver to lock the shelves in place.

7 Apply two coats of satin polyurethane to the base assembly, upper reveal frame, and top.

8 With the finish dry, clamp the upper reveal frame to the top. The reveal frame sits back from the top's edge ¾" all around. Drill pilot and counter-sunk shank holes through the reveal frame into the top, as seen in **10–7** (*page 175*). Drive the screws.

Assemble the Shelf Unit

1 Lay one side (A/C) on the floor with the cam housings up. Insert the shelves (B/E) and bottom shelf (B/D), as shown in **10–8**.

2 Position the other side on the upturned shelves, engaging the shelf studs in the cam-housing sockets. Turn the cams to lock in the shelves.

3 Clamp the base assembly (F/G/H/I/J) and top assembly (I/J/K) to the shelf unit. The base stretcher/side frame (F/G) should be flush with the shelf unit's edges. The top (K) should overhang ½" all around. If you are building a double unit, tightly clamp the units together side to side, with the ends and edges flush, before mounting the base and top assemblies. Drill pilot and countersunk shank holes through the base assembly into the bottom shelf, and through the top shelf into the top assembly, as shown in **10–7**. Drive the screws, and remove the clamps.

Make the Boxes

1 Cut the box sides (L); top and bottom (M); and, if you are building a drawer box, cut the drawer shelf (N) to size.

2 Rip the box side banding (O), top/bottom banding (P), and drawer shelf banding (Q) to width, and cut them about ½" longer than their mating ply-wood panels. Plane, glue, and clamp the bandings to their mating parts as you did for the sides (A) and bottom shelf (B).

3 With the glue dry, sand the banding flush with the panels' faces. Trim the banding ends flush with their respective panels' ends.

4 Lay out the locations of the 1" holes for the knockdown fittings' cam housings on the sides (L), where dimensioned on **10–5** (*page 174*). Because the cam-housing holes for the drawer shelf in the drawer box are slightly below center, mark the bottom ends of the drawer box sides, and measure these hole locations from the marked ends.

5 Cut the grooves for the back (R) in the box sides (L) and top and bottom (M) with a regular blade in your tablesaw, where shown on **10–5**, **10–9** and the Drawer Box drawing in **10–11** (*page 178*). To make a good fit for the plywood back, cut the grooves in two passes. If making a drawer box, pair up the drawer box sides so you have right- and left-hand sides.

6 As before, press the cam housings into the sides. Use the jig to drill stud pilot holes in the top, bottom, and drawer shelf ends. Drive the studs.

7 Clamp a box together, and check the groove-to-groove dimensions. Cut the box back (R) to size. Note that the grain runs vertically.

8 To make the rear edge of the drawer shelf (N/Q) fall inside the drawer box back (R), rip ½" off its rear edge, giving the drawer shelf assembly a finished width of 13½".

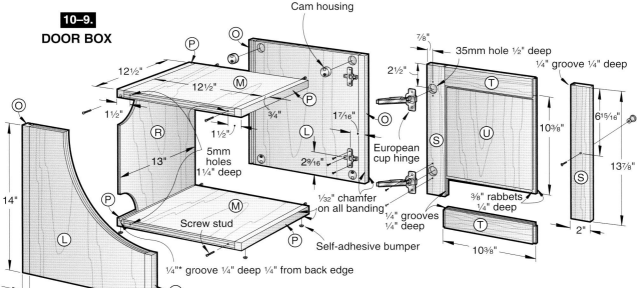

10–9.
DOOR BOX

Cam housing

7/8"
35mm hole 1/2" deep
1/4" groove 1/4" deep

12½"
12½"
2½"
6¹⁵⁄₁₆"
1½"
¾"
1⁷⁄₁₆"
10⅜"
1½"
European cup hinge
13"
5mm holes 1¼" deep
2⁹⁄₁₆"
13⅞"
14"
⅜" rabbets ¼" deep
2"
¹⁄₃₂" chamfer on all banding
¼" grooves ¼" deep
Screw stud
Self-adhesive bumper
¾"
12½"
¼"* groove ¼" deep ¼" from back edge
10⅜"
¾"
*Thickness of ¼" plywood

9 Rout a ¹⁄₃₂" chamfer on all the banding edges and ends. Sand the box parts to 220 grit, and apply the finish.

Make a Frame-and-Panel Door

1 Cut the stiles (S) and rails (T) to size. Install a ¼" dado blade in your tablesaw, and cut ¼"-deep grooves centered in the thickness of the rails and stiles, where shown on **10–10**. To ensure centered grooves, first make test cuts in scrap that is the same thickness as your parts, adjusting the fence as necessary. When you are satisfied that the fence is correctly positioned, cut the grooves in the stiles (S) and rails (T).

2 With the ¼" dado blade in your tablesaw, form the tenons on the ends of the rails (T). Test the fit of the rail tenons in the stile grooves by first making cuts in your scrap piece.

3 Clamp your door frame together, and check the groove-to-groove dimensions. Cut the panel (U) to size. With a ⅜" dado blade in your tablesaw, form a centered tongue on the panel that fits the frame parts' grooves and leaves a ⅛" reveal. To keep from chipping veneer at the corners, first form the cross-grain tongues, and then the parallel-grain tongues. Sand the panel to 220 grit.

4 To enhance the reveal, stain the panel's tongue with the same stain used on the mahogany parts. Apply masking tape to the tongue's shoulder to keep stain from bleeding onto the panel's surface.

5 Once the stain is dry, squeeze glue into the grooves. Use glue sparingly so that it does not squeeze out into the reveal. Clamp the door together, making certain it is square and flat.

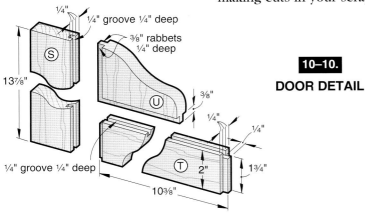

¼"
¼" groove ¼" deep
⅜" rabbets ¼" deep
13⅞"
⅜"
¼"
¼"
¼" groove ¼" deep
2"
1¾"
10⅜"

10–10.
DOOR DETAIL

10–11.
DRAWER BOX

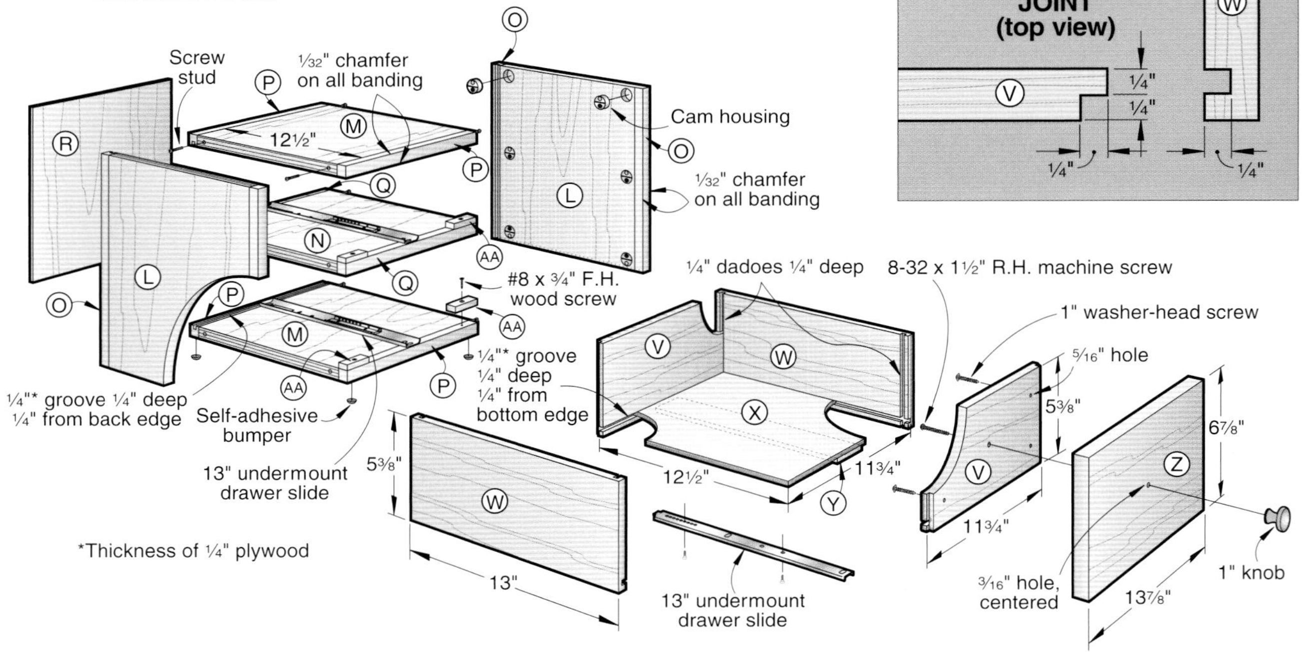
Screw stud
1/32" chamfer on all banding
12 1/2"
Cam housing
1/32" chamfer on all banding
#8 x 3/4" F.H. wood screw
1/4" dadoes 1/4" deep
8-32 x 1 1/2" R.H. machine screw
1" washer-head screw
5/16" hole
5 3/8"
6 7/8"
1/4"* groove 1/4" deep 1/4" from bottom edge
1/4"* groove 1/4" deep 1/4" from back edge
Self-adhesive bumper
13" undermount drawer slide
5 3/8"
12 1/2"
11 3/4"
11 3/4"
13"
13" undermount drawer slide
3/16" hole, centered
13 7/8"
1" knob
*Thickness of 1/4" plywood
O
P
M
L
R
Q
N
AA
V
W
X
Y
Z

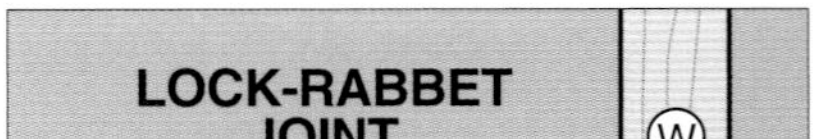
LOCK-RABBET JOINT (top view)
W
V
1/4"
1/4"
1/4"
1/4"

6 Mark the hinge-cup hole locations on the back of the door's stile, where shown on **10–9** (*page 177*). Chuck a 1½" Forstner bit in your drill press, and drill the ½"-deep holes. Drill the 3⁄16" knob hole, where shown. Sand the door to 220 grit, and apply the finish.

7 Mark horizontal and vertical centerlines for the hinge plates on one side (L/O), where shown on **10–9**. Position the plates on the centerlines, and drill the pilot holes.

Construct a Pair of Drawers

1 Plane enough lumber to ½" thickness for the drawer fronts/backs (V) and sides (W). Cut the parts to size. Install a ¼" dado blade in your tablesaw. Cut the rabbets in the fronts/backs and the dadoes in the sides to form the lock-rabbet joint shown on the Lock-Rabbet Joint drawing in **10–11**. Cut the ¼"-deep grooves in the parts for the bottoms (X), according to the Drawer Box drawing in **10–11**. Use a regular blade in your tablesaw, making two passes to match the thickness of the ¼" plywood.

2 Drill the four 5⁄16" holes in the fronts (V) for mounting the drawer faces (Z), where shown. The faces are fastened to the drawers with washer-head screws. The oversize holes allow you to adjust the faces' positions during final assembly. Sand all the drawer parts to 220 grit.

3 Dry-assemble the drawer parts to check their fit, and measure for the bottoms (X). Cut the bottoms to size. Then apply glue to the lock rabbets and grooves, and clamp the drawers together.

4 Resaw a ¾ x 2½ x 12" board in half and plane it to ¼" thickness for the drawer slide cleats (Y). Glue and clamp the cleats to the drawer bottoms, centered where shown on the Drawer Box drawing in **10–11**.

5 Cut the drawer faces (Z) to size. Drill centered 3⁄16" holes for the knobs. Sand the faces to 220 grit. Apply finish to all the drawer parts.

6 Resaw and plane a ⅜ x ¾ x 8" blank for the glides (AA).

Cut them to length, and drill centered, countersunk shank holes. Set the glides aside.

Assemble the Boxes

1 Position the glides (AA) on the drawer box bottom (M/P) and drawer shelf (N/Q), per the Drawer Box drawing in **10–11**. Drill pilot holes, and screw the glides in place.

2 Remove the optional rear bracket from the under-mounted drawer slides, and separate the drawer and carcase members. Carefully centering the carcase members, and keeping their front ends flush with the front edges of the bottom and shelf, screw them in place.

3 Insert the top, bottom, and drawer shelf studs in the cam housings of one side of the door and drawer boxes. Lock them in place. Slide the backs into the grooves. Mate the other sides with the protruding studs, and lock the cams.

4 Screw the hinge plates to the door box. Press the hinges into the cup holes, and using the holes in the cup flanges as guides, drill the pilot holes. Drive the screws. Install the knob, and snap the hinges onto the plates. Turn the adjustment screws to center the door on the box.

5 Turn the drawers upside down. Carefully centering the slides' drawer members, and keeping their front ends flush with the drawers' front edges, screw them in place. Slide the drawers into the box, and check to see if they are square in their openings. If not, the slides' slotted holes allow for adjustment.

6 To mount the lower drawer face (Z), place the drawer box on a flat surface. Pull the bottom drawer out far enough to accommodate the heads of small C-clamps or bar clamps. Clamp a drawer face to the drawer, as shown in **10–12**. Remove the drawer and, centering the bit in the 5⁄16" holes in the drawer front (V), drill pilot holes into the drawer face (Z). Then drive washer-head screws, and remove the clamps.

7 Mount the upper drawer face in the same manner, this time placing the upper face on a 1⁄8"-thick spacer resting on the top edge of the lower drawer face. Clamp, drill, and drive the screws.

8 Check the alignment of the drawers and faces with the drawer box and each other. Make any necessary adjustments to the positions of the drawer slides and drawer faces. When you are satisfied with the alignment, using the holes in the drawer faces as guides, drill the knob screw holes through the drawer fronts. Using the 1½"-long machine screws that come with the latter, screw the knobs in place.

9 To keep the door and drawer boxes from slipping around on the shelves, adhere four self-adhesive bumpers to the bottom of each box.

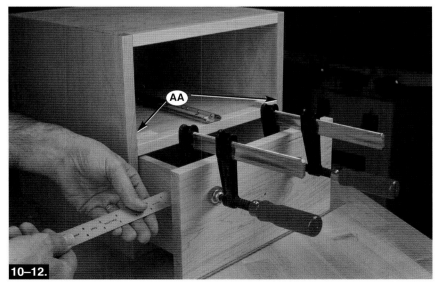

10–12.

Place a 1⁄16"-thick spacer underneath the drawer face, and clamp it, centered, to the drawer. The upper drawer was removed to show the placement of the slide's carcase member and the glides (AA).

SHOP TIP

Guidelines for Driving Screws Into Melamine

Read this before you drive a single screw into melamine. Unlike solid-wood fibers, which tend to be crushed when you drive a screw into them, the glue and wood particles in melamine-laminated particleboard tend to bulge up at the point where the screw enters the surface.

To avoid this, always drill pilot holes into melamine. For the 1", 1¼", 1¾", and 2" deck screws used throughout this project, ⁷⁄₆₄" pilot holes work well.

Also, in addition to drilling a countersunk hole for the screwhead, it helps to countersink a hole in the area where the pilot hole enters the second piece of material, as shown in 10–13. This gives the particleboard material a place to go so that it doesn't bulge up and interfere with the pieces already fastened tightly together.

10–13.

LAUNDRY CENTER

Although doing laundry doesn't rank high on anyone's list of fun activities, this feature-packed project helps make wash-day work as pleasant and efficient as possible. It has storage aplenty, a rod for air-drying clothes, bulletin board, and shelf, and a light to help spot stains. It ties all these features plus appliances into a tidy, hardworking assembly.

Build the Large Cabinet

1 From ¾" melamine-laminated particleboard (often referred to simply as "melamine"), cut the two 24 x 80" side panels (A).

2 On both panels, apply melamine edge banding to one long edge (the front edge in the assembled cabinet) and one short edge (the bottom edge of the cabinet). Use a clothes iron set on high heat to apply the banding, as shown in **10–14**. Be sure to keep the iron moving during application.

3 Mark one of the panels with dado and rabbet locations according to **10–21** *(page 184)*. Repeat making these markings on the other panel (the right side of the cabinet), keeping in mind that the right side must be a mirror image of the left.

CUTTING DIAGRAM FOR LAUNDRY CENTER

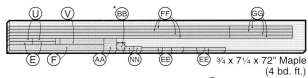
¾ x 7¼ x 72" Maple
(4 bd. ft.)

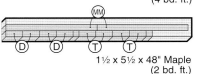
1½ x 5½ x 48" Maple
(2 bd. ft.)

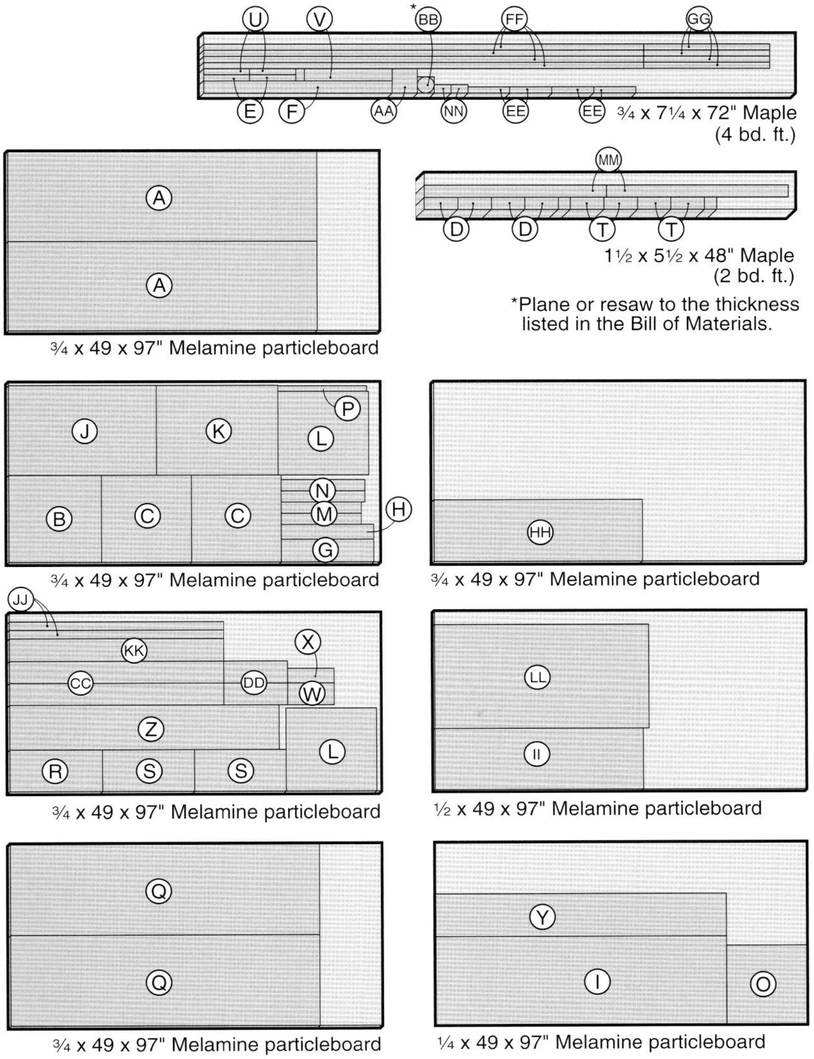

*Plane or resaw to the thickness
listed in the Bill of Materials.

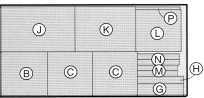
¾ x 49 x 97" Melamine particleboard

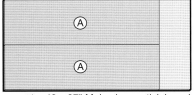
¾ x 49 x 97" Melamine particleboard

¾ x 49 x 97" Melamine particleboard

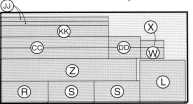
¾ x 49 x 97" Melamine particleboard

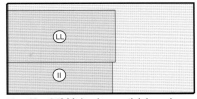
½ x 49 x 97" Melamine particleboard

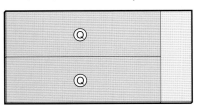
¾ x 49 x 97" Melamine particleboard

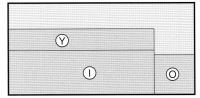
¼ x 49 x 97" Melamine particleboard

MATERIALS LIST FOR LARGE CABINET

| PART | FINISHED SIZE | | | MTL. | QTY. |
	T	W	L		
A sides	¾"	24"	80"	ME	2
B top	¾"	23¼"	24"	ME	1
C fixed shelves	¾"	23¼"	23¾"	ME	2
D* bottom cleats	1½"	1½"	4"	MA	4
E* upper front cleats	¾"	¾"	5¼"	MA	2
F upper back cleat	¾"	1½"	22½"	MA	1
G top fixed panel	¾"	6"	24"	ME	1
H bottom fixed panel	¾"	4"	24"	ME	1
I back	¼"	23¼"	75¼"	ME	1
J upper door	¾"	24"	38³⁄₁₆"	ME	1
K lower door	¾"	24"	31⁷⁄₁₆"	ME	1
L shelves	¾"	22⅜"	23½"	ME	2
M drawer front/back	¾"	3"	20¾"	ME	2
N drawer sides	¾"	3"	21¾"	ME	2
O drawer bottom	¼"	21¾"	20"	ME	1
P drawer-slide filler	¾"	1½"	23"	ME	1

* Cut parts marked with * oversized, and trim to
finished size according to instructions.
Materials Key: MA = Maple; ME = Melamine-
laminated particleboard.

MATERIALS LIST FOR SMALL CABINET

| PART | FINISHED SIZE | | | MTL. | QTY. |
	T	W	T		
Q sides	¾"	24"	80"	ME	2
R top	¾"	11¼"	24"	ME	1
S fixed shelves	¾"	11¼"	23¾"	ME	2
T* bottom cleats	1½"	1½"	4"	MA	4
U* upper front cleats	¾"	¾"	5¼"	MA	2
V upper back cleats	¾"	1½"	10½"	MA	1
W top fixed panel	¾"	6"	12"	ME	1
X bottom fixed panel	¾"	4"	12"	ME	1
Y back	¼"	11¼"	75¼"	ME	1
Z door	¾"	12"	69¾"	ME	1
AA rod swivel block	¾"	3"	3"	MA	1
BB rod end	½"	2" dia.		MA	1

* Cut parts marked with * oversized, and trim to
finished size according to instructions.
Materials Key: MA = Maple; ME = Melamine-
laminated particleboard.

10–14.

*Apply the front banding edge last.
That way, the joint between the
front and bottom banding isn't
visible from the front.*

4 Chuck a ¾" straight bit
in your router, and adjust
it to cut ⅜" deep. Clamp a
straightedge to your panel
to cut the dadoes and
rabbets, as shown in **10–16**
(*page 182*).

5 Build the hole-drilling
jig shown in **10–18** (*page
183*). Next, drill the ¼" shelf-
support holes ⅜" deep, where
shown in **10–20**. To do this,

MATERIALS LIST FOR LIGHT HOUSING AND SHELF/CORKBOARD

PART		FINISHED SIZE				
		T	W	L	MTL.	QTY.
LIGHT HOUSING						
CC	front /back	¾"	6"	55½"	ME	2
DD	ends	¾"	6"	16½"	ME	2
EE*	corner cleats	¾"	¾"	4¾"	MA	4
FF	front /back cleats	¾"	¾"	52½"	MA	4
GG	end cleats	¾"	¾"	15"	MA	4
HH	bottom	¾"	16½"	54"	ME	1
II	top	½"	16½"	54"	ME	1
SHELF/CORKBOARD						
JJ	shelf supports	¾"	2¼"	55½"	ME	2
KK	shelf	¾"	6"	55½"	ME	1
LL	back	½"	28"	55½"	ME	1
MM	back cleats	1½"	1½"	22"	MA	2
NN	ends	¾"	2¼"	4⅜"	MA	2

*Cut these parts oversized, and trim them to finished size according to instructions.
Materials Key: MA = Maple; ME = Melamine-laminated particleboard.
Supplies: 125° full-overlay hinges (7); 3½" matte chrome wire pulls (3); 20" bottom-mounting drawer slides (2); 48" single-tube fluorescent light fixture; single-pole pull switch; grounded plug; 10'-long 16/3 insulated electrical cord; 11¼ x 42½" white ½"-grid diffuser panel; 1" chrome shower rod, 42" long; 1" conduit clip; 5⁄16" floor levelers (8); 5⁄16" T-nuts (9); ¼" pin shelf supports; 1", 1¼", 1¾", and 2" deck screws; ¼ x 22 x 58" corkboard; 5⁄16 x 1¾" roundhead machine screw; 5⁄16" washer; white melamine edge banding.

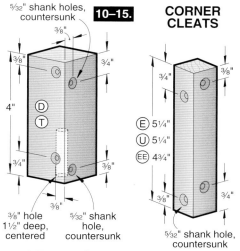

5⁄32" shank holes, countersunk

10–15.

CORNER CLEATS

3⁄8"
3⁄8"
¾"
4"
D
T
¾"
3⁄8"
3⁄8"
3⁄8" hole 1½" deep, centered
5⁄32" shank hole, countersunk

LEVELING CLEATS

¾"
3⁄8"
¾"
E 5¼"
U 5¼"
EE 4¾"
3⁄8"
¾"
5⁄32" shank hole, countersunk

align the end of the jig with the center dado in the cabinet sides, as shown in **10–17**.

6 Cut the top (B) and the two fixed shelves (C) to size, according to the Materials List. Band the front edges of all three panel pieces.

7 Cut a 1½ x 1½ x 17" maple blank, and crosscut it into four 4" lengths for the bottom cleats (D). Drill the holes and countersinks, as shown in the Leveling Cleats drawing in **10–15**. Attach to the bottom of the sides (A), where shown in **10–20** and **10–21** (*page 184*).

8 Cut a ¾ x ¾ x 11" maple blank, and crosscut it into two 5¼" lengths for the upper front cleats (E). Drill the holes and countersunk holes, where shown in the Corner Cleats drawing in **10–15**. Attach to the sides (A), where shown.

9 Apply glue to the dadoes and the top rabbet. Clamp together parts A, B, and C and check for square, as shown in **10–19**.

10 Cut the ¾ x 1½ x 22½" upper back cleat (F) from maple. Attach the cleat to the top (B), where shown.

11 Cut the top fixed panel (G) and bottom fixed panel (H) to size. Band all edges. Attach both panels to the cabinet as shown, being careful to align their edges flush with the top and bottom of the case.

12 Cut the 23¼ x 75¼" back (I) from ¼" melamine. Place the back into the rabbet on the case, and attach with 1" deck screws. Use six screws evenly spaced along the long edges, and two screws for the top and fixed dividers.

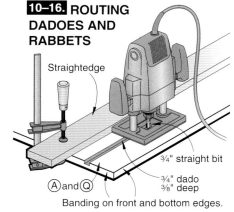

10–16. ROUTING DADOES AND RABBETS

Straightedge

¾" straight bit
A and Q
¾" dado 3⁄8" deep
Banding on front and bottom edges.

10–17.

The hole-drilling jig helps prevent wobbly shelves by ensuring uniformly spaced pin shelf supports.

13 Tap ¼" T-nuts into the ⅜" holes in the ends of the leveling cleats. Thread a floor leveler into each T-nut.

14 Cut the upper door (J) and lower door (K) to size. Band all edges. Drill holes for

125° full-overlay hinges, where shown. Install the 3½" matte chrome wire pulls, where shown in **10–20**.

15 Attach the hinges to the doors with their accompanying screws. Locate and drill

holes for the other half of each hinge that attaches to the carcase side, where shown on **10–21** (*page 184*). Attach the doors to the carcase, and adjust the hinges according to their accompanying instructions.

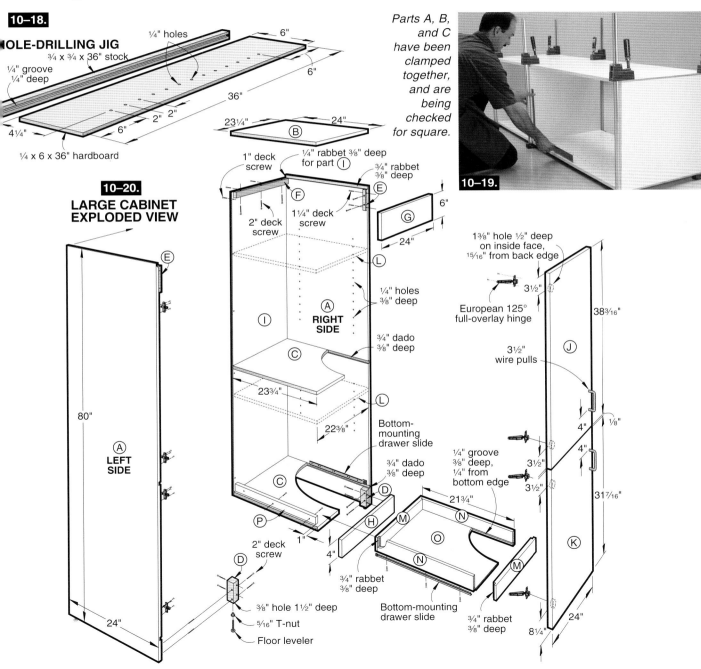

10–18.

OLE-DRILLING JIG

¾ x ¾ x 36" stock

¼" holes

¼" groove ¼" deep

6"

6"

36"

4¼"

2" 2"

6"

¼ x 6 x 36" hardboard

Parts A, B, and C have been clamped together, and are being checked for square.

10–19.

10–20.
LARGE CABINET EXPLODED VIEW

23¼" 24"

(B)

¼" rabbet ⅜" deep for part (I)

1" deck screw

¾" rabbet ⅜" deep

(F)

(E)

2" deck screw

1¼" deck screw

(G)

6"

24"

80"

(E)

(A)
LEFT SIDE

(I)

(A)
RIGHT SIDE

(L)

¼" holes ⅜" deep

¾" dado ⅜" deep

(C)

23¾"

(L)

22⅜"

Bottom-mounting drawer slide

¾" dado ⅜" deep

(C)

(P)

(D)

(H)

(M)

(N)

(O)

(N)

(M)

21¾"

1"

4"

¾" rabbet ⅜" deep

Bottom-mounting drawer slide

¾" rabbet ⅜" deep

2" deck screw

(D)

⅜" hole 1½" deep

5/16" T-nut

Floor leveler

24"

1⅜" hole ½" deep on inside face, 15/16" from back edge

3½"

European 125° full-overlay hinge

3½" wire pulls

(J)

38³/16"

4"

4"

⅛"

31⁷/16"

¼" groove ⅜" deep, ¼" from bottom edge

3½"

3½"

3½"

(K)

24"

8¼"

10–21. LARGE CABINET, LEFT-SIDE

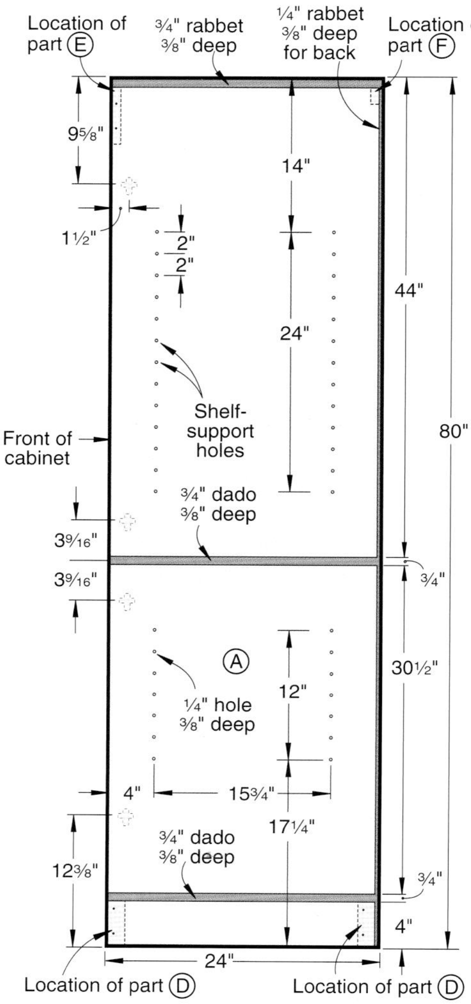
Location of part E
¾" rabbet ⅜" deep
¼" rabbet ⅜" deep for back
Location of part F
9⅝"
14"
1½"
2"
2"
44"
24"
80"
Front of cabinet
Shelf-support holes
¾" dado ⅜" deep
3⁹⁄₁₆"
3⁹⁄₁₆"
¾"
A
30½"
¼" hole ⅜" deep
12"
4"
15¾"
17¼"
¾" dado ⅜" deep
12⅜"
¾"
4"
24"
Location of part D
Location of part D

10–22. SMALL CABINET, RIGHT-SIDE

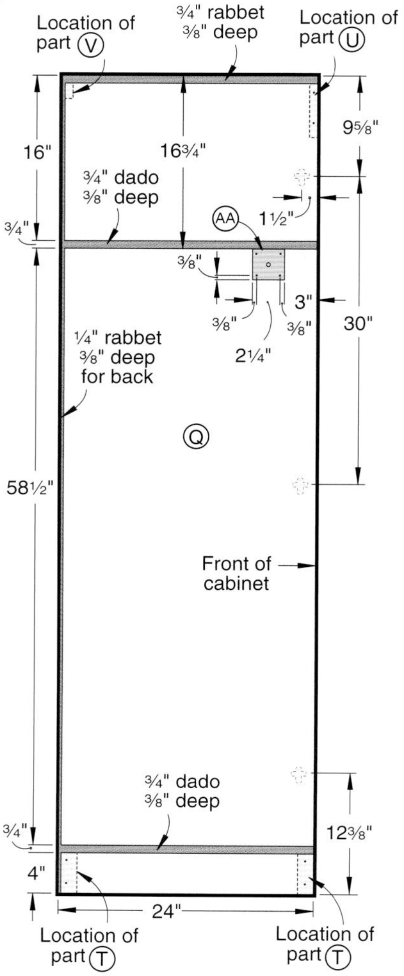
Location of part V
¾" rabbet ⅜" deep
Location of part U
16"
16¾"
9⅝"
¾" dado ⅜" deep
AA
1½"
¾"
⅜"
3"
⅜"
⅜"
2¼"
30"
¼" rabbet ⅜" deep for back
Q
58½"
Front of cabinet
¾" dado ⅜" deep
12⅜"
¾"
4"
24"
Location of part T
Location of part T

16 Cut two shelves (L) to size. Band the front edges only.

Add a Drawer to the Large Cabinet

1 Cut the drawer front/back (M) and drawer sides (N) to size. Band the top edges of all four pieces, and the ends of the front and back.

2 Cut a ¾" rabbet ⅜" deep on the ends of the front and back. Using a ¼"-wide dado set, cut ⅜"-deep grooves ¼" from the bottom edges of the drawer front, back, and sides.

3 Cut the 21¾ x 20" drawer bottom (O) from ¼" melamine.

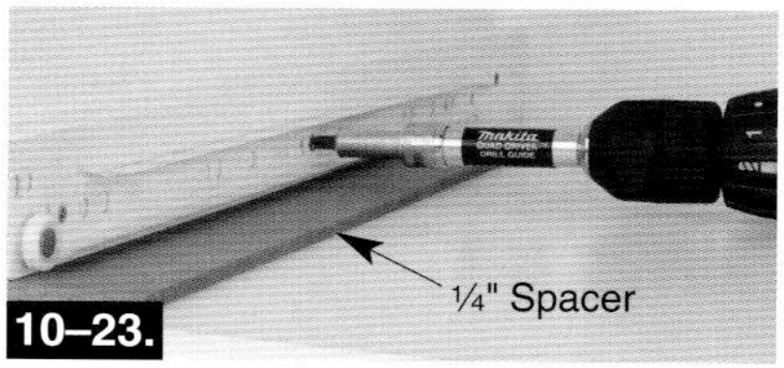
¼" Spacer
10–23.

To precisely position the drawer slides, place a ¼"-thick spacer underneath them as you fasten them with screws.

> SHOP TIP
>
> **How to Cut Clean Melamine Edges**
>
> **The thin plastic outer layers on melamine-laminated particleboard can chip easily when sawn, leaving unsightly edges. To minimize this chipping, do the following:**
>
> **1 Align your tablesaw's rip fence perfectly parallel with the blade.**
>
> **2 Use a sharp blade with plenty of teeth (10" carbide blades made especially for cutting melamine have 80 teeth).**
>
> **3 Orient the melamine sheet face side up when cutting it with a tablesaw.**
>
> **4 The previous rule is reversed for handheld circular saws and jigsaws—orient the melamine face side down when using these tools.**

Apply glue to the rabbets and grooves, and assemble the drawer, as shown in **10–20** (*page 183*).

4 Cut the 1½ x 23" drawer-slide filler (P) from ¾" melamine, and band its top and front edges. Attach to the case, where shown.

5 Place a ¼"-thick scrap spacer under each drawer slide, and position them along the side (A) and drawer-slide filler (P), where shown. Position the fronts of the slides 1" from the front edge of the carcase, and attach them with the screws provided. (See **10–23**.) Attach the other half of the slides to the drawer bottom, where shown.

Build the Small Cabinet

1 From ¾" melamine, cut the two 24 x 80" side panels (Q).

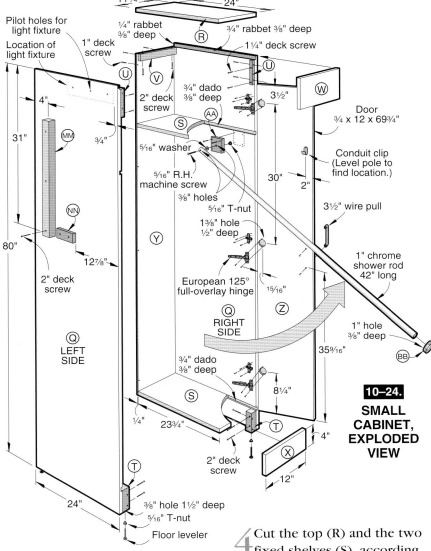

Pilot holes for light fixture

Location of light fixture

11¼"

24"

¼" rabbet ⅜" deep

¾" rabbet ⅜" deep

1" deck screw

1¼" deck screw

4"

31"

¾"

80"

2" deck screw

12⅞"

24"

¾" dado ⅜" deep

2" deck screw

3½"

Door
¾ x 12 x 69¾"

Conduit clip
(Level pole to find location.)

30"

2"

3½" wire pull

1" chrome shower rod 42" long

¼"

23¾"

⅜" hole 1½" deep
5⁄16" T-nut

Floor leveler

5⁄16" washer

5⁄16" R.H. machine screw

⅜" holes

5⁄16" T-nut

1⅜" hole ½" deep

European 125° full-overlay hinge

15⁄16"

35⁄16"

8¼"

4"

12"

1" hole ⅜" deep

2" deck screw

RIGHT SIDE

LEFT SIDE

10–24.
SMALL CABINET, EXPLODED VIEW

On both large panels apply plastic banding to the front and bottom edges.

2 Mark one of the panels with dado and rabbet locations, according to **10–22**. Repeat these markings on the other panel (the left side of the cabinet), keeping in mind that the left side must be a mirror image of the right.

3 With a straightedge, router, and ¾" straight bit, cut the ⅜"-deep dadoes and rabbets.

4 Cut the top (R) and the two fixed shelves (S), according to the Materials List. Band the front edges of all three panels.

5 Cut and drill four bottom cleats (T), as described in *Step 7* of the section "Build the Large Cabinet." Attach to the bottom of the sides (Q), where shown in **10–22** and **10–24**.

6 Cut and drill two upper front cleats (U) as described in *Step 8* of "Build the Large Cabinet." Attach the cleats to the sides (Q), where shown.

7 Apply glue to the dadoes and the top rabbet. Clamp together parts Q, R, and S.

8 Cut the ¾ x 1½ x 10½" upper back cleat (V) from maple. Attach the cleat to the top (R), where shown.

9 Cut the top fixed panel (W) and bottom fixed panel (X) to size. Band all edges. Attach both panels to the cabinet, as shown, being careful to align their edges flush with the top and bottom of the case.

10 Cut the 11¼ x 75¼" back (Y) from ¼" melamine. Place the back into the rabbet on the case, and attach.

11 Tap ¼" T-nuts into the ⅜" holes in the ends of the leveling cleats. Thread a floor leveler into each T-nut.

12 Cut the ¾ x 12 x 69¾" melamine door (Z). Band all edges. Drill holes for 125° full-overlay hinges, where shown. Also install a 3½" matte chrome wire pull.

13 Attach the hinges to the door with the screws

10–25.
ROD MOUNTING DETAIL

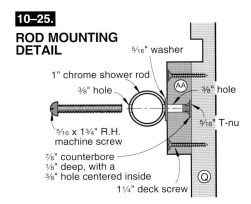

1" chrome shower rod

5⁄16" washer

⅜" hole

⅜" hole

5⁄16" T-nut

5⁄16 x 1¾" R.H. machine screw

⅞" counterbore ⅛" deep, with a ⅜" hole centered inside

1¼" deck screw

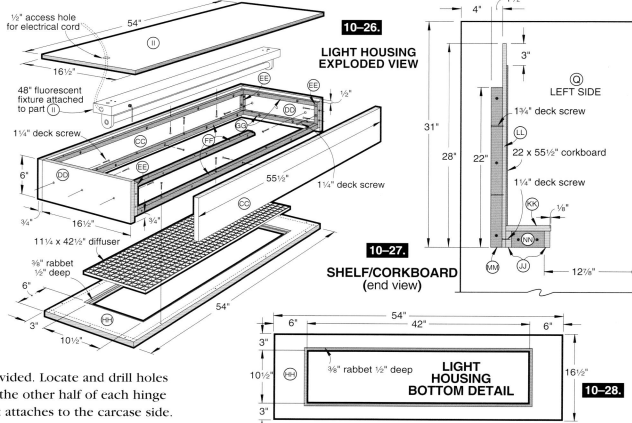

½" access hole for electrical cord

54"

16½"

48" fluorescent fixture attached to part (II)

1¼" deck screw

6"

¾"   16½"   ¾"

11¼ x 42½" diffuser

⅜" rabbet ½" deep

6"

3"

10½"

10–26.

LIGHT HOUSING EXPLODED VIEW

½"

55½"

1¼" deck screw

54"

10–27.

SHELF/CORKBOARD (end view)

1½"
4"
3"
31"
28"   22"
1¾" deck screw
(LL)
22 x 55½" corkboard
1¼" deck screw
⅛"
12⅞"

(Q) LEFT SIDE

10–28.

54"
6"   42"   6"
3"
10½"
3"
⅜" rabbet ½" deep

LIGHT HOUSING BOTTOM DETAIL

16½"

---

provided. Locate and drill holes for the other half of each hinge that attaches to the carcase side. Attach the door to the carcase, and adjust the hinges as needed.

14 Cut the 3 x 3" rod swivel block (AA) from ¾" maple. Drill a centered, ⅛"-deep, ⅞" counterbored hole on one face; then drill a ⅜" hole, centered on the counterbore, through the block, as shown in **10–25**. Attach the rod swivel block to the inside of the right side of the case, as shown in **10–24** and **10–25**.

15 Attach the 1"-diameter, 42"-long chrome shower rod. Swing the rod to a level position, and attach a supporting conduit clip to the inside of the door, where shown.

16 Cut a ½"-thick, 2"-diameter maple disc to make the rod end (BB). Bore a centered 1" hole, ⅜" deep, on one side of the rod end (BB), and attach it to the end of the rod with epoxy.

Making the Fluorescent Light Fixture

1 Cut the front/back (CC) and ends (DD) to size. Band the bottom edge and ends of the front and back, and the bottom edge of the ends.

2 Rip a ¾ x ¾ x 20" maple blank for the corner cleats (EE). Crosscut it into four pieces,

each 4¾" long. Drill each cleat, as shown in the Corner Cleats drawing in **10–15** (*page 182*). Attach the cleats to the ends with 1¼" deck screws, where shown in **10–26**.

3 Clamp the front, back, and ends together, being careful to align their ends and edges flush. Fasten them with 1¼" deck screws driven through the remaining holes in the corner cleat blocks.

4 Rip four ¾ x ¾ x 52½" maple front/back cleats (FF), and four ¾ x ¾ x 15" maple end cleats (GG). Attach two FF cleats

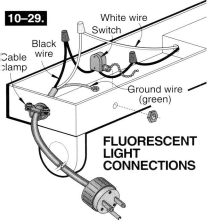

10–29.

White wire
Switch
Black wire
Cable clamp
Ground wire (green)

FLUORESCENT LIGHT CONNECTIONS

to the front and back, between the bottom ends of the corner cleats, where shown. Use five evenly spaced 1¼" deck screws. Follow the same procedure to attach two GG cleats to the ends, but use two screws. Set aside the unused FF and GG cleats for now.

5 Cut the ¾ x 16½ x 54" melamine bottom (HH). With a jigsaw, cut the opening where shown in the Light Housing Bottom Detail drawing in **10–28**.

6 Rout a ⅜" rabbet ½" deep around the edge of the opening using a piloted ⅜" rabbeting bit.

7 Place the bottom into the light housing frame and screw it to the FF and GG cleats with 1¼" screws.

8 Cut a plastic light-diffuser panel to 11¼ x 42½". Place it into the rabbet in the bottom.

9 Attach the remaining FF and GG cleats between the top ends of the corner cleats in the same way you attached the other FF and GG cleats.

10 Cut the ½ x 16½ x 54" melamine top (II).

11 Add a single-pole pull switch, electrical cord, and plug to a 48" single-tube fluorescent light, as shown in **10–29**. Mount the light to the center of the top (II). Drop the switch's pull chain through the grid of the light diffuser. Drill a ½" hole through the top (II), and feed the electrical cord through it.

Make the Shelf/Corkboard

1 Cut the shelf supports (JJ), and shelf (KK) to size. Glue and clamp these shelf-assembly parts together, using the Shelf/Corkboard drawing in **10–27** as a guide.

2 Cut the 28 x 55½" back (LL) from ½" melamine. Clamp two ¼ x 1 x 60" strips of wood 3" from the edges, as shown in **10–30**. Use a short-nap roller to apply contact cement between the strips.

3 From ¼" cork, cut a 22 x 55½" panel and apply contact cement to one face. Attach the cork to the back (LL), and remove the wood strips.

4 Attach the JJ/KK assembly to LL with six evenly spaced 1¼" screws.

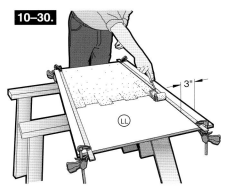

10–30.

Applying contact cement between wood strips on the back of the laundry center.

Final Assembly

1 Cut the back cleats (MM) and ends (NN) to size. Attach to the sides of the large and small cabinets, where shown in **10–24**.

2 Clamp the light housing between the two cabinets. It should be set back ¾" from the front edge of the cabinets and be flush with their tops. Screw the housing to the sides with 1¼" deck screws.

3 Slide the shelf/corkboard unit between the cabinets and set it down on the ends (NN). Drill two evenly spaced holes through the back cleats (MM), and fasten the shelf/corkboard with countersunk 1¾" deck screws.

4 When placing the finished unit in your washing area, attach the cabinets securely to a wall to prevent them from tipping forward. Do this by driving fasteners through the upper back cleats (F, V) and into wall studs, concrete, or masonry block. You're done!

INDEX

Adjustable shelf standards, 21
Air-dried lumber, 13
Acrylic artist's colors, 28
Acrylic, use for displaying shelves, 23
Alcohol-based dyes, 26
Alder (red), uses of, 11
All-in-one finishing products, 29, 30
Appleply, matching to project and budget, 16–17
Arcs, making, 71
Artist's oils, 28
Arts & Crafts storage unit
  bottom shelf, 71, 72, 73
  description of, 68
  finish, 73
  legs, 68, 69
  panels, 71, 72, 73
  rails, 69, 70, 71
  top, 71 72, 73
Ash
  and shelf sag, 22
  uses of, 11
Bald cypress, uses of, 11
Baltic birch, matching to project and budget, 16–17
Banding, applying, 174
Barrister's bookcase
  assembly, 92, 93
  base, 90, 91, 92
  carcase, 86, 87–88, 89
  cutting diagram, 85
  description of, 85
  door, 89, 90
  finish, 92
  top, 90, 91, 92
Basic fasteners, 19, 20, 21
Basswood, uses of, 11
Beech, and shelf sag, 22
Bendable plywood, matching to project and budget, 16–17
Birch
  and shelf sag, 22
  use for country hall seat, 156–161, 162
  uses of, 11
Bird's-eye maple, 30
Blotching, 27, 28
Board feet
  guidelines, 13
  how to determine, 13
Bookcases
  barrister's, 85, 90–93
  full-length, 94, 95–99, 100
  in three styles, 101, 102–110
Book dimensions, 23
Box nail, 20
Brad, 20

Bristle brush, 31
Bull door catch, 20
Burnt umber glaze, 28
Butt hinge, 20
Butternut, uses of, 11
Cabinets
  CD or DVD storage, 128 – 132
  collector's, 134, 135–138, 139
  doors for, hanging, 58
  hardware for, 20, 21
  pine hutch, 40, 41–49
  Shaker, 37–40
  system of, 171, 172–180
  three-piece, 74–78
  traditional sideboard, 50–60
C and Better Select boards, 12
Carriage bolt, 20
Catches, types of, 20, 21
CD or DVD storage cabinet
  assembling, 132
  carcase, 128, 129–131, 132
  description of, 128
  drawers, 128
  finish, 132
  materials list, 129
Cedar
  use for heirloom chest, 163–168
  uses of, 11
Ceramic pull, 20
Cherry
  cabinet, on workstation, 119, 120–127
  plywood, cabinet combination, 74–82
  and shelf sag, 22
  Shaker cabinet, 37–39, 40
  uses of, 11
Circular saw
  and board's good face, 19
  blade for, and tear-out, 19
  blade to use with, 15
"Climb-cutting" with a router, 91
Clutter, conquering, 6
Collector's cabinet
  base, 137
  case, 135, 136, 137
  crown, 137
  description, 134, 135
  door, 138
  finish, 139
  hardware, 139
  hinged panel, 137
  utilizing space with, 6
Color wheel, 28
Combination blade, 15
Common nail, 20
Computer workstation
  assemble the project, 126, 127

carcase, 119, 120–122, 123
  description of, 119
  doors, 124, 125, 126
  drawers, 123, 124
  drop leaf, 124, 125, 126
  finish, 126, 127
Corrugated fastener, 20
Country projects
  bookcase100, 101–110
  entertainment center, 62, 63–67, 68
  hall seat, 156–162, 163
Cove molding, clamping, 78
D Select boards, 12
Danish oils, 29
Dark end grain, dealing with, 28
Decorative ceramic knob, 20
Decorative ceramic pull, 20
Decorative corner reinforcement, 20
Decorative pull, 20
Door catches, 20
Drawer slide, 20
Drop-front writing desk
  carcase, 114, 115
  dadoes and rabbets, 113, 114
  doors, 118, 119
  drawer unit, 115, 116, 117
  drop leaf, 117, 118
  edge-glued panels, 112, 113, 114
  finish, 118
  materials list, 112
  shelves, 114, 114
Drywall screw, 20
Dust bumps, removing, 31, 35
Dyes and pigmented stains, difference between, 25, 26
Dye/pigment stains, 29
Electronic media storage unit
  assembling the project, 72
  finish, 73
  legs, 68, 69
  panels, 71, 72
  rails, 69, 71
  shelf, 71, 72
  top, 71, 72
Engineered wood, 14
Entertainment centers
  cabinet combination, 74–83
  country, 62, 63–67, 68
  showtime storage, 68, 69–73
European-style hidden hinge, 20
FAS 1-Face boards, 12
Fasteners, 20, 21
Fender washer, 20
Finishes
  clear, 30, 31–33, 34
  guidelines for applying, 24, 25

staining, 25, 26–28, 29
  as a woodworking activity, 8
Finish nails, 20
Finish washers, 20
Finnish birch, matching to project and budget, 16–17
First & Seconds (FAS), 11
Flathead wood screw, 20
Friction door catch, 20
Front-mount offset hinge, 20
Full-length bookcase
  basic cabinet, 94, 95, 96
  cutting diagram, 94, 95
  description of, 94
  face frame, 96, 97, 98
  finish, 100
  moldings, 97, 98, 99, 100
  shelves, 100
Full-wrap inset hinge, 58
Gels, 29
Glass, use for displaying shelving, 23
Glazing, 29
Glue squeeze-out, dealing with, 105
Green boards, removing moisture from, 13
Hanger screw, 20
Hardboard
  guide, for drilling shelf support holes, 123
  matching to project and budget, 16–17
Hardwood
  description of, 11
  grades, 12, 13, 14
  plywood, matching to project and budget, 16–17
  uses of, 11
Heartwood, 27
Heirloom chest
  base, 167, 168
  cutting diagram, 164
  finish, 168
  frame, 163, 165, 166
  hardware, 168
  lid molding, 167, 168
  liner, 166, 167
  materials list, 164
Hickory, uses of, 11
High-density overlay plywood, matching to project and budget, 16–17
Hinges, types, 20, 21
Hutch cabinet
  assembling the cupboard, 49
  cap, 44, 45
  carcases, 42
  crown, 44, 45
  cutting diagram, 41
  description of, 40
  doors, 47, 48
  face frames, 42, 43, 44
  finish, 48

materials list, 41
  part blanks, 42
  shelves, 45, 46, 47
  skirts, 44
  top, 44
Invisible hinge, 20
Japan colors, 28
Jointer, trimming plywood with a, 19
Kiln-dried lumber, 13
Knob, 20
Knockdown cabinet system
  assembly of the shelf unit, 177
  base, 175, 176, 177
  boxes, 177, 178, 180
  carcase, 173, 174, 175
  cutting diagram, 172, 173
  description of, 171
  drawers, 179, 180
  frame-and-panel door, 178, 179
  materials list for, 172
  top, 175, 176, 177
Lacquer, spray, 30
Lag screw, 20
Laundry center
  cutting diagram for, 181
  description of, 181
  drawer for large cabinet, 185
  final assembly, 188
  fluorescent light fixture, 187, 188
  large cabinet, 181, 182–184, 185
  shelf/corkboard, 183, 188
  small cabinet, 182, 185, 186, 187
Library storage
  barrister's bookcase, 85, 86–93
  bookcase in three styles, 100, 101–110
  full-length bookcase, 94–99, 100
Liquid dyes, 26
Machine bolt, 20
Magnetic door catch, 20
Mahogany
  and shelf sag, 22
  uses of, 11
Maple
  and shelf sag, 22
  use for knockdown cabinet system, 170–180
  uses of, 11
Masonry lag shield, 20
Medium-density fiberboard
  matching to project and budget, 16–17
  and shelf sag, 22
Medium-density overlay plywood, 16–17
Melamine
  cutting clean edges on, 184
  driving screws into, 180

matching to project and budget, 16–17
Moisture content of boards, 13
Molding stock, 12
National Hardwood Lumber Association, and grading of hard wood boards, 11
Nongrain-raising dyes, 29, 30
Oak
  plywood, use for bookcase, 100, 101–110
  plywood, use for traditional sideboard, 50–60
  and shelf sag, 22
  storage cabinet 128–132
  uses of, 11
  white, use for barrister's book case, 85–93
Oil-based polyurethane
  advantages of, 31
  applying, 31
Paint finish, 34, 35
Paint job, repairing a, 35
Particleboard
  matching to project and budget, 16–17
  and shelf sag, 23
  use for laundry center, 180–187
Penetrating oil
  advantages of, 32
  applying, 32, 33
  on jewelry case, 30
  unique properties of, 30
Phillip's head screw, 20
Pigmented stains, 25, 26
Pine
  drop-front writing desk, 112, 113–118, 119
  entertainment center, 62, 63–67, 68
  hutch made of, 40, 41–49
  knotty, used on bookcase, 100, 101–109, 111
  ponderosa, uses of, 11
  red, uses of, 11
  southern yellow, uses of, 11
  white, uses of, 11, 30
Pivot hinge, 20
Planing, effects of, 13
Plastic wall anchor, 20
Plywood
  cherry, use for bookcase, 100, 101–110
  cherry, use for cabinet combina tion, 74–82
  cutting characteristics of, 7
  description of, 14
  exposed edges of, 8
  filling edges of, 34
  matching to project and budget, 16–17
  oak, for bookcase, 100, 101–110
  oak, for sideboard, 50–60

and shelf sag, 22
technique for cutting, 14, 15, 16, 17
walnut, for full-length bookcase, 94–99, 100
Polyurethane
on buffet, 30
oil-based, advantages of, 31
oil-based, applying, 31
on sideboard, 30
unique properties of, 30
Poplar, uses of, 11
"Prefinished" particleboard, 23
Primer coats of paint, 34, 35
Pulls, 20
Raw sienna glaze, 28
Raised grain, 27
Raised-panel door, making, 47
Roller door catch, 20
Roundhead wood screw, 20
Router
climb-cutting with a, 91
cutting cove molding with a, 76, 78
trimming plywood with a, 15, 18
Sapwood, 27
Scraper, removing dust bumps with a, 31
Screws
driving into melamine, 180
types of, 19, 20
"S-Dry" boards, 13
Selects, 12
Shaker bookcase
base, 106, 107
case, 100, 101–105
cutting diagram, 101, 102
description of, 100
finish, 110
materials list, 102
Shaker cabinet
adding a drawer, 40
basic case, 37, 38–39, 40
cutting diagram, 37
finish, 40
materials list, 39
Sheet goods
cutting on a table saw, 14
exposed edges of, 8
guide to, 14–18, 19
matching to project and budget, 16–17
Shelves
bracket systems, 21, 22
drilling pin holes in, 42
reinforcing, 22, 23
sag in, preventing, 22, 23
size of, determining, 23
span limits, 22

support holes, drilling with a hardboard guide, 123
supports for, handmade, 21
supports for, with metal sleeves, 104
Shelving-grade boards, 13
Shop-grade boards, 12, 13
Shop tips
arcs, making, 71
banding, applying, 173
cabinet doors, hanging, 58
dado cuts, preventing tear-out when making, 130
doors, making simply, 47
glue squeeze-out, 105
melamine, cutting clean edges on, 184
melamine, driving screws into, 180
rabbet for glass, cutting, 91
repetitive layout marking, 174
shelf-pin holes, drilling quickly and accurately, 42
shelf support holes, drilling using a hardboard guide, 123, 148
shelf supports with metal sleeves, 104
Sideboard
case, 53, 54, 55
cutting diagram, 50, 51
description of, 50
doors, 56, 58
face frame, 55, 56
finish, 60
materials list, 51
shelves and top, 59, 60
sides, 51, 52, 53
wine racks, 60
Side-mount offset hinge, 20
Slothead screw, 20
Softwood plywood
description of, 11
grades, 12, 13
matching to project and budget, 16–17
uses of, 11
Spray lacquer
applying, 31, 32
on lamp, 30
unique properties of, 30
Staining guidelines
all-in-one products, 29
applying stains, 26, 27
dyes and pigmented stains, 25, 26
dye/pigment stain, 29
gels, 29
nongrain-raising dye, 29
oil/varnish mixture, 29

problems, preventing and solving, 27, 28, 29
Steel rule, hanging cabinet doors with a, 58
Straight-edge guide, when cutting plywood, 19
Tablesaw
cutting dadoes with, 117
cutting half-laps with, 77
cutting plywood with, 14, 15, 18, 19
Teak, uses of, 11
Three-piece cabinet combination
assembly of project, 81, 82
banding and molding, 75, 76–78
carcase, 74, 75
finish, 81, 82
flipper-door hardware, 79, 80, 81
side cabinets, 81
television insert, 78, 79
Toggle bolt, 20
Traditional sideboard
case, 53, 54, 55
cutting diagram, 50, 51
description of, 50
doors, 56, 58
face frame, 55, 56
finish, 60
materials list, 51
shelves and top, 59, 60
sides, 51, 52, 53
wine racks, 60
Uneven board color, dealing with, 27
Walnut
plywood, for full-length bookcase, 94–99, 100
and shelf sag, 22
uses of, 11
Water-based polyurethane
advantages of, 33
applying a, 33, 34
on sideboard, 30
unique properties of, 30
Writing desk
carcase, 114, 115
dadoes and rabbets, 113, 114
doors, 118, 119
drawer unit, 115, 116, 117
drop leaf, 117, 118
edge-glued panels, 112, 113, 114
finish, 118
materials list, 112
shelves, 114, 114
Zero-clearance tablesaw insert, 15

METRIC EQUIVALENTS CHART
Inches to Millimeters and Centimeters
MM=MILLIMETERS   CM=CENTIMETERS

INCHES	MM	CM	INCHES	CM	INCHES	CM
1/8	3	0.3	9	22.9	30	76.2
1/4	6	0.6	10	25.4	31	78.7
3/8	10	1.0	11	27.9	32	81.3
1/2	13	1.3	12	30.5	33	83.8
5/8	16	1.6	13	33.0	34	86.4
3/4	19	1.9	14	35.6	35	88.9
7/8	22	2.2	15	38.1	36	91.4
1	25	2.5	16	40.6	37	94.0
1 1/4	32	3.2	17	43.2	38	96.5
1 1/2	38	3.8	18	45.7	39	99.1
1 3/4	44	4.4	19	48.3	48	101.6
2	51	5.1	20	50.8	41	104.1
2 1/2	64	6.4	21	53.3	42	106.7
3	76	7.6	22	55.9	43	109.2
3 1/2	89	8.9	23	58.4	44	111.8
4	102	10.2	24	61.0	45	114.3
4 1/2	114	11.4	25	63.5	46	116.8
5	127	12.7	26	66.0	47	119.4
6	152	15.2	27	68.6	48	121.9

C R E D I T S

Special thanks are due to the following people or companies for their contributions:

David Ashe, for project design in Chapter 7
Marty Baldwin, for photographs in Chapters 2, 3, 4, 5, 7, 9, 10, and 11
Kevin Boyle, for text in Chapters 4 and 10 and project designs in Chapters 4, 6, 7, 8, 10, and 11
Tim Cahill, for illustrations in Chapters 2 and 10
Larry Clayon, for text in Chapter 3
James Downing, for illustrations in Chapter 4 and project designs in Chapters 5 to 10
Kim Downing, for illustrations in Chapters 5 to 9
Owen Duvall, for text in Chapters 4, 6, 8, 9, and 11
Randall Foshee, for illustrations in Chapter 9
Kerry Gibson, for text in Chapter 3
Chuck Hedlund, for text in Chapters 3 to 8, 10, and 11 and project design in Chapter 5
Burdette Heikens, Carefree Arizona, for project design in Chapter 11
Mike Henry, for illustrations in Chapter 6
John Hetherington, for photographs in Chapters 3, 9, and 10
Hopkins Associates, for photographs in Chapters 4, 5, 6 and 8
Lorna Johnson, for illustrations in Chapters 4, 5, 7, 9, 10, and 11
Jim Kascoutas, for photographs in Chapter 9

Marlen Kemmet, for text in Chapters 3, 5, 6, 8, and 9 and illustrations in Chapters 4 and 5
Bill Krier, for text in Chapter 10
Jim Kull, for text in Chapter 3
Bill LaHay, for text in Chapter 7
Roxanne LeMoine, for illustrations in Chapters 3 to 11
Jim Maw, for project design in Chapter 11
Jeff Mertz, for illustrations in Chapter 6 and project designs in Chapter 8 and 11
Mike Mittermeier, for illustrations in Chapter 11
Carson Ode, for illustrations in Chapter 10
Jim Pollock, for text in Chapter 3
Robert J. Settich, for text in Chapter 5
Douglas E. Smith, for photographs in Chapter 9
David Stone, for text in Chapter 2
Studio Au, for photographs in Chapter 3
Jan Svec, for text in Chapters 3, 4, 6, 7, 8, 10, and 11
Kent Welsh, for project design in Chapter 9
Raymond L. Wilber, for text in Chapter 2
Bill Wright, for building a project in Chapter 10
Dean Young, for project design in Chapter 4
Bill Zahn, for illustrations in Chapters 4 and 9

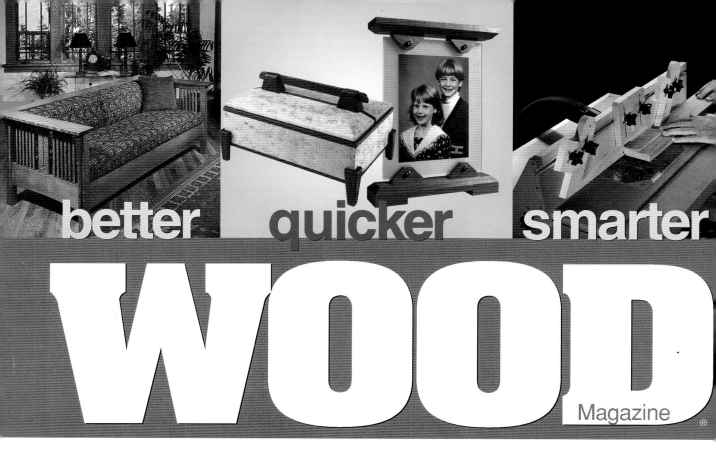